Criminalized Mothers, Criminalizing Mothering

Criminalized Mothers, Criminalizing Mothering

EDITED BY

Joanne Minaker and Bryan Hogeveen

DEMETER

DEMETER PRESS

The publisher gratefully acknowledges the the financial assistance of the Government of Canada through the Canada Book Fund.

Canadä

Demeter Press
140 Holland Street West
P. O. Box 13022
Bradford, ON L3Z 2Y5
Tel: (905) 775-9089
Email: info@demeterpress.org
Website: www.demeterpress.org

Demeter Press logo based on the sculpture "Demeter" by
Maria-Luise Bodirsky <www.keramik-atelier.bodirsky.de>

Printed and Bound in Canada

Library and Archives Canada Cataloguing in Publication

Criminalized mothers, criminalizing mothering / edited by Joanne Minaker and Bryan Hogeveen.

Includes bibliographical references.
ISBN 978-1-926452-01-2 (pbk.)

1. Mothers--Effect of imprisonment on. 2. Women prisoners. 3. Female offenders. 4. Mother and child. 5. Marginality, Social. 6. Criminal justice, Administration of--Social aspects. I. Hogeveen, Bryan Richard, 1972-, author, editor II. Minaker, Joanne Cheryl, 1974-, author, editor

HV8738.C74 2015 306.874'3086927 C2015-900634-1

For our daughter, Maylah.
May she choose to (or not to) mother in the context of care, support, and love.

Table of Contents

Acknowledgements

The book you hold in your hands is the result of the hard work and dedication of several excellent people who deserve our warm gratitude. Our sincere appreciation goes to Andrea O'Reilly for her pioneering work in this area and tremendous encouragement and support. Thank you to all the contributors for their exceptional work, commitment and industry. Many thanks to the production team at Demeter Press (Andrea, Angie, and Katherine). We acknowledge the support of our family and friends. Always, we are grateful for our children, Ayden, Taryk, and Maylah. You inspire us. We also appreciate the time and space our sabbaticals provided to devote to this book project.

I am so appreciative to have a partner in writing, in parenting, and in life who offers his respect, support, strength, care, and love to me each day. Thank you, Bryan, for reminding me: *Do you,* encouraging me in my pursuits, and for your unwavering commitment to our shared vision inside our home and beyond.

—Joanne Minaker

A special debt of gratitude goes to my co-editor and partner in life. I am grateful for, and admire, your tireless dedication to all things social justice. This book is a monument to your devotion and a testament to your passionate commitment to creating meaningful change through caring relationships.

—Bryan Hogeveen

From Criminalizing Mothering to Criminalized Mothers

An Introduction

JOANNE MINAKER AND BRYAN HOGEVEEN

Now time for proper packing, labelling then just shipping packages so Teagan and I can enjoy the upcoming festivities, celebrations, and beautiful loving Christmas time—feeling thankful.

LISA BALSTONE POSTED THESE LINES to her Facebook page only days before her daughter's death (Holmes). As this book goes to press, headlines such as, "Surrey mom charged with murder in death of her eight-year-old girl, who was found in trunk of car" (Saltman) and "Psych assessment ordered for South Surrey mother charged with murder" (Holmes) cannot escape our notice. Tragic, sad, and painfully distressing—these words only begin to describe Teagan's premature death. Feelings of sympathy for a little girl murdered come (almost) naturally; more difficult is empathy for her mother who is accused of the crime.

The fastest growing prison population worldwide, more and more women are living in cages and most of them are mothers (Balfour and Comack). This alarming trend has huge ramifications for women, children, and communities across the globe (Sudbury). *Orange Is the New Black* notwithstanding, empathy for mothers behind bars and concern for criminalized mothers in the community is in short supply (Kerman). Mothers are criminalized for their vulnerabilities and for making unpopular but difficult choices under material and ideological conditions not of their own choosing. *Criminalized Mothers, Criminalizing Mothering* shines a spotlight on mothers who are, by law or social regulation, criminalized, and examines their troubles and triumphs. Unlike the Netflix series *Orange is the New Black,* this book offers a critical and compassionate lens on social (in)justice, mass incarceration, and collective miseries women-as-a-group experience (e.g., economic inequality, gendered violence, devalued care work, lone-parenting etc.). This book is about mothers' encounters with systems of control, confinement, and criminalization, but also their experiences of care.

Criminalized Mothers, Criminalizing Mothering broadens the scope of criminalization in order to more fully understand criminalizing as a complex and nuanced process that is intimately connected to forces of social exclusion and marginalization. Power relations and systemic issues—poverty, street entrenchment, colonialization, and patriarchy—figure prominently in the analyses. Taken together, this volume complicates dominant narratives about criminalization and motherhood. The authors demonstrate that while motherhood is generally valued, mothers (especially marginalized mothers) are habitually devalued, their rights violated, and their capacity to parent put on trial, all of which can have devastating consequences for women and their families. We maintain that practices and penalties of criminalization emerge inside and outside of formal criminal justice and correctional systems; criminalization—or the threat of being criminalized—impacts all mothers, especially women who transgress hetero-normative boundaries or mother at the social margins.

Mothering with multiple marginalizations comes with the risk of criminalization for violating the law and/or offending social-cultural codes. Mothers who find themselves subject to criminalization are placed in the space of "Other," puzzlingly unseen but hyper-visible. We conceptualize "criminalizing mothering" as the complex process of scrutiny, surveillance, and social sanction characterized by perceiving some mothering *as criminal*, and through legal and extra-legal practices (formal and informal regulation) treating some women as deviant, dependent, and/or dangerous mothers, which undermines mothers' authority and authenticity. Discourses and practices of maternal criminalization are part of a wider, disturbing trend that Meda Chesney-Lind and Michele Eliason call the "demonization of marginalized women and girls" (29). We argue that a wider cultural acceptance of practices that criminalize particular forms of mothering makes criminalizing certain mothers—especially ones at the margins—more likely.

In this introduction we situate the criminalization of mothering in the wider empirical and theoretical literature and outline the structure of the book. First, we discuss feminist scholarship on motherhood and criminalized women. Next, we present the chapters in the book and weave together analyses of representations and lived experiences, stories of struggle and strife, and social and legal regulation of "deviant" and/or "criminal" mothers. We critique an unequal playing field that sets women up for failure, the practices that punish mothers for failing to conform or for fighting back, and the systems that marginalize rather than empower, control instead of care.

Criminalizing particular forms of mothering and certain mothers involves broader questions of social justice. Women whose mothering is at odds with social norms and cultural expectations are more likely to be criminalized. The criminalization of poverty makes women more vulnerable to abuse, extreme poverty, homelessness, and responding to these circumstances in deviant and criminal ways. Cultural stereotypes about maternal characters bound by age, class, race, and gender shape policies that criminalize mothers. Powerful constructions of poor, young, unmarried, non-white mothers as deviant and in need of regulation and/or punishment rather than deserving of support and care are not historical relics. Blaming mothers for situations like poverty, homelessness, or children's exposure to violence, as we will see in this book, directs our attention away from pressing concerns: access to resources to care for and provide for children. What can be done to support rather than criminalize mothers?

The contributors tell stories of mothers who find themselves—and their mothering—the object of state-sponsored control, punishment, social surveillance, stigma, practices of social exclusion, and public scrutiny. Our aim is to hear the voices of the mothers themselves, especially marginalized women who are socially excluded and/or penalized and called to account for inadequate care giving, such as mothers living with HIV, mothers in abusive relationships, and incarcerated mothers. We hope to create a space for envisioning how social justice for all mothers and children is possible.

Criminalized Mothers, Criminalizing Mothering is the first book of its kind to examine both the experiences of mothers criminalized through criminal justice processing and extra-legal regulation of mothering in marginalized social locations. The collection was born of our effort to grapple with the relationship between criminalized mothers as a group and criminalizing mothering as a process. We sought out chapters that investigate how women (re)build their lives in the face of, or with the threat of, criminalization, and illuminate the conditions and contexts under which marginalized women care for themselves and their children.

Interdisciplinary and international in scope, *Criminalized Mothers, Criminalizing Mothering* examines some of the challenges women around the world face as they mother at the social margins with limited access to resources to care for themselves and their children. It features scholarship in diverse fields (including sociology, women's health, women's studies, criminal justice, criminology, psychology, and motherhood studies) and new research conducted in Canada, the United States, Brazil, Trinidad and Tobago, England, and Israel.

LOCATING THE SOCIAL REGULATION OF MOTHERS

Recent media headlines such as "Working Mom Arrested for Letting Her Daughter Play Outside" (referring to Debra Harrell) (Friedersdorf) and "'Octomom' Charged with Welfare Fraud in California" (referring to Nadya Schulman) (Rogers), illustrate that criminalization of mothers proliferates. In her 2012 *New York Times* article, "The Criminalization of Bad Mothers," Ada Calhoun describes the case of Alabama mother Amanda Kimbrough. In April 2008, Amanda Kimbrough was arrested after the death of her son (who was born premature) and mandated to undergo drug treatment and parenting classes. Her two daughters were removed from her care. Police charged Kimbrough with chemical endangerment of a child, a crime that carries a mandatory sentence of ten years to life. She pled guilty and received ten years in prison.

Informal regulatory mechanisms also police the behaviours of mothers like Harrell, Shulman and Kimbrough. The mother who deviates from cultural scripts simultaneously contradicts and reifies a long-standing belief that the good mother is supposed to selflessly care for her children (O'Reilly, "Rocking the Cradle"). Women who are perceived to live and act outside of these sensibilities are treated, informally and/or formally, as "Other." The "criminalized mother" as "Other" betrays overarching societal assumptions about gender, care, and control. Namely, the "good mother" does not harm her child, and mothers are supposed to be primarily responsible for protecting their children from harm (Hays). What's more, causing harm (or merely being blamed for social harm) and failure to protect, warrant scrutiny, control, and punishment. The chapters in this collection reveal the consequences for mothers when they are criticized, shamed, and called to account for *failing* to provide for and protect their children.

THEORETICAL FRAMING

Through the lens of maternal subjects and with a keen eye to both the discursive and material practices that criminalize mothering, *Criminalized Mothers, Criminalizing Mothering* brings together scholarship mainly operating in silos, namely feminist criminology and motherhood studies, and begins to bridge the gap in the literature between criminalization and mothering.

Beginning with Adrienne Rich's *Of Woman Born*, Sara Ruddick's maternal thinking, and Andrea O'Reilly's prolific analyses, motherhood studies has evolved into a field rich in depth and breadth. This impressive scholarship has identified the "contradictions of motherhood" (Hays) and continues to examine a plethora of issues that impact mothers, from work and the economy to childcare and parenting practices (Thurer; Douglas and Michaels; Hays; O'Reilly *Mother Outlaws*).[1] Judith Stadtman Tucker encapsulates the (contested) dominant ideology of motherhood:

> The belief that children's optimal growth and development are directly and exclusively related to the quality and quantity of maternal care they receive, and caring mothers

> always put children's needs ahead of their own. (210)

A criminalized mother is an Other, outside of the "caring mothers" category. As long as dominant cultures paradoxically value motherhood and devalue mothers, the criminalized mother, and women equated to her, will be branded as unworthy citizens and *bad* mothers. The criminalization of mothers is a significant and timely area of scholarship because women are called to account for more than law violations when they are criminalized; their mothering practices are on display, and, at times, on trial. In *Incarcerated Mothers: Oppression and Resistance*, editors Gordana Eljdupovic and Rebecca Jaremko Bromwich situate mothering by women who end up incarcerated in the context of their lives at the margins, in all its stigma, shame, and deviance. They argue that:

> when women from the margins do mother, they place value on themselves and on children that the society in which they live has deemed unworthy of investment. Mothers from the margins may "resist" imposed perceptions and negative stereotypical or ideological assessments of their mothering, and yet, maintain values stemming from mothering in high regard and of utmost importance. (6)

Women who commit crimes defy the law and betray their gender (Balfour and Comack). From the pivotal work of Carol Smart to vibrant contemporary critical scholarship, feminist criminologists have challenged male-stream narratives of women and crime, produced analyses that have centred criminalized women's experiences, and, in the process, offered new ways to understand women's troubles with the law (Smart, *Women, Crime and Criminology;* Smart, *Feminism and the Power of Law*; Rafter and Heidensohn; Cain; Gelsthorpe and Morris). Feminist scholars like Patricia Carlen, Margaret Shaw, and Elizabeth Comack have demonstrated the association between victimization and criminalization. Others have shown how racism and poverty compound this connection (Chesney-Lind and Eliason; Monture-Angus). In their classic piece "Criminalized

Mothers: The Value and Devaluation of Parenthood Behind Bars," Angela Moe and Kathleen Ferraro argue that motherhood itself and particularly when combined with other factors, like drugs, poverty, and abuse, is a pathway to crime. Ferraro and Moe argue: "The ability to mother one's children according to social expectations and personal desires depends ultimately on one's access to the resources of time, money, health, and social support" (14). Feminist scholars link the feminization of poverty to women's exponential rate of criminalization (Allen, Flaherty and Ely). Elizabeth Comack, for her part, argues: "[a]s more and more women are confronted with the task of making ends meet under dire circumstances, the link between poverty and women's lawbreaking becomes more obvious" (39). One key finding—that the struggle to provide and care for child(ren) brings many women into conflict with the law—deserves closer consideration. Feminist criminologists have identified processes outside criminal justice systems that manage and regulate women's lives.[2] Extending this study, *Criminalized Mothers, Criminalizing Mothering* explores how criminalized women are disciplined and regulated *as mothers,* how criminalization impacts mothering, and the ways in which women resist practices of surveillance and marginalization.

Marlee Kline maintains that motherhood ideology constructs mothering as compulsory "only for those women considered 'fit,' and not for women who have been judged 'unfit' on the bases of their social location" (120-121). The ideology of the good mother is embedded in class, race, sexuality, ability, ethnicity, and age hierarchies. It privileges a dominant mothering approach very few women can embody and lifestyles many cannot afford. In 1995, Marlee Kline argued: "Thus, motherhood is better conceptualized as a privilege than a right, a privilege that can be withheld, both ideologically and in more material ways, from women who are not members of dominant groups in society or who are otherwise considered unfit" (122).

Twenty years later, the contradictions between motherhood and criminalization demands our concern. As the chapters in this book demonstrate, mothering figures prominently in incarcerated women's lives. Put simply, *to criminalize*, according to most dictionary definitions, is "to turn a person into a criminal." The power to criminalize is the law's most formidable role (Balfour and Comack). Gillian Balfour and Elizabeth Comack argue that criminalization is complicated because law deals not simply in objective facts, but in ideology and discourse. In the courts, legal actors evaluate women against gendered expectations as well as against violations of the criminal code.[3] Determining the legally relevant facts of a case, they assert, requires legal actors to engage in "deciphering or translation," making judgments "on the legal subjects themselves, in terms not only of what they have *done*, but also of *who* they are, and on the social settings or spaces in which they move" (9-10, emphasis added). This deciphering is gendered, racialized, and class compounded (Razack; Balfour and Comack). Dominant ideologies about *good motherhood* and *good womanhood* influence how the police, courts, and corrections staff treat and interpret a woman and evaluate her behaviour. Extra-legal processes—social work, health care and medicine, child welfare—also function to criminalize certain kinds of mothering through a discourse and set of practices that blame, shame, and punish mothers.

Njoki Nathani Wane contends:

> Assumptions about which women can and cannot be mothers or good mothers are a form of social control embedded in the capitalist mode of production and rooted in patriarchal systems. Ideally, assumptions about who constitutes a good mother would not be based on one model of mothering, but would be determined in culturally and community specific contexts. (111)

Minaker found that women mother in the context of contradiction, experiencing motherhood "in the space between" oppression and resistance. Mothering in the context of marginalization and criminalization is fraught with difficulties stemming from the material realities of women's lives and their experiences of social exclusion, imprisonment, violence, racism, and poverty. Women who resist systemic conditions of their lives through acts of violence, criminal activity, or political activism face additional barriers, regulation, surveillance, criminalization, and the threat of punishment.

CRIMINALIZING MARGINALIZED MOTHERS

Mothers, historically and today, are controlled, regulated, scrutinized, and pathologized on account of their believed inability to care for and protect their child(ren) (Donzelot; Mosher; Swift and Callahan). A discourse of child neglect has become a powerful way to "manufacture" bad mothers (Swift). Renee Heikamp may have the dubious distinction of being "Canada's Most Notorious Bad Mother," a representation that obscures her status as a young, homeless, marginalized mother (Robson 217). After the inquest into the death of Jordon Desmond Heikamp, who died while under the care of Ontario Children's Aid in 1997 of chronic starvation, Renee Hiekamp (Jordan's nineteen-year-old, homeless mother) and Angela Martin (Jordan's assigned social worker) were charged with negligence. In her review of newspaper coverage of the case, Krista Robson examined how the media and public constructed Renee Heikamp as a "bad mother," reinforcing hegemonic notions of "good" mothering. Melissa Gills claims that the inquest was about "the capability of Renee Heikamp to parent. It [was] not an inquest into a fundamentally problematic system that allows a 19-year-old youth to receive full blame for the death of an infant supposedly under the care of the Ontario child welfare system" (6). Relying on this discourse, the Coroner's report (Ontario) decontextualized Renee's choice to feed her baby diluted formula from her material reality and her lack of other choices. A mother's access to the resources and supports necessary to care for her family depends on her social location. As circumstances of women's lives deteriorate and support systems erode under the weight of state retrenchment, resources for care become harder to come by for lone-mothers and those without the social capital to attain a secure, living wage. In chapter fifteen of this volume, Hogeveen and Minaker demonstrate the plight of young, marginalized mothers who struggle to transform their material circumstances.

Charges laid against substance-using women provide another

illustration of how particular kinds of mothering are subject to criminalization. Hope Ankrom was the first woman prosecuted on an abuse charge for using drugs during her pregnancy in Alabama. Complex social and ethical issues concerning drug (ab)use during pregnancy get obscured when women like Hope are cast as "Drug-Dependent Mothers" and held blameworthy for child endangerment (Gustavsson). Alabama's chemical-endangerment law empowers the state to lay charges and prosecute substance-using women. Under this law, mothers' addiction becomes a criminal issue, not a health issue. The assumption underlying such prosecution is that mothers are not supposed to harm their children in *any* way, under any circumstances. As Nora Gustavson explains, when women are constructed as "agents of harm" criminalization is the legitimate response (65). A wider social discourse of maternal blame justifies claims of women's irresponsibility. Research demonstrates women's drug use is connected to a host of other factors, including depression, physical and emotional abuse, poverty, lack of adequate housing, poor nutrition, and inadequate health care (Boyd and Marcellus; Toscano). Yet, the most recent object of regulation in the War on Drugs, which began in the 1970s, primarily targeted to low-income and racialized neighbourhoods, is the pregnant, drug-dependent woman (Moe and Ferraro). It appears that managing the "risk" to the unborn takes precedence over supporting the mother-to-be through her pregnancy and alleviating the pressures from systemic barriers or other conditions that lead to challenges mothers and children might face. Despite mounting opposition from reproductive rights groups, doctors, and medical organizations who are opposed to criminalization and argue that it makes vulnerable women less likely to seek drug treatment, states like Tennessee continue to criminalize mothers.[4] As the state gains more access to women's wombs through technology and legal intrusion, women might eventually be held accountable for *everything* and *anything* they do during pregnancy, and a wide spectrum of maternal practices may become subject to state regulation. This dystopian scenario is not pure fiction. Case in point: in Indiana, Bei Bei Shuai is serving a prison sentence for her suicide attempt, one that resulted in the death of her fetus.[5]

OUTLINE OF THE BOOK

Criminalized Mothers, Criminalizing Mothering explores the uneasy tensions between mothering and criminalization. The chapters explore the struggles, resilience, and contradictory experiences of criminalized mothers and challenges public discourses about mothering at the margins. Under what material and discursive conditions do mothers at the margins and criminalized women mother? As resources to care for themselves and their children are unevenly distributed, how do mothers—especially those at the social margins—respond, cope, and re-imagine their lives?

We chose to organize the book into two sections that each attend to the book's main theme of criminalized motherhood. Part 1, Discourses and Practices of Maternal Criminalization, examines criminalization through maternal regulation and formal criminal justice processing. The chapters in this section cover different subject matter, from maternity homes for young mothers to international law on child abduction, and each furthers our understanding of the discourses and/or practices that act to criminalize particular forms of mothering. Part 1 emphasizes the conditions under which mothers are marginalized by social location and injustice, including violence, gender inequality, poverty, racism, and age hierarchies. The authors illustrate how mothers are active agents subjected to legal regulation, not passive recipients of intrusions into their lives.

Part 2, Maternal Narratives/Beyond Criminalization, amplifies mothers' voices and acts of resistance. Each chapter attempts to unravel the tensions faced by criminalized mothers and/or uncover alternatives to the social and cultural processes that criminalize *particular forms of* mothering. These chapters show how, in the face of challenge and disadvantage, mothers—both imprisoned or/and regulated in the community—demonstrate strength, resilience, and the wherewithal to push the limits of social exclusion with dignity, grace, and care.

One theme unites the chapters in the book: the tensions and openings within the space of marginalized and criminalized mothering. In what follows we present the chapters and show how each piece contributes to our understanding of the impact of legal and extra-legal processes of criminalization on mothers and mothering.

The book opens with a poem written by Melissa Bigstone during a painful period of her adolescence, a time when she was struggling with new mothering and involvement with child welfare. Creative expression provides a window into her vulnerability and, we hope, invites the kind of compassion necessary for personal change and social transformation.

PART 1: DISCOURSES AND PRACTICES OF MATERNAL CRIMINALIZATION

We can learn about processes of maternal criminalization by looking to the past and to the dominant responses to "deviant" mothers, but important lessons about criminalized mothers are also visible when social actors challenge those practices. In "Treasures: Multiple Economies of Reproduction at the Beulah Rescue Home for Unmarried Mothers, Edmonton, Alberta, 1909-1963," Amy Kaler explores what she calls "the physical and symbolic nexus for the management of illicit pregnancy." She examines the circulation of babies and virtue in "the social imaginary" in twentieth-century Edmonton at the Beulah Rescue Home for unmarried mothers. Kaler depicts Beulah as a site of multiple economies of reproduction. She argues that social value is generated through some pregnancies, but not through others, and thereby links "stratified reproduction to the much wider field of the political economy of reproduction." Her analysis explores the way the Beulah institution and its discourse transformed unmarried pregnant women and their infants.

The following two chapters explore how law shapes public perceptions of "fit" mother and "unfit" mothers. Extra-legal factors like a mother's presumed capacity to parent, economic resources, and culture play a determining role. Impoverished women (e.g., poor women of colour in the United States and Aboriginal women in Canada) are entangled with criminal justice and other regulatory systems in ways that are tied to their role and identity as (often sole care-giving) mothers. For example, entrenched negative representations of Aboriginal mothers as "unfit" reinforce "the pervasive, critical glare of the state" (Cull 141) and child protection involvement on the grounds of failure to protect or provide. This view fails to place contemporary Aboriginal mothering practices in the context of colonization and its destructive consequences, and also ignores a resurgence of cultural teachings aimed at Aboriginal families and communities.

The case of Indigenous mothering illustrates how criminalizing motherhood is class-compounded and racialized. Laura Landertinger and Josephine L. Savarese both focus on the plight of Indigenous mothers in Canada. In different ways they each investigate the "bad mother" in child welfare discourse and how practices of regulation impact criminalized mothers' lives. In "Settler Colonialism and Carceral Control of Indigenous Mothers and their Children: Child Welfare and the Prison System," Laura Landertinger interrogates what she calls the "bio-politics of settler colonialism" and how it reinforces the marginalization of Indigenous mothers. She argues that two overlapping techniques of surveillance, the child welfare system and the prison system, have detrimental impacts on Indigenous mothers.

Continuing the theme of child welfare intervention as a tool to criminalize mothers/mothering, Josephine L. Savarese investigates how gendered and racialized frameworks determined child welfare involvement in the case of Laura, an Indigenous mother constructed as threatening to her children's wellbeing after her daughter Sara disappeared. In "Theorizing Soft Criminalization and Surveillance in the Child Welfare System: Analyzing *Re S.F.*," Savarese reviews the appeal decision, *Re S.F.* and argues that both criminal justice and child protection systems in this case surveil an Indigenous mother's life for non-conformance with dominant norms.

Michelle Hughes Miller explores the concept of mother blame and its impact on organizational policies and practices of youth justice. In "Mothering Outside-In: Confined Children and Mothering under State Paternalism," Hughes Miller shines a light on the mothers left in the community when systems of care and control detain their children. She asks: How do juvenile justice system policies manage the mothers of juveniles detained within the system? To examine this question she critically reflects on the way mother-blame dictates "the boundaries of separated mothering within the juvenile justice system in the United States."

The next two chapters continue the theme of maternal responsibility, though the focus shifts outside North America. In "Criminalizing Motherhood: Examining the Hague Convention on International Child Abduction," Rebecca Jaremko Bromwich offers a legal analysis of discrimination of mothers who flee abuse with their children. Jaremko Bromwich argues "the Convention puts children and mothers at risk of harm." She points out how the Hague Convention fails to recognize domestic violence. The law, Jaremko Bromwich illustrates, exposes already marginalized and vulnerable mothers to the risk of criminalization for efforts to protect themselves and their children from witnessing or experiencing violence.

Next, we move from women's experiences of violence to their engagements with violence. Mothers accused of child murder—and social responses to women presumed to be "monsters"—signify the way criminal mother is an oxymoron. In their book *When Mothers Kill,* Michelle Oberman and Cheryl Meyer drew on qualitative interviews with mothers who were imprisoned for causing a child's death to paint a picture in stark contrast to the cold, uncaring, homicidal woman in the public imagination of "killer moms." The authors gave voice and visibility to the plight of women who lacked social supports, had inadequate mechanisms to cope with the stress of motherhood, and felt isolated and vulnerable in their experiences of violence, isolation, and hopelessness.

Following this approach, two authors in this section (Hijin Park and Hollis Moore) tackle the trouble of and for mothers who kill their children. Hijin Park illustrates how constructions of race, nation, gender, class, and citizenship intersect with media representations of criminalized mothers in contemporary Calgary, Canada. In "Race, Nation and Citizenship in 'Mothers Who Kill Their Children': The Case of Rie Fujii," Park provides "a structural analysis that accounts for how race, gender, class, and nation intersect in the context of Canadian white settler nationalism." She argues that media discourse bolsters law's power to criminalize in the case Rie Fuji, a mother behind bars for killing her children.

The next chapter takes another historical turn to explore changing perceptions of motherhood at the intersections of law and medicine. In "Legal and Medical Maneuvers: The Attitude of the Legal and Medical Systems to Ellen Harper Who Murdered Her Infant Daughter in 1878," Tamar Hager explores the English legal and medical systems in the late nineteenth century. Hager uses Ellen Harper's story to show how medicine and law served to reinforce the patriarchal view that mothers are not autonomous but rather exist for the sake of their own children. She suggests that the case of Ellen Harper "exposes the contradiction between the written law, which has perpetuated the past, and the actual attitude of the courts and the medical establishment towards mothers who had murdered their children."

"Pregnant, Incarcerated, and Overlooked: Shedding Light on Pregnancy in Juvenile Detention Centres" explores the psychological and social issues surrounding young women who find themselves both incarcerated and pregnant. Based on a feminist understanding of women's health, Keri O'Neal and Wendy Watson offer a literature synthesis of existing research about pregnant, incarcerated adolescents. They explore the social and cultural contextual factors associated with pregnancy for incarcerated young women, and demonstrate that the unique physical, emotional, and social needs of this group are often overlooked. They call for greater scholarly and policy consideration of pregnant teenagers housed in correctional detention facilities.

PART 2: MATERNAL NARRATIVES/BEYOND CRIMINALIZATION

In her poem "Turning to One Another," Margaret Wheatley suggests "there is no power greater than a community discovering what it cares about." She reminds us to ask "what's possible?" rather than what is wrong. Othering practices inside and outside the criminal justice and correctional systems will continue to socially exclude marginalized mothers until we hear their voices, take their claims seriously, and recognize their rights. The chapters in this section foreground the voices of women behind bars and living at the social, economic, and political margins of their communities. The contributors underscore mothers' stories of courage, care, resistance, and resiliency.

Some mothers experience criminalization and/or are at risk of being criminalized for stigmatized social identities. In their chapter "(M)othering with HIV: Resisting and Reconstructing Experiences of Health and Social Surveillance," Saara Greene, Allyson Ion, Dawn Elston, Gladys Kwaramba, Stephanie Smith, and Mona Loutfy draw on narrative interviews with seventy-seven women to explore themes at work in the health and social care system for mothers living with HIV in Ontario, Canada. They argue that mothers living with HIV are policed both formally vis-à-vis the criminalization of HIV non-disclosure law and informally by being under the constant surveillance of health and social care professionals. The authors examine the complex interplay of socially constructed notions of motherhood, HIV-related stigma, and gender, race, and class, and ask how professionals can play a more supportive role.

The professionals working within the social and criminal justice systems that mothers encounter influence the extent to which women feel cared for and/or criminalized. In "Do You Have My Son?" Criminalization and the Production of (Un)Relatedness in Brazil," Hollis Moore analyses the "disappearance" of the son of Ivete, a female remand prisoner. Moore situates the event within the broader context of Ivete's life history and explores the ways institutions, discourses, and structures shape and are shaped by practices of (un)relatedness. A focus on one woman's fraught experiences of care/control offers important lessons about criminalized women's struggles and the demanding conditions under which marginalized women mother.

From Brazil to the remote islands of Trinidad and Tobago, we find women all over the world wrestling with the divide between how they see themselves and how others view them. In "Mothering at the Margins: The Case of Incarcerated Women in Trinidad and Tobago," Talia Esnard and Kimberly Okpala explore the challenges incarcerated mothers face within their family relationships and with mother-child separation, inside and outside of prison. How do incarcerated mothers redefine and reclaim already fractured maternal identities and practices? Using a case study, the authors give voice to the experiences of twelve incarcerated mothers in Trinidad and Tobago's prison. Esnard and Okpala argue that incarceration of mothers, with its connection to gender and cultural and class position, exacerbates the complexities of women's lives. Indeed, criminalized mothers confront many paradoxes as they negotiate and define their maternal identities and practices.

The theme of contradiction continues in Caroline McDonald-Harker's chapter. "Mothering in the Context of Domestic Abuse and Encounters with Child Protection Services: From Victimized to 'Criminalized' Mothers" offers a rare glimpse into the complicated plight of mothers living in abusive relationships. In this extensive qualitative study, mothers in domestic abuse relationships find a space to tell their stories. McDonald-Harker argues that surveillance and maternal regulation largely characterized the women's encounters with child protection agencies and the criminal justice state. She suggests that listening to mothers' stories is a necessary step to creating more caring communities where women and their children can access the services and support they need.

Poor and marginalized mothers who experience increased surveillance and decreased social care find themselves along the victimization-criminalization continuum. Racialized women are disproportionately represented in women's prisons (Chesney-Lind and Eliason). Renita L. Seabrook and Heather Wyatt-Nichol tell the stories of criminalized mothers, many of whom are Latina and African American, in "Marginalization and Hope: Personal Narratives of Previously Incarcerated Mothers." Based on interviews with sixteen previously imprisoned mothers now enrolled in a re-entry program in Baltimore City, Maryland, the authors use critical race theory and feminist standpoint theory to examine the women's plight and what is possible for reunification with their children. Seabrook and Wyatt-Nichol argue that mothers "are often punished again through obstacles to successful transition into the community—barred from assistance programs, finding meaningful employment, and in reestablishing the mother-child relationship." Despite these obstacles many mothers are hopeful they can rebuild their lives.

Mothering can provide an opportunity to transition to a new lifestyle and can construct new identities, even in the most marginal social spaces and among the most disadvantaged. Hogeveen and Minaker offer a story of transformation in "'Something Worth Living For': Young Criminalized Mothering." Hogeveen and Minaker draw on interviews with young mothers living at the margins in Edmonton, Canada to highlight how criminalized mothers navigate the demands of parenting as they transition away from the harms and hostility of street life. The chapter is based on a case study of Jenna, a former street-involved youth who transformed from a young mother at the margins to a stable and secure life with her husband and son. Meaningful, positive life changes become possible when a mother (no matter her age, social status, or background) is welcomed into a community of care.

The book closes with a short essay called, "My Mothering Story: A Mother, a Daughter, a Fighter," in which Melissa Bigstone shares her story of healing and hope. Melissa describes her childhood growing up in the child welfare and youth justice system, her entanglements with child welfare with her own children, and her quest for social justice for other marginalized mothers. A role model in her community, Bigstone reminds us of the power of transformative care and the resilience of the human spirit.

CONCLUSION

> Their futures are not hopeless. Many have survived circumstances worse than incarceration and will continue to survive despite insurmountable odds. We must recognize this and choose to support them through the process, instead of ignoring, spacegoating, and criminalizing them. (Moe and Ferraro 160)

At a time when women are the fastest growing segment of the prison population worldwide and when two thirds of incarcerated women are mothers, consideration of the criminalization of mothers is timely and vital (Comack and Balfour). We have opened the window into the material and symbolic realities of mothering at the margins. The chapters in this book reveal how women living at the social margins and within impoverished environments are most likely to have their maternal rights infringed upon and be subject to criminal justice or child welfare intervention. Scholars from diverse fields have come together to explicate the hardships and harrowing experiences of women who mother in the context of criminalization.

All criminalized women are not marginalized, and all marginalized women do not become criminalized. However, problematizing the relationship between mothering and criminalization is critically important so we can understand why the most marginalized mothers are most likely to be incarcerated, separated from their children, blamed, shamed, and made "Other." Thoughtful consideration of systemic issues and personal struggles can open new possibilities for building alternative, more caring, and inclusive social systems.

Being empathetic to each other's struggle and strength is part of a quest toward social justice. It recognizes our shared humanity and demands openness to seeing beyond the social constructions, stigmatization, and discourses that perpetuate us versus them. The complex lives of mothers who are criminalized cannot be reduced to popular representations of "poor mothers," "young mothers," or "violent mothers" etc. Within these pages, the eclectic contributors also offer stories of hope and care, narratives of resilience, and new possibilities for meaningful change. For radical social transformation, we must imagine a future where *all mothers* could be "mother outlaws." In Andrea O'Reilly's ("Mother Outlaws") terms, these mothers have agency, authority, autonomy, and authenticity to engage in mothering *of their own choosing*. If we are to recognize the value and necessity of a broad community of care for all mothers and children, we must bridge the (material and discursive) divide that separates mothers. For the sake of all mothers and children everywhere, we must close the chasm between mothers and "Other" mothers.

Our hope with this book is to humanize criminalized mothers by offering a window into the social contexts that condition and contour the lived realities of criminalized mothering. May the dialogue the book stimulates bring us closer to empowering all mothers to make choices about how they mother free of coercion and violence. The stories shared here remind us that up against powerful forces of criminalization and control, mothers are strong in their resolve, resilient in their ability to transform their lives, and have the courage to be bold with their care.

Remember, you don't fear people whose story you know. Real listening always brings people closer together. Trust that meaningful conversations can change the world.
—Margaret Wheatley

ENDNOTES

[1]See over 50 Demeter Press titles and the *Journal of the Motherhood Initiative for Research and Community Involvement.*
[2]For example, Shelley Gavigan and Dorothy Chunn point to the direct effect of neoliberal provincial government clawbacks to services (e.g., shelters, public housing, daycare, and food banks) on women's vulnerability to domestic violence and risk of criminalization for welfare fraud.
[3]In other spheres, from schools to workplaces, in child welfare offices to hospitals, and within their communities, individuals and institutions judge mothers against cultural expectations of who they are and who they are *supposed* to be.
[4]In 2013 the State of Tennessee enacted the Safe Harbor Act, which protected the custody rights of mothers, giving them priority for treatment in drug treatment centres. Tennessee women found to be using drugs while pregnant can now be criminally charged for harm done to their infants, after Gov. Bill Haslam signed legislation that went into effect July 1, 2014.
[5]Mississippi law how enables prosecutor's to charge women (like Rennie Gibbs, whose pregnancy resulted in a stillborn birth) with "depraved heart murder." This charge has a life sentence with no parole until age 65. Under South Carolina's "viable fetuses" law of October 2003, Regina McKnight became the first American woman convicted for murder for using cocaine while pregnant. She remains in prison serving a twelve-year sentence for murder (Talvi).

WORK CITED

Allen, Suzanne, Chris Flaherty, and Gretchen Ely. "Throwaway Moms: Maternal Incarceration and the Criminalization of Female Poverty." *Journal of Women and Social Work* 25.2 (2010): 160-72. Print.

Balfour, Gillian and Elizabeth Comack. *The Power to Criminalize: Violence, Inequality and the Law*. Halifax: Fernwood, 2004. Print.

Boyd, Susan and L. Marcellus. *With Child: Substance Use During pregnancy, A Woman-Centred Approach*. Halifax: Fernwood, 2007. Print.

Cain, Maureen. "Towards Transgression: New Directions in Feminist Criminology." *International Journal of the Sociology of Law* 18 (1990): 1-18. Print.

Calhoun, Ada. "The Criminalization of Bad Mothers." *New York Times* Web. 19 July 2014.

Canadian Human Rights Commission, *Protecting Their Rights a Systematic Review of Human Rights in Correctional Services for Federally Sentenced Women*. (Ottawa: Canadian Human Rights Commission, 2003) at 6. Print.

Carlen, Patricia. *Women, Crime and Poverty*. Milton Keynes: Open University Press, 1988. Print.

Comack, Elizabeth and Gillian Balfour. *Criminalizing Women: Gender (In)Justice in Neo-Liberal Times*. Halifax: Fernwood, 2006. Print.

Chesney-Lind, Meda and Michelle Eliason. "From Invisible to Incorrigible: The Demonization of Marginalized Women and Girls." *Crime Media Culture* 2.1 (2006): 29-47. Print.

Cull, R. (2006). Aboriginal mothering under the State's gaze. In D. Lavell-Harvard & J. Lavell (Eds.), Until our hearts are on the ground: Aboriginal mothering, oppression, resistance and rebirth, (pp.141-156). Toronto, ON: Demeter Press.

Donzelot, Jacques. *The Policing of Families*. New York: Pantheon Books, 1979. Print.

Douglas, Susan J. and Meredith W. Michaels. *The Mommy Myth: The Idealization of*

Motherhood and How It Has Undermined Women. New York: Free Press. 2004. Print.

Eljdupovic, Gordana and Rebecca Jaremko Bromwich. *Incarcerated Mothers: Oppression and Resistance*. Bradford: Demeter Press, 2013. Print.

Ferraro, Kathleen J. and Angela M. Moe. "Mothering, Crime and

Incarceration." *The Journal of Contemporary Ethnography.* 32(1) (2003): 9-40. Print.
Friedersdorf, Conor. "Working Mom Arrested for Letting Her 9-Year-Old Play Alone at Park." *The Atlantic* Web. 27 November 2014.
Gavigan, Shelley, and Dorothy Chunn. "From Welfare Fraud to Welfare as Fraud: The Criminalization of Poverty". *Published Articles & Book Chapters.* Paper 90, 2006. Web. 3 May 2014.
Gills, Melinda Vandenbeld. *From Need to Risk: The Neoliberal Construction of the "Bad" Mother.* Munk School Briefings. Toronto: Monk School of Global Affairs, University of Toronto. n.d. Print.
Gelsthorpe, Loraine and Allison Morris. "Feminism and Criminology in Britain." *British Journal of Criminology* 28.2 (1988): 93-110. Print.
Gustavsson, Nora S. "Pregnant Chemically-Dependent Women: The New Criminals." *Affilia* 6 (1991): 61-73. Print.
Hays, Sharon. *The Cultural Contradictions of Motherhood.* New Haven: Yale University Press, 1996. Print.
Holmes, Tracy. "Psych assessment ordered for South Surrey mother charged with murder." *Peace Arch News* Web. 12 December 2014.
Kerman, Piper. *Orange Is the New Black: My Year in a Women's Prison.* New York: Random House, 2011. Print.
Kline, Marlee. "Complicating the Ideology of Motherhood: Child Welfare Law and First Nation Women." *Law: Feminist Theory and the Legal Regulation of Motherhood.* Ed. Martha Fineman and Isabel Karpin. New York: Columbia University Press, 1995. 118-141. Print.
Minaker, Joanne. "The Space Between: Mothering in the Context of Contradiction." *Moms Gone Mad: Oppression and Resistance.* Ed. Gina Wong Bradford: Demeter Press, 2012. 124-140. Print.
Moe, Angela and Angela Ferraro. "Criminalized Mothers: The Value and Devaluation of Parenthood from Behind Bars." *Women and Therapy* 29.3,4 (2006): 135-164. Print.
Monture-Angus, Patricia. "Women and Risk: Aboriginal Women, Colonialism, and Correctional Practice." *Canadian Woman Studies/les cahiers de la femme* 19 (1999): 24-9. Print.
Mosher, Janet. "Intimate Intrusions: Welfare Regulation and Wom-

en's Personal Lives." *The Legal Tender of Gender: Law, Welfare and the Regulation of Women's Poverty.* OÑATI International Series in Law and Society. Ed. Shelley Gavigan and Dorothy Chunn. Oregon: Hart Publishing, 2010. 165–188. Print.

Oberman, Michelle and Cheryl Meyer. *When Mothers Kill: Interviews from Prison.* New York: New York University Press, 2008. Print.

Ontario: Office of the Chief Coroner. *Report on the Inquest into the Death of Jordan Desmond Heikamp.* Toronto, September 2002. Print.

O'Reilly, Andrea. *Rocking the Cradle: Thoughts on Motherhood, Feminism and the Possibility of Empowered Mothering.* Toronto: Demeter Press, 2006. Print.

O'Reilly, Andrea. *Mother Outlaws: Theories and Practices of Empowered Mothering.* Toronto: Women's Press, 2004. Print.

Orange is the New Black, Netflix Series. [Film/series accessed online follows this format: Film Title. Director name. Distributor, Year of Release. Name of Service Provider. Medium of Publication. Day Month Year of Access. [pls provide]

Rafter, Nicole Hahn and Frances Heidensohn. "Introduction: The Development of Feminist Perspectives on Crime." *International Feminist Perspectives in Criminology: Engendering a Discipline.* Ed. Nicole Hahn Rafter and Frances Heidensohn. Philadelphia: Open University Press, 1995. Print.

Razack, Sherene. *Race, Space and the Law: Unmapping a White Settler Society.* Toronto: Between the Lines, 2002. Print.

Rich, Adrienne. *Of Woman Born: Motherhood as Experience and Institution.* New York, Norton and Company, 1976. Print.

Robson, Krista. " 'Canada's Most Notorious Bad Mother': The Newspaper Coverage of the Jordan Heikamp Inquest." *Canadian Review of Sociology and Anthropology* 42.2 (2005): 217-32. Print.

Rogers, John. 'Octomom' charged with welfare fraud in California. *Yahoo News* January 14, 2014. Web. 2 March 2014.

Ruddick, Sara. *Maternal Thinking: Towards a Politics of Peace.* Boston: Beacon Press, 1989. Print.

Saltman, Jennifer. Web. "Surrey mom charged with murder in death of her eight-year-old girl, who was found in trunk of car." *The*

Province December 12, 2014. Web. 12 December 2014.
Shaw, Margaret. "Women in Prison: A Literature Review." *Forum* 6.1 (1994): 13-18. Print.
Smart, Carol. *Feminism and the Power of Law*. New York: Routledge, 1989. Print.
Smart, Carol. *Women, Crime and Criminology: A Feminist Critique*. Boston: Routledge & Kegan Paul, 1976. Print.
Stadtman, Judith Tucker. "Rocking the Boat: Feminism and the Ideological Grounding of the Twentieth-First Century Mothers' Movement." *Feminist Mothering*. Ed. A. O'Reilly. New York: State University of New York Press, 2008. 205-218. Print.
Sudbury, Julia, ed. *Global Lockdown: Race, Gender, and the Prison-Industrial Complex*. London: Routledge. 2004. Print.
Swift, Karen. *Manufacturing "Bad Mothers": A Critical Perspective on Child Neglect*. Toronto: University of Toronto Press, 1995. Print.
Swift, Karen and Marilyn Callahan. *At Risk: Social Justice in Child Welfare and Other Human Services*. Toronto: University of Toronto Press, 2009. Print.
Talvi, Silja J. A. "Criminalizing Motherhood." *The Nation Magazine* December 11, 2003. Web.10 June 2014.
Thurer, Shari L. *The Myths of Motherhood*. New York: Houghton Mifflin Company, 1994. Print.
Toscano, Vicki. "Misguided Retribution: Criminalization of Pregnant Women Who Take Drugs." *Social Legal Studies* 14 (2005): 360-86. Print.
Wane, Nathani Njoki. "Reflections on the Mutuality of Mothering Women, Children and Othermothering." *Journal for the Association for Research on Mothering*. 2 (2004): 105-116. Print.
Wheatley, Margaret. "Turning to One Another." Web. December 12, 2014.

Part I:
Discourses and Practices of Maternal Criminalization

1.
For My Kids

A Poem

MELISSA BIGSTONE

It seemed like a normal day, woke up got ready and I was on my way,
But little did I know that all would be lost,
I was hoping and praying I could go back in the past,
Wishing it didn't happen so fast,
Now all I can do is wait, and do my best to fight this fate,
Wondering why this happened to me!
Is there something I didn't see?
I know some day this will grow on me,
I just got to move on and hope to see,
I know now that the best things in life don't come for free,
I hope that this will all end soon by the time spring comes and the flowers are ready to bloom,
I want to do it right next time, I do not wanna miss no warning signs,
'Cause I wake up every day not knowing what to say,
Just thinking about that one day I woke up thinking it was an ordinary day....

This poem is for my kids. I miss them a lot.
Written January 2, 2010.

2.
Treasures

Multiple Economies of Reproduction at the Beulah Rescue Home for Unmarried Mothers, Edmonton, Alberta, 1909-1963

AMY KALER

> *If ours were a task associated with world markets, [with] changing values and production in material gains and losses the problem would not be so distressing, but since we live and work with human lives ... ours is a very different undertaking. ... So we go on week after week casting bread upon the waters and trusting the promise that we shall find it after many days.* (Beulah Archives, "1936 Anniversary"[1])

> *How about doing some part of your Christmas shopping in the basement of the Legislative building this year? What could make a grander Christmas present than a darling baby?* (Beulah Archives,"Baby Adoption a Christmas Gift Idea")

HOW DO BABIES BECOME CHRISTMAS GIFTS, and what does this have to do with markets, gains, and losses? In this chapter, I examine the circulation of babies and the circulation of virtue in the "social imaginary" of a home for unmarried mothers in twentieth-century Edmonton. By "social imaginary" I mean the shared values, visions, and beliefs which animated collective social action, so that certain strategies come to be seen as both desirable and necessary. The intersection of 137th Avenue and 99th Street in Edmonton, Alberta, Canada is today a nondescript bit of inner-ring suburbia, dominated by an ageing mall, rush hour traffic, and franchised "family restaurants." For more than half of Edmonton's history, however, it was the site of the Beulah Rescue Home for unmarried mothers, and the physical and symbolic nexus for the management of illicit pregnancy. Here, I analyze Beulah as a site of multiple economies of reproduction generated through the efforts of the Beulah staff and wider society to contain, redeem, and transform unmarried pregnant women and their infants.

The first historians and sociologists studying the governance of pregnancies outside normative frameworks of marriage did so from a deviance/psychology perspective in which the pathologization or de-pathologization of individual girls was at issue (e.g., Friedman; Rains; for an overview see Brush; Spensky; Solinger). More recent work, strongly influenced by feminist theory and Foucault, has moved away from the question of individual deviance to focus on unmarried mothers as the subjects of governance, enmeshed in the biopolitics of their times (e.g., Reeves; Murray; Levesque; Little; Strange). This body of work also draws from the influential idea of stratified reproduction developed by Shellee Collen and popularized through the widely cited work of Faye Ginsburg and Rayna Rapp on reproduction and social theory. As they put it, stratified reproduction refers to the hierarchies of social value assigned to the childbearing practices of different groups of women, so that "the concept of stratified reproduction helps us see the arrangements by which some reproductive futures are valued while others are despised" (3).[2]

The idea that social value is generated through some pregnancies, but not through others, links stratified reproduction to the much wider field of the *political economy of reproduction* (Greenhalgh; Greenhalgh and Li; Browner; Kaler, "Who Has Told You"; Kaler *Running After Pills*; Rapp; Ginsburg and Rapp). In the political economy perspective, reproduction is imagined as a situationally contingent, socially directed process, in which the accumulation, consumption, and distribution of resources are shaped by asymmetric power relations among individuals and collectives. In this paper, I too take political economy as a point of departure. However, while most authors speak of *a* or *the* political economy of reproduction, I want to suggest that reproduction under any circumstances consists of *multiple* simultaneous economies, symbolic and material, which intersect, reinforce, and contradict one another.

By "economies" here, I mean observable patterns in the accumulation, distribution, conversion, and circulation of valued resources, whether those resources are concrete or symbolic.[3] To illustrate the ideas of multiple simultaneous economies, I look at two distinct patterns of accumulation, distribution, and circulation of resources at work in twentieth-century Alberta, brought into existence through the work of the Beulah Rescue Home. These are what I call the *economy of feminine virtue*, by which I mean the attribution of goodness and innocence to individuals. This attribution is convertible into entitlement and claims on other forms of resources; and *the economy of babies*, focussing on the distribution of the adoptable infants born at Beulah. The pregnant women who came to Beulah were regarded not as "damaged goods" or incorrigible sinners, but as unfortunate victims, whose downfall contained the seeds of their redemption, through their babies.

The first economy is mainly symbolic; the second is as concrete and corporeal as it is possible to be. Yet these two economies intersect with each other and are mutually dependent. The interdependence of these economies is perhaps most obvious in the words used to describe them—both the feminine virtue of the "fallen" women who became pregnant and the babies themselves were frequently referred to as "treasures," "precious," and even "jewels." The material and discursive work needed to assign value to these entities, both symbolic and corporeal, and to accumulate and distribute this value is the subject of this chapter.

A focus on political economies is slightly different from a focus on individualized "deviance" or a Foucauldian focus on governance and discipline. With a political economy approach, I am examining not so much the workings of power, as a biopolitical approach would do, as I am the different modalities of circulation. The entities which circulate in these economies include both the very corporeal in the form of babies, and the very abstract, in the form of particularly feminine virtues. These entities may be commodified, decommodified, and transformed one into another. Discussion of subjectivity and subject formation, one of the mainstays of Foucauldian approaches, here takes a backseat to tracing the movement of things and ideas through institutional and discursive spaces.

Beulah assisted women variously designated as "unfortunate," "fallen," "in trouble" and "in a certain way" between 1909 and 1964. Beulah provided them with residential accommodation before, during, and after the birth of their child, along with medical services and efforts at social and moral rehabilitation of the so-called disgraced mothers within a Christian ethos that stressed compassion and forgiveness. The home was also the centre of distribution for the children born of these pregnancies, whether these children were taken by their biological mothers immediately after birth; boarded at Beulah until the biological mothers could secure accommodation and retrieve their children; placed for adoption with other families; or turned over to the custody of the provincial Department of Neglected Children, later the Department of Social Welfare.

This chapter is based on the records of Beulah Home kept in the Provincial Archives of Alberta. These records consist largely of the vast personal papers of some of Beulah's longest-serving staffers, who maintained detailed scrapbooks,[4] ledgers, and correspondences. The continuity of these staffers, particular Mary Finley, who was the superintendent from 1921 until 1964, long-serving nurse Olivia Eidsath, and board of directors leader Charles Hill, meant that many ideas and practices at Beulah remained consistent across its decades of existence, although the Home was most active in the late 1910s through the 1940s. Records containing details of individual clients, including their own accounts of their circumstances, are protected by Canada's privacy legislation, meaning that the voices of the clients themselves are necessarily obscured by institutional texts.

AN OVERVIEW OF BEULAH

Edmonton, site of Beulah, is the capital of the province of Alberta in western Canada. Edmonton has historically functioned as a frontier city, the gateway to Canada's vast northwest. A boom-and-bust cycle in agriculture, land, and mineral resources has dominated Edmonton's economy since the beginning of the twentieth century.

Beulah Rescue Home began in 1909 as an offshoot of the Beulah Rescue Mission which catered to the growing transient urban population. The word "Beulah" appears in the book of Isaiah in the Christian bible as an alternate name for Israel, a blessed and prosperous land. Of particular significance to this paper, "Beulah" is often translated literally as "a married woman." The mission was run by the Mennonite Brethren in Christ, although its literature describes it as "nondenominational." The Mission was initially focussed on providing food, shelter, and a large dose of evangelism to indigent men, but from its first days, the presence of women and girls in Edmonton's demi-monde were pressing, as the Mission workers encountered women in the sex trade, alcoholic women, and women with unplanned, "illegal" pregnancies. In 1909, a house was rented to shelter these women away from the men and named the Beulah Rescue Home. While the Mission remained to cater for men, the new Home, with its connotations of domesticity, would be for women. In 1911, a purpose-built Home was opened on what was then the outskirts of Edmonton at 99th St and 137th Ave, on agricultural land donated by a prominent businessman. This spatial relocation marked the true beginning of Beulah as a home for unmarried pregnant women, as distinct from an institution catering to women in all forms of distress, separating out the girls who might yet be redeemed from their "fall" into unmarried motherhood and those who were unregenerate participants in the demi-monde. The Beulah Board of Directors approved this move because it enabled them to keep the "girls who had been deceived" separate from "the women of the underworld" (i.e. sex trade workers) (Beulah Archives, "Beulah Home Board of Directors Minutes 1913"). Beulah thus effected a literal spatial sorting of women as Madonnas and whores.

By its seventh anniversary in 1916, Beulah could claim to have "rescued" ninety girls in the preceding year, with seven girls and four babies in residence on the annual "open day," when the population of Edmonton was invited to tour Beulah.[5] The annual intake of women grew steadily through the next four decades, peaking at about 170 intakes per year in the late 1950s. Throughout these decades, Beulah was run by its matron and superintendent Mary Finlay, a deeply religious woman who began work for Beulah in the 1910s, left briefly for a marriage ending in early widowhood, and returned as superintendent in 1922, a position she retained until retiring in 1964. Her staff consisted of a cadre of "baby nurses" and general assistants, many of them also very long-serving, and the services of a group of Edmonton doctors who attended births in Edmonton hospitals, and later when Beulah's own hospital wing was opened in 1927, at the Home itself.

Beulah does not appear to have been run along the models of other maternity homes in North America and Europe, when compared to accounts by Levesque, Petrie, Solinger, Murray, Garrett, Luddy, Thane and others. In these accounts, such homes appear as sites for the routinized production of shame and correction, like the infamous Magdalen laundries of Ireland. Beulah, however, partook in a religiously motivated ethos which was more akin to "Christian maternalism" (Minaker). This ethos emphasized love, compassion, and forgiveness for those girls who were willing to accept being rescued.

These young women's acceptance entailed incorporation into a model "family" at the home. Beulah clients were encouraged to think of the staff as mothers and grandmothers, and their fellow clients as sisters, even though their residence with this "family" was a matter of weeks or months. In the matron's monthly report to the Board of Directors, when giving an account of how many women or infants joined the family or left, the entire population of the Home—clients, staff, and babies—are referred to as "the Beulah family." What the clients themselves thought of this familialization is not known, although Beulah's files contain many letters from former clients and staff claiming nostalgia and affection for the particular atmosphere of the home.

In 1944, one girl wrote:

> I certainly miss everybody. Every time I get the blues there is only one place that I usually want to go to again. I'd often walk over in the evening only I'm so afraid I will run into someone I know. I always think of chapel Thursday night and Sunday school on Sunday and I really wish I could attend them again. Honestly I really miss all the things I enjoyed so, there with all of you. (Beulah Archives, "Annual Report 1944")

This testimony was used in the same annual report for fundraising purposes, which may make it suspect, but other handwritten letters, apparently sincere, suggest that Beulah Home was remembered well, or at least was a better alternative than other possibilities for single women at the time, both as clients and staff. One staff member remarked: "Beulah, home for the staff, for the precious girls, and for the darling little babies ... oh how I want to come home, how I want to be part of that precious fellowship that you will be sharing" (Beulah Archives, letter from "N Pratt", September 9, 1949).

Beulah's main sources of revenue were fees paid by the inhabitants themselves to cover medical costs and the costs of boarding their baby for up to a year (until it was either turned over to the provincial welfare department for adoption or taken home by the biological mother) and donations. Donors to Beulah were a cross-section of Alberta philanthropy, including small-town Women's Institutes, which contributed knitted blankets and socks; wealthy local women; church groups; municipal authorities from whose rural districts the Beulah clients came; the Edmonton Community Chest (later the United Way); and newspaper readers who were encouraged to sponsor a baby or a mother for as little as fifty-nine cents a day (Beulah archives, "Did You Know [Facts About Beulah Home]," 1931).

These efforts were enthusiastically supported by the local press, who ran frequent features in which the tragedies of the clients' backgrounds were juxtaposed with the brief idyllic period of quasi-family life they found at Beulah. The local press also co-operated in ventures such as the Christmas adopt-a-baby drive (of which more later), and the 1928 appeal for $5000 one-dollar bills: "The babies are reaching out little hands to YOU now. Have you sent your dollar? Mail it NOW please" (Beulah Archive, "Babies needing help"). Much of the imagination and energy of Beulah's staff went into crafting these appeals to different audiences, framing the women, the circumstances of their pregnancies, and their babies in such a way as to generate the greatest amount of compassion and donation possible.

The demographic makeup of Beulah clients is hard to ascertain. Finlay and the Beulah administration had an interest in representing their clientele as young girls barely out of childhood and still partaking in the innocence of childhood, which has led them to be easy picking for deceptive older men, as distinct from the "hard cases," the older women who had sex repeatedly outside marriage for money or for pleasure and who were not welcomed at Beulah's rural idyll. Beulah's clientele were almost always referred to as "girl-mothers" or "child-mothers," and the short biographical sketches that accompanied appeals for funds focussed on barely adolescent girls, often bereft of mothers themselves. One particular story about a fourteen-year-old girl who found herself pregnant appeared repeatedly.

However, other evidence suggests that Beulah's clientele may not have been entirely or even predominantly children or "girl-mothers." Because Beulah was primarily privately supported, it was not required to complete detailed annual reports on the composition of its clients, so figures are hard to come by. Nonetheless, a 1947 article on Mrs. Finlay's long service reported that "Mothers have come from various fields and occupations.... Included are waitresses, clerks and factory workers 36 *percent*; domestic workers 20 *percent*; girls living previously at home 19 *percent*; in professions 18 *percent*; school girls 6 *percent*." Thirty years earlier, at Beulah's sixth anniversary festivities, the matron Mrs. White informed that audience that 28 girls had been helped over the course of the year thus far, but in her breakdown of numbers, only five were listed as being under eighteen.

Beulah's clients came to the Home through self-referral, referral by doctors and by Edmonton's social welfare department, and, especially in the early years, through the police department. Fees were charged, beginning at $130 for three months stay, including the doctor's fee for delivery, a charge which "shall be made in all instances against the father of the child where he is found" (Beulah Archive, Board of Directors Minutes, March 27, 1925). In many cases, the municipal welfare department paid the charges; in an unknown number of other cases, the client could "work off" her fees after the child's birth by doing work around the Home, including caring for the babies in the nursery. The average length of stay appears to have been around three months.

Once the babies were born, clients had the option of keeping the baby with them or placing the baby for adoption by making the infant a ward of the state. In the literature on maternity homes, the question of just how much freedom the clients had in making decisions about their children's future is prominent, with many accounts of women being coaxed, coerced, or deceived into agreeing to have their child adopted. At Beulah, the subtle pressures that may have been exerted on clients to place for adoption are lost to history. Nonetheless, the written record suggests that the Beulah administration was openly supportive of clients keeping their babies, even in the earliest years when the stigma of unmarried motherhood was strongest. The increasing number of "girls making good and keeping their babies" was described as "an encouraging result" for 1924, and the 1925 Annual Report noted approvingly that "there is a growing sympathy for the mother who keeps her child and we trust that this will continue to increase" (Beulah Archives, Board of Directors Minutes, January 29, 1924 and Annual Report 1925).

Beulah clients who chose not to place their child for adoption but were unable to set up a living situation which could accommodate a baby were able to board their babies at Beulah until they were able to reclaim them. In theory, babies could be boarded for a year; in practice, some were boarded well into toddlerhood. The cost of boarding a baby in the 1930s was $5.00 per month.

Beulah's 1929 Christmas letter to donors stated that 50 percent of the babies were kept by their mothers and the other 50 percent were available for adoption. This ratio appears to have fluctuated between a half and a third throughout the decades, and appears substantially lower than the average for Canadian maternity homes, in which during the 1950s approximately 80 percent of babies were placed for adoption (Petrie).

If Beulah looked favourably on mothers keeping their children, other Edmonton institutions did not. As late as the 1950s, the Beulah Board of Directors expressed concern about other bureaucrats, especially in the provincial department of child welfare, pressuring mothers to place their children for adoption. Part of this pressure apparently involved telling unmarried pregnant women to give birth at the city hospital, where it was easier to separate mother and baby, rather than at Beulah:

> [The superintendent of the child welfare department] seems quite convinced that it is better to persuade every mother to give up her baby. They can go to a local hospital and if they wish never see their baby and leave as soon as able. [The deputy superintendent,] I believe, is also urging this measure—for the sake of the baby, they say. ... We are anxious to help rebuild character in the girl and also give the baby a reasonable start in life. (Beulah Archives, Superintendent's Report)

By the 1950s, Beulah's work was slowing down. The number of clients per year peaked in 1955 at 171, and then began to decline. Hospital facilities had become more accessible and more accommodating to unmarried women, and fewer sought out the discretion of Beulah. Reforms to social welfare regulations had also made it more feasibly for single mothers to raise their children, so the role of Beulah in brokering adoptions was no longer as necessary. In 1963, the nursery at Beulah was closed and all infants moved to a central city facility. By 1979, following the liberalization of laws governing contraception and abortion, the Home itself was closed, and in 1983 the Beulah Rescue Home was officially dissolved. The Mary A. Finlay Manor for senior citizens took its place nearby.

AN ECONOMY OF VIRTUE

As Nurse Pratt's letter makes clear, Beulah was fuelled by affect and morality. In this, it was similar to other maternity homes in which emotion, especially "feminized" emotions of pity, compassion, and affection, drove (or were accused of driving) the work of the home. Kunkel quotes critics of American maternity homes complaining about the "superheated emotional atmosphere of pseudo-moral indignation" in the homes, and the "maudlin sentimentality" with which the staff regarded the clients and one another (26; see also Murray). Kunzel disagrees with this harsh assessment, pointing out that in the gendered division of charity work in the early twentieth century, "emotion, intuition, empathy and piety ... were the tools of the trade of womanly benevolence" (24). At Beulah, this emotional expression centred on the figure of the young "child-mother" divested of her most precious currency, her sexual purity, and animated the institutional effort of raising the value of that currency again.

Affect and morality thus blended in what I am calling the "economy of virtue" at Beulah, an economy in which clients, staff, and even adoptive parents partook. I am using the term "virtue" in the same narrow sense as it is was used in the Beulah archives, to refer to an intrinsic gendered value or worth, located in but distinct from the self, grounded in sexual history but not reducible to it. For the clients of Beulah, their virtue was imagined as a precious form of capital which they had either lost or been cheated of through fraudulent transactions, but which could be replenished through the investment of time, emotion, sacrifice, and spiritual grace. Clients were never considered "ruined" at Beulah. Instead, they were perceived as being at a low point in their fortunes, but redeemable.

How did these women lose their virtue? The Beulah archive presents one hegemonic narrative: a young virgin, always referred to as a "girl" and usually described as being without family protection, is tricked into sexual activity with predatory men and to her own surprise and terror, becomes pregnant. A Moravian minister associated with Beulah opined that "some of these poor girls get an awful shock when they find out what bitter tears the results of sin can bring" (Beulah Archives, "Twenty-Five Years of Rescue Work at Beulah Home" 27). Edmonton is figured as a city of vice, in which a "transient class" of men flourished, creating temptations for a girl to "spend" her treasured virginity in the same bars and hotels where men spent their wages. A typically melodramatic example of this narrative of loss and expenditure was probably written by the first matron of Beulah, Elizabeth Chatham:

> We have scores of young women from the old country [Great Britain].... The wages paid for domestic service here are much better than at home and they expect to help their people by their earnings, but alas! Their plans and good intentions are spoiled for the trap has been laid! They are left broken hearted, robbed of their virtue, with the prospect of becoming a mother and facing the world in

> disgrace.... She makes the acquaintance of a stranger who does not care, only to ruin her. And then who is there to take care? She is a stranger in a strange city, her loved ones are far away and anyway the awful thought of disgracing her father's home haunts her until the suggestion to end it all comes. She can make her way through the dark to the edge of the Saskatchewan [river] to end her misery, and who cares if she does? ...I have listened to stories like this more than once.... These young girls come in from a homestead to take work in a hotel or café where they can earn good wages. Are they attacked? Oh no, the agent of evil comes along and tells them they can earn more money and have nicer clothes and possess jewelry and many of these poor ignorant girls consent to have more money and fine clothes and jewelry at the cost of the most sacred endowment God could bestow on a woman. (Beulah Archives, "Fallen and Unfortunate Women")

Without intervention, the girl who has "fallen" could be headed for an even worse fate as a prostitute:

> The young mother is left with one or more children to support. Under this burden the pressure of temptation comes. It is sharp and keen. Their life of only five years in the [illegible] pool of this evil is worse than a thousand deaths. Oh the horror of those years. Cut off from loved ones, she would not for the world let her people know and she feels no one cares. So she suffers and suffers a slave and diseased, her only prospect is death. Soon she will hear that fateful sentence: "She that is [illegible] let her be [illegible] still, and she that is filthy, let her be filthy still." Soon she will be lying where so many others have lain, in a morgue, awaiting a pauper's funeral. (Beulah Archives, "Rescue work in Edmonton")

This imagery of disease and filth resonates with the metaphors found throughout the "purity" and "moral reform" movements in English Canada (e.g., Valverde). However, the filth could be cleansed and the sickness cured, although it required great effort by the women entrusted with this task. Only through careful and altruistic investment of time, money, dedication, and spiritual grace can the fallen girl regain the virtue she has lost.

Advocates at Beulah Home were emphatic that client-saving was a form of investment, in which emotion, time, and spiritual grace would turn a profit:

> What does it pay to make all this sacrifice for the unfortunate girl? It is true she has been robbed of the priceless treasure of woman's virtue, she has fallen among thieves who have wounded her, robbed her and left her half dead: she is an expectant mother and must face the unspeakable sorrow of bringing into the world a nameless babe.... There is not only hope, but the possibility of a noble and useful life. (Beulah Archives, "Twenty-Five Years of Rescue Work at Beulah Home," 17)

Beulah representatives, especially when addressing faith-based audiences, turned this narrative into a profoundly gendered economy of prodigality, expenditure, and the replenishment of moral capital, suggesting that the clients of Beulah, because they were women, were both more vulnerable to the loss of virtue and more able to attain a greater level of moral virtue than "fallen" men:

> Some may ask—why the effort? Why spend money, time and lives? Why not work for the protection of the pure girl? Why give all the attention to the prodigal girl? Here is the answer. Did you ever notice that it is only one gospel records the story of the prodigal boy. He deliberately went astray [and was] glad he went home [and] received a welcome, ring, robe, fatted calf and a merry time. No mention of his name or what he did afterwards. The prodigal girl [Mary Magdalene] is down too, but enticed away. All the four gospels record it and give her name. She was so lost that seven devils possessed her. Was she redeemed? Yes [she was] first at the tomb, sent by the risen Christ to tell the disciples of his resurrection, the first messenger of the

> glorious truth. Do you wonder why we do it now? (Beulah Archives, "Sunday, January 25, 1914")

While other maternity homes also used the Magdalene as a symbol of sin and/or forgiveness (indeed, the notorious Irish asylums for women deemed promiscuous or sexually overactive were known generically as "Magdalen homes"), in Beulah discourse she was not merely a fallen woman, but a stand-in for girls who had been robbed of all their virtue, like the prodigal son and his wealth, but who go on to regain far more than they lost, in the form of spiritual grace. The story of the Magdalene's witness to the risen Christ was used to demonstrate that the kindness and compassion which Jesus showed the fallen woman paid off abundantly through her elevation to timeless sanctity; and that by analogy, investment in the Magdalenes of Edmonton would reap abundant rewards.

Was this narrative of "girl-mothers" seduced and abandoned typical of the real experiences of women who came to Beulah? Their own accounts are lost, but case files from the provincial agents responsible for enforcing the *Children of Unmarried Parents Act* (CUPA), which required men to assume the costs of children they had fathered out of wedlock, including paying for their stay at Beulah, suggest a much wider range of experiences. The situations in these case files cover everything from consensual relations between partners in a committed relationship to frank rape. Almost none of the cases in the CUPA files follow the dominant Beulah narrative, which is not surprising. In developing an economy of virtue surrounding unmarried pregnant women, iconic images and affect-laden representations of young girls who had lost their most precious treasures were better currency than accounts of actual pregnancies.

If young mothers had lost their virtue and the *precious treasure* of their womanhood, Beulah would help them re-accumulate it, even as the Home provided pragmatic help with the logistics of pregnancy and birth. The primary value-creating activity of the Home was Christian evangelism. Early annual reports, although inconsistent in format, record the number of "girls professing conversion" (21 in 1914) and the number of religious services held (104 in 1924) as well as the number of clients admitted and babies born. Beulah routines included daily prayer meetings as well as formal church services and Sunday school once a week, and one of the visiting pastors from the Moravian church noted approvingly that "it will be utterly well with [Beulah clients] if their spirit will bow in abject obedience of faith at the feet of the savior of men" (Beulah Archives, "Twenty-Five Years of Rescue Work").

The Beulah administration collected, and reprinted in fund-raising documents, letters they had received from grateful clients which express a spiritual gratitude, suggesting magnitude of the efforts to bring the "girls" to Jesus. These letters include frequent references to the relief of the writer's "sin-sick soul" by their conversion experience at Beulah, and their gratitude at being brought to Christianity.

Alongside religion, however, there was an arguably even more powerful process for restoring value to clients. This was through the deployment of domesticity in Beulah, through both the passing on of gender-appropriate housekeeping skills and through the replaying of normative familiality, especially normative mother-daughter relations, in symbolic form. Both the physical and the interpersonal environment were strategically manipulated to create an archetypal home, an engine of replenishment and rejuvenation for women who had lost their most valuable possessions.

The tremendous faith that Beulah staff placed in the transformative strength of "hominess" was typical of maternity homes of the day. The Crittenton Homes, the largest chain of such facilities in the United States, were founded on a belief in "the redemptive power of domesticity," which was thought to be "curative for women who had flouted domestic conventions" by nonmarital sex (Kunzler). In Toronto, managers of homes of very different religious denominations took a common pride in the "homelikeness" and "family atmosphere" of their institutions (Murray 260).

At Beulah, domesticity was equated with light and redemption. The imagery of light, in particular, is striking, especially in the context of a moral order in which disgrace was equated with darkness, as Valverde points out (38-40). When a permanent facility was built on what was then the outskirts of Edmonton, newspapers gushed over the brightness and charm of the home:

> Sunlight floods the Beulah Home north of the city.... And the nursery where five tiny babies sleep and eat and cry and sleep some more is sunniest of all, and spotlessly clean. These conditions exist throughout the home, and if a clean bright environment has any influence on a disheartened or careless girl, that influence working silently in the Beulah home is a strong one. (Beulah Archives, "A Home Which Tries to Rectify the Unnamed Sins of Society")

And on the occasion of Beulah's fifth anniversary:

> The Beulah home is an ideal place in an ideal spot and one can hardly imagine a more homelike shelter for the girls. The large sunny rooms, the two verandahs, the two acres of ground, the conservatory and the pretty furnishings throughout tend to develop the love of a quiet, pretty home and are indeed a revelation to many of the girls who have never had a chance to grow in a domestic atmosphere. (Beulah Archives, "Beulah Mission Established Five Years Ago Does Good Work among the Fallen Ones")

Clients were trained in domestic arts of cooking, cleaning, and decorating, partly as vocational preparation for domestic service (which was often presumed to be the destiny of Beulah clients who did not marry), and partly for the morally regenerative effects of housekeeping.

Even more important than the physical effects of domesticity was the replaying of familial relations. It was presumed that clients' parenting and family relationships had not been adequate, and that Beulah would be their first encounter with normative family life. In effect, the "girl-mothers" were returned to a state of childhood, where the deficiencies in their original formation could be remedied through an accelerated immersion in both the spiritual and the practical work of Christian family life.

> There in an atmosphere of love and sympathy, they are sheltered and cared for, and in a real Christian home—often their first experience of such surroundings—they are

> given a new vision of life. So effective is this morally that the in very few cases does the girls sink back into the old life. (Beulah Archives, "Where Girls find Help")

In superintendents' reports to the board of directors and in speeches and texts prepared for supporters, Beulah was constantly referred to as a "family," with the births of new babies duly noted as "additions to our Beulah family." Clients were encouraged to think of one another as "sisters," and Beulah often used letters from former clients nostalgic for the "family" they found at the home. The superintendent, the matron, and the nursing staff were positioned as surrogate mothers who could provide the love and guidance that the clients had been deprived of as daughters.

> Many of the girls who come to the home ... become mothers when they themselves were most in need of a mother's protection. How different their lives might have been had they had a mother's love and careful supervision! (Beulah Archives, "Twenty-Five Years of Rescue Work" 21)

Beulah could stand in as a second mother for such girls, but the absence of appropriate maternal guidance could never be entirely recuperated: "This stream of broken girlhood is so sad. How we would like to grant a full and gracious release and return these little girls to their parents and friends without even a memory of so sad a chapter in their past" (Beulah Archives, "1928 Anniversary Report").

At Beulah, the investments the clients of spiritual guidance and recuperative domesticity paid dividends. These dividends were noted in the Beulah files in the form of girls who regained their feminine value, primarily by marrying and having their own families, but also by living useful lives caring for others. Weddings of former Beulah clients were always prominently noted in annual reports (with care taken to preserve the anonymity of the bride) and as early as 1912, some former clients held their weddings at Beulah, with the virginal trappings of weddings gowns and veils. In 1926, the annual report noted approvingly that "indeed we have a fine record of at least 25 percent of our girls being married in the past five years." Stories of girls who married respectably, or who took up caring professions such as nursing or teaching were often inserted into newspaper articles and documents produced by Beulah. Several former clients went on to missionary work in Canada and abroad. A promotional piece from the 1930s, purportedly consisting of extracts from letters written by former clients, informed supporters that,

> in the past six years, 292 young women have been at Beulah Home. Today 31 percent are married and living in established homes; 53 percent are living with their parents or earning a living in some honest way; three per cent are unknown at present; and only five per cent have not made as good as we would wish to see, the other eight percent make up the present family [i.e. were presently living at Beulah]. (Beulah Archives, "That Bundle of Letters")

The redemption of these clients marked the full cycle of the economy of virtue at Beulah—virtue as a feminine form of wealth and the birthright of all women, which was lost or stolen and then, through careful investments in spirituality and domesticity, recreated and redistributed to those from whom it had been dispossessed, through careful investments in spirituality and domesticity.

AN ECONOMY OF BABIES

If the notion of an economy of virtue seems somewhat abstract, the economy of babies at Beulah was solidly corporeal, sometimes distressingly so to twenty-first-century sensibilities. The main units of value in this economy were the "little treasures," the babies born to Beulah clients. Economic metaphors are unavoidable in describing the distribution and circulation of these infant resources, which sometimes took the form of something very close to a market.

In the early years of Beulah, babies were in surplus. Some babies, as noted earlier, were boarded at Beulah by their biological mothers until the mothers were able to retrieve them, but the real problem was babies awaiting adoption, who could remain at Beulah for a year or more. Newspaper articles emphasized the overabundance of infants at the home and promoted funding drives to extend the nursery facilities so that more adoptable babies could be accommodated and not transferred as quickly into the provincial foster care system, widely acknowledged as under-regulated and haphazard.

To find homes for these babies, Beulah and its supporters advertised the children, stressing their beauty, winsomeness, and capacity to give affection. As noted earlier, the major annual event at Beulah was the anniversary open day, during which visitors were encouraged to tour the nurseries. The babies on display were visibly divided into those which were available for adoption and those which were not, by means of tags attached to cribs or to the infants themselves. The local newspapers faithfully covered the open day, promoting the event in advance and describing the attractive babies on offer:

> The nurseries were fresh and attractive with their aquamarine tinted walls and their bunny-designed curtains. Here were the babies, some sleeping peacefully through all the excitement, other protesting loudly, some just indifferent. Like dainty flowers they were dressed in palest pink, green and blue, and a winsome dark eyed Japanese baby was adorable in canary yellow. ... But upon many of the cribs was the poignant printed statement: I am for adoption. (Beulah Archives, "More Babies Adopted from Beulah Home")

Individual babies were also singled out by their attractiveness:

> Belle has blue eyes and a lot of that sub-bronze red hair that is after all the last word in feminine beauty and she has the happiest disposition imaginable. From her cot in the sunny baby cottage, Belle gurgles and coos and looks with bright eyes at passersby. In her own particular language she is saying "please missus, I'd love to come to your house and make you realize just what a treasure I am." Belle is just one of ten babies who are for adoption at Beulah Home at this time. (Beulah Archives, "Redheaded Baby Would Like to Win Parents")

The desires of parents for adoptable babies, as well as the desires of the babies for parents, were discursively and affectively mobilized to drive the circulation and redistribution of children. Empty maternal hearts were described as filled by the adoption of a baby.

> Dimples and baby smiles, blue eyes and brown, is it any wonder that almost any day one may see a car drawn up at the doors of the Beulah home while some woman is satisfying the hunger of her heart and some man is enjoying the instinctive pride of fatherhood when such babies as those at the home can be adopted for keeps? (Beulah Archives, "Beulah Home Builds Again")

The investment in adoption was sure to pay dividends, not only in the private joy babies brought to the family but also in the creation of useful public citizens. In the 1940s, when the first "generation" of babies born at Beulah had grown to adulthood, advertisements from Charlie Hill's office and promotional material from Beulah noted that Beulah babies were now serving their communities as businessmen, Sunday school teachers, successful farmers, and so forth. In a 1944 typescript for an address to the Community Chest, special mention is made of Beulah boys now serving in the Army (Beulah Archives, "Questions and answers for Community Chest 1944").

All the babies were described as "treasures" and "precious," but some evidently commanded higher value than others. Most notably, girl babies were more desirable to prospective parents than boys, so that on open days

> ...sturdy boy babies kick their legs and coo to no account, so long as the adjoining crib holds a girl baby. This is one of the few instances where the girls have the advantage.... It is strange that no one wants a boy baby. Every prospective adopter wants blue-eyed girls and the homes cannot keep up with the demand for these fair maidens. (Beulah Archives, "Sixteen Babies Rejoice: Beulah Home Nursery Completed")

While gender evidently stratified babies' attractiveness to prospective parents, racial or ethnic background did not appear to stratify the babies. As noted above, babies with Asian parentage were described as "winsome" and "dainty," while babies with African parentage were similarly exoticized, in terms which grate on present-day sensibilities: "One of our treasures is a chocolate baby girl with big black eyes and a kinky curly head. She is learning to swing and an order has been sent in for a swing set" (Beulah Archives, "1930 Christmas Card").

In 1948, an appeal to donors claimed that,

> there's no racial discrimination for babies at the Beulah Home. Babies of all races and nationalities will have a happy life. ... [For instance] Dovie, a pretty negro child of eight and a half months, will have a better start in life if our coffers are filled. (Beulah Archives, "These Bright Beulah Home Babies Need Community Chest Support")

Aboriginal children were never mentioned, and the staffers at Beulah appear to have been oblivious to the existence of Edmonton's growing urban aboriginal population. It is not clear whether the absence of aboriginal women and children is due to racist attitudes that may have led women to avoid Beulah; or because aboriginal women who became pregnant outside of marriage utilized other options for pregnancy and delivery, such as remaining within their communities and families or seeking assistance from the Catholic church; or whether other forces were at play.

In the 1930s and '40s, the number of adoptable babies at Beulah was rising sharply due to the combined effects of the depression, which was forcing families off farms and young women into employment and precarious autonomy in Edmonton, and to the later garrisoning of American troops in Edmonton, which resulted in more non-marital sex and pregnancy. In addition, as the depression took hold some women who had been boarding their babies at Beulah were no longer able to afford the $5.00 weekly charge, and released the baby for adoption. These same conditions also led to a decrease in the demand for adoptable babies, as marriages were postponed and economic uncertainty led to greater reluctance on the part of potential parents to bring a child into their family. As a result, the effort to "sell" Beulah babies to the public was ratcheted up several notches, and the babies were advertised as delightful additions to households.

This intensification owed much to the interventions of Charles "Uncle Charlie" Hill, a child welfare inspector since 1923 who made his way to the top of the bureaucratic hierarchy as superintendent of child welfare in the 1940s, and who had strong ties to Beulah in his professional capacity and as a volunteer member of the Board of Directors. Hill was a flamboyant and controversial figure, whose aggressive approach to "placing out" adoptable children led to an apparent commercialization of adoptive parenting, and of the babies themselves.

For Hill, Beulah was a reliable source of babies of known parentage, professionally cared for and meeting standards of desirability, as distinct from the other children who came under his care through abandonment, neglect, or facilities for the delinquent. Accounts of his term as superintendent suggest that he personally signed off for the adoptions of 12,000 children. It is not clear how much of this volume of business came from Beulah, but certainly the great majority of Beulah Home adoptions went through Hill, and the Home was one of his promotional showpieces. A 1938 newspaper article titled "Baby Adoption a Christmas Gift Idea" urged readers:

> How about doing part of your Christmas shopping in the basement of the Legislative Building [where the provincial child welfare offices were located] this year? ... "What could make a grander Christmas present than a darling baby?" Mr. Hill asks, revealing that he now has for adoption some of the finest babies he has ever seen in his 24 years as official "baby man" for the provincial government. (Beulah Archives, "Baby Adoption a Christmas Gift Idea")

Two years later, the stock of available babies was even better, as Hill told the newspapers that he intended to place thirty babies in thirty homes in one week:

> [Hill] wants to place those 30 babies in 30 good homes and

> is sure they will go fast. Because this year Mr. Hill says he has just about the finest assortment of babies on hand he has ever seen and he has been in the baby business for a good many years. Who knows? Perhaps in this collection there is the future prime minister of Canada or the president of the CPR.... He is anxious to show his present stock-in-trade and is certain that one look at any of the present supply will win a prospective parents' heart. (Beulah Archives, "30 Babies Wait for Homes")

Hill also emphasized that the babies could be taken "on trial" and returned or exchanged if they proved unsatisfactory or showed evidence of any hereditary defects.

Hill's style was also evident in gimmicks such as the "Silver Seven," seven infants chosen to be advertised in the Edmonton newspapers in the weeks leading up to Christmas, with exhortations to readers to "make themselves the best Christmas present" (Beulah Archive, "Orphans! We Want a Home"). The babies were named and photographed, and thereby personalized to readers:

> Merry Christmas, folks! We know it's a little early, but how's chances to spend Christmas with you? We'd like to hang our little pink and blue sox on somebody's mantelpiece and have a real Christmas in a real home of our own with a real mummy and daddy. ... That's the Silver Seven, Mr. and Mrs. Edmonton. All they want is a home and a daddy and a mummy. It doesn't have to be a wealthy home, just a home where they'll be appreciated and pay it back some time with brimful and overflowing, with love and affection. Just call ... [and] you can make yourself the best Christmas present anyone could give you—on of these sturdy little Canadians. (Beulah Archive, "Orphans! We Want a Home")

It is impossible to say how the Beulah staff reacted to the marketing of their infants. However, Beulah staff lent their names and images to articles and brochures about Hill's programmes which celebrated the success of Alberta's baby exports. Hill claimed that "letters come from all over Canada and the U.S. asking to adopt babies," and Finlay concurred that "many of our children are adopted by American couples. Only this week a baby boy left for California with his new parents, ... and we received a picture and a glowing account of one of the babies who was adopted by a home in Nevada" (Beulah Archives, "Mrs. M Finlay, Foster Mother to Babies at Beulah Home"). In a fundraising brochure from the late 1940s, the attractiveness of Beulah babies on the international adoption circuit was similarly stressed through quotes from letters from American adopting parents:

> My trip to Edmonton seems just like a dream.... I can think of nothing but praise for the Canadian people and my children will never be ashamed of having come from your great country.... I certainly was impressed by your Beulah Home, the place where we found our children.
>
> Satisfied beyond words! We have a little child from the Beulah Home and the joy we have already experienced has been far beyond our expectation and we are sure this little life will turn many lonely hours into joyous ones. (Beulah Archives, "A Memento of Beulah Home")

In 1948, however, the high-turnover, high-volume economy of babies in Alberta was dealt a huge blow by an investigation into child welfare in the province conducted by Charlotte Whitton (then a muckraking journalist, later the first woman mayor of Ottawa) at the behest of the Imperial Order of the Daughters of the Empire (IODE), whose members worried that child welfare services in general were under-regulated and run as personal fiefdoms. Whitton uncovered plenty of evidence that child welfare services were mismanaged, but the biggest bombshell of her report were allegations that highly placed bureaucrats in child welfare were taking cash for adoptions, turning the metaphorical baby market into a literal market.[6] Hill was not named directly in the report, but given his centrality in adoptions, he was clearly the target of the allegations.

Whitton alleged that Americans, particularly in the border states, were arranging international adoptions entirely by mail, with no oversight of the adoptive homes and no vetting of the prospective adoptive parents. Babies could be picked up in Edmonton, or even delivered directly to their new homes by couriers. Whitton's report was wildly controversial in Alberta but attracted international attention. *Time Magazine* described her as "one of the most determined women in the Dominion [of Canada]," and cast her as David to Charlie Hill's Goliath ("Determined Woman"). Whitton was attuned to the circulation of adoptable babies as an economic matter, as she wrote:

> If these babies are suitable for adoption, they are a valuable national asset and the whole Alberta policy [of expediting adoptions to the United States] is puzzling; if they are not suitable for placement, it is a dastardly thing to send them to foster [and adoptive] homes in a friendly neighboring country. ("Determined Woman")

The provincial government held a commission of inquiry into the allegations in the Whitton/IODE report, and, perhaps not surprisingly, found that there was no solid evidence of babies being sold. Nonetheless, the Howson Commission concluded that cross-border adoptions should be terminated. Staff from Beulah Home gave testimony at the inquiry, stating that their role in the circulation of adoptable babies was founded in compassion and empathy with birth mothers. They stated that mothers were never pressured to sign over their valuable infants for adoption, and that furthermore Beulah had never received advice or instructions from the provincial government about how to increase the number of babies available for adoption.

With the cross-border baby-selling scandal, the hard-sell approach to the distribution of Beulah babies came to an end. Newspapers continued to run pictures of adorable infants in their best clothes who would "be at home to visitors to the nursery" every year on Beulah's open days (photo caption, undated but probably 1957), but the adopt-a-baby-week and Silver-Seven mode of distributing children had come to a close. As the volume of adoptable infants declined through the 1960s, both because more mothers were keeping their infants and because more were giving birth in standard hospitals rather than Beulah's specialized facilities, the economy of babies became less fraught and more standardized within the provincial bureaucracy.

CONCLUSION

I want to return to the discussion of intersecting multiple economies with which this chapter opened. I have here described the processes operating in two realms, one primarily discursive, the other primarily corporeal, but both partaking of discourse and corporeality. Gendered virtue, as a symbolic resource, was understood as something that could be illicitly taken from girls through theft and fraud. However, this loss could be recouped through careful investment of time, prayer, compassion, and donations, resulting in spiritual and psychological dividends to both the individual and her society. The consequence of that loss of virtue, the baby, was subject to market forces bound up with the fluctuations of supply and demand over the decades, and caught up in processes of distribution which often veered perilously close to commodification.

The relationships between these economies are complex, and not always self-evident. The most obvious form of relation is isomorphism, as pregnant women and adoptable babies were imagined in structurally similar ways. Both the women and the babies existed outside of normative families, and both women and babies were positioned as minors in need of rescue and maternal love in order to transform their lives and recuperate them. Both babies and mothers had the potential to overcome unsuccessful beginnings to become valuable members of society as a consequence of the kindness they met with at Beulah. The power of this positioning of the "child-mothers" was such that it persisted even when other evidence of the women's lives, such as their ages or the details of the experiences that had led them to become pregnant, contradicted the view of them as hapless children.

However, the more profound relationship between the two economies is more alchemical than isomorphic. The babies, adorable and adoptable, were a transfiguration of the tragedies that had attended their coming into being. In the imaginative discourse of

Beulah, the depletion of virtue, the depletion of feminine treasure through non-marital sex, is transformed into another kind of treasure, in the form of babies. The loss of virtue was thus converted into something of tremendous value—a baby. These infant treasures could not exist without the loss of their mother's greatest treasure, her feminine virtue. In this way, the abject dross of the seduced and deceived woman became the golden treasure of the baby (sometimes almost literally golden, if the rumours of baby-selling have any validity). The intrinsic value of these babies to hopeful adoptive parents, to Charlie Hill, and as precious individuals within the Christian ethos of Beulah, approached if not surpassed the loss of value experienced by their mothers when they became pregnant without marriage. Babies and feminine virtue were acquired, depleted, distributed, and transformed one into the other.

ENDNOTES

[1]Unless otherwise noted, all archival references are to the unsorted Beulah Rescue Home files held in the Provincial Archives of Alberta, Edmonton, accession PR 1971.007 – 1 Beulah Home.
[2]For a particularly well-worked out example of the use of this concept, see Roberts 1997.
[3]This idea of multiple economies of reproduction is indebted to Pierre Bourdieu's idea of multiple convertible forms of capital (Bourdieu 1986), but the concept of capital, even fungible capital, is insufficient to represent the dynamics of accumulation, depletion, investment, and valuation in which Beulah was imbricated.
[4]While the scrapbooks contain many newspaper articles about Beulah, the scrapbook keepers were not always scrupulous about dating the clippings. I thus infer the year or month of publication based on the clipping's location in the chronological order of the scrapbooks.
[5]The annual "open day," usually held on the anniversary of Beulah's move to 137th Avenue, became a major fundraising and public relations event. Newspapers published stories and features leading up to the open day, cars were hired to transport visitors without their own transportation to the Home, tea and food were

served, and the programme featured inspirational speakers from Beulah and the broader evangelical community. The high point of the open day was a tour of the home, including the specially decorated nurseries full of well-scrubbed and charming babies.
[6]The time was ripe for concerns about baby-selling, in the wake of the scandals surrounding the Ideal Maternity Home in Nova Scotia, where babies were openly sold to American would-be parents for upwards of $1000, while the biological mother would be told her baby had died. Many unmarketable babies were neglected by the staff and died.

WORK CITED

Beulah Archives. Provincial Archives of Alberta, Edmonton, accession PR 1971.007 – 1 Beulah Home

Beulah Archives. "1928 Anniversary Report"

Beulah Archives. "1930 Christmas Card"

Beulah Archives. "1936 Anniversary Report"

Beulah Archives. "30 Babies Wait for Homes," undated newspaper clipping, probably December 1940

Beulah Archives. "A Home Which Tries to Rectify the Unnamed Sins of Society," undated newspaper clipping, probably 1909

Beulah Archives. "A Memento of Beulah Home," undated pamphlet, probably 1947

Beulah Archives. Annual Report 1925

Beulah Archives. Annual Report 1944

Beulah Archives. "Baby Adoption a Christmas Gift Idea," undated newspaper clipping, probably November 1939.

Beulah Archives. "Babies needing help," undated newspaper clipping, probably January 1928

Beulah Archives. Beulah Home Board of Directors Minutes 1913

Beulah Archives. Beulah Home Board of Directors Minutes March 27 1925, PAA 93.359 Beulah Home minutes

Beulah Archives. Beulah Home Board of Directors Minutes January 29 1924, PAA 93.359 Beulah Home minutes

Beulah Archives. "Beulah Home Builds Again," undated newspaper clipping, probably 1928

Beulah Archives. "Beulah Mission Established Five Years Ago

Does Good Work Among the Fallen Ones," undated newspaper clipping, probably 1914
Beulah Archives. "Did You Know [Facts About Beulah Home]," pamphlet, 1931
Beulah Archives. "Fallen and Unfortunate Women," undated typescript, probably 1911
Beulah Archives. "These Bright Beulah Home Babies Need Community Chest Support," undated typescript, probably 1948
Beulah Archives. Letter from "N Pratt," September 9, 1949
Beulah Archives. "More Babies Adopted from Beulah Home," newspaper clipping, September 14 1936
Beulah Archives. "Mrs. M. Finlay, Foster Mother to Babies at Beulah Home," newspaper clipping, September 28 1945
Beulah Archives. "Orphans! We Want a Home," undated newspaper clipping, probably November 1947
Beulah Archives. "Questions and Answers for Community Chest 1944," undated typescript but probably 1944.
Beulah Archives. "Redheaded Baby Would Like to Win Parents," undated newspaper clipping, probably 1930
Beulah Archives. "Rescue Work in Edmonton," undated handwritten speech, probably 1909
Beulah Archives. "Sixteen Babies Rejoice: Beulah Home Nursery Completed," undated newspaper clipping, probably 1923
Beulah Archives. "Sunday January 25 1914," typescript speech
Beulah Archives. "Superintendent's Report to Board of Directors 1955," PAA 93.359 Beulah Home minutes
Beulah Archives. "Twenty-Five Years of Rescue Work at Beulah Home," undated pamphlet, probably early 1920s
Beulah Archives. "That Bundle of Letters," typescript speech, undated, probably 1935
Beulah Archives. "Where Girls Find Help," undated newspaper clipping, probably 1919
Bourdieu, Pierre. "The Forms of Capital." *Handbook of Theory of Research for the Sociology of Education.* Ed. John Richardons. New York: Greenwood Press, 1986. 241-258. Print.
Browner, C. H. "Situating Women's Reproductive Activities." *American Anthropologist.* 102.4 (2000): 773–788. Print.
Brush, Lisa D. "Worthy Widows, Welfare Cheats: Proper Woman-

hood in Expert Needs Talk About Single Mothers in the United States, 1900 to 1988." *Gender & Society* 11.6 (1997): 720-46. Print.

Collen, Shellee. "'Like a Mother To Them': Stratified Reproduction and West Indian Childcare Workers and Employers in New York." *Conceiving the New World Order: The Global Politics of Reproduction.* Ed. Faye D. Ginsburg and Rayna Rapp. Berkeley: University of California Press, 1997. 78-102. Print.

"Determined Woman." *Time* August 4 1947. Print.

Friedman, Helen L. "Why Are They Keeping Their Babies?" *Social Work* 20.4 (1997): 322. Print.

Garrett, Paul Michael. "The Abnormal Flight: The Migration And Repatriation Of Irish Unmarried Mothers." *Social History* 25.3 (2000): 330-43. Print.

Ginsburg, Faye and Rayna Rapp, eds. *Conceiving the New World Order: The Global Politics of Reproduction.* Berkeley: University of California Press, 1995. Print.

Greenhalgh, Susan ed. *Situating Fertility: Anthropology And Demographic Inquiry.* Cambridge: Cambridge University Press, 1995. Print.

Greenhalgh, Susan and J. Li. "Engendering Reproductive Policy and Practice in Peasant China: for a Feminist Demography of Reproduction." *Signs: Journal of Women in Culture and Society* 20.3 (1995): 601-633. Print.

Kaler, Amy. "'Who Has Told You To Do This Thing?' Towards a Feminist Interpretation of Contraceptive Diffusion in Rhodesia 1970-1980." *Signs: Journal of Women in Culture and Society* 25.3 (2000): 677-708. Print.

Kaler, Amy. *Running After Pills: Gender, Politics and Contraception in Colonial Rhodesia.* New York: Heinemann, 2004. Print.

Kunzel, Regina G. "The Professionalization of Benevolence: Evangelicals and Social Workers in the Florence Crittenton Homes 1915 To 1945." *Journal of Social History* 22.1 (1988): 21-43. Print.

Levesque, Andree. *Making and Breaking the Rules: Women in Quebec 1919-1939.* Trans. Yvonne Klein. Toronto: McClelland Stewart. 1994. Print.

Little, Margaret Jane Hillyard. *No Car, No Radio, No Liquor Permit: The Moral Regulation of Single Mothers in Ontario*

1920-1997. Toronto: Oxford University Press, 1998. Print.

Luddy, Maria. "Unmarried Mothers in Ireland, 1880-1973." *Women's History Review* 20.1 (2011): 109-26. Print.

Minaker, Joanne. "Sluts and Slags: The Censuring of the Erring Female." *Criminalizing Women: Gender and (In)Justice in Neoliberal Times*. Ed. Gillian Comack and Elizabeth Balfour. Toronto: Fernwood Press, 2014.

Murray, Karen Bridget. "Governing 'Unwed Mothers' in Toronto at the Turn of the Twentieth Century." *Canadian Historical Review* 85.2 (2004): 253-76.

Petrie, Ann. *Gone to An Aunt's. Remembering Canada's Home for Unwed Mothers*. Toronto: McClelland and Stewart, 1998. Print.

Rains, Prudence M. "Moral Reinstatement." *American Behavioral Scientist* 14.2 (1970): 219-222. Print.

Rapp, Rayna. "Gender, Body, Biomedicine: How Some Feminist Concerns Dragged Reproduction to the Center of Social Theory." *Medical Anthropology Quarterly* 15.4 (2001): 466-477. Print.

Reeves, Josephine. "The Deviant Mother and Child: The Development of Adoption as an Instrument of Social Control." *Journal of Law and Society* 20.4 (1993): 412-426. Print.

Roberts, Dorothy E. "Race, Gender, and Genetic Technologies: A New Reproductive Dystopia?" *Signs: Journal of Women in Culture and Society* 34.4 (2009): 783-804. Print.

Solinger, Rickie. *Wake Up Little Susie: Single Pregnancy And Race Before Roe v. Wade*. 2nd ed. New York: Routledge, 2000. Print.

Spensky, M. "Producers of Legitimacy: Homes for Unmarried Mothers in the 1950s." *Regulating Motherhood: Historical Essays on Marriage, Motherhood and Sexuality*. Ed. Carole Smart. London: Routledge, 1992. 100-118. Print.

Strange, Carolyn. *Toronto's Girl Problem. The Perils and Pleasures of the City, 1880-1930*. Toronto: University of Toronto Press, 1995. Print.

Thane, Pat. "Unmarried Motherhood in Twentieth-Century England." *Women's History Review* 20.1 (2011): 11-29. Print.

Valverde, Mariana. *The Age of Light, Soap and Water: Moral Reform in English Canada 1885-1925*. Toronto: University of Toronto Press. Print.

3.
Settler Colonialism and Carceral Control of Indigenous Mothers and their Children

Child Welfare and the Prison System

LAURA LANDERTINGER

THIS CHAPTER EXAMINES THE INTERSECTIONS of settler colonialism, child welfare, and the prison on the lives of Indigenous mothers and their children. Michel Foucault reminds us that the emergence of biopower inscribed racism (in its "modern," statist form) in the mechanisms of the normalizing state (*History of Sexuality* 149). Racism, thus, is not an effect but rather a *means* of creating a "biologized" internal Other against whom society must defend itself (Stoler 59). The existence of those deemed undesirable is constructed as problematic or even threatening to the well-being of the dominant majority. By this logic the (literal and social) death of the internal Other (i.e. the inferior, degenerate, abnormal) "will make life in general healthier: healthier and purer" (Foucault *Society* 255) for the dominant majority.

Such an idea becomes especially powerful in a settler-colonial state, such as Canada. To ensure its proliferation, the settler society must not only strive for the elimination of the Indigenous nations (through extermination, containment, and assimilation), but must simultaneously establish a new social body on the expropriated landmass (Wolfe). For this reason, a colonial settler society is inherently eliminatory in that the dominant culture must "destroy to replace" (Wolfe 390). Colonial settlement literally signifies the displacement of Indigenous peoples (Morgensen 59). The mere existence, let alone proliferation, of Indigenous peoples is counterproductive to the colonial project. Andrea Smith argues that in a settler colonial society, the creation of the Indigenous person as the internal Other is effected "through the metaphorical transformation of Native bodies into a pollution of which the colonial body must constantly purify itself" (*Conquest* 9). Through this, Indigenous peoples are rendered "inherently rapable, their lands inherently invadable, and their resources inherently extractable" (Smith "American Studies" 312).

Smith further points out that colonialism is a fundamentally *gendered* project that depends on the subjugation and management of Indigenous women (Smith *Conquest,* "Queer Theory"; Leigh). Drawing on Ann Stoler, Smith explains that, "Native women are bearers of a counter-imperial order and pose a supreme threat to the dominant culture. Symbolic and literal control over their bodies is important in the war against Native people" (*Conquest* 15). Seen as (literal and symbolic) "bearers" of a counter-imperial order, the management of Indigenous mothers and their children is foundational to the heteropatriarchal settler colonial project. As such, it is in the mutually reinforcing colonial narratives of Indigenous "womanhood" and "motherhood" that one can discern some of the core tenants of colonial control in Canada today.

This chapter traces such mutually reinforcing narratives by, first, focussing on the construct of the "unruly" Indigenous woman and, subsequently, the construct of the "unfit/bad" Indigenous mother. Drawing on a document analysis and discourse analysis of 198 newspaper articles published in 2010 in the *Edmonton Journal*, the *Calgary Herald*, the *Winnipeg Free Press*, and the *Brandon Sun*,[1] I examine how these two narratives span, legitimize, and reinforce two major systems of colonial control in Canada: the prison system and the child welfare system. In what is to follow I analyze the child welfare system and the prison system as two overlapping techniques of surveillance, control, and punishment that perpetuate the heteropatriarchal colonial logic of elimination.[2] Brown and Bloom point out that in neoliberal states, "both penal systems and child welfare systems converge to create an ever-expanding carceral population made up of poor families" (152).[3] Extending their insight to an analysis of settler colonialism, I argue that this dual form of state control perpetuates a colonial relationship that takes part in the building of a normatively white settler nation, effected primarily through the management of Indigenous women.[4] Through the constructs of the "unruly" Indigenous woman and the "unfit/bad" Indigenous mother—narratives that portray Indigenous women as innately immoral, violent, and neglectful—Indigenous women come to signify the unruly racial Other who needs to be managed, if need be through violence and coercion, and by extension whose children need to be "protected" by the settler society. Such narrative devices not only construct an Indigenous population in need of management/colonial rule, but simultaneously normalize a dominant settler society whose "geo-political self evidence" (Rifkin qtd. in Razack "Space of Difference" 89) is once more re-affirmed.

INDIGENOUS PEOPLES AND CARCERAL PUNISHMENT

This volume is being published at an important time. After decades of neoliberal restructuring and austerity measures combined with the current government's "tough-on-crime" approach, we are witnessing changes to the Canadian justice system and the state's approach to carceral punishment. Despite falling crime rates, the conservative government under Prime Minister Stephen Harper is bound on prison reform/expansion and has succeeded in implementing its omnibus crime bill (Bill C-10) in 2012. Bill C-10 means tougher jail sentences, restrictions to parole, longer waiting times for pardons, harsher sentences for youth, and mandatory minimum sentences. With laws and policies that create more punishable crimes and hence produce more criminals, Bill C-10 increases the numbers of prisoners[5] in federal and provincial institutions as well as the length of time prisoners have to spend behind bars (CCPA-MB; Wesley Group 2).

Marginalized groups are the most affected by the prison system (see, for example, Alexander; Smith and Stanley; Díaz-Cotto; Pate; Sudbury; Ross). Race, class, gender, sexuality, and disability are all factors that intersect in powerful ways to influence one's likelihood of incarceration. There is a direct link between austerity measures and the gutting of social services on the one hand, and increasing numbers of people driven into poverty and a rising prison population on the other. Not only are poor people surveilled to a higher degree (see, for example, Maki), but when people are placed in precarious situations they must often engage in various survival strategies that may increase poverty-related "crimes" for which "offenders" will be punished. In Canada, the carceral web is tightest around Indigenous peoples, and in particular Indigenous women and mothers, as they are the most likely to be incarcerated by the settler state.

The logic of prison organizes the white settler colony along particular gendered, classed, and racial lines, managing Indigenous peoples in highly colonial ways. According to Correctional Investigator Howard Sapers, Indigenous peoples make up approximately four percent of the population in Canada, and constitute 22.8 percent of prisoners in federal institutions (OCI "Annual Report 2013-2014"). This means that almost one-in-four prisoners in federal penitentiaries today are of Indigenous ancestry. These numbers are even more pronounced in federal facilities in the Prairies, with Indigenous peoples making up 55 percent of prisoners at the Saskatchewan Penitentiary and 60 percent at the Stony Mountain Penitentiary in Manitoba (OCI "Spirit Matters"). In provincial jails, the situation is even more outrageous. In 2005, Indigenous peoples represented 14.9 percent of the population in Saskatchewan, but represented 81 percent of persons taken into provincial custody (OCI "Spirit Matters"). Moreover, the disproportionate rate at which Indigenous peoples are taken into in the federal prison system continues to grow. Since 2001, the number of Indigenous prisoners has increased by 56 percent (OCI "Spirit Matters").

Furthermore, once under the control of the penal system, Indigenous peoples are more severely punished than non-Indigenous prisoners. Once convicted, Indigenous peoples are released later in their sentence (Mann; OCI "Annual Report 2009-2010"), they are more likely to be placed in maximum security institutions, and they must serve more time of their sentence behind bars than non-Indigenous prisoners (OCI "Spirit Matters"). Parole boards dismiss Indigenous prisoners' requests for parole at a higher rate than those from non-Indigenous prisoners (Mann; see also OCI "Annual Report 2009-2010"). If they are granted parole, they are also more likely to have their parole revoked and be returned to prison (OCI "Spirit Matters"). Once inside the prison, prison guards treat Indigenous peoples harsher than non-Indigenous prisoners. Indigenous peoples are more likely to be confined in segregation cells than non-Indigenous prisoners (OCI "Spirit Matters"; Mann) and they are also more often the targets of physical violence by prison guards—or what the institution calls "use of force interventions" (OCI "Spirit Matters").[6]

The logic of prison, as a gendered and racialized form of surveillance and punishment, functions in particularly oppressive ways towards Indigenous women. Indeed, the Canadian state incarcerates Indigenous women at higher rates than anyone else. Not only is poverty a reality for many Indigenous women prisoners (Monture "Confronting Power" 25), but they also come up against the ubiquitous authoritarian culture of excessive heteropatriarchal masculinity and whiteness inside (and outside) the prison walls. When we remind ourselves that settler colonialism is a fundamentally gendered project, it should come as no surprise that the incarceration rate for Indigenous women is even higher than for Indigenous men (see OCI "Spirit Matters"; Wesley Group 1; Monture-Angus "Women and Risk" 25). Indigenous women have been, and continue to be, the fastest growing group of people incarcerated by the Canadian state (OCI "Annual Report 2009-2010"). The number of Indigenous women prisoners has increased drastically over the last decades. Between 1981 and 2002, the number of imprisoned Indigenous women more than doubled (Sinclair and Boe 17) and over the past ten years, the number of Indigenous women prisoners shot up by nearly 90 percent (OCI "Spirit Matters").[7] Currently, Indigenous women make up an incredible 33 percent of women sent to federal prisons (OCI "Spirit Matters"). This means that one-in-three women prisoners is an Indigenous woman. In some provincial jails, it is estimated that Indigenous women make up between 90-99 percent of prisoners (EFS; Porter; AJIC "Jails").

COLONIAL ANXIETIES AND THE "UNRULY" INDIGENOUS WOMAN

The coercive management of Indigenous women is justified by a variety of colonial narratives. Patricia Monture argues that "[t]he relationship between the colonial legacy, the portrayal of women as violent and increasingly as dangerous, and the racialization of Aboriginal women are interwoven strategies used by correctional systems" ("Confronting Power" 31). Yet, this also begs the question, if Indigenous women are portrayed as violent threats, what is it that they are threatening? What is at stake that demands a "solution" to the "problem" that Indigenous women pose? According to a former prisoner, recalling her experience in the Prison for Women in Kingston, "[s]ecurity classifications were applied to us because as native women, we were seen as a collective, a war party, that posed a risk to the good order of the institution" (qtd. in NWAC "Aboriginal Women's" 29). Constructed as internal dangers (Foucault *Society* 216) to the well-being of the settler state and more specifically to "the good order of the institution," Indigenous women are rendered dangerous and uncontrollable in the colonial imaginary. The "unruly Indigenous woman" emerges as a threat to white heteropatriarchal rule. Such a discourse lends legitimacy to their incarceration and justifies the use of violence against them.

Within the prison, an institutional solution for how to manage the "violent" and "unruly" Indigenous woman includes, first, classifying her as such and, second, handling her with a stern approach. According to a report by the Canadian Human Rights Commission (CHRC), Indigenous women are disproportionally classified as "maximum security" prisoners (Parkes and Pate; see also Wesley Group). Indeed, almost 50 percent of women prisoners who are tagged with the "maximum security" label are Indigenous women (OCI "Annual Report 2009-2010"). Such a label may even be the institutional answer to prisoners' acts of "non-compliance"—an act in and of itself taken as "unruly" behaviour. For example, according to a report on the treatment of Indigenous women in the former Prison for Women (P4W) in Kingston, "Aboriginal women, under maximum security at Prison for Women, were prejudged as violent, uncontrollable, and unmanageable because they refused to co-operate when male guards ordered them to remove their clothes in population" (NWAC "Aboriginal Women's" 29). As Horii puts it, "With no power, few uncoerced choices are available and that includes the choice to say, 'No', which is the most terrifying consequence of being a prisoner" (105). Further, prison guards place Indigenous women prisoners more frequently into segregation cells than non-Indigenous women, and once segregated they are forced to stay in solitary confinement for longer (Parkes and Pate).[8]

Coercive control through gendered violence inside and outside the prison remains a powerful strategy in the colonial management of Indigenous women. As Smith has shown, the colonization of Indigenous peoples always went hand in hand with femicide and rape ("American Studies" 312). In the present context, the hundreds of "missing" and murdered Indigenous women are a gruesome reminder of how rampant this deadly strategy is (see NWAC "Sisters in Spirit"). Horrific accounts of physical abuse, sexual assault, rape, and gang rape of Indigenous women, for example, by the colonizers' police (see HRW 46-65) exemplify how gendered violence is used as a tool of patriarchy, white-supremacy, and colonial subjugation. For example, Gabriella P. alleges that, on multiple occasions, RCMP officers drove her to remote locations and gang-raped her. Afterwards, she recounts, "[t]hey threatened that if I told anybody they would take me out to the mountains and kill me and make it look like an accident" (in HRW 59). Perhaps as a "keepsake," Gabriella reported that the RCMP officers kept her underwear. This violence is normalized to such an extent that, for the likelihood of such an outcome, a community worker from the same town as Gabriella P. said that "she keeps packages of underwear for women living on the streets because other women have reported to her that they have been sexually assaulted by police and had their underwear confiscated" (HRW 60).

Once confined within a prison cell, and hence at the mercy of their keepers, Indigenous women prisoners (as any female prisoners) are especially vulnerable to abuse and harassment. This may manifest through such simple acts as the intentional withholding of tampons or pads during menstruation (Acoby "Interview"), to physical and sexual violence by prison guards—a disturbing reality that has been known for decades and which numerous studies continue to point out (see, for example, Faith; Parkes and Pate; Horii).[9]

Women prisoners abused by prison guards have no recourse,

or even access to effective complaint or grievance processes (see Parkes and Pate 259) since these are handled "internally" and hence rarely result in punitive measures for the perpetrators. Sometimes complaints are even submitted to and handled by the very same prison staff against whom the report was filed (Parkes and Pate 271). Consequently, the violence women may face as a form of retaliation is a very real threat. Similarly, women in maximum security prisons—half of which are Indigenous women—who do file a complaint may subsequently be classified as "difficult to manage" or as failing in their "institutional adjustment" (Parkes and Pate 272). Being punished for filing a complaint through such a label means that these women may be prevented from being reviewed for a reduction of their security classification and hence will be kept in prison for longer. In one instance, a former prisoner at the Surrey Pre-trial Service Centre in British Columbia came forward (a second time) after her release in 2011, to speak out against the sexual assault she had to endure by one of the prison guards. During her incarceration—after being sexually assaulted multiple times by the same guard—she turned to other prison staff for help, with the result that she was "placed in segregation and heavily medicated for five months" ("Alleged Sex Assault"). Thus, the consequences of speaking out against one's abuser may be institutional violence (being labelled "unruly," which can mean solitary confinement, forced medicalization, increased "use of force" against her) or retaliatory violence by the perpetrator.

As Sherene Razack continues to remind us, anything can be done to a person who is considered less than human ("Space of Difference," *Casting Out*, "Gendered Racial Violence"). Indigenous women are marked as "threatening," "unruly," and in need of management. Once locked in cages, they are held in a coercive space designed for punishment. It is a space in which whiteness, excessive masculinity/patriarchal control, and absolute authoritarian rule are institutionalized as the norm. It is also a space in which violence routinely occurs, and in which violence done to prisoners is not recognized as violence as such. In such spaces, Razack argues "violence may occur with impunity" and "[b]odies from respectable spaces may also violate with impunity" ("Gendered Racial Violence" 143).

CONSTRUCTING THE "UNFIT/BAD" INDIGENOUS MOTHER

Being considered "threatening," "unruly," and "violent" in the colonial imagination intertwines with perceptions of Indigenous women's in/aptitude for motherhood. Bonita Lawrence remarks that the removal of Indigenous children has consistently been justified by a settler imagination of Indigenous mothers as dysfunctional, irresponsible and thus not equipped to take care of their own children (113; see also Kline). Such insights align with my own findings after conducting a discourse analysis of newspaper articles that make reference to Indigenous mothers.

In all four examined newspapers the Indigenous mother emerges as the archetype of an unfit mother. Not simply are Indigenous women's abilities to mother rendered suspect, but more forcefully, they are portrayed as in violation of every quality of a "good" mother. Indigenous mothers are always portrayed as neglectful, usually incompetent, and oftentimes outright abusive.[10]

In a commonly recurrent narrative, newspaper articles portray Indigenous mothers as substance abusers and "pregnant drunks." Indeed, articles from all four newspapers[11] bring Indigenous women in connection with drug and alcohol abuse. Labels such as "drunk" or "drug addict" (Simons "College Girls," "Let's Protect Kids," "Slain Toddler"), "alcoholic mother" (Gelinas and Ibrahim), or "the drunken woman" (Santin; "Kenora Officer") are commonly used to describe Indigenous women. This "type" of woman is portrayed as selfish, irresponsible, and someone who puts her own desire for alcohol and drugs above any considerations for her child. This mother is also imagined to drink during pregnancy and hence is said to produce children who suffer from Fetal Alcohol Spectrum Disorder (FASD). She is so irresponsible in this regard, as some articles state, that it may be best to prevent her from having children altogether—if need be through forced sterilization. Such a view, for example, is advocated in two medical columns by Dr. Gifford-Jones and in the comments he received from his readers (published as part of the second column).[12] In his professional opinion, "good sense dictates" that one must stop this "maternal madness" (Gifford-Jones "Should Women") and sterilize mothers who produce "FAS-children." One of his readers responded with the following: "We have a large native population and as a social worker I've been aware of this tragedy for years. I know a family with five FAS children. They are always in jail, show no remorse, and they will never change. Please keep writing about controversial issues" (qtd. in Gifford-Jones "Flood of Comments"). Perhaps finding the forced sterilization of women somewhat harsh, a different reader instead suggested "adding birth-control pills to cheap liquor" (qtd. in Gifford-Jones "Flood of Comments").

Newspaper accounts furthermore portray Indigenous women as excessively sexual and promiscuous. This "type" of woman is usually depicted as a prostitute or simply someone who is willing to exchange sexual favours to feed her drug and alcohol addiction. This particular stereotype seems to be a contemporary version of an image previously identified as the "easy squaw" (see Anderson 106; Acoose 39); a woman portrayed as "inherently dirty" and tainted by "sexual sin" (Smith *Conquest* 10). Lacking any rights to bodily integrity (Smith *Conquest* 10) she is imagined as nothing more than a "vessel" for "sexual release" (Maracle 16, 24) for white men. This stereotype, in which racism and sexism intersect, renders Indigenous women "sexually violable" (Smith *Conquest* 10) and, as exemplified above, condones sexual violence against them. The image of the promiscuous Indigenous mother is further connected to racial anxieties over increased fertility. This woman is imagined as having "too many" children, getting pregnant usually "too early" in their life, and bearing the children of multiple men.

Meshing with the discourse of the violent and threatening Indigenous woman discussed above, Indigenous mothers are similarly imagined as also posing a threat to their offspring. They are said to be physically abusive towards their children and newspaper articles document this abuse through extremely graphic accounts (see, for example, McIntyre "Mom in Shelter"; Welch "Sinclair Inquiry," "Little Phoenix," "Baby Phoenix"). Yet even if the mothers are not abusive themselves, failure to protect their children from harm seems to be constructed as equally indicative of their incompetence. For example, articles blame Indigenous mothers for failing to protect their children from abusive men (see, for example, Gelinas and Ibrahim; McIntyre "Jail Dad"; Hughes). Discourses of "mother-blame," of course, are nothing new (see

Landsman; Strega et al; Gustafson; Scourfield; Ladd-Taylor and Umansky). As elaborated by Strega et al., even in cases of physical or sexual abuse by a father-figure, oftentimes "what mother did not do is seen as more serious and more blameworthy than what father (or another male perpetrator) did" (706). Add racism to a discourse of mother-blame, and the Indigenous mother emerges as the quintessential "unfit mother." She embodies the racialized and class-based stereotype of the irresponsible, substance-abusing, promiscuous "bad mother" whose behaviour inflicts harm on her offspring. Her attitude towards her children extends from negligence on the one hand to physical abuse on the other. These narratives not only justify but indeed necessitate the removal of Indigenous children to "save" them from their "unfit" mothers.

CARCERAL MOTHERHOOD AND INTERSECTING FORMS OF COLONIAL GOVERNANCE

As is the case with the prison system, Indigenous mothers are also the most commonly targeted group by child welfare authorities. Studies have shown that once child welfare workers enter a home, Indigenous children are more likely to be removed than non-Indigenous children (29 percent compared to 11 percent respectfully) (MacLaurin et al.). Once removed, they are more likely to be placed in permanent rather than temporary care, and thus tend to stay in the system for longer and are less likely to return to their families (MacLaurin et al.). Indigenous children also constitute the fastest growing percentage of children entering the system (MacDonald and MacDonald). Between 1995 and 2001, the number of First Nation children placed in provincial custody across Canada rose by 71.5 percent (Gough et al.). In 2011, almost half (48.1 percent) of all children under the age of 14 who lived in foster care were Indigenous children, while constituting 7 percent of the below-14 child population in Canada (Statistics Canada 5). Similar to the rates of incarceration for adults, the statistics are even more pronounced in the Prairies. For example, in Manitoba, the 2010 report by the Manitoba Office of the Children's Advocate (OCA) to the legislative assembly indicates that 86 percent of children in Manitoba's custody were Indigenous children (OCA 11).

As has been documented by various authors, the wholesale removal of Indigenous children by the colonial settler society constitutes a genocidal practice (Monture-Angus *Thunder in My Soul* 193) that is affected through breaking the bonds to family, nation, and land, and through its assimilatory function for the children (LaDuke; Chrichlow; see also Blackstock, Brown and Bennett). Different than other practices of colonial population control, such as outright extermination (Stevenson 2), forced starvation (Lawrence 31), sexual violence against Indigenous women (Weaver), sterilization abuses (Grekul, Arvey and Odynak), and oppressive policies of the Indian Act that seek to (literally) "define" Indigenous peoples "out of existence" (Lawrence), this particular strategy takes as its focus the removal of the children. It is also a practice that has a long history. As Fournier and Crey point out, from its very inception, Canada's "Indian policy" sought to sever the bond between Indigenous children and their communities (17). During each new era of Indigenous-settler relations, the settler society fashioned new reasons and corresponding tactics to transfer Indigenous children from their nations to the colonial body (Fournier and Crey). This was achieved by placing them in residential schools, foster care, or handing them over to white bourgeois settler families for adoption during the now infamous "Sixties Scoop" (Walmsley; Monture-Angus *Thunder in My Soul* 191-215). As one Indigenous grandmother exclaimed during a social justice gathering in which I participated, "The CAS [Children's Aid Societies] are the new residential schools." This assertion rings true when we consider that the number of Indigenous children in state custody has never been higher. It is estimated that there are now potentially three times more Indigenous children institutionalized through the child welfare system than there ever were through the residential school system (Blackstock). Expressed differently, the colonial management of Indigenous children through their systemic and systematic removal and institutionalization began in 1878 with the emergence of the residential school system and continues through child welfare to this day.

The child welfare system is a looming presence in the lives of most women prisoners. This is because the vast majority of women prisoners are young, single mothers (Faith; OCI "Annual

Report 2009-2010"). Being separated from their children is a reality for all imprisoned mothers. Maintaining contact with their children is quite difficult for women behind bars (OCI "Annual Report 2009-2010"). Telephone calls from prison are costly and covering expenses for visits (e.g., transportation and possibly accommodation) can be impossible hurdles. These costs increase, of course, the further away from home the mother is incarcerated. Indigenous women primarily face these difficulties as they are less likely permitted to serve their sentences in their community than non-Indigenous women (Parkes and Pate). In interviews conducted by Cunningham and Baker with 45 women prisoners, few of the mothers interviewed indicated that their children had visited them in prison. For many, the distance between their own location and their children's was too far and hence transportation costs would be too expensive. Others did not want their children to enter the prison (Cunningham and Baker 9). Indeed, some mothers want to spare their children from seeing them behind bars and from going through dehumanizing security procedures, such as metal detectors, drug dogs, ion scanners, and possible frisk- or strip-searches (see John Howard Society).

There is another hurdle that impacts Indigenous women in particular. Being labeled a "maximum security" prisoner, as most Indigenous women are, has consequences that impact their relationship to their children. Not only does such a classification determine how harsh and complete a person's punishment will be, it also influences one's eligibility for parole. This means that Indigenous women are less likely granted parole than other women prisoners and are thus separated from their children for longer periods of time. Mothers who are classified as "maximum security" prisoners may even be denied contact to their children altogether (see *Turner v. Burnaby*; CAEFS 38-39).

One of the most difficult aspects for imprisoned mothers, however, may be finding someone to look after their children while in prison. When a mother has to go to prison, she will have to find an alternative caretaker (such as her partner, other family members, or friends) to look after her children. However, given that the majority of mothers going to prison are the sole supporters of their children, it is often difficult to find an alternative caregiver. Yet, if the mother is unable to find someone, child welfare authorities will take custody of the child (CAEFS 30). Similarly, if the mother does find an alternative caretaker, but child welfare authorities deem them "inappropriate"—a likely outcome given the colonial discourses surrounding Indigenous motherhood—social workers will similarly place the child with child welfare services.

Thus, the entangled functions of the child welfare and the penal system are especially evident when it comes to imprisoned single mothers. When a mother is ordered to go to prison and hence is no longer able to care for her child, Child Welfare laws (such as section 37(2) of the Child and Family Services Act in Ontario) provide the legal basis for considering the child "in need of protection" and social workers may thus apprehend them as they see fit. In other words, when the penal system incarcerates and thus physically removes a mother from her child, the child welfare system will classify the mother—due to her physical absence—as "unable to provide care" for the child, meaning that she may lose custody. This is especially ironic given that, oftentimes, the crimes for which women are incarcerated are the outcomes of various survival strategies adopted to provide for themselves and their children with gravely insufficient resources (Faith; see also Horii).[13] Once an imprisoned mother has lost her child to child welfare authorities, regaining custody of her child upon release is extremely difficult if not impossible (CAEFS 29). As discussed above, this "difficulty" may be attributed to the fact that gendered and racial discourses already portray Indigenous mothers as utterly unfit. The additional fact that they were convicted of a crime and subsequently imprisoned is imagined as further evidence of their degeneracy (see also Faith). These mothers are depicted as failing to properly manage their own lives, let alone take care of their children. As an Indigenous woman at the Portage Correctional Institution put it:

> You come to jail and you sit here; your kids, your whole family is all split up. Child and Family Services ... have a way of getting involved.... They say you're not a good mother. They, too, don't listen to the person that has been through here. They haven't seen a mother look after her kids

> all those years. That's what they call you an unfit mother or you're not good enough to look after your own kids and who else can you turn to? If you go back to welfare, they tell you the same thing. It's all the same run around. (qtd. in AJIC "Aboriginal Women")

It is further important to note that many Indigenous women prisoners were themselves removed from their parents by child welfare services and grew up as wards of the state (AJIC "Jails"). This corresponds to Monture's assertion that "The child welfare system feeds the youth and adult correctional systems" (*Thunder in My Soul* 194).

CONCLUSION: "NATIONAL EMBARRASSMENT" OR THE PROMISE OF SETTLER COLONIALISM

Given that most women prisoners are young mothers, combined with the knowledge that one-in-three is an Indigenous woman, I believe it necessary to acknowledge that it is, in fact, Indigenous mothers who are the most disproportionally incarcerated group by the Canadian settler state. Given also that Indigenous mothers are the most likely to lose their children to the child welfare system, it seems that Indigenous mothers are not "allowed" to mother without encountering the coercive functions of the settler state. Constructed as utterly "violent" and "neglectful," the Indigenous mother emerges as the archetypical "bad mother" in the colonial imaginary. It is she who must be managed—through surveillance, control, and/or punishment (for example, through sexual violence, by being locked in a cell, and/or by having her children taken)—and it is her children who must be "protected" by the colonial settler society. The white heteropatriarchal settler state effectively enmeshes Indigenous peoples in a web of surveillance and carceral control, and places both Indigenous children and adults in "institutions of confinement" (Monture-Angus *Thunder in my Soul* 193). Prisons are filled with Indigenous mothers, while child welfare institutions are full of their children. The child welfare system and the prison system thus emerge as two intersecting institutional frameworks through which settler colonial power over Indigenous peoples is authorized and enacted. Mechanisms around child welfare and carceral punishment are part of a racialized knowledge production that not only construct a "colonisable" Indigenous population, but also create and maintain dominant settler subjectivities defined in contradistinction to those whom they claim to rule. It is through these institutions that white settler subjects re-affirm and normalize their position as dominant and superior, and Indigenous peoples are constructed as subjects to be managed.

Thousands of pages of government reports have been written (see Monture-Angus "Women and Risk"; Wesley Group 1) and numerous task forces were created (see NWAC "Aboriginal Women's" 27) to address the disproportionate incarceration rate of Indigenous peoples. Yet, for decades, repeated calls for meaningful institutional change have gone unanswered (see Parkes and Pate 261).[14] The Canadian Bar Association (CBA) even calls the disproportionate incarceration of Indigenous peoples a "national embarrassment" (Ernst). While the CBA's statement may be well intentioned, it also speaks to a common anxiety among settlers of having their self-image as benevolent citizen-subjects jeopardized, and seemingly rests on the assumption that the Canadian settler society is built on anything *but* the dispossession of Indigenous peoples. I argue that the large-scale institutionalization of Indigenous peoples in the Canadian penal system and child welfare system is not an aberration in an otherwise egalitarian state. This is not a story about a system "gone wrong"; this is a story about a system gone right.

Settler colonization is not an event but a *structure* (Wolfe 388). As part of this "structure," law manages the relationship between Indigenous peoples and the settler society (Razack "The Space of Difference"). As Luana Ross reminds us, the genocide of Indigenous peoples has never been against the law. The Canadian legal framework is not set up to work in favour of Indigenous peoples, but rather perpetuates their oppression (see Monture-Angus *Thunder in My Soul* 196). This is not only the case when it comes to the Indian Act, an obvious example of an oppressive body of colonial law that was founded on heteropatriarchal notions of white supremacy and established with the explicit aim of controlling Indigenous peoples (see Lawrence 31). It also applies to child welfare laws and the penal system, which are based on the same settler colonial logic. For example, the removal of Indigenous children by the settler society is sanctioned through different legal frameworks, such as the Indian Act, provincial laws concerning health and welfare, and provincial child welfare statutes. This legal framework reproduces a white settler society that normalizes its position over Indigenous peoples. Through these laws, the settler subject is defined as the one who possesses the unquestioned right to enter Indigenous communities, judge the welfare of their children, and remove them as they see fit.[15] Through such colonial encounters, the white settler emerges as the dominant subject whose power is continuously re-enforced. It is also through law that Canada's colonial history and present are rendered invisible. Through law—particularly visible in trials and court hearings (see, for example, Razack "Gendered Racialized Violence" 126, "The Space of Difference")—Indigenous peoples are pathologized, imagined as dysfunctional and damaged, owing to some innate inadequacy or cultural inferiority. Anything *but* colonialism is considered as the cause for Indigenous peoples ending up in prisons or for their children as wards of the state. As Razack so aptly put it, "Settlers *become* owners of the land through what is both a narrative and a performance" ("The Space of Difference" 88; emphasis in original). Racial narratives are essential for Europeans to imagine themselves as rightful owners of Turtle Island. When settlers can imagine Indigenous peoples as too dysfunctional to live law-abiding lives, too abject to take care of themselves, too damaged and too neglectful to take care of their children, then consequently we can also imagine Indigenous peoples as too dysfunctional to govern the land (Razack "The Space of Difference" 88).

In such a context, I deliberately write against those who would argue for "institutional reforms" or "improvements" to the child welfare system or the prison system, by making them more "efficient," "sensitive," or "culturally appropriate." To think of alternatives outside the current child welfare and prison system in regards to Indigenous peoples is a radical notion and it has to start with Indigenous self-determination and self-governance. In the words of Thomas-Muller: "Today, we are still confronting the violence of colonization. It has manifested in many forms that I don't care to list. One thing that is clear to me, however, is that ... the answer always has and continues to be sovereignty and self-determination over our land and life" (220). Real transformative change can only take place outside the context of settler colonial control. Self-governing autonomy for Indigenous peoples cannot be established in any real or meaningful way within the colonial state structure and its institutions (Smith "Queer Theory", "American Studies"; Alfred *Peace, Power, Righteousness*, "Radical Imagination"; Coulthard; Turner). It cannot happen in a context in which the colonizer polices, surveils, judges, and imprisons, and where the colonized must prove their worthiness whether they are "good enough" to raise their own children or "adjusted enough" to be released on parole. Conditions of possibility ought to be in place for Indigenous mothers to be able to mother their children. It is highly unsettling to have to state that Indigenous peoples have to have autonomy to look after their own offspring. Such a transformation certainly goes beyond the judicial system and social services, but speaks to a larger project of decolonization. This also means that white settlers have to come to know themselves *as* settlers/colonizers, interrogate our participation in regimes of violence, and acknowledge the sovereignty of the Indigenous nations whose territories the Canadian state rests within.[16]

ENDNOTES

[1]This number corresponds to the articles and editorials on Indigenous child welfare matters that were published from January 1st to December 31st by the four examined newspapers. Articles and editorials were identified through database searches with the following search criteria: "Any" of the following terms "aboriginal," "native," "(i)ndigenous," "First Nation" in combination with "foster care" or "child welfare" or "child intervention" or "children and youth services" or "child and family services." This set of data was then coded into sub-groups of: "mother," "father," "man or men," "woman or women," and "child(ren)."

[2]In doing so, I follow the lead of Patricia Monture who first made the connection between the child welfare and the criminal justice

system as two intersecting mechanisms of colonial governance.

[3]In this paper, neoliberalism is broadly conceived as follows. With its economic axioms of privatization and deregulation, neoliberalism dictates that governments ought not to interfere with the workings of "the market." As such, the market—both concept and practice—informs a new manner of governmental rationality and practice (Winnubst 82; Foucault *Birth of Biopolitics* 32). Yet, more than mere economic doctrine, neoliberalism entails an extension of economic rationality into all areas of life. As such, it constitutes a new social ontology and epistemology (see Winnubst 81-88) that are indeed foundational to biopolitics (Foucault *Birth of Biopolitics*). One of the biopolitical outcomes of neoliberalism is (re)production of racialized and gendered structures of poverty, violence, and punishment on a national and international level (see, for example, Goldberg; Kuokkanen; Mohanty). This also means that for certain groups of people, the state is not "disappearing." On the contrary, in relation to Indigenous peoples, the state continues to reassert its sovereignty and authority; the management of Indigenous peoples through state surveillance and punishment remains rigid and absolute.

[4]By "white-nation" I refer to a society that structurally and institutionally favours those from (Western) European backgrounds and where the definition of who counts as a "national subject" is explicitly raced (Thobani). Thus, with the term "white nation" I do not refer to a population that is primarily "white" in appearance (indeed millions of racialized immigrants have been "admitted" to Canada), but in terms of power relations. Furthermore, I acknowledge that there are vast differences in power relations among settlers, based on race, class, gender, sexuality, and ability. Indeed, we live in a settler society that is based on heteropatriarchy and white supremacy in which certain subject positions are rewarded while others are marked for deadly violence. Thus, when I refer to "the settler society," I primarily have in mind white settlers and their descendants (see Mackey 89).

[5]I deliberately use the term "prisoner" instead of the problematic term 'offender." For as Gayle Horii so powerfully states, "*Prisoner* is the only correct term to describe a person locked into a cage or cell within a facility not of one's choice and whose quality of

existence therein depends upon the keeper(s).... The continual use 'offender' justifies everything done to 'an inmate in the name of the law'" (108, emphasis in original).

[6]"Use of Force" refers to the use of chemical agents (e.g., tear gas), pepper spray, taser stun guns, fire arms, and "other" physical violence against prisoners.

[7]In comparison, the number of incarcerated Indigenous men increased by 35 percent for the same period (OCI "Spirit Matters").

[8]For a very powerful piece on solitary confinement refer to "Solitary" by Renée Acoby, an Ojibwe prisoner from Manitoba who was forced to spend seven years in solitary confinement and continues to serve an "indeterminate' (i.e. life) sentence behind bars.

[9]While there exist certain safeguards under the National Protocol that (at the very least) are supposed to decrease the possibilities through which prison staff are able to harass and abuse women prisoners—for example, male guards are supposedly precluded from doing night rounds, unit and bed checks, and strip searches—they are rarely followed by CSC staff (CHRC cited in Parkes and Pate 260).

[10]This applies to all newspaper articles that make a reference to Indigenous mothers. In all of them, there was but *one* article which included a quote from the mother of a missing Indigenous woman who referred to her daughter as someone who "enjoyed being a mom" (see Greene). This was the only positive representation of an Indigenous mother—and it came from a relative, which may be interpreted as biased.

[11]See, for example, Simons "College Girls", "Let's Protect Kids", "Slain Toddler"; Gelinas and Ibrahim; Welch "Chiefs Ruled"; Gifford-Jones "Flood of Comments"; Rabson; McIntyre "Mom in Shelter"; Giroday and Welch; Santin; "Kenora Officer"; Hitchen.

[12]Dr. Gifford-Jones is the pen name of Dr. Ken Walker, graduate of the University of Toronto and Harvard Medical School. He has a regular medical column which is published in 70 Canadian newspapers, several U.S. newspapers and the Epoch Times which is published in a number of European countries.

[13]As one Indigenous woman put it, "It starts with the welfare system ... because I am a mother with kids and in order to do that, I had to do my crime. In order to barely live on welfare, I had to do my

crime. You do get help from welfare, but it's just barely enough to live. From there, you get involved with your crime and after that then you get picked up, you go to jail and when they look at you they call you nothing but a thief or whatever you've done" (qtd. in AJIC "Aboriginal Women").

[14]Even after the Task Force on Federally Sentenced Women (TFSSW) and its publication "Creating Choices", which did connect colonialism and gender in its analysis, and which finally led to the closure of the infamous P4W in Kingston, as well as the creation of "Aboriginal healing lodges," the situation of women prisoners did not improve. In fact, it enabled the construction of more prisons. Now, women who are classified as maximum-security prisoners are imprisoned in more secure facilities than was possible under the old in the Prison for Women in Kingston (Monture "Confronting Power" 26; see also Hannah-Moffat).

[15]Imagine, for example, the reaction if, instead, Kanien'kehá:ka walked into Tiohtiá:ke (Montreal) to remove white settler children because they deemed it "in the children's best interest" to do so?

[16]It needs pointing out that this should not be read as a call for the settler society to "grant" self-determination to Indigenous peoples. Self-governance or self-determination cannot be "granted" or "bestowed' by the colonial settler state for it is something that is already possessed (Turner). This is a call for prison abolition. This is a call to cease the occupation and to stop the violence.

WORKS CITED

Aboriginal Justice Implementation Commission (AJIC). "Chapter 11: Jails." *Volume 1: The Justice System and Aboriginal People. Report of the Aboriginal Justice Inquiry of Manitoba.* 1999. Web. 12 March 2013.

Aboriginal Justice Implementation Commission (AJIC). "Chapter 13: Aboriginal Women." *Volume 1: The Justice System and Aboriginal People. Report of the Aboriginal Justice Inquiry of Manitoba.* 1999. Web. 12 March 2013.

Acoby, Renée. "Interview." *The Fifth Estate* CBC Interviewer: Hana Gartner. 26 Nov. 2010. Web. 22 March 2013.

Acoby, Renée. "Solitary." Just Blog. A Rittenhouse Production.

22 November 2012. Web. 13 March 2013.

Acoose, Janice. *Iskwewak: Neither Indian Princesses nor Easy Squaw*. Toronto: Women's Press, 1995. Print.

Alexander, Michelle. *The New Jim Crow: Mass Incarceration in the Age of Colorblindness*. New York: The New Press, 2012. Print.

Alfred, Taiaiake. *Peace, Power, Righteousness. An Indigenous Manifesto*. Oxford: Oxford University Press, 2009. Print.

Alfred, Taiaiake. "What is Radical Imagination." *Affinities: A Journal of Radical Theory, Culture, and Action* 4.2 (2010): 5-8. Print.

"Alleged Sex Assault by Jail Guard Triggers Lawsuit." *CBC News* 18 Jan. 2012. Web. 12 March 2013.

Anderson, Kim. *A Recognition of Being: Reconstructing Native Womanhood*. Toronto: Sumach Press, 2000. Print.

Blackstock, Cindy, Ivan Brown and Marlyn Bennett. "Reconciliation: Rebuilding the Canadian Child Welfare System to Better Serve Aboriginal Children and Youth." *Putting a Human Face on Child Welfare: Voices from the Prairies*. Ed. I. Brown, F. Chaze, D. Fuchs, J. Lafrance, S. McKay, and S. Thomas Prokop. Prairie Child Welfare Consortium/Centre of Excellence of Child Welfare, 2007. Print.

Blackstock, Cindy. "First Nations Child and Family Services: Restoring Peace and Harmony in First Nations Communities." *Child Welfare: Connecting Research Policy and Practice*. Ed. Kathleen Kufeldt and Brad McKenzie. Waterloo: Wilfred Laurier University Press, 2003. Print.

Brown, Marilyn and Barbara Bloom. "Colonialism and Carceral Motherhood: Native Hawaiian Families Under Corrections and Child Welfare Control." *Feminist Criminology* 4.2 (2009): 151-169. Print.

Canadian Association of Elizabeth Fry Societies (CAEFS). "Human Rights in Action: Handbook for Women in Provincial Jails in Ontario." 2010. Web. 12 March 2013.

Canadian Centre for Policy Alternatives Manitoba Office (CCPA-MB). "Fact Facts: Bill C-10: The Truth about Consequences." 1 March 2012. Web. 12 March 2013.

Coulthard, Glen S. "Subjects of Empire: Indigenous Peoples and the 'Politics of Recognition' in Canada." *Contemporary Political*

Theory 6 (2007): 437–460. Print.

Crichlow, Wesley. "Western Colonization as Disease: Native Adoption and Cultural Genocide." *Canadian Social Work* 5.1 (2003): 88-107

Cunningham, Alison and Linda Baker. "Invisible Victims: The Children of Women in Prison." Centre for Children & Families in the Justice System. Dec. 2004. Web. 12 March 2013.

Díaz-Cotto, Juanita. *Chicana Lives and Criminal Justice: Voices from El Barrio*. Austin: University of Texas Press, 2006. Print.

Elizabeth Fry Society of Manitoba (EFS). "Fact Sheet: Human and Fiscal Costs of Prison." EFS. 2005. Web. 12 March 2013.

Ernst, Trinda. "Ten Reasons to Oppose Bill-C10." *Toronto Star* 14 Nov. 2011. Web. 12 March 2013.

Faith, Karlene. *Unruly Women: The Politics of Confinement & Resistance*. 2nd ed. New York: Seven Stories Press, 2011. Print.

Foucault, Michel. *The History of Sexuality: An Introduction, Volume I*. New York: Random House Inc, 1990. Print.

Foucault, Michel. *"Society Must Be Defended": Lectures at the College de France, 1975-1976*. Trans. David Macey. New York: Picador, 2003. Print.

Foucault, Michel. *The Birth of Biopolitics: Lectures at the Collège de France, 1978-1979*. Trans. Graham Burchell. New York: Picador, 2010. Print.

Fournier, Suzanne and Crey, Ernie. *Stolen from Our Embrace*. Toronto: Douglas & McIntyre Ltd, 1997. Print.

Gelinas, Ben and Ibrahim, Mariam. "Homicide Victim had Violent Past; Body of 25-Year-Old Man Found on Stairs in River Valley." *Edmonton Journal* 18 May 2010. B1. Print.

Gifford-Jones, W. "Should Women Who Deliver Fetal Alcohol Syndrome (FAS) Children Be Sterilized?" DocGiff: Your Resource for No Nonsense Medical and Healthy Lifestyle Advice. 6 Feb. 2010. Web. 12 March 2013.

Gifford-Jones, W. "Flood of Comments Pours in on Sterilizing FAS Mothers." Column. *Winnipeg Free Press* 26 Feb. 2010: A23. Print.

Giroday, Gabrielle and Welch, Mary Agnes. "Racism Blamed for Violence. Families Want More Steps Taken to Solve Killings of Native Women." *Brandon Sun* 22 April 2010. Print.

Goldberg, David T. *The Threat of Race: Reflections on Racial*

Neoliberalism. Malden, MA: Wiley-Blackwell, 2008. Print.
Gough, Pamela, Nico Trocmé, Ivan Brown, Della Knoke, and Cindy Blackstock. "Pathways to the Overrepresentation of Aboriginal Children in Care." CECW Information Sheet #23E. Toronto, ON, Canada: University of Toronto, 2005. Print.
Greene, Crystal. "Sending Prayers for Missing Women." *Brandon Sun*. 22 Dec. 2010. Print.
Grekul, Jana, Krahn Arvey and Dave Odynak. "Sterilizing the 'Feeble-Minded': Eugenics in Alberta, Canada, 1929-1972." *Journal of Historical Sociology* 17.4 (2004): 358-384. Print.
Gustafson, Diana. "The Social Construction of Maternal Absence." *Unbecoming Mothers: The Social Production of Maternal Absence*. Ed. Diana Gustafson. Binghamton, New York: Haworth Clinical Practice, 2005. Print.
Hannah-Moffat, Kelly. *Punishment in Disguise: Penal Governance and Federal Imprisonment of Women in Canada*. Toronto: University of Toronto Press, 2001. Print.
Hitchen, Ian. "House Arrest for Possessing Crack Cocaine." *Brandon Sun*. 10 Dec. 2010. Print.
Horii, Gayle K. "Processing Humans." *An Ideal Prison? Critical Essays on Women's Imprisonment in Canada*. Ed. Kelly Hannah-Moffat and Margaret Shaw. Halifax: Fernwood Publishing, 2000. Print.
Hughes, John. "8-Year Sentence Sought for Incest." *Brandon Sun*. 26 Feb. 2010. Print.
Human Rights Watch (HRW). "Those Who Take Us Away: Abusive Policing and Failures in Protection of Indigenous Women and Girls in Northern British Columbia, Canada." 13 Feb. 2013. Web. 22 March 2013.
John Howard Society of Ontario. "Visiting a Loved One Inside? A Handbook for People Visiting a Prisoner at an Adult Correctional Facility in Ontario." 2011. Web. 12 March 2013.
"Kenora Officer Shoots Knife-Wielding Woman." *Brandon Sun* 9 June 2010. Print.
Kline, Marlee. "Child Welfare Law, 'Best Interest of the Child' Ideology, and First Nations." *Osgoode Hall Law Journal* 30.2. (1992): 375-425. Print.
Kuokkanen, Rauna. "Globalization as Racialized, Sexualized Vi-

olence." *International Feminist Journal of Politics* 10.2 (2008): 216-233. Print.

Ladd-Taylor, Molly and Lauri Umansky. *"Bad Mothers": The Politics of Blame in Twentieth Century America.* New York: New York University Press, 1998. Print.

LaDuke, Winona. "Foreword." *At the Risk of Being Heard: Identity, Indigenous Rights and Postcolonial States.* Ed. Bartholomew Dean and Jerome Levi. Ann Arbor: University of Michigan Press, 2003. Print.

Landsman, Gail Heidi. "Doing Everything Right: Choice, Control and Mother-Blame." *Reconstructing Motherhood and Disability in the Age of 'Perfect' Babies.* New York: Routledge, 2009. Print.

Lawrence, Bonita. *"Real" Indians and Others: Mixed-Blood Urban Native Peoples and Indigenous Nationhood.* Vancouver: University of British Columbia Press, 2004. Print.

Leigh, Darcy. "Colonialism, Gender and the Family in North America: For a Gendered Analysis of Indigenous Struggles." *Studies in Ethnicity and Nationalism* 9.1 (2009): 70-88. Print.

MacDonald, Nancy and Judy MacDonald. "Reflections of a Mi'kmaq Social Worker on a Quarter of a Century Work in First Nations Child Welfare." *First Peoples Child and Family Review: A Journal on Innovation and Best Practices in Aboriginal Child Welfare Administration, Research, Policy & Practice* 3.1 (2007): 34-45. Print.

Mackey, Eva. *The House of Difference: Cultural Politics and National Identity in Canada.* Toronto: University of Toronto Press, 2002. Print.

MacLaurin, Bruce, Nico Trocmé, Barbara Fallon, Cindy Blackstock, Lisa Pitman, and Megan McCormack. "A Comparison of First Nations and non-Aboriginal Children Investigated for Maltreatment in Canada in 2003." CECW Information Sheet #66E. Toronto: Factor-Inwentash Faculty of Social Work, University of Toronto, 2008. Print.

Maki, Krystle. "Neoliberal Deviants and Surveillance: Welfare Recipients under the Watchful eye of Ontario Works." *Journal of Surveillance and Society* 9.1 (2011): 47-63. Print.

Mann, Michelle. "Good Intentions, Disappointing Results: A Progress Report on Federal Aboriginal Corrections." Office of the Correctional Investigator. Government of Canada, 2009. Web. 22 March 2013.

McIntyre, Mike. "Jail Dad for Years of Abuse: Crown – 8-year Termillm Sought for Molester, 68." *Winnipeg Free Press* 26 Feb. 2010. A12. Print.

McIntyre, Mike. "Mom in Shelter Killed Her Little Girl – Toddler Severely Abused, Manslaughter Hearing Told." *Winnipeg Free Press* 25 Nov. 2010. A4. Print.

Maracle, Lee. *I Am Woman: A Native Perspective on Sociology and Feminism*. Vancouver: Press Gang Publishers, 1996. Print.

Mohanty, Chandra Talpade. "Women Workers and Capitalist Scripts: Ideologies of Domination, Common Interests and the Politics of Solidarity." *Feminist Genealogies, Colonial Legacies, Democratic Futures*. Eds. M. Jacqui Alexander and Chandra Talpade Mohanty. New York: Routledge, 1997: 3-29. Print.

Monture-Angus, Patricia. *Thunder in My Soul: A Mohawk Woman Speaks*. Halifax: Fernwood Publishing, 1995. Print.

Monture-Angus, Patricia. "Women and Risk: Aboriginal Women, Colonialism, and Correctional Practice." *Canadian Woman Studies/les cahiers de la femme* 19.2 (1999): 24-29. Print.

Monture, Patricia. "Aboriginal Women and Correctional Practice: Reflections on the Task Force on Federally Sentenced Women." *An Ideal Prisons? Critical Essays on Women's Imprisonment in Canada*. Ed. Kelly Hannah-Moffat and Margaret Shaw. Halifax: Fernwood Publishing, 2000. Print.

Monture, Patricia. "Confronting Power: Aboriginal Women and Justice Reform." *Canadian Woman Studies/les cahiers de la femme* 25.3 (2006): 25-33. Print.

Morgensen, Scott. "The Biopolitics of Settler Colonialism: Right Here, Right Now." *Settler Colonial Studies* 1 (2011): 52-76. Print.

Native Women's Association of Canada (NWAC). "Aboriginal Women's Healing Lodge: An NWAC Report." 1993. Web. 12 March 2013.

Native Women's Association of Canada (NWAC). "What Their Stories Tell Us: Research Findings from the Sisters in Spirit Initiative." 2010. Web. 22 March 2013.

Office of the Children's Advocate of Manitoba (OCA). "Annual Report." Winnipeg, Manitoba. 2010. Print.

Office of the Correctional Investigator (OCI). "Annual Report of the Office of the Correctional Investigator 2013-2014." Government of Canada. 2014. Web. 1 Dec. 2014.

Office of the Correctional Investigator (OCI). "Spirit Matters: Aboriginal People and the *Corrections and Conditional Release Act.*" Government of Canada, 2012. Web. 12 March 2013.

Office of the Correctional Investigator (OCI). "Annual Report of the Office of the Correctional Investigator 2009-2010." Government of Canada, 2010. Web. 12 March 2013.

Parkes, Debra and Kim Pate. "Time for Accountability: Effective Oversight of Women's Prisons." *Canadian Journal of Criminology and Criminal Justice.* 48 (2006): 251-285. Print.

Pate, Kim. "Advocacy, Activism and Social Change for Women in Prison." *Canadian Woman Studies/les cahiers de la femme* 25.3 (2006): 81-84. Print.

Porter, Jody. "Kenora Jail Holds 'Shocking' Number of Aboriginal Women." *CBC News* 30 Oct. 2012. Web. 12 March 2013.

Rabson, Mia. "Relatives of Missing Women Band Together." *Winnipeg Free Press* 3 Aug. 2010: A7. Print.

Razack, Sherene. "The Space of Difference in Law: Inquests into Aboriginal Deaths in Custody." *Somatechnics* 11 (2011): 87-123. Print.

Razack, Sherene. *Casting Out: The Eviction of Muslims from Western Law and Politics.* Toronto: University of Toronto Press, 2008. Print.

Razack, Sherene. "Gendered Racial Violence and Spatialized Justice: The Murder of Pamela George." *Race, Space, and the Law: Unmapping a White Settler Society.* Ed. Sherene Razack. Toronto: Between the Lines, 2002. 121-156. Print.

Ross, Luana. *Inventing the Savage: The Social Construction of Native American Criminality.* Austin: University of Texas Press, 1998. Print.

Santin, Aldo. "'The Officer Was Scared, She Panicked' No Need to Shoot Woman: Witness." *Brandon Sun.* 9 June 2010. Print.

Scourfield, Jonathan. *Gender and Child Protection.* Houndmills, Basingstoke: Palgrave MacMillan, 2003. Print.

Simons, Paula. "'College Girls' Overcome Foster Care, Choose 'White' Way Out." *Edmonton Journal* 13 Feb 2010: B1. Print.

Simons, Paula. "Let's Protect Kids, Rather Than Criminals' Privacy; Alberta's Dysfunctional Child-Welfare System Screams for an Overhaul." *Edmonton Journal* 12 Aug 2010. A3. Print.

Simons, Paula. "Slain Toddler Came Second to Privacy." *Calgary Herald* 13 Aug 2010: A12. Print.

Sinclair, Roberta Lynn and Roger Boe. "Canadian Federal Women Offender Profiles: Trends from 1981 to 2002 (Revised)." Ottawa: Research Branch, Correctional Service Canada (CSC). 2002. Print.

Smith, Andrea. "Queer Theory and Native Studies: The Heteronormativity of Settler Colonialism." *GLQ: A Journal Lesbian and Gay Studies* 16.1-2. (2010). 41-68. Print.

Smith, Andrea. *Conquest: Sexual Violence and American Indian Genocide*. Cambridge: Southend Press, 2005. Print.

Smith, Andrea. "American Studies without America: Native Feminisms and the Nation-State." *American Quarterly* 60.2 (2008): 309-315. Print.

Smith, Nat and Eric A. Stanley, eds. *Captive Genders: Trans Embodiment and the Prison Industrial Complex*. Oakland, CA: AK Press, 2011. Print.

Statistics Canada. "Aboriginal Peoples in Canada: First Nations People, Métis and Inuit. National Household Survey, 2011". Government of Canada. 2013. Web. 12 May 2013.

Stevenson, Winona. "Colonialism and First Nations Women in Canada." *Scratching the Surface: Canadian Anti-Racist Feminist Thought*. Ed. E. Dua and A. Robertson. Toronto: Women's Press, 1999. Print.

Stoler, Ann Laura. *Race and the Education of Desire: Foucault's History of Sexuality and the Colonial Order of Things*. Durhman and London: Duke University Press, 2006. Print.

Strega, Susan, Claire Fleet, Leslie Brown, Lena Dominelli, Marilyn Callahan, and Christopher Walmsley. "Connecting Father Absence and Mother Blame in Child Welfare Policies and Practice". *Children and Youth Services Review.* 30 (2008): 705-716. Print.

Sudbury, Julia, ed. *Global Lockdown: Race, Gender, and the Prison-Industrial Complex*. New York: Routledge, 2004. Print.

Task Force on Federally Sentenced Women (TFFSW). "Creating Choices: The Report of the Task Force on Federally Sentenced Women." Correctional Service Canada. Government of Canada.

1990. Web. 12 March 2013.

Thobani, Sunera. *Exalted Subjects: Studies in the Making of Race and Nation in Canada*. Toronto: University of Toronto Press, 2007. Print.

Thomas-Muller, Clayton. "The Seventh Generation." *This is an Honour Song: Twenty Years Since the Blockades*. Ed. Leanne Simpson and Kiera L. Ladner. Winnipeg: Arbeiter Ring Publishing, 2010. Print.

Turner v. Burnaby Correctional Centre for Women, 24 W.C.B. (2d) 250. 1994. Print.

Turner, Dale. 2006. *This is Not a Peace Pipe: Towards a Critical Indigenous Philosophy*. Toronto: University of Toronto Press, 2006. Print.

Walmsley, Christopher. *Protecting Aboriginal Children*. Vancouver: University of British Columbia Press, 2005. Print.

Weaver, Hilary. "The Colonial Context of Violence: Reflections on Violence in the Lives of Native American Women." *Journal of Interpersonal Violence* 24.9 (2009): 1552-1563. Print.

Welch, Mary Agnes. "Chiefs Ruled CFS Agency, Review Finds – Council Skimmed Money Earmarked for Children." *Winnipeg Free Press* 12 Feb. 2010: A8. Print.

Welch, Mary Agnes. "Sinclair Inquiry Could Begin This Fall – Child's Mother Decides Not to Appeal Sentence." *Winnipeg Free Press* 28 July 2010: A7. Print.

Welch, Mary Agnes. "Little Phoenix's Killer Appealing to High Court." *Winnipeg Free Press*. 30 July 2010: A9. Print.

Welch, Mary Agnes. "Baby Phoenix Inquiry Still On Hold – Province Wants to Wait Till Killer's Appeal Done." *Winnipeg Free Press* 25 Nov. 2010: A4. Print.

Wesley Group. "Marginalized: The Aboriginal Women's experience in Federal Corrections." The Wesley Group, Public Safety Canada. 2012. Web. 12 March 2013.

Winnubst, Shannon. "The Queer Thing about Neoliberal Pleasure: A Foucauldian Warning." *Foucault Studies*. 14 (2012): 79-97. Print.

Wolfe, Patrick. 2006. "Settler Colonialism and the Elimination of the Native." *Journal of Genocide Research* 8.4 (2006): 387-409. Print.

4.
"Sadly ... it appears the mother ... saw more of the police ... than [she] did [her] children"[1]

Theorizing Soft Criminalization in the Child Welfare System: An Analysis of *Re S.F.*

JOSEPHINE L. SAVARESE[2]

> *No justice system will ever alleviate all suffering or fear, but if it is to be a legitimate source of order, it should, at least, avoid burdening those in pain with the additional suffering of despair. After all that has passed, a different story could start with this: that there be no spaces where we will not, as a society, honour the enormity of another's horror and loss.*
>
> —Hadley Friedland (142)

IN THIS CHAPTER, I unite the troublesome fronts of marginality, Othering, and surveillance to investigate the plight of the Indigenous mothers who are at the intersections of the discriminatory regimes of child welfare and criminal justice. The proceedings from *Re S.F.*, a child protection hearing involving an Indigenous mother from a Saskatchewan First Nation, given the pseudonym Laura in the 2008 trial, were scrutinized to investigate the nation state reliance's on the child welfare system to bolster surveillance and to position Indigenous mothers as the "expected," disdained, "bad" mother. On July 9, 2008, the Honourable Madam Justice Janet E. McMurtry of the Saskatchewan Court of Queen's Bench, Family Law Division, ordered the gradual return of the six children to their mother's care after a lengthy trial. Laura lost custody of her five oldest children after Sara, her five-year-old daughter, went missing. Laura was a "dedicated, but imperfect parent" who deserved the opportunity to re-unite her family (*Re S.F.* 2008 at para 178). Justice McMurtry determined the children's needs were "best met" by placing them with their mother (2008 at para 184). In 2009, the Saskatchewan Court of Appeal unanimously overturned the trial decision arguing theJustice made legal errors. The matter was reviewed by the Honourable D. E. Wayne McIntyre in 2011 with reasons reported in *Re S.F.* 2014.

Through a comparison of the varied *Re S.F.* findings, including the 2008 trial decision, the 2009 appellate ruling, and the 2014 rehearing, I describe ways Laura was positioned as an outsider to mainstream order and cast as a deserving recipient of reproach. Laura's case is afforded analytical weight in this detailed exploration because it dramatically illustrates the integration of punitive scripts in family law. This amounts to what I consider a "softer" form of criminalization because Indigenous women are sanctioned through the less visible controls commonly associated with community corrections described by scholars including MaDonna Rose Maidment (2006) and Shoshana Pollack (158-174). The circulation of racialized, gendered narratives in family court decisions like *Re S.F.* frames an Indigenous mother as the permanent Other, justifying increased criminalization. Research affirming Indigenous parenting, including *Indigenous Mothering, Family and Community: International Perspectives* edited by Dawn Memee Lavell-Harvard and Kim Anderson, informs this chapter because it gives credence to the trial justice's appraisal of Laura's strengths. Harvard and Anderson's collection provides authority for the contextualized, more culturally appropriate evaluation of Laura's parenting by Justice Janet McMurtry.

In the 2009 appellate judgment and the 2014 review decision, Laura is characterized as the prototypical aberrant norm violator lacking the material resources and disciplinary practices associated with "good mothering." Through oversight and surveillance, evidence was produced rendering Laura largely unredeemable and in need of regulation. Her body was presented as consumed by risk, thereby jeopardizing her children's security. The Saskatchewan Court of Appeal emphasized the Ministry of Social Services' reports on Laura including her neglect of the children and her "excessive use of alcohol or drugs" (*Re S.F.* 2009 at para 10), the domestic violence in the home, Laura's incarceration for three months for soliciting and curfew violation, her irregular family visitations and frequent moves, sometimes due to eviction. The Ministry's claim that Laura was not addressing her addictions was restated (*Re S.F.* 2009 at para 4) though Laura completed residential treatment in 2006. The 2014 decision meticulously outlines Laura's maternal failings, presenting a compelling case of defilement and inadequacy.

By troubling many of the seemingly neutral findings of facts, I suggest the child welfare system and the criminal justice system promulgate the same or comparable discourse on the lives of Indigenous women as disrupted and in need of regulation. This chapter offers fresh insights on the criminalization of mothers in the child welfare context through illustrations from the *Re S.F.* cases. Prior studies establish that criminalizing motherhood is class compounded and racialized (Monture 1-17). There is need, however, for futher analysis on the interrelationships between the two systems given their mutual authority to render mothers abject. Theorizing Laura's situation helps probe Caitlin Janzen and colleagues' piercing question posed in "*Nothing Short of a Horror Show": Triggering Abjection of Street Workers in Western Canadian Newspapers* (142-162).With her colleagues, Janzen queries "what is at stake for dominant culture should abjected bodies begin to count as 'bodies that matter' (144). In this chapter, I attempt to take up their question through a close read of the three *Re S.F.* decisions.

This chapter does not attempt to determine the best placement for Laura's children. It aims to problematize the pronounced institutional negativity that undermined her custody claim. During the protracted legal proceedings, Laura moved from a central to a more nominal figure in her children's lives. In 2014, Justice D.E.W. McIntyre found that Laura "largely disappeared from the lives of her children and had little contact with the Ministry" in 2010 and 2011 (*Re S.F.* 2014 at para XXVIII). This contradicted Justice Janet McMurtry's 2008 finding Laura's children were "very connected to her" and "[wanted] to be with her" (*Re S.F.* 2008 at para 178). During the trial, Ministry officials acknowledged the children had strong bonds to each other and to their mother (*Re S.F.* 2008 at para 172).

Drawing from diverse strands of critical race oriented feminist thought, I theorize that Laura's struggles are more understandable given the systemic and interpersonal violence she has experienced, including childhood sexual abuse, domestic violence and the loss of her five-year-old daughter, Sara, from a mysterious abduction in 2004. For theorist Sara Ahmed, stories like Laura's can offer an "instructive lesson" by challenging us to consider ways marginalized women are silenced (396). As a result, Laura's experiences with the mainstream justice system can teach us "how to hear, listen, and read differently in the collective project of struggling for justice, and bearing witness to injustice" (Ahmed 396).

PART I: BACKGROUND DISCUSSION

The Legal History

Laura's involvement with the Ministry began in 1994 when her eldest daughter, Serena, was one year old. After that time, the Ministry was regularly involved with Laura's growing family: Riley born in 1995, twins Tara and Sara born in 1998, Carson born in 2000, and Anna born in 2003. The application for an order for Jonah, born in 2007, was amalgamated into the trial. The 2014 review hearing incorporated Laura's youngest son, Jeremy, born in 2010. Both Jonah and Jeremy were apprehended at birth due to the Ministry's protection concerns.[3] The children were fathered by three partners, John, Tom, and Dale.

By November 2007, there were fifty-three Mobile Crisis Reports or emergency interventions in the family. With her partners, Laura had entered into eight parental services agreements and five voluntary agreements with the Ministry allowing temporary placements by the 2008 trial (*Re S.F.* 2008 at para 10). An important turning point occurred in 2006 when Laura opposed the long-term placement of her then-five children in state care. A protection hearing or trial took place on intermittent dates between January 7 and April 22, 2008 resulting in an order for the children's return. Justice McMurtry acknowledged Laura's "troubled parenting history" yet emphasized Laura's deep affection for her children (*Re S.F.* 2008 at para 163).

Based on the antagonistic approach, Justice McMurty concluded: "The Ministry failed this family" (*Re S.F.* 2008 at para 189). She urged the Ministry to offer supports to help the family "recover" (*Re S.F.* 2008 at Para 189). Laura's stubbornness, commitment to her partner, Dale, and failure to access resources were factors in the "great delay in being reunited with her children" (*Re S.F.* 2008 at para 181).The Ministry's appeal was heard in September 2008. The Court of Appeal issued its decision in November 2009 overturning Justice Janet McMurty's ruling.

The Court of Appeal particularly rebuked Justice McMurtry's critique of an emergency apprehension on July 21, 2004, shortly after Sara's disappearance. When Ministry staff unexpectedly entered the family home, Laura requested time for the children to finish breakfast, pack their clothes and prepare for the relocation. These requests were denied and the children were immediately removed by social workers assisted by four to six police officers. Justice McMurty described the event as follows: "The resulting scene was chaotic; children and mother crying and the children carried off under the glare of TV cameras" (*Re S.F.* 2008 at para 54). After the apprehension, Laura and Dale became "distraught" and found coping difficult (*Re S.F.* 2008 at para 8). For Justice McMurty, the apprehension partially explained the "gulf of distrust" between Laura and the Ministry (*Re S.F.* 2008 at para 166). Following Sara's abduction, Ministry staff visited the home two to three times daily (*Re S.F.* 2008 at para 56) yet provided no warning of the removal plan. Justice McMurtry stated: "In the midst of a tragedy, instead of helping Laura, the Ministry took away her children" (*Re S.F.* 2008 at para 163). In contrast, the appellate court critiqued the trial justice for conducting a "collateral attack," or unwarranted strike, on the Ministry's decision (*Re S.F.* 2009 at para 38).

Laura unsuccessfully attempted to appeal to the Supreme Court of Canada to reverse the appellate findings (L.K. v. Minister of Social Services for Saskatchewan, 2010). Laura asked the Supreme Court to re-affirm the right to state funded counsel in the protection setting guaranteed by s. 7 of the *Canadian Charter of Rights and Freedoms* (Saskatchewan Legal Aid Commission, *Appellant's Memorandum of Argument*). She identified several instances when she lacked advocacy. After the 2004 apprehension, for example, Laura signed an agreement in July 2004 granting short term custody of the five children to the Ministry. At trial, she reported being unsure of her options. She thought she had to sign the agreement "to get her children back" (*Re S.F.* 2008 at para 61). The next meeting between Laura and the Ministry took place in October 2004 (*Re S.F.* 2008 at para 60). When the first formal court order was imposed on October 11, 2005, Laura was temporarily incarcerated in Pine Grove, the provincial women's correctional institutional in Prince Albert, Saskatchewan (*Re S.F.* 2008 at Paragraph 79). Although Laura appeared by telephone from the women's prison under restrictive conditions, she was described by the appellate court as having "attended" the Chambers hearing (*Re S.F.* 2009 at para 19). Arguably, Laura consented to childcare arrangements without appreciating the difficulty of reversing the protection related track record. Her vulnerability raises the need for public policy reform to ensure families are supported throughout protection proceedings (Savarese 2011).

When the appeal was denied by the Supreme Court, Justice McIntyre of the Saskatchewan Court of Queen's Bench reviewed the Ministry's protection concerns at a hearing in 2011 for the five youngest children, Carson, Tara, Anna, Jonah, and Jeremy. Serena and Riley were no longer in the Ministry's care. The Ministry presented evidence on its protection concerns in regard to Laura. The hearing ran from the morning into the mid-afternoon, even though Laura failed to appear and the matter was uncontested (*Re S.F.* 2014 at paras IV-VI). In 2014, the court issued a long-term order for the continued placement of Tara, Carson, and Anna in foster care. Laura's contact, C. M., was designated as "a person of sufficient interest" or appropriate caregiver for Laura's youngest sons, Jonah and Jeremy.

THE SIGNIFICANCE OF SARA'S DISAPPEARANCE

The disappearance of Sara, one of Laura's twin daughters, on July 5, 2004 from the family home in Regina, Saskatchewan shadows this case. For the past decade, the Regina Police Service has searched for Sara with few meaningful leads. In 2014, the Service re-issued the reward for information on Sara's abduction, doubling the fund to $50,000. Given the haunting backdrop of Sara's abduction, this paper aims to demonstrate that institutional bias towards missing and murdered women complicated the state's response to Laura.

The focus on Laura's motherly limitations implies she is responsible, if only through carelessness, for Sara's disappearance. The events on Sara's last evening at home are described in *Re S.F.* 2008 and 2014. In brief, Serena, then age eleven, was left in charge of the five younger children after her mother, Laura, and stepfather, Dale, left at different points. The inconsistent adult supervision may have factored in the crime. However, the evidence produced by the Ministry at trial was pronounced too "scant" by Justice McMurtry to permit "conclusions" on "the adequacy of the children's supervision" (*Re S.F.* 2008 at Para 52).[4] Importantly, Laura and her family were identified clients of the Ministry at the time of Sara's disappearance, meaning that multiple guardians were charged with Sara's safety.

Prior to Sara's disappearance, a worker from an Indigenous child welfare agency, Aboriginal Family Services, visited the family twice per week (*Re S.F.* 2008 at para 36). A new worker, C.P., called upon Laura on June 22, 2004. The home was described as unclean with "dirty dishes, toys and food" strewn through the living room (*Re S.F.* 2008 at para 37). Laura claimed her noticeable track marks resulted from former drug use. C.P. and Laura agreed to meet the next week for case planning. The failure to meet was not explained at the trial, although this was clearly an important oversight. Sara disappeared two weeks later (*Re S.F.* 2008 at para 37).

PART 2: HIGHLIGHTING SARA AS A YOUNG MISSING INDIGENOUS WOMAN, PROBLEMATIZING LAURA AS "SOCIAL WASTE"

In this section, I reason that the appellate and reviewing court's pronounced fixation with Laura's "failings" replicates broader discourses on the disappearance of Indigenous women by foregrounding parental failings to "explain" Sara's victimization (García-Del Moral 33-62). By restating the Ministry's claim the parents "live in an environment of violence, risk and danger," the appellate judgment suggests negative life choices were causal in Sara's abduction (*Re S.F.* 2008 at Para 40). This version of events implies Laura and Dale jeopardized the children beyond neglect.

The appellate and subsequent 2014 judgment incorrectly treat

Laura's behaviour as the central variable determining harm. Collectively, Laura and her children were disproportionately vulnerable to victimization due to gender, race, and class-based markers. Caitlin Janzen and her colleagues identify the intricate structural inequities underpinning violent victimization, such as Sara's 2004 abduction. They state:

> A whole system of supporting violations and discourses establishes the conditions under which certain bodies are continuously victimized. It is these insidious forms of violence—racism, colonization, patriarchy, misogyny, and capitalism among them—that permit more visible acts to occur, and to occur with impunity. (Janzen et al. 142- 43)

From this insight, I argue the attribution of fault to Laura individualizes blame and ignores the commonality between Sara's removal and other similar cases. That Sara is only one of the many Canadian Aboriginal women exposed to extreme violence showcases the social (in)justice informing the case. Race, gender, and social economic status pre-determined victimization in every instance. Wendee Kubik, Carrie Bourassa, and Mary Hampton urge reforms to promote safety for Indigenous women and children (18-34). Fixation with maternal inadequacy diverts attention from the comprehensive strategies needed to address the underlying factors causing Indigenous women's marginalization (NWAC).

In support of calls for social justice, advocates for missing and murdered Indigenous women have emphasized the indifference and even hostility towards the women (Amnesty International, *Stolen Sisters*; Amnesty International, *No More Stolen Sisters*). Based on a qualitative review of Mexican newspapers and the Canadian coverage of Robert Pickton's trial, Paulina García-Del Moral concluded news sources in Canada and Mexico cast missing women as "social waste" marked by excess and abjection (36). Sara was a young child without the indicators of degeneracy attributed to other disappeared women. Ironically, Laura has been characterized as possessing the vice typically associated with disappeared women. In García-Del Moral's terminology, Laura was portrayed as "social waste" marked by abject humanity.

While largely absent from the court judgments, systemic race, gender, and class factors rendering Indigenous women vulnerable to violence are prominent in the research. Kirsten Gilchrist argues mainstream "texts," generated by institutions including the print media, position Aboriginal women for vicious disciplining by stressing their deviance (373-390). These dehumanizing accounts foster indifference to violent victimization and often lead to impunity. In 2013, Human Rights Watch criticized the "apparent apathy" demonstrated by the police to the frequent disappearances and murders in northern British Columbia (8). The disinterest generated "a persistent and well-publicized stain on Canada's human rights record" (Human Rights Watch 8). Inadequate action and reform mean Indigenous women/girls disappear in unacceptably high numbers.

While advocates attribute the disappearances to socio-environmental factors, trial evidence indicates Laura internalized responsibility for Sara's abduction. Kathy Depko, a counsellor with a Saskatchewan community based agency, began working with Laura in September 2004. She summarized the 44 sessions held with Laura in her trial testimony. In his 2014 review, Justice McIntyre limits his review to comments made on Laura's addictions, including Kathy Depko's observation Laura was "high on cocaine, t's and r's and weed" at meetings (*Re S.F.* 2014 at para XV). Alternatively, the 2008 trial judgment incorporates sympathetic passages from Ms. Depko's testimony. Laura admitted to her counsellor Sara might not have "gone missing" if "perhaps ... she had changed her life earlier" (*Re S.F.* 2008 at para 63). Laura was "very open and honest" with Kathy Depko, even acknowledging drug misuse (*Re S.F.* 2008 at para 63). This suggests her admission of guilt was also truthful. Irrespective of Laura's self-blame, countless researchers attribute the disappearances of Indigenous women to broader structural factors that they argue warrant a fuller examination.

The revelations in *Re S.F.* (2008) on the Ministry's (mis)handling of the file suggests that other institutions beyond the criminal justice system need to be investigated for possible bias towards disappeared and murdered Indigenous women and their families. The possibility the rhetoric of child protection may shield officials who chastise families confronting profound loss deserves the challenge attempted here. By exposing details of the more hidden story of state harm towards Laura and her family, my hope is to amplify the calls for a national public inquiry into the missing and murdered Indigenous women in Canada, estimated in 2014 to number at over one thousand (RCMP).

PART 3: CONSIDERING SOFT CRIMINALIZATION AND SURVEILLANCE

Recent scholarship, while "embryonic" in linking surveillance and child welfare practices, brings attention to the more covert aims that may underlie state interventions into families (Wrennall 304). Lynne Wrennall's view that a watchful, suspicious state operates within the child welfare context under the guise of promoting children's best interests helps to theorize the Ministry's surveillance of Laura (304-324). For Wrennall, families are short-changed when parental shortcomings are magnified to satisfy a policing function. Wrennall labels the child welfare system a "Trojan Horse" that often harms children and families even while trumpeting benevolent aims. Disadvantaged, largely Indigenous clientele, shoulder the system's discriminatory impacts:

> The evidence establishes that children and their families are processed by a system that is patently manifesting the effects of class bias, compounded by gender bias and racial bias, undertaking investment decisions that further exacerbate inequality. The system is especially ferocious in regard to Indigenous Peoples as part of a strategy of dispossession that leaves Indigenous People bereft of what they value most, their children, their land, their connection to the earth. (Wrennall 318)

Re S.F. 2009 and 2014 starkly illustrate the child welfare's system capacity for disdain and discriminatory action towards an Indigenous mother and her family. In this text, Justice McMurty's ruling is considered more praiseworthy because she refused to narrowly cast Laura as a harmful mother. Her findings are paralleled in qualitative research by Comack and Brickley (1-36). They found criminalised women "are neither bad *or* good, monsters *or* normal sisters, miscreants *or* nuns" (24, emphasis in original). The interviewees shared stories confirming the "Violent Woman," or, in Laura's case, the "neglectful" mother, "can be both good *and* bad at the same time" (Comack and Brickley 24).

In fact, Laura performed well on certain indicators, including those valued by mainstream protocols. Justice McMurty heard testimony on the strong family bonds. Rhonda, the original foster mother who left Saskatchewan, testified on the children's views of Laura. They were reported to "idolize" their mother (*Re S.F.* 2008 at para 117). The next foster mother, Rose, stated the older children wanted to return home while the younger children were neutral. Laura missed visits yet was present for "every birthday, Christmas, Easter and Thanksgiving celebration" (*Re S.F.* 2008 at para 136). Serena's life improved "markedly" after she returned to Laura's care in early 2008 (*Re S.F.* 2008 at para 179). With Laura's encouragement, Serena returned to school and accessed anger management counselling through a local youth centre. The Ministry was less proactive and took two months to provide a $15.00 bus pass for Serena's transport to school (*Re S.F.* 2008 at para 158).

Laura also made personal progress in the immediate aftermath of the 2008 trial decision. A new worker, Ellen McGuire, was assigned in August 2008 (*Re S.F.* 2014 at para XXIII). Ms. McGuire replaced M.T. who was openly hostile to Laura. Ms. McGuire reported Laura obtained a larger home, attended school, and evidenced better "self-esteem," presumably with the promise of re-gaining custody (*Re S.F.* 2014 at para XXIV). While the Ministry's appeal was pending, workers noticed Laura resumed substance use with observable signs by Christmas 2008. She lost her home and dropped out of school. Laura regularly missed visits with the children. She placed meetings with her family support worker 'on hold' in March 2009 (*Re S.F.* 2014 at para XXIV).

The individualized, correctional approach adopted by the appellate and reviewing courts reduces a complicated story to a narrow frame that discredits Laura—and other Indigenous mothers more generally—by circulating negative accounts of her life. It downplays the damaging consequences of colonialism and the systemic legacy of trauma. Laura Landertinger suggests accounts like those in *Re S.F.* contribute to the ongoing marginalization of Indigenous peoples by replacing histories of "political, economic and institutional violence" with explanations of "inherent inadequacy" (146). Reports of "Canadian benevolence," including stories of protecting Aboriginal children, work in tandem with "colonial narratives" to "spin a discursive web that naturalizes colonial control, while denying its very existence" (Landertinger 146).

PART 4: ANALYSIS AND FINDINGS

In this section, I identify selections from the case where gendered, racialized surveillance and the over-usage of the state's criminalization power documented by scholars such as Margaret A. Jackson (197-208) are evident. I contend the 2009 and 2014 *Re S.F.* cases show criminal overreach through a less visible form, namely family law. I theorize that Justice McMurty's efforts to apply a re-integrative, restorative framework were rebuked because her approach threatened mainstream order by refusing the discourse of individualized blame. Through a qualitative investigation of the *Re S.F.* decisions inspired by Janzen et al.'s analytical approach (144-145), I link the child welfare system with the criminal process. Findings in the appellate (2009) and review (2014) judgments are cited to illustrate that the retributive scripts found in prosecutions also inform family law. Henderson's research on the ways western paradigms disadvantage Indigenous culture/knowledge helps to explain the damaging consequences of the court's emphasis on Laura's weaknesses (1-56).

A careful read of the record reveals a more complicated state of affairs, including Laura's affection for her children. The 2014 decision states, for example, that Laura was responsible for locating C.M, Jonah and Jeremy's caregiver ("When Jeremy was born, the mother identified C.M. as a potential resource for Jeremy," *Re S.F.* 2014 at para XXII). While recognizing Laura's love for her children, Justice McIntyre devotes more attention to Laura's parental shortcomings (*Re S.F.* 2014 at para XLII).

Theme 1: Racialized Depictions of the "Bad" Mother

This section tracks ways the "bad" mother was reinserted into the judicial narratives, reversing the trial justice's findings on Laura's mothering capacity. More generally, insights from critical victimologists, Colleen Anne Dell and Jennifer M. Kilty, help to explain the harsh treatment of Aboriginal women by the courts (51-68). While researching Aboriginal women drug users, their analysis fosters critical insights on the *Re S.F.* 2009 appellate and 2014 review decisions. Dell and Kilty maintain substance users are depicted as the typical "offender" due to operation of gender, race, and class bias. Aboriginal women like Laura are presumed always and already offenders. This casts Indigenous women as deserving punishment because they are presumed incorrigible. In the child welfare context, they must overcome the presumption of maternal lack.

In correspondence with Dell and Kilty's concerns, the maligning of Laura undermined her custody application. For example, *Re S.F.* 2014 sets out Laura's history of substance use, noting her alcohol use began at age eleven and escalated to Talwin, Ritalin, and cocaine by adulthood (*Re S.F.* 2014, para XIII). In addition to early onset substance use, Laura's failure to maintain an orderly household was described. Drug paraphernalia and used needles were visible to social workers. One worker who visited the home on October 28, 2011 described the kitchen as "dirty with garbage laying about." The bedroom furnishings were "mattresses on the floor" (*Re S.F.* 2014, para XXVII). As critical race feminist scholars emphasize, the inclusion of this information is not accidental (Ahmed 377-398; Razack 91-130). Laura's flagrant violations of dominant norms of respectability situate her outside of "normalcy."

The negative characterization of Laura seems to have resulted in persistent surveillance by the Ministry, particularly after Sara's abduction. Justice McMurtry stressed that no evidence was produced at trial linking Laura to Sara's disappearance. In fact, Laura fully cooperated with the investigation providing at least eight interviews (*Re S.F.* 2008 at para 45). Although never connected to the crime, Laura believed she was policed rather than encouraged. Justice McMurty noted: "In Laura's view, the Ministry has confined itself to collecting evidence against her, rather than attempting to re-unify the family" (*Re S.F.* 2008 at para 175). When the assigned worker, M.T., learned Serena missed classes, he informed the Ministry, not Laura. He placed the results of a positive screening for substance use on Laura's file with no attempt to problem-solve with Laura on her relapse. Wrennall's argument that child welfare practice amounts to a "strategy of subjugation" where state agents use their discretion to apply an "intensely aggressive expression of discipline" brings insight to the Ministry's engagement with Laura (305).

One example seems to particularly demonstrate the Ministry's continued oversight. In July 2005, the worker, M.T., unexpectedly approached Laura around the one-year anniversary of Sara's disappearance and the apprehension of the siblings. Justice McMurty stated:

> On July 23, 2005, M.T. saw Laura walking down the street, carrying her personal belongings in a box. He offered her a ride. She smelled of alcohol, but was not intoxicated. She said she and Dale were still together but would not be living together. M.T. asked her to sign another s. 9 [voluntary placement] agreement. He testified that Laura told him that "she was having a tough time with things." (*Re S.F.* 2008 at para 75)

This passage confirms Laura's grief through her statements to the worker. At the time, she was homeless, somewhat intoxicated and taken off guard. Even so, M.T. pressed her for a decision on the children's placements, seeming to typify Wrennall's worry that state agents prioritize surveillance over a supportive function.

An alternative concern to state oversight is the Ministry's failure to offer needed supports to Laura. Hadley Friedland's claim that the legal system excessively surveils while under-protecting Indigenous peoples thereby creating a disordering effect seems to find expression in Laura's interactions with the Ministry (Friedland 105-142). The withdrawal of supports for Laura's rehabilitation made mother/child reunification unlikely. Among many examples, Laura's requests for a "healing circle" with Aboriginal agencies were not acted on (*Re S.F.* 2008 at para 92). The fitness pass she requested for recreation with the children was not provided (*Re S.F.* 2008 at para 92). The apparent apathy to her well-being is also notable in the 2014 court's response to the domestic violence Laura experiences. The police reported nine incidents for domestic violence or intoxication between August 2009 and August 2011 (*Re S.F.* 2014 at para XXVI). One report stated that Dale was at the home covered in blood and holding a hammer (*Re S.F.* 2014 para XXV). Another time, law enforcement intervened because Dale threatened to conduct a 'murder suicide' with a knife (*Re S.F.* 2014 para XXI). Domestic violence was, according to Justice D.E. Wayne McIntyre, an "ever present" part of Laura's life (*Re S.F.* 2014 para XXXV). The pressing issue the judge faced was ensuring the children did not conclude domestic violence was "normal" in relationships (*Re S.F.* 2014 para XXXII).

While very important, this solution offers no support to Laura or to Serena, an occasion witness. Efforts by Caitlen Janzen and her colleagues' to probe mainstream society's willingness to relegate certain bodies to the margins may shed insight on the seeming indifference to Laura's plight. They encourage us to question "why some women are left behind in "uninhabitable" and "unlivable' zones" (Janzen et al. 149). Justice Janet McMurty expressed greater concern by prohibiting Dale from residing with Laura once the 2008 order for the children's return was implemented "because his substance abuse [brought] with it the potential for violence" (*Re S.F.* 2008 at para 182).[5]

The 2014 Queen's Bench review decision appears to endorse the state's apathy to Laura by connecting her to what Razack (2000) labels "degenerate spaces" (cited in Janzen et al. 145). Statements by Justice D.E. Wayne McIntryre in 2014 clearly link Laura to the racialized domain of the "street" reinforcing her parenting unsuitability. Justice McIntryre describes C.M., the designated caregiver for Jonah and Jeremy, as an outreach worker for a church that provided "*street* level" ministry "to prostitutes and those living on the *street*." Laura met C.M. when she visited the outreach bus with Dale for "food, prayer and warmth from the *street*" (all above citations are to *Re S.F.* 2014 para XXII, emphasis added). The repeated references place Laura in the abandoned, lawless zones described by Caitlin Janzen and her team as beyond the "respectability of privileged white spaces" (145). Justice McIntyre decontextualizes Laura's problems by attributing her struggles to her inability to "successfully deal with [her] challenges" (*Re S.F.* 2014 at para XLII). As a victim of violence, drug user, failed housekeeper, user of street outreach, and an occasional street-based sex worker, Laura is deemed nominal in ways accounted for by Janzen et al. She is captured in a "double-bind." As "The Other," Laura is "always excluded from normalcy, yet constantly judged by a code she many not subscribe to and will never measure up to" (Janzen et al. 152).

Theme Two: Considering the Disappearance of a "Daughter X"

In this section, I speculate on possible reasons Sara's disappearance is routinely downplayed in the 2009 appellate and 2014 decisions, depicting her life as one that is not grievable. The Saskatchewan Court of Appeal referred to Sara as "a daughter X," a twin sister to Tara or T.K. (*Re S.F.* 2009 at para 16). The other parties are referred to by their initials. Sara's disappearance caused what was described as a "destablizing crisis" in the family (*Re S.F.* 2009 at para 16). This terminology appears cautious when the profound loss of a young child is considered. Referring to Sara as "X" portrays her as an absence rather than an absent presence, remembered by her family and community members. The 2014 decision is similarly brief. It states: "On July 6, 2004, one of the mother's children ... was reported missing" (*Re S.F.* 2014 Para XVI). Justice McIntyre stated the child subjected to the *reported* disappearance was not included in the protection file, as if that possibility existed. These statements obscure Sara's victimization by describing her disappearance in ambiguous terms minimizing the decade-long investigation into her whereabouts. Her disappearance is "normalized" as a child protection matter masking the violent crime.

Backgrounding the crime reinforces Laura as a hardened norm violator who is careless and indifferent to her children. In this position, Laura does not command us to review the borders of respectability that offer privileges to some while denying them to others. Reasoning with Paulina García-Del Moral, we are asked to solidify the distinctions separating "'clean and proper' bodies, subjects and social orders" (35) from degenerate Others, like Laura, who present a threat of "contamination." This implies we are not permitted outrage for Laura as a beleaguered Indigenous mother of a very young missing daughter.

While not made prominent, Sara's abduction shadows the *Re S.F.* cases in ways that seem to generate panic in regard to Laura. Sara Ahmed helps to theorize the state's seemingly feverish efforts to denounce Laura (377-398). Ahmed states: "What is important, then, is that the narratives that seek to preserve the present through working on anxieties of death as the necessary consequence of the demise of social forms also seek to locate that anxiety in some bodies, that then take on fetish qualities as objects of fear" (394). For Ahmed, bodies like Laura's "engender even more fear." While threatening to settler colonialist formations, such bodies cannot be pacified and "threaten to pass by" (394).

PART 5: MAKING TRUTHS, MAKING WORLDS

Laura's treatment by child welfare agencies exemplifies what I label "soft" criminalization in reference to the expansion of carceral ideology enabled by child welfare policies and practices. Because racialized women are increasingly deemed problematic, feminist scholars are documenting their heightened scrutiny by enforcement agencies. Chesney-Lind and Eliason situate the upward trends in women's criminalization globally (29-47). They expose the increasingly harsh responses to women, particularly those like Laura who are impoverished and marginalized, who veer from stereotypical feminine norms. Brown and Bloom's findings that criminal and child protection justice ensnare Indigenous Hawaiian women are relevant to Canadian Aboriginal women. Like their northern counterparts, Native Hawaiian women are the targets of "neo-liberal policies that hold them accountable for the historical and structural injustices that shape their current situations" (165). Yasmin Jiwani establishes that various surveillance techniques and technologies support Canada's retributive turn by documenting the "failings" of the underclass thereby justifying punitive interventions (13-31).

Regardless of concerns raised by the 2010 Saskatchewan inquiry, *For the Good of Our Children and Youth* (Saskatchewan Child

Welfare Review Panel), the rhetorical strength of the child welfare system's claims means it operates with limited challenge and accountability. While interventions are sometimes warranted for children's safety, the supports offered by the child welfare system are often motivated by disdain, are culturally inappropriate and insufficient in scope. Laura Landertinger explains the over-representation of Indigenous families in child welfare systems through Foucaldian bio-political theory. Landertinger states: "The Native-as-Others is marked as deviant, intrinsically pathological and irredeemable. Indigenous peoples, as a group, are seen as standing outside definitions of normality and bourgeois respectability. Such constructions blame Indigenous peoples for their social ills" (146). The deficient responses ignore the systemic drivers of child welfare and criminal justice involvement, thereby leaving oppression and historical trauma unchallenged.

Blackstock and Trocmé recommend culturally appropriate community development strategies to realize children's well-being and long-term security (12-33). The failure to rebuild Indigenous nations has resulted in a growing tide of Indigenous children entering care, further weakening future generations. Community-based innovations could eliminate the widespread, colonial inspired removal of Indigenous children—the predominant model of child welfare for over a century.

The apprehension of Laura's children demonstrates that the still-colonial nation state resorts to this strategy with insufficient reservation. The treatment afforded Laura and her family reveals ways the child welfare system provides an ideological and practical gateway for the harder strategies in Canadian public policy as "tough" justice gains momentum. In 2012, the Wesley Group for Public Safety Canada reported the numbers of imprisoned Aboriginal women increased by approximately ninety percent in the last decade making them the fastest growing offender population (Wesley). Societal reforms needed to realize anti-racism and social, political, and cultural equality are obscured when individual shortcomings are magnified.

The court's pronounced focus on Laura's transgressions reinforces the white settler parenting standards that disadvantage Indigenous mothers in the protection system. The judicial findings are significant according to Sara Ahmed's reasoning because they are presented as factual and beyond challenge. Ahmed asserts: "To 'make truths' is to make worlds" (377). The courts' preoccupation with dominant societal truths about Indigenous culpability generally, and Laura's "guilt" more specifically, undermine the alternative truths that afford Laura more humanity and worth. Laura's knowledge as a member of an oppressed community is silenced beyond the trial judgment. Greater attentiveness to her narrative might reveal the everyday influence of historic trauma as a lived reality for Indigenous mothers, thereby bringing insight to the discriminatory conditions that facilitated Sara's disappearance.

PART 6: CONCLUSIONS: A CALL FOR EXPANDED SPACES OF "HONOUR"

In this chapter, I investigated the troubling interplay between the child welfare system and the criminal justice system through a critical read of the three *Re S.F.* decisions. I suggested the two parallel systems bolster repression of Indigenous women, like Laura, by penalizing their non-compliance with mainstream guidelines. This oversight negated Laura's status as a crime victim warranting empathy. Rather than supporting the family, agency officials investigated Laura's failings to compose a decisive record of her deviancy. As an applied case study, *Re S.F.* showcased the normalized, everyday surveillance of families and mothers identified as protection risks.

This paper problematized the use of child protection claims to transfer blame to Laura by magnifying her individualized failings. This approach serves to criminalize her and forestalls a comprehensive investigation into the varied factors that may have facilitated Sara's abduction, including child welfare inadequacy. The persistent rebukes appear to be pushing Laura further to the margins, according to a close read of the 2014 Queen's Bench judgment. As Laura blends deeper into the "street," her drug-related problems appear more severe and her ties to her surviving children appear weaker, ensuring their existence is characterized by significant loss. Friedland's conclusion that the contemporary Canadian justice system creates chaos and exercises a "disordering influence" for the Indigenous peoples who experience its punitive over-reach is dramatically illustrated through the Ministry's approach to Laura (142). While the quest for a more effective, less colonial justice system is on-going, we might begin to expand the spaces of "honour" where "another's horror and loss" are recognized (Friedland 142). At a minimum, Laura and her children deserve this respect as they rebuild their lives over a decade after the disappearance of their daughter and sister, Sara.

Alarmed by disappearances like Sara's, organizations (including the Native Women's Association of Canada, Amnesty International, Human Rights Watch) and individuals (including James Anaya, former United Nations Special Rapporteur on the Rights of Indigenous Peoples and Rinelle Harper, the 16-year-old survivor of a nearly fatal attack in Winnipeg in 2014) have called for a national investigation into Indigenous women's systemic vulnerability to victimization, to the extreme of homicide. In this chapter, I have similarly rejected diversionary tactics that attribute responsibility to Indigenous women for the violence they disproportionately experience. The preoccupation with Laura's "criminality" obscured the importance of Sara's disappearance even though her unresolved abduction remains a pressing story.

ENDNOTES

[1]*Re S.F.* SKQB 179. Saskatchewan Court of Queen's Bench. 2014. Canadian Legal Information Institute. Web. 30 June 2014 (at Para XXVIII).

[2]Dijonna Brooks, student of Criminology and Criminal Justice, St. Thomas University provided valued research assistance. I also thank the organizers of the international conference, *Missing Women: Decolonization, Third Wave Feminisms, and Indigenous People of Canada and Mexico*, University of Regina, August 14-17, 2008, particularly for the inspiring stories from mothers of missing daughters.

[3]The pseudonyms used in the 2008 trial for the children and adults are retained in this chapter.

[4]In his 2014 decision, Justice McIntryre reported at para XVI (*Re S.F.* 2014) that Laura and Dale's house was in "complete disarray"

on July 6th when Sara was discovered missing. Furthermore, it "appeared as if there had been a party recently." These statements are not attributed to any source nor were these observations part of the trial judgment.

[5]During the trial, Laura testified Dale was an important support to her. She stated she felt like she was "always going to be sad." Dale helped her not to be "so sad all the time" and was "very attentive." (*Re S.F.* 2008 at para 99).

WORKS CITED

Ahmed, Sara. "The Politics of Fear in the Making of Worlds." *International Journal of Qualitative Studies in Education* 16.3 (2003): 377-398. Taylor and Francis Online. Web. 10 November 2013.

Amnesty International Canada. *Canada: Stolen Human Sisters: A Rights Response to Discrimination and Violence against Indigenous Women in Canada.* Ottawa: Amnesty International Canada, 2004. Web. 3 May 2013.

Amnesty International Canada. *No More Stolen Sisters: The Need for a Comprehensive Response to Discrimination and Violence against Indigenous Women in Canada.* Ottawa: Amnesty International Canada, 2009. Web. 3 May 2013.

Blackstock, Cindy and Nico Trocmé. "Community-Based Child Welfare for Aboriginal Children: Supporting Resilience through Structural Change." *Social Policy Journal of New Zealand* 24.12 (2005): 12-33. Print.

Brown, Marilyn and Barbara E. Bloom "Colonialism and Carceral Motherhood: Native Hawaiian Families under Corrections and Child Welfare Control." *Feminist Criminology* 4.2 (2009): 151-169. Web. 5 June 2012.

Chesney-Lind, Meda and Michele Eliason. "From Invisible to Incorrigible: The Demonization of Marginalized Women and Girls." *Crime, Media, Culture* 2.1 (2006): 29-47. Web. 10 May 2013.

Comack, Elizabeth and Selena Brickey, "Constituting the Violence of Criminalized Women." *Canadian Journal of Criminology and Criminal Justice* 49.1 (2007): 1-36. Web. 10 May 2013.

Dell, Colleen Anne and Jennifer M. Kilty. "The Creation of the

Expected Aboriginal Woman Drug Offender in Canada: Exploring Relations between Victimization, Punishment, and Cultural Identity." *International Review of Victimology* 19.1 (2013): 51-68. Web. 10 May 2013.

Friedland, Hadley. "Different Stories: Aboriginal People, Order, and the Failure of the Criminal Justice System." *Sask. L. Rev.* 72 (2009): 105-142. Web. 10 May 2011.

García-Del Moral, Paulina. "Representation as a Technology of Violence: On the Representation of the Murders and Disappearances of Aboriginal Women in Canada and Women in Ciudad Juarez." *Canadian Journal of Latin American and Caribbean Studies* 36.72 (2011): 33-62. Web. 10 May 2013.

Gilchrist, Kristen. " 'Newsworthy' Victims? Exploring Differences in Canadian Local Press Coverage of Missing/Murdered Aboriginal and White women." *Feminist Media Studies* 10.4 (2010): 373-390. Web. 10 May 2013.

Henderson, James Youngblood. "Postcolonial Indigenous Legal Consciousness." *Indigenous Law Journal* 1 (2002): 1-56. Print.

Human Rights Watch. *Those Who Take Us Away: Abusive Policing and Failures in Protection of Indigenous Women and Girls in Northern British Columbia, Canada*. Human Rights Watch, 13 February 2013. Web. Accessed 3 May 2013.

Kubik, Wendee, Carrie Bourassa, and Mary Hampton. "Stolen Sisters, Second Class Citizens, Poor Health: The Legacy of Colonization in Canada." *Humanity & Society* 33.1-2 (2009): 18-34. Web. 10 May 2013.

Jackson, Margaret A. "Canadian Aboriginal Women and Their 'Criminality': The Cycle of Violence in the Context of Difference." *Australian & New Zealand Journal of Criminology* 32.2 (1999): 197-208. Web. 10 May 2013.

Janzen, Caitlin, et al. "'Nothing Short of a Horror Show': Triggering Abjection of Street Workers in Western Canadian Newspapers." *Hypatia* 28.1 (2013): 142-162. Web. Accessed 10 May 2014.

Jiwani, Yasmin. "Trapped in the Carceral Net: Race, Gender, and the 'War on Terror." *Global Media Journal, Canadian Edition* 4.1 (2011): 13-31. Web. 10 May 2013.

Landertinger, Laura Christine Luise. "The Biopolitics of Indigenous Reproduction: Colonial Discourse and the Overrepresentation of Indigenous Children in the Canadian Child Welfare System." Master's Thesis, Queen's University, 2011. Web. 3 May 2013.

Lavell-Harvard, Dawn Memee and Kim Anderson, eds. *Indigenous Mothering, Family and Community: International Perspectives.* Bradford: Demeter Press, 2014. Print.

Maidment, MaDonna Rose. *Doing Time on the Outside: Deconstructing the BenevolentCommunity.* Toronto: University of Toronto Press, 2006. Print.

Monture, Patricia A. "Vicious Circle: Child Welfare and the First Nations." *Canadian Journal Women & Law* 3 (1989): 1-17. Web. Accessed 2 May 2011.

Native Women's Association of Canada (NWAC). *Fact Sheet: Root Causes of Violence Against Aboriginal Women and the Impact of Colonization*, n.d. NWAC. Web. 5 June 2014.

Pollack, Shoshana. "'I'm Just Not Good in Relationships': Victimization Discourses and the Gendered Regulation of Criminalized Women." *Feminist Criminology* 2.2 (2007): 158-174. Web. 3 May 2012.

Razack, Sherene H. "Gendered Racial Violence and Spatialized Justice: The Murder of Pamela George." *Canadian Journal of Law and Society* 15 (2000): 91-130. Web. 10 May 2013.

Royal Canadian Mounted Police (RCMP). "Missing and Murdered Aboriginal Women: A National Operational Overview." Royal Canadian Mounted Police, May 27, 2014. Web. 5 June 2014.

Saskatchewan Child Welfare Review Panel. *For the Good of Our Children and Youth: A New Vision, A New Direction.* Government of Saskatchewan, December 2010. Web. May 3, 2013.

Saskatchewan Legal Aid Commission, Regina Rural Area Office. Appellant's Memorandum of Argument. *L.K. v. Minister of Social Services for Saskatchewan.* Supreme Court of Canada, December 2009. Saskatchewan Legal Aid Commission. Print.

Savarese, Josephine L. "The Disappearance of 'a Daughter X' and the Reappearance of the *Vicious Circle* of Child Welfare and First Nations." Canadian Law and Society Association, Fredericton, New Brunswick, 29 May 2011. Print.

Wesley, Mandy. *Marginalized: The Aboriginal Women's Experience in Federal Corrections.* Aboriginal Corrections Policy Unit, Public Safety Canada, 2012. Web. 3 May 2013.

Wrennall, Lynne. "Surveillance and Child Protection: De-mystifying the Trojan Horse." *Surveillance & Society* 7.3/4 (2010): 304-324. Web. 10 May 2012.

CASES CITED

L.K. v. Minister of Social Services for Saskatchewan. CanLII 25911. Supreme Court of Canada. 2010. Canadian Legal Information Institute. Web. 3 May 2012.

Re S.F. 2008. July, 9. Regina. F.S.M. No. 80 of 2001. Saskatchewan Court of Queen's Bench. Print.

Re S.F. 2009. SKCA 121. Saskatchewan Court of Appeal. Canadian Legal Information Institute. Web. 3 May 2012.

Re S.F. 2014. SKQB 179. Saskatchewan Court of Queen's Bench. Canadian Legal Information Institute. Web. 30 June 2014.

5.
Mothering Outside-In

Confined Children and Mothering Under State Paternalism

MICHELLE HUGHES MILLER

MY STUDY BEGINS with an unfortunately too-common story: a child lives in a space removed from her parents/caregivers. The reason for and discourse around the child's separation will vary. Perhaps the child was "relocated" by children and family services or "placed" into a substance abuse or mental health facility. Too often, the youth is "detained" by the juvenile justice system. Regardless of the reason for the separation, once entered into the systems of care and control, the child becomes ruled by policies and practices, which, in the United States, are often legally mandated to be "in her best interests." And so does the child's mother.

In this paper I consider how the issue of maternal blame affects organizational policies and practices that dictate the boundaries of separated mothering in relation to the juvenile justice system in the United States. My discussion centers on the question: How do juvenile justice system policies manage the mothers of juveniles detained within the system? Using this one representative domain, which contributes to the design and experience of separated mothering, I present some initial thoughts on how institutional discourse integrates, or fails to integrate, mothers and mothering as it manages the time, experiences, and interactions of the juveniles under its control.

Throughout, I consider how juvenile facilities contribute to a criminalizing of mothers of detained juveniles by invoking elements of maternal-blame and maternal responsibility in their organizational practices.

BACKGROUND AND THEORETICAL FOUNDATIONS

Despite media accounts of juvenile crime and an image of violent juvenile delinquents (Surette 66), rates of juvenile delinquency are declining in the United States and in Florida, currently at their lowest level since 1986 (Florida Department of Juvenile Justice). While this decline in arrest, detention, commitment, and probation has sparked a reduction in juveniles in Florida's juvenile justice system, the number of juveniles brought into the system each year is still over 50,000, with over 3,000 of those juveniles actually detained in secure facilities (Florida Department of Juvenile Justice). Outside the juvenile justice system, a growing network of prevention and intervention programs is designed to pre-empt juvenile justice entry through enhanced interactions and surveillance of juveniles deemed "at-risk" for juvenile justice involvement. So, while judicial interventions are declining, extra-judicial management of juveniles is increasing. The United States is witnessing a diversification in our surveillance of juveniles, reflected in the parceling out of the responsibility for identifying and responding to youthful misbehavior (in all its range and complexity) from the increasingly fractured juvenile justice system to other social institutions. Two examples of this include the proliferation of zero-tolerance policies in schools (Mackey and Stefkovich 243) and the expanded use of prescription drugs to manage children's behaviours at home and in public (see e.g., Warner 117). So, at the same time delinquents are being referred to other systems, thereby shrinking the size of the justice population, these other systems are expanding the pool of juveniles that can be brought into the juvenile justice system to include less traditional delinquents. As Fagan claims:

> we incarcerate children because their homes are too dangerous or criminogenic; because they are both delinquent and mentally ill or addicted to intoxicants and there are no other appropriate placements; because they need therapies that are unavailable elsewhere, even though they pose no security risks; because they are homeless; because they are sexually active at young ages; or because we think they may commit some crime in the near future. (44)

Florida statistics echo this claim: less than half of all commitments to juvenile facilities in 2011/2012 were for juveniles who had committed felonies ("Demographic Profile"). Instead, twenty percent of all committed juveniles in that year were committed simply because they had violated some aspect of their probation, not because of additional offenses. Official discipline, in this sense, is much more inclusive than we imagine.

So why do we surveil, discipline, and sometimes detain our juveniles across these institutional domains? I argue that our concern is not solely with the children and the fear of their uncontrolled (uncontrollable?) behaviours. Instead, this increased surveillance and dispersed intervention reflects, I believe, two parallel social transformations: (1) an increased ability to engage in surveillance and intervention developed through decades of scholarship on the causal explanations of children's misbehaviour and social, legal, and medical research on strategies to address it; and (2) a larger societal concern and intensive debate about the state of our families and their ability to manage and care for youth—rooted in concerns about changes in family structure, family economic stability and, specifically, changes in the institution of motherhood. In short, I argue that the management of our youth across these domains is driven, in part, by our collective worry about the effects of "bad mothering."

Before addressing the construction of bad mothering and maternal blame, I want to delve more deeply into two related issues: first, separated mothering, and what it means when mothers are legally separated from their children, given social responses to the child's behaviours; and second, which children and which mothers are most likely to experience this particular form of motherhood control.

SEPARATED MOTHERING

I define separated mothering narrowly in this paper because of my interest in mothers of juveniles detained by the juvenile justice system. I am concerned about separated mothering *initiated by state actions because of actions of the juvenile, not because of abusive or neglectful actions of the mother.*[1] My interest is in the cases in which mother-blame exists, without evidence of abuse or neglect. While separated mothering is not uncommon, the management or control of mothers by initiating separated mothering situations is relatively "unnatural" to our legal/social/economic processes. We have court rulings that encourage/enforce parental rights[2] for children and parental obligations to children, and that specifically restrict state involvement in parental actions without compelling state interest. Case law from custody, divorce, adoption, and foster care cases has included the incorporation of a theory of attachment that encourages parent-child interaction because of its presumed effect on child welfare (Maroney 474). It has also included U.S. Supreme Court rulings on family rights and responsibilities within the private sphere (see Meyer v. Nebraska; *Pierce v. Society of Sisters*). Such rulings construct parental responsibility in terms of a geometric triangle representing the separate interests of parent, child, and the state. Parental prerogative in raising and disciplining children—of defining and managing their own parenting behaviours—is offset by the state's *parens patriae* power to ensure the basic welfare of children and their development into productive citizens. So at home, Rosenbury (833) argues, parents have the authority to self-design parenting practices, losing this authority to the state only in cases of abuse or neglect. However, Meyer (141) notes this is not entirely true. We do manage some of parents' behaviours. Two cases in point: Troxel v. Granville allows states to force visitation; and we demand vaccinations and hold home-schoolers accountable for the "outcome" of their schooling. But generally, the space of the home creates strong expectations of parental liberty.

These rulings reflect a public collective interest to have children be the responsibility of parents, including mothers, and for mothering to be self-constructed. But once we leave the home with its presumption of parental control and children enter the public world—like their school—Rosenbury (869) suggests that parents lose ground to object to state intervention and parenting control that may lead to separated mothering. Parents' interests don't evaporate in public settings, but the state's interests increase when conduct is in "public." Delinquent acts, then, as public acts, provide an opportunity for the state to assert its interests by directly intervening with the juvenile and the parent because the family has failed to perform their socialization responsibilities adequately in the private sphere. Zero tolerance policies in particular create the potential for the balance of authority to self-define mothering to tip toward the state.

In light of my specific focus on the mothering of detained children, I find Rosenbury's (879) arguments about "spaces between," where the control of the family or the state is not dominant, but rather is contested, intriguing. Daycare, church, camps, private treatment centers, etc. are all locations where the state's interests do not automatically supersede the parents, and vice versa. Who has responsibility and authority for managing parenting in these "spaces between"? What rights beyond choice of enrollment/placement do parents have, especially in terms of interactions with their children in these contested locations? Juvenile Detention centers, on the surface, seem like domains within which the state's interests rule, where state paternalism might be most dominant. However, as parents enter these facilities and as they manage their interactions with their children within these facilities, is it possible for the spaces to be transformed from state-controlled into lived "spaces between," spaces where mothering might be able to be owned by the mothers? The distinction is an important one, as Ben-Ishai (154) notes. In her discussion of state paternalism she differentiates between two forms. In the first, the state creates policies and rules that restrict the autonomy or choices of its subjects—in this case, rejecting the potentiality of self-defined separated mothering. But paternalism can also be seen as autonomy-enhancing in that it can create opportunities for participants (i.e. mothers) to "challenge oppressive social structures" (153). The question becomes, how are mothers integrated into juvenile justice? The more mothers retain some autonomy in mothering, the more we can envision detention centers as "spaces between."

Despite little research on mothers' experiences of separated mothering of detained juveniles, one study does illustrate the issue of parental autonomy. The researchers found that parents of recently detained juveniles expressed differing sentiments about how they were treated by the juvenile justice system (Church et al. 20). Some parents felt as if their parental authority had been summarily eclipsed by the power of the state, and expressed frustration with the loss. Others interpreted the juvenile justice system as a "partner" (17) who would support their efforts to rein in the behaviours of their troubled child. Still others welcomed the authority of the juvenile justice system to provide needed discipline for a child with behavioural issues. While this research gives us little guidance about the appropriate ways for state and parent to interact in this potential "space between," it does call into question a strictly paternalistic response to mothers that ignores their ability to self-construct mothering.

WHICH CHILDREN? AND WHICH MOTHERS?

Which children become separated from their mothers through juvenile justice processes? The racialization of the juvenile justice system is just as apparent as for its adult counterpart. Juveniles of colour are disproportionately likely to be pulled into the system of juvenile justice, to be adjudicated delinquent, to be detained within juvenile facilities, and to be transferred, when the crime and circumstances warrant, to the adult system ("Demographic Profile"). This racialization of juvenile justice has been resistant to change, despite research and policies designed to address it (Fagan 44). Economic marginalization also is clearly implicated in patterns of juvenile detention. Indeed, historical concerns about lower class juveniles were implicit in the development of the juvenile justice system itself (see Krisberg and Austin 22). The race ethnicity-class intersection also mattered historically, with native children, in particular, vulnerable to separated mothering at the whim of state actors more concerned about assimilation than family integrity (Marr).

We can also question the extent to which poor children and children of colour are more likely to be brought under the auspices of state control because of who their mothers are (Flavin 112). Maternal scholars have argued that not all mothers, nor their children, are evaluated equally. Walkerdine and Lucey (231) remind us that surveillance of mothers is driven by class, with corresponding valuations of mothers driven by the middle class yardstick of "good mothering" presumed by the ideology of intensive mothering (Hays *x*). In particular, Walkerdine and Lucey (227) argue that we are much more likely to pathologize the parenting of working class mothers than middle class mothers because of the ways they are perceived to respond less effectively to their children's needs. In terms of race, Patricia Hill Collins ("Shifting the Center" 319) is much more specific in explaining why black children are removed from black households: "Physical and/or psychological separation of mothers and children, designed to disempower individuals, forms the basis of a systematic effort to disempower racial ethnic communities."

MOTHER-BLAME

This leads us to the question of maternal blame. The expansion of surveillance of juveniles is facilitated by continuing concern about the risks to children from their parents, namely mothers, who are perceived to harm or neglect their children with little concern that such behaviours might negatively affect their offspring. Such concerns lead to increased surveillance of mothers, facilitated by cultural tropes of bad mothers and legalized management of families through the various systems of justice and control. Yet one has but to consider the expansiveness of the "new momism" representations in media and popular culture that put unrealistic expectations on women to be perfect, all engaging (and engaged) mothers (Douglas and Michaels 4-5) to see the myriad ways in which mothers can fail their children beyond abuse or neglect. Actors in our social institutions, including the juvenile justice system, then intervene because they believe they have to; *someone must protect* the children from the failures of their mothers. We are collectively convinced that the inappropriate behaviours of children are because of, in part, the inappropriate behaviours (or characters) of their mothers, a maternal blame that we often internalize, as well (Thurer 341).

Why does this matter? In the world of criminalization, the fallout of punishment frequently reaches and/or attaches itself to those not explicitly criminalized (Schaffner 412). Often we think of our children as the innocent victims of their mothers' and fathers' behaviours; when parents are criminalized, we argue, their children are adversely affected also. But the fallout can occur in the other direction. As we monitor our children's behaviours through increasingly punitive zero tolerance policies at school, expanded community policing in our neighbourhoods, regulatory demands associated with welfare and low-income support, and through medicalized demands for "appropriate" juvenile behaviours defined by ever more inclusive diagnoses, such surveillance trickles up to the parents—or, more typically, to the mothers. As Schaffner (412) claims: "...the juvenile justice system has shifted from waging a 'war on crime' to waging a 'war on criminals' parents.'"

This deferred criminalization can be seen as one element of the mother-blame that permeates our society (Thurer 343). Arguing that every pathology of children is, at some point, analyzed in terms of its maternal roots, Thurer considers the impossibility of mothers of children caught in the web of societal (and psychological) review effectively justifying any of their mothering behaviours:

> [C]ommon sense has given way to an obsession with the mother-child relationship. Yet even a cursory examination reveals this preoccupation to be a linear way of thinking. At worst, it makes a scapegoat of mom; even at best, it leads to an over-emphasis on what she does, at the expense of a broader understanding of child development. It obscures the importance of family dynamics, of the social environment, life events, and the character and inner psychodynamics of the child. (335)

Other theorists posit that mothers will always fail (Douglas and Michaels 12) because the expectations of mothering are so unrealistic that to do otherwise is unimaginable, even for the most privileged mothers who tend to be white, heterosexual, married, and upper class. Yet it is one thing to argue that mother-blame is ubiquitous because of an ideology of intensive mothering (Hays 8) that demands maternal sacrifice and fulfillment. It is quite another to seek out explanations for juvenile behavior in the mothering the delinquents receive. For the former, mothers, at least, are socialized into unrealistic expectations and occasionally have the privilege and/or support to "talk back" to these demands (see e.g., Schaffner 425). For the latter, as Thurer (339) points out, presumptions of cause and effect are linear: as juvenile misconduct is identified, in true investigatory fashion experts trace this behaviour back to its roots in the childhood experiences of the offender. Defending oneself for past inadequacies is daunting; defending oneself without the ability to contextualize those past inadequacies might be impossible. The parents in Schaffner's (419) study, for instance, who were participating in parenting skills classes as a mandatory part of their juvenile's probation expectations, found themselves continually confronting the attitude that they did not know how to parent, which is why their children were delinquents. Though the parents sometimes resisted this description of themselves as failed parents by using what Schaffner calls "emotional resistance" (426), they frequently found their comments about love, worry, and fear negated by probation officer "teachers" extolling them to engage instead in discipline, authority, and control.

Thus, in the world of juvenile justice, juveniles enter as miscreants, their mothers often questioned as the primary source of the delinquent behaviours of their children. Research encourages this understanding of mothers. "Bad" mothering that leads to juvenile antisocial behaviour (including delinquency) includes such items as: smoking during pregnancy (Ellis, Widmayer and Das 333), parental monitoring (De Los Reyes et al. 1418), getting divorced (DeGarmo and Forgatch 229), being employed when they endorse traditional gender expectations (DeCoster 600), using coercive discipline (Forgatch et al. 193), and, most importantly, not being sufficiently emotionally connected to their children (Mack et al. 63). In making these discoveries researchers have even used mothers as the reporters of their children's behaviours (see e.g., De Los Reyes et al. 1419), using their own reports against them. Not surprisingly, in this context of widespread mother-blame, maternal behaviour has been much more widely evaluated in terms of its effect on juvenile delinquency than paternal behaviours (Shaw and Gross 98). And the results are fairly consistent: researchers discover that it is mothering, and especially how mothers interact with their children, that is most closely correlated to delinquency (Hoeve et al. 777; Mack et al. 63).

This finding is driven, in part, by a related phenomenon: a correlation between lone parent households and delinquency (see e.g.,

Kierkus and Hewitt 123). And, it is largely the alleged pathology of lone mother households, the dominant form of single parent households in the U.S. (Livingston) that holds researchers' attention (see e.g., Holmes, Jones-Sanpei, and Day 379). Jackson and Mannix (151) claim: "Single mothers have become the stigmatized 'other.'" Frankly, a significant number of delinquent children grow up in households headed by lone mothers (Sickmund 31). Yet again, identity matters. Hill Collins ("The Meaning of Motherhood" 275) and Roberts (13) remind us that mothering for African-American mothers has historically been viewed pejoratively, with such controlling images as the matriarch and the mammy tossed around to denigrate black mothers regardless of their family structure. Unfortunately, even when scholars recognize variables including racism and failed economic policies that help explain the correlation between household structure and delinquency (see e.g., Morse 53), these understandings sometimes only shift the blame from lone mothers (in the "wrong" household structure) to lone mothering (women parenting in the "wrong" ways). A case in point is my own article on delinquency, which questioned the relative importance of family structure. We argued that family structure was much less relevant in predicting involvement in minor delinquency than what parents teach and how they interact with their children (Hughes Miller, Esbensen and Freng 21). By default, this still held mothers accountable for how well they socialized their children into norms of conformity, a type of mothering responsibility identified by Ruddick (104).

It is important to note that these are not just empirical studies that define and perpetuate mother-blame, but rather analyses driven by widely repeated theoretical arguments within the social sciences. Parenting, more likely mothering, has been implicated in theories as diverse as Miller's (14) Subcultural Theory and Agnew's (58) General Strain Theory, *inter alia*. As an example, in the General Theory of Crime proposed by Gottfredson and Hirschi (97) the child is purportedly set on a path toward delinquency if his parents (read: mothers) do not use effective parenting to create children with self-control. Empirical research testing this theory has supported the basic premise: effective parenting affects children's self-control, which is correlated with engagement in delinquency (see, e.g., Hay

725). In other words, parenting/mothering affects children's criminality. Does this endemic emphasis on mother-blame influence, then, how the juvenile justice system interacts with mothers?

STUDY APPROACH AND FINDINGS

My research question for this project is: *How do juvenile justice system policies manage the mothers of juveniles detained within the system?* To answer this question I analyze discourse from the Florida Department of Juvenile Justice, including program descriptions, research, training manuals, and assessment reports. I then couple this state-wide discursive research with a more intensive look at the official policies and procedures of one short-term juvenile detention facility. The facility houses males and females ages 8-18 in secure placement for up to 21 days. The short-term nature of the placement makes the question of mother involvement quite telling, as the facility has little time to negotiate ongoing interactional patterns. Instead, policies become definitive standards for relationships and thus articulate expected mothering practices and juvenile justice personnel actions in facilitating mother-child interactions.

Analysis involved two stages. First, using the manifest content of the documents I identified every instance where relevant terms were mentioned or discussed and coded both the use of language and the expressed purpose of the terms. I specifically looked for the terms: parent, mother, father, family. These identified text comments were then content analyzed for additional themes using open coding procedures. I then reconsidered the identified text to look for latent themes related to interaction, blame, and responsibility. Lastly, I re-sorted the text to allow for open coding of latent themes.

I present my findings by focusing on the primary themes that arose from the data. This involved looking at how families were defined by juvenile justice policy, and how access, interactions, and knowledge are controlled. Finally, I consider maternal responsibilities, as dictated in institutional policy.

The documents I reviewed typically used gender-neutral language (parent) rather than specifically mentioning mothers. Because of the demographics of parents of detained juveniles, the predominance of mother-blame as a key cause of juvenile delinquency, and gender differences in caregiving and parenting in our society, I interpret the term "parent" to refer primarily to "mother." I also, in agreement with Gazso (45), believe "that gender-neutral policy is gendered and has deeply gendered consequences." Gender-neutrality may also serve to silence mothers' personal voices and expertise by homogenizing their experiences through this neutral language, thus opening up the possibility of a reassertion of the authority of the expert voice (Cole 172). Thus, I consider these policies as overwhelmingly defining and managing the relations between mothers and their detained children and I use this understanding in my analysis.

In presenting these themes it is first important to acknowledge that juvenile justice agencies train their focus on the juvenile, not the family. Under the tag line, "Our Children, Our Future," the Florida Juvenile Justice system describes research-driven processes and agencies that are purported to meet the educational, psychological, social, and sometimes spiritual needs of the child. The institutions that manage delinquents keep their emphasis on those activities and individuals who are perceived as capable of contributing to the overarching mission of the Florida Juvenile Justice system: "To increase public safety by reducing juvenile delinquency through effective prevention, intervention and treatment services that strengthen families and turn around the lives of troubled youth" (Florida Department of Juvenile Justice).

INTEGRATING MOTHERS

What roles do families play in juvenile justice detention? The legislative intent of detention centers, according to state law, specifies that detention centers are to: "Preserve and strengthen the youth's family ties whenever possible" (Florida Department of Juvenile Justice). As I discuss the strategies used to allegedly fulfill this intent, it is helpful to remember the balance of concern endorsed in case law that recognizes interests held by three parties: the state, the juvenile, and the parent/mother. As a site of punishment for "troubled youth," the interests of the juvenile tend to be secondary to the interests of the detention facility. There is the potential for juvenile justice policies to treat families, particularly mothers, as important to the success of their endeavour by incorporating them into programming. Yet, as I will show, juvenile justice policies tend to discursively acknowledge maternal interests in their children, while administratively negating mothers' authority to engage in mothering.

CONSTRUCTING "FAMILY"

Detention facility policy specifies who can visit detained juveniles and who will be notified by agency staff during the course of the juveniles' detention. These rules privilege biological and legal relationships: parents, grandparents, and legal guardians. According to regulations at each facility, other individuals may be allowed to visit if the court orders it. This process maintains state control over juveniles' visitors, thereby controlling the size and composition of the juveniles' support network.

It is possible that the inclusion of grandparents on this list of expected visitors is because of strong legislative support for grandparents' rights in Florida and the significant number of grandparents who are living with and/or responsible for the care of their grandchildren. Current estimates suggest that over 450,000 grandparents in Florida are living with their own grandchildren, 36.6 percent of which are primarily responsible for their grandchildren. Not surprisingly, almost two-thirds (63 percent) of those responsible grandparents are female (US Census Bureau). Florida also has a presumption of relative caregiving in foster care, dictating that reasons to reject relative care must be specified if the child is being placed with the state in lieu of relative care. Such provisions essentially prioritize who can be officially recognized "othermothers" (Hill Collins "The Meaning of Motherhood" 278) and, for purposes of this research, interact with detained juveniles.

Despite the incorporation of grandparents, the list of standard allowable family members excludes many individuals who may be part of a juvenile's support network, including siblings, intimates, or other members of their community. Such control over visitors may appear to be warranted for safety and security reasons, yet it does little to enhance juveniles' relationships in ways that may be of importance to them. Thus, this tight control over juvenile contacts serves the discursive purpose of defining the appropriate family structure for juveniles, while managing their outside interactions in ways aligned with facility goals, if not the legislative intent to preserve and strengthen juveniles' relationships. For mothers, automatic inclusion on this list eases their ability to continue mothering their detained child, yet only if they can maneuver through the labyrinth of access, discussed below. Yet it is also important to note that by endorsing the mother-juvenile relationship this policy also sets into motion the responsibilities embodied by the designation of family, and the blame that can flow from it.

CONTROLLING ACCESS

> "Visitation is an important component of a youth's stay in detention and is encouraged and supported by detention staff." ("Programs-Facilities")

The most obvious way that juvenile facilities manage mothering is through their control of time and space—in this case, both for the juveniles and their mothers. By limiting access to the juvenile the facility maintains its authority over both parties; by allowing access to the juvenile only through the facility, through the personnel of the facility, and only in designated time blocks or methods, the state manages mothering activities. I address these issues, below.

Mothers are allowed direct access to their detained juveniles in three ways: 1) via telephone; 2) via mail; and 3) via visits to the facility. Telephone contact is unidirectional. Couched in terms of juvenile and parental rights, all juveniles are allowed to phone their parents, free of charge, when first arriving at a facility. After that, all phone calls to their parents are collect. If the mother cannot financially accept the charges for this phone call, the juvenile will be allotted one free ten-minute phone call every week. Timing of these telephone calls is variable, but is typically dictated by the scheduling of the facility. Little regard is made of the availability schedule of the mother. Mothers are not allowed to phone their children during their stays in the detention facility. Juveniles are also allowed and/or encouraged to write their parents two letters per week. These letters are voluntary, but seen as a source of contact—again, unidirectional—between the juvenile and their parents. Mothers are also allowed to write their children at the facility, but such mail "can" be subject to inspection.

While both telephone contacts and mail contacts are considered an element of juvenile and parental rights, these rights are more akin to privileges as both can be abridged based upon staff's assessment of the behaviour of the juvenile. Thus, contact between juveniles and their mothers can be refused or limited, based upon assessments beyond the mothers' knowledge, and sometimes for trivial violations of rules rather than safety concerns. Stated differently, juveniles can lose the right to contact their family support network as a form of punishment for violation of facility rules. Maternal contact, then, becomes a way to discipline the juveniles in the facility.

Finally, juveniles who have successfully managed their behaviour may have visitors to the facility. The Florida Department of Juvenile Justice requires facilities to make at least one hour of visitation available per week.[3] The detention facility analyzed in this paper has three designated visitation hours per week: Wednesdays, 7:00 to 8:00 pm; and Saturdays and Sundays from 1:00 to 2:00 pm. These designated times allow us to ask whether juvenile justice officials considered any of the following questions in establishing their visitation policies: What is the purpose of family contact? In what ways is communication most likely to "preserve and strengthen family ties"? How does regulating the times, types, and interactional exchanges support and/or negate that goal? In response, a critical assessment of the management of visitation illustrates that, rather than a means to encourage family bonding, family visitation is a behaviour management tool that strengthens the authority of the facility over the detained juveniles and shifts the mother-juvenile relationship. As Fagan (43) describes it: "Juvenile corrections, whether located in a human warehouse or a therapeutic community, is designed mainly to control its residents and restrict their personal freedoms."

CONTROLLING INTERACTIONS

Where and how visitation occurs is also relevant, as it illustrates that the interactions themselves are carefully monitored to meet facility goals. The facility is explicit about the appropriate nature of exchange between juveniles and mothers. Visitation is to take place in a "designated area or room of the facility that contributes to a safe and secure environment." Above all, visitation is managed as a security issue, with explicit rules about conduct for both family members and juveniles specified. At any point during the visitation, the visit can be cancelled if either party becomes "disruptive or uncooperative," failing to follow staff orders. Disruptive behaviour is further described as behaviour that reflects strong emotions, thus facilities insist upon a particular type of emotional exchange during these necessarily brief encounters. Such emotion management (see e.g., Hochschild 19) may be difficult given the nature of the interaction and the potential seriousness of the exchange. Yet emotions must be managed, because visitation itself is a type of discipline: the penalty for disruption can be prohibition of future visits.

A further consideration for facilities is the content of these exchanges. All visitors must be prepared to be electronically searched and are not allowed to bring any personal items into the facility at the risk of being charged with a 3rd degree felony. In stating this, the facility manages whether and how mothers are expected and/or allowed to provide resources to their children. The facility manual states:

> Clothing and personal hygiene items are provided for all youth. The detention center provides supplies and clothing for the youth. Detained youth are not permitted to have money. Gifts are discouraged.... Snacks are provided.... ("Programs-Facilities")

In short, during the limited contact times it is strongly suggested that mothers not bring anything to their children in the way of personal clothing, money, gifts, or food. Cultures that create intimacy through breaking of bread are dissuaded from using that process in these facilities. Even hegemonic values of consumption contained in the new momism are rejected here: mothers are not allowed to address any perceived privation through material means. While this is a way for the facility to manage the juveniles and issues of competition or jealousy, concerns about how this may limit mothers' ability to share anything tangible with their children, and thus to assert a hegemonic "good mother" identity, are irrelevant.

MANAGING MOTHER'S KNOWLEDGE: THE LANGUAGE OF NOTIFICATION

In addition to tightly controlling how and when mothers interact with their children, facilities manage access and interaction by managing the distribution of knowledge about their residents. The message for mothers in terms of information about their children is very specific: all information about detained juveniles is managed by facility personnel and, though parents have rights to particular types of information, the manner and timing of notification is dictated by facility concerns. Mothers also have the right to know where their child is being held, including if they are moved to a different facility. In addition, staff are expected to make "reasonable effort" to notify parents if their child receives medical care or escapes from the facility. Since mothers are required to give the facility their telephone number, reasonable effort may involve just a telephone message. In terms of hearings at the facility related to their juvenile's detention, mothers are invited to attend an initial confinement hearing. If their child who is being detained is under ten years of age, the court is obligated to consider the parents' wishes for placement in deciding the appropriate facility for detention.

A study by Church et al. (14) on the perceptions of parents who are newly informed about their child's detention is informative here. Parents, who were overwhelmingly female, reported that they were frustrated, confused, and even angered by the information they received from juvenile justice center staff about their child's detention. Often, this was because they were given insufficient or inaccurate information—as if the parts of the juvenile justice system were not working together. This frustration is understandable if we consider what is not on the list of required information to be shared with mothers: the juveniles' progress, disciplinary actions, evaluations, desire to communicate with their mothers, successes, interactions with other family members and/or justice system actors (including attorneys), or any other aspects of the juveniles' daily lives that might facilitate stronger bonds between mothers and their children. Conceivably, all such information can be shared with the mothers through their contact with the juveniles—if they have been able to manage contact through one of the restricted means previously discussed.

For some of the parents in Church and his colleagues' study (15), initial notification of their child's detention started them on a process of losing control over their children and over their own parenting processes for those children. Thus it is reasonable to question the extent to which the juvenile justice system asserts parental authority in any of their policies, or even shares authority with parents during their children's detention. I turn to this issue next.

ASSERTING MOTHERS' RESPONSIBILITY

Two themes emerged from the data on responsibility: maternal availability and financial viability. These expectations flow through the juvenile justice policies. For instance, contact between the mother and her child is dictated by facility policies, making mothers reactive to the demands of the agency. Her flexibility in availability is therefore mandated. Timing is managed around the facility's interests such that mothers' schedules are dictated to, rather than negotiated with. Other mother responsibilities related to work, transportation, others' needs, personal health or abilities are all negated in this exchange.

The same is true in terms of the presumption of financial viability. Transportation to and from the facility are to be managed by the mothers, which begs questions of distance, time, and resource access to private or public transportation. Work responsibilities, and the potential to adjust work schedules and manage corresponding potential income loss are not acknowledged. Telephone calls and postage are at the expense of mothers, and demand stability of households and "home" that may not be warranted for all mothers. Generally, the discourse in the policies reflects classist and sexist assumptions about mothers' abilities to realize contact that align, in part, with the presumption that mothers will be available at any time for their children, whose needs should come first.

But these assumptions about maternal availability and economic resources are not just implicit in facility policies. Florida statute dictates a more direct financial responsibility for the parents of detained juveniles. According to F.S. 985, parents are billed monthly for their share of the cost of juvenile detention, which amounts to $5/day in secure facilities, and $1/day if the juvenile is not detained but is under state supervision (i.e. probation). The "Cost of Care" brochure available on the department's website considers detention a joint responsibility between parents and the state, and frames the issue as "positive parental involvement":

> Positive parental involvement is crucial. A joint effort between the parents and the State improves the quality of life for our children and provides safer neighborhoods for all of us... Together we can reduce juvenile crime. (Florida Department of Juvenile Justice)

If mothers cannot afford to pay this cost, it can be waived by completing a form available at the detention center, though approval of the waiver is not a given. If the juvenile stays for the entire 21 days, this would be over $100, which is in addition to any attorney fees, transportation fees, or other financial responsibilities held by the mother. It is clear that this expectation is a mark of commitment to the juvenile, and a sign that the parent will be a positive influence on the child upon release.

DISCUSSION

It is clear from my review of the policies of the facility and the Florida Juvenile Justice system that parents are expected to be involved with their children while they are under state control. Doctrine dictates the why of this involvement: the goal of strengthening families. It also dictates the how, when, where, and who.

Unfortunately, the disconnect between the ideology of parental inclusion and the practice of parental involvement leaves many mothers, and potentially their children, struggling to manage their relationships in ways that are familiar to them. If mothers can arrange to interact face to face with their children during the few hours they are available, they cannot express strong emotions or share material goods/gifts during those exchanges. If they cannot arrange those visitations, they are dependent on the scheduling and rules of the facility to receive phone calls or letters. And, always, their interactions are subject to disruption because rather than being essential to the juveniles' well-being, they are tools of behaviour management employed by the facility for any of a host of infractions. The ambivalence about mothering detained children contained in these policies actually reflects quite a strong sentiment: this is not a "space between" where mothers can negotiate their mothering alongside state interests, to benefit the juveniles. Instead, in this short-term facility mothering is tangential to the process, though expected and managed in a nod to state rules.

What explains this state-centered quasi-inclusion of mothering? While we can assert the needs of safety and security at such facilities as a predominant concern, such issues seem to not justify the visitation restrictions and are remarkably incapable of justifying the type of information control and other contact limitations seen here. Instead, I would argue that the ambivalence toward mothering demonstrated in these policies may be driven by an acceptance of mother-blame as a component of the criminalizing of mothers. If, as I have argued, justice personnel accept the theories and research that find fault in mothering for children's misbehaviour, why should they work to find strategies for maternal involvement in juvenile justice? And, if all mothers are questionable parents, because of the link between mothering and delinquency, there is no reason to differentiate between mothers who are abusive and neglectful and those who were deficient in some other perhaps hidden way, such as failing to fulfill the ideology of intensive mothering. Facility personnel don't know, necessarily, how mothers have "failed." But they may accept the premise that at least on some level, the mothers of the juveniles who are now part of their caseload did, indeed, fail. Mother-blame, rooted as it is in misogyny (Jackson and Mannix 156) and perpetuated by masculinist systems—such as the juvenile justice system—can be expressed by these staff in ways detrimental to the mother-child relationship yet in line with these institutional policies. The result is criminalizing of these mothers through maternal control, as a strategy to manage their children.

How mothers are integrated into juvenile justice policies is not just relevant for the time that their children are detained. Rather, children leave these facilities and, often, return home. If mothering has been paternalistically regulated during their detention, how can it be a source of support for them when they return? Indeed, research on reentry suggests that parents and home circumstances are key ingredients for successful juvenile reentry and that targeted interventions to improve family systems lead to less recidivism than interventions targeting the juveniles themselves (Abrams and Snyder 1792; Martinez and Abrams 170). A targeted family intervention, however, requires actually acknowledging mothers and integrating them into the juvenile justice system by changing the ways we think about access, information, and responsibility. Without such recognition and interventions, some families return to pre-existing negative behavioural patterns (Martinez and Abrams 173). Nevertheless, research has suggested that valuing the family system is not always the case among juvenile justice personnel. Probation officers who endorsed punitive responses to delinquency were less likely to seek engagement with the parents of their probationers than those who endorsed more rehabilitative strategies that encouraged family involvement (Schwalbe and Maschi, 402). It is no wonder that parents report feeling disempowered by their interactions with juvenile justice personnel (Garfinkel and Nelson 27).

Of course this conclusion rests upon data not gathered here, that is, the attitudes of facility personnel toward mothers and mothering. Another voice is also absent in this study: those of the mothers themselves. How mothers manage their relationships while their children are detained is a question largely unaddressed in the literature. I am particularly concerned about race ethnicity and class differentials in maternal engagement with the juvenile justice system, given the disproportionate detainment of low income and juveniles of colour. I believe there is a power in the resistance to hegemonic definitions of motherhood embodied in the lived mothering of mothers of colour. Such mothering exists within racist and classist surveillance practices. Given this, we can learn from mothers of colour how mothering of confined children can be done in ways that recreate homeplace, to use hooks' (267) term, across bars, across time, and despite the watchful eyes of the panopticon (Henderson, Harmon and Houser 235). Homeplace is not just home, but home that has a radical, political dimension because of its mere presence in the context of an oppressive society. Is it possible for mothers of detained children to create homeplace for their separated children within the context of the detention facility? If our goal for juvenile justice really was to strengthen families and prepare our children for their future, facilitating the construction of homeplace, even within a detention facility, and rejecting the criminalizing of mothers alongside and because of their detained children, would be a route to that end.

ENDNOTES

[1]A great deal of research acknowledges that some mothers engage in abuse and neglect of their children. This discussion is beyond the scope of this chapter.

[2]As much as possible, I invoke the motherhood literature to answer the questions of the paper. But, research and policies often invoke gender-neutral terminology, and I choose to use their terms in citing their findings.

[3]Some longer term facilities provide for more intensive interactions. Using the discourse of "invitation," such facilities notify mothers of upcoming court dates and relevant meetings, inviting the mothers to attend via telephone or in person. Mothers may also be invited to participate in therapeutic sessions.

WORKS CITED

Abrams, Laura S. and Susan M. Snyder. "Youth Offender Reentry: Models for Intervention and Directions for Future Inquiry."

Children and Youth Services Review 32 (2010): 1787-1795. Print.

Agnew, Robert T. "Foundation for a General Strain Theory of Crime and Delinquency." *Criminology* 30.1 (1992): 47-87. Print.

Ben-Ishai, Elizabeth. "The New Paternalism: An Analysis of Power, State Intervention, and Autonomy." *Political Research Quarterly* 65.1 (2012): 151-165. Print.

Church II, Wesley T., Gordon Macneil, Shadi S. Martin, and Debra Nelson-Gardell. "What Do You Mean My Child Is in Custody? A Qualitative Study of Parental Response to the Detention of Their Child." *Journal of Family Social Work* 12 (2009): 9-24. Print.

Cole, Barbara. "Mothers, Gender and Inclusion in the Context of Home–School Relations." *Support for Learning* 22.4 (2007): 165-173. Web. 15 October 2013.

DeCoster, Stacy. "Mothers' Work and Family Roles, Gender Ideologies, Distress, and Parenting: Consequences for Juvenile Delinquency." *The Sociological Quarterly* 53 (2012): 585-609. Print.

De Los Reyes, Andres, Kimberly L. Goodman, Wendy Kliewer, and Kathryn Reid-Quiñones. "The Longitudinal Consistency of Mother–Child Reporting Discrepancies of Parental Monitoring and Their Ability to Predict Child Delinquent Behaviors Two Years Later." *Journal of Youth and Adolescence* 39 (2010): 1417-1430. Print.

DeGarmo, D. S. and M. S. Forgatch. "Early Development of Delinquency within Divorced Families: Evaluating a Randomized Preventive Intervention Trial." *Developmental Science* 8 (2005): 229-239. Web. 14 October 2013.

Douglas, Susan J. and Meredith W. Michaels. *The Mommy Myth: The Idealization of Motherhood and How It Has Undermined All Women*. New York: The Free Press, 2004. Print.

Ellis, Lee, Alan Widmayer, and Shyamal Das. "Maternal Smoking during Pregnancy and Self-Reported Delinquency by Offspring." *Criminal Behaviour and Mental Health* 22 (2012): 325-335. Print.

Fagan, Jeffrey. "The Contradictions of Juvenile Crime and Punishment." *Daedulus* Summer (2010): 43-61. Print.

Flavin, Jeanne. "Slavery's Legacy in Contemporary Attempts to Regulate Black Women's Reproduction." *Race, Gender, and Punishment: From Colonialism to the War on Terror*. Ed. Mary Bosworth and Jeanne Flavin. Camden, MA: Rutgers University

Press, 2006. 95-115. Web. **20 October 2013.**

Florida Department of Juvenile Justice. 2012. Web. **29 October 2010.**

Florida Department of Juvenile Justice. "Demographic Profile." 2012. "Web. **29 October 2010.**

Florida Department of Juvenile Justice. "Programs-Facilities." 2010. Web. 29 October 2010.

Forgatch, Marion S., Zintars G. Beldavs, Gerald R. Patterson and David S. DeGarmo. "From Coercion to Positive Parenting: Putting Divorced Mothers in Charge." *What Can Parents Do? New Insights into the Role of Parents in Adolescent Problem Behavior.* Ed. Margaret Kerr, Hakan Statin, Rutger C.M.E. Engels. West Sussex, England: John Wiley and Sons, 2008. 191-209. Web. 20 October 2013.

Garfinkel, Lili Frank and Renelle Nelson. "Promoting Better Interaction Between Juvenile Court, Schools, and Parents." *Reclaiming Children and Youth* 13:1 Spring (2004): 26-28. Print.

Gazso, Amber. "Gendering the 'Responsible Risk Taker': Citizenship Relationships with Gender-Neutral Social Assistance Policy." *Citizenship Studies* 13.1 February (2009): 45-63. Print.

Gottfredson, Michael R. and Travis Hirschi. *A General Theory of Crime.* Stanford: Stanford University Press, 1990. Print.

Hay, Carter. "Parenting, Self-Control, and Delinquency: A Test of Self-Control Theory." *Criminology* 39.3 August (2001): 707–736. Print.

Hays, Sharon. *The Cultural Contradictions of Motherhood.* New Haven: Yale University Press, 1998. Print.

Henderson, Angela C., Sandra M. Harmon and Jeffrey Houser. "A New State of Surveillance: Applying Michel Foucault to Modern Motherhood." *Surveillance and Society* 7.3/4 (2010): 231-247. Web. 20 October 2013.

Hill Collins, Patricia. "The Meaning of Motherhood in Black Culture and Mother-Daughter Relationships." O'Reilly 274-289.

Hill Collins, Patricia. "Shifting the Center: Race, Class and Feminist Theorizing about Motherhood." *Mothering: Ideology, Experience & Agency.* Ed. Evelyn Nakano Glenn, Grace Chang and Linda Rennie Forcey. New York: Routledge, 2007. 311-330. Print.

Hochschild, Arlie Russell. *The Managed Heart: The Commercial-*

ization of Human Feeling. Berkeley: University of California Press, 2012. Print.

Hoeve, Machteld, Geert Jan J. M. Stams, Claudia E. van der Put, Judith Semon Dubas, Peter H. van der Laan, and Jan R. M. Gerris. "A Meta-analysis of Attachment to Parents and Delinquency." *Journal of Abnormal Child Psycholology* 40 (2012): 771-785. Print.

Holmes, Erin K., Hinckley Jones-Sanpei, and Randal D. Day. "Adolescent Outcome Measures in the NLSY97 Family Process Data Set: Variation by Race and Socioeconomic Conditions." *Marriage & Family Review* 45.4 (2009): 374-391. Print.

hooks, bell. "Homeplace: A Site of Resistance." O'Reilly 266-273.

Hughes Miller, Michelle, Finn-Aage Esbensen and Adrienne Freng. "Parental Attachment, Parental Supervision and Adolescent Deviance in Intact and Non-Intact Families." *Journal of Crime and Justice* 22 (1999): 1-29. Print.

Jackson D, and J. Mannix. "Giving Voice to the Burden of Blame: A Feminist Study of Mothers' Experiences of Mother Blaming." *International Journal of Nursing Practice* 10 (2004): 150-158. Print.

Kierkus, Christopher A. and John D. Hewitt. "The Contextual Nature of the Family Structure/Delinquency Relationship." *Journal of Criminal Justice* 37.2 March–April (2009): 123-132. Print.

Krisberg, Barry and James Austin. *Reinventing Juvenile Justice*. Newbury Park, CA: Sage, 1993. Print.

Livington, Gretchen. *The Rise of Single Fathers: A Ninefold Increase Since 1960*. Pew Research Report: Social and Demographic Trends. 2013. Web. 15 October 2013.

Mack, Kristin Y., Michael J. Leiber, Richard A. Featherstone, and Maria A. Monserud. "Reassessing the Family-Delinquency Association: Do Family Type, Family Processes, and Economic Factors Make a Difference?" *Journal of Criminal Justice* 35 (2007): 51-67. Print.

Mackey, Hollie J. and Jacqueline A. Stefkovich. "Zero-tolerance Policies and Administrative Decision Making: The Case for Restorative Justice-Based School Discipline Reform." *Global Perspectives on Educational Leadership Reform: The Development and Preparation of Leaders of Learning and Learners of*

Leadership (Advances in Educational Administration, Volume 11). Ed. Anthony H. Normore. Emerald Group Publishing Limited, 2010. 243-262. Web. 14 October 2013.

Maroney, Tarry A. "In Family Law, Love's Got a Lot to do with it: A Response to Phillip Shaver." *Virginia Journal of Social Policy & the Law* 16:2 (2009): 471-491. Print.

Marr, Carolyn J. *Assimilation Through Education: Indian Boarding Schools in the Pacific Northwest*. University of Washington Libraries, 2013. Web. 14 October 2013.

Martinez, Damian J. and Laura S. Abrams. "Informal Social Support among Returning Young Offenders: A Metasynthesis of the Literature." *International Journal of Offender Therapy and Comparative Criminology* 57.2 (2013): 169–190. Print.

Meyer, David D. "The Geography of Family Privacy." *University of Pennsylvania Pennumbra* 156 *University of Pennsylvania Law Review Pennumbra* 136 (2007): 136-150. Print.

Meyer v. Nebraska. 262 U.S. 390, 399. U.S. Supreme Court. 1923. Web. **6 November 2010.**

Miller, Walter. "Lower Class Culture as a Generating Milieu of Gang Delinquency." *Journal of Social Issues* 14.3 (1958): 5-20. Print.

Morse, Jennifer. "Parents or Prison?" *Policy Review* 120 (August-September 2003): 49-60. Print.

O'Reilly, Andrea, ed. *Maternal Theory: Essential Readings*. Toronto, Canada: Demeter Press, 2007. Print.

Pierce v. Society of Sisters. 268 U.S. 510, 534-35. U.S. Supreme Court. 1925. Web. **6 November 2010.**

Roberts, Dorothy. *Killing the Black Body: Race, Reproduction and the Meaning of Liberty*. New York Vintage, 1998. Print.

Rosenbury, Laura A. "Between Home and School." *University of Pennsylvania Law Review* 155 *University of Pennsylvania Law Review* 833 (2007): 833-898. Print.

Ruddick, Sara. *Maternal Thinking: Toward a Politics of Peace*. Boston, Massachusetts: Beacon Press, 1995. Print.

Schaffner, Laurie. "Families on Probation: Court-Ordered Parenting Skills Classes for Parents of Juvenile Offenders." *Crime & Delinquency* 43.4 (1997): 412-437. Print.

Schwalbe, Craig S. and Tina Maschi. "Patterns of Contact and Cooperation Between Juvenile Probation Officers and Parents of

Youthful Offenders." *Journal of Offender Rehabilitation* 49.6 (2010): 398-416. Web. 14 October 2013.

Shaw, Daniel S. and Heather E. Gross. "What We Have Learned about Early Childhood and the Development of Delinquency." *The Long View of Crime: A Synthesis of Longitudinal Research*. Ed. A. M. Liberman. New York: Springer, 2008. 79-127. Web. 15 October 2013.

Sickmund, Melissa. "New Survey Provides a Glimpse of The Youth Reentry Population." *Corrections Today* April (2005): 30-31. Web. 14 October 2013.

Surette, Ray. *Media, Crime and Criminal Justice: Images, Realities and Policies*. 4th ed. Belmont, C: Wadsworth, 2011. Print.

Thurer, Shari L. "The Myths of Motherhood." *Maternal Theory: Essential Readings*. Ed. Andrea O'Reilly. Toronto: Demeter Press, 2007. 331-344. Print.

Troxel v. Granville. 530 U.S. 57. U.S. Supreme Court. 2000. Web. **6 November 2010.**

United States Census Bureau. *American Community Survey*. U.S. Census Bureau, 2011. Web. 25 March 2013.

Walkderdine, Valerie and Helen Lucey. "It's Only Natural." *Maternal Theory: Essential Readings*. Ed. Andrea O'Reilly. Toronto: Demeter Press, 2007. 224-236. Print.

Warner, Judith. *We've got Issues: Children and Parents in the Age of Medication*. New York: Riverhead Books, 2010. Web. 10 October 2013.

6.
International Law Criminalizing Motherhood

Examining the Hague Convention on International Child Abduction

REBECCA JAREMKO BROMWICH

THE HAGUE CONVENTION on the Civil Aspects of International Child Abduction, 1980,[1] is a powerful legal tool. Because it has been adopted directly into the domestic law of many countries, including Canada, it provides a means by which children can be returned to their country of habitual residence after they have been removed from it. However, in general, the Convention does not provide assistance if a mother flees abuse with her children. This chapter explores how the Convention may, in effect, act to criminalize rather than support mothers who experience abuse within the home.

A 2011 study that statistically analyzed Hague Convention applications made across 60 signatory countries in 2008 demonstrates that the failure of the Convention to recognize domestic abuse is highly problematic. Domestic violence allegations are not rare in Convention cases. To the contrary, it is in fact in the *majority* of Hague Convention cases where allegations of serious domestic abuse are made.[2] A large majority (69 percent) of the abductors in the 2008 cases surveyed were mothers fleeing alleged abuse (Lowe).

As currently interpreted, in Canada the Convention puts children and mothers at risk of harm while also exposing already marginalized and vulnerable mothers to a risk of criminalization for efforts to protect themselves and their children from witnessing or experiencing violence. Using the Convention, abusive parents—usually men—can forcibly return children even in the face of domestic violence. Such forced returns leave mothers with no good options. They have to choose between risking arrest and criminal charges for leaving a jurisdiction where they may have no status other than as their husband's spouse and the alternative prospect of almost certainly suffering further abuse as well as risking harm to their children.

This chapter explores doctrinal interpretation of the Convention in cases from Canada to examine the extent to which the Convention, as currently interpreted in Canada, recognizes domestic violence. Unfortunately, the Convention, when incorporated into Canadian domestic law, brought with it a regressive discourse of zero sum "rights" in wives and children, re-inscribing patriarchal thinking that decades of feminist and otherwise progressive law reform painstaking sought to transform. I argue that the Convention should be amended to provide for consideration of domestic violence, and to remove from its definitions and structure assumptions about property rights in children and the authority of fathers. Absent such amendments, actors within Canada's justice system should exercise agency by broadening the scope of what is considered "grave risk of harm" to children.

INTERNATIONAL CHILD ABDUCTION: THE HAGUE CONVENTION

The Hague Convention on the Civil Aspects of International Child Abduction is the primary means by which nation states have come together to protect children against international abduction. The Convention is a multilateral between over 60 countries that is intended to prevent abduction of children across international borders, to facilitate return of abducted children, and to protect the rights of custodial parents.

More specifically, the objectives of the Convention, as provided in Article 1, are "to secure the prompt return of children who have been wrongfully removed to or retained in any Contracting State," and "to ensure that rights of custody and of access under the law of one Contracting State are effectively respected in the other Contracting States." Article 12 provides that where a child has been "wrongfully" removed to or retained, an order will be made for return of the child to the country of his or her habitual residence. Custodial parents can make application for return unless more than a year has passed since the wrongful removal or retention and the child is now settled in his or her new environment. Not all countries are signatories to the Convention; however, in Canada the Convention has profound and far-reaching implications.

The Convention operates in the following manner where abduction is alleged. Article 12 of the Convention provides the parent left behind with the remedy of having the "abducted" child forcibly returned to him or her where it is found that a child was wrongfully removed from that parent's jurisdiction pursuant to Article 3.[3] A hearing will be held in the country where the children are found. At this hearing, a judge will determine whether the child has been wrongfully removed, and whether the remedy of return should be granted. The burden of proof to show that there has been a breach of Article 3 is on the party bringing the Hague Convention application, the "petitioner." Where a child is found to have been unlawfully removed or retained, a *prima facie* case will have been made for return of the child to the petitioner parent.

The onus will then shift to the respondent parent to defend his or her action in removing the child. Return will not be forced in all circumstances. In some circumstances the responding parent may have a defence. The application must have been made promptly upon the child's removal to be successful. Article 12 allows that, if the child has been settled in the jurisdiction to which he or she was removed for in excess of one year, he or she will not be forcibly returned to the petitioner. Article 13 affords a court hearing a Hague Convention application the discretion not to return a child when that child is of sufficient age and maturity to expresses his or her opinion and indicates a desire not to be returned.

More significantly from the perspective of mothers fleeing abuse, Article 13 (b) allows that the child will not be returned to the petitioner's jurisdiction where the respondent can show that such a return would place the child in question at a grave risk of harm. This "grave risk of harm" exception could conceivably be interpreted to include the harm a child will suffer when he or she witnesses domestic violence, as is recognized under Canadian domestic family law. As such, this "grave risk of harm" defence, interpreted purposively, could be used as an avenue for argument by a domestic violence survivor to defeat the remedy of return.

ENFORCEMENT

In general, rights to which state's parties have agreed in principle under international law cannot be enforced by individual citizens of those states. The Convention is an exception to this general rule because laws of the signatory parties "incorporate" the agreement by expressly stating in their own statutes (or domestic law) that the document forms part of the law of those countries.[4]

In Canada, the Hague Convention has been incorporated into domestic law and can be enforced. In Ontario, for example, section 46 of the Children's Law Reform Act (CLRA) incorporates the Hague Convention into the province's domestic law. In Saskatchewan, the *International Child Abduction Act,* 1996 is the legislation that does this. Similar legislation exists across Canada. Although they are to bear in mind treaty obligations, Canadian courts must apply domestic law in interpreting the phrase "habitual residence." For instance, in Ontario this is done by reference to section 22 of the CLRA, as was made clear in the decision *Medhurst v Markle*, which is discussed in more detail below.

The significance of the remedy of return provided by Article 12 of the Hague Convention must not be underestimated. The Hague Convention is a law that can force return of children to abusive homes and indirectly force return of their mothers, placing the vulnerable mothers at risk of criminalization and both mothers and children at risk of harm.

GENDER BLINDNESS AND PARENTAL RIGHTS

The Hague Convention is "gender blind," meaning it makes no reference to whether it is a male or female parent abducting the child. Consequently, the Convention is also blind to the transnational problem of woman abuse. It was not written in contemplation of the possibility that a mother's abduction of her children could be in the best interests of the child.

The Convention was drafted in contemplation of a malevolent abduction by someone, a parent or otherwise, with either a direct intention to harm the child, or a disregard of the child's best interests. Such an abductor might be a parent seeking to subvert custody rulings made against him or her, or might be a third party acting with the intention of exploiting the child.

While, under the Convention, gender is formally irrelevant, it applies in a world where gender does, of course, matter very much. Debates about the Convention at the time of its signing did have gendered aspects. These debates assumed the problem the Convention would remedy would be a male abductor taking a child by force to a venue where the custodial regime was more favourable to him.[5] Also publicized were cases of American or Canadian parents left behind. However, the prospect of a mother fleeing from an abusive partner with whom she and her children lived in a jurisdiction where authorities are unwilling or unable to protect her or her children from his violence was not discussed (Weiner).

Child custody is defined within the structure, definitions, and purposes in the Convention. By incorporating the Convention into Canadian domestic law, the current system also incorporates understandings of relationships between parents and children and between spouses that reflect gendered authority structures within patriarchal legal regimes. The defined and implicit concepts underlying the protection conferred by the Convention are drawn from many legal systems. Definitions of terms in the Convention emerged from discussions between representatives of nation states, many of whose family law regimes still protect parental, but more specifically and particularly, *paternal rights* of property in children.[6] Further, the question for a court in a jurisdiction to which a child has been removed is to factually determine who has custody rights under another jurisdiction's rules.

The central matter protected by the Convention is *not* the child's best interests but parental "*rights* of custody." Judges hearing applications for return under the Convention make a zero sum decision about who has a right to the child. The very idea that there is such a thing as a parental *right* to custody does not coincide with the notion of custody under Canadian law. Further, under the Convention, Canada will effectively enforce custodial determinations decided under regimes where understandings of woman abuse are very significantly less developed than they are in this country.

While, as discussed below, historically, Canadian fathers had property in their spouses and children (Mason 1994), the idea that anyone can have a "right" to custody of a child has been expressly rejected in reforms to Canadian family law. Canadian statutes were quite deliberately amended to remove the notions of property in women and children. Enforcement of the Convention under Canadian law results in contemplation by Canadian courts of concepts and arguments that rely upon antiquated, patriarchal understandings of parental relationships that diverge from the concepts to be considered by courts when a child taken by a parent within Canada.

The gender blindness of the Convention is also discordant with Canada's *Immigration and Refugee Board Guidelines*.[7] These guidelines enable woman refugees to seek status in Canada when they flee domestic abuse in jurisdictions where their safety is inadequately protected. Because of this disconnect, women who have strong claims for refugee status on the basis of domestic violence, and who would almost certainly gain custody of their children under the domestic "best interests" test can face the spectre, resulting from the Hague Convention, of harassment and coercion in the form of petitions by abusive partners for return of their children to countries where the women's victimization by abuse has been ignored or permitted.

The Convention as currently interpreted subjects many domestic violence victims who cross international borders with their children to the remedy of return of those children to their home country. As will be discussed below, in cases dealing with the Convention in Canada and elsewhere, courts have disregarded allegations of woman abuse, holding that they are irrelevant to the determination of whether a child should be returned to the petitioning parent.

WOMAN ABUSE: AN INTERNATIONAL PROBLEM

Although long hidden from view by masculinist research agendas and questions as well as a culture of silence around problems in the "private sphere" of the home, feminist scholarship in Canada and elsewhere has revealed since the 1970s that woman abuse is a problem of distressing magnitude in Canada, as well as internationally (Senn).[8] Statistics Canada's 2010 Statistical Profile on Family Violence in Canada found that females have more than double the risk of males of falling victim to domestic violence (Statistics Canada, *Family Violence* 2010). According to the agency, Status of Women Canada, as of 2004, half of Canadian women (51 percent) have been victims of at least one act of physical or sexual violence since the age of sixteen (Status of Women Canada 11). Canada is not alone in having to contend with the problem of woman abuse. International statistics also speak to high numbers of women being battered each year. For example, one United States study indicated that each year, one million American women suffer nonfatal violence by an intimate partner (United States Dept. of Justice 3). This is in addition to the women killed by their partners.

A feminist perspective examines domestic violence as a gendered problem related to patriarchy and unequal social power. Overwhelmingly, the aggressors in intimate partner violence are male. Victims of female-perpetrated domestic violence are considerably less likely to experience more serious forms of violence (Canadian Center for Justice Statistics 14-16). Gender is not the only factor in abuse. Other systemic inequalities in social power also contribute to disproportions in who suffers abuse. Race, class, sexual orientation, and ability intersect with the experience of abuse in ways that compound the vulnerability of women who are not easily identified as "able" and "white" (see Razack). Further, the extent to which state protection is available to women who have suffered abuse at the hands of their intimate partners is highly variable internationally (UNICEF).

Where women are abused, children are at risk. Isolation and threats against children are tools used by many men (Domestic Abuse Intervention Project). Abusers use myriad tools to maintain their power over their intimate partners and children, including systemic complicity and overt co-operation in nations and regions where woman abuse is accepted. Even where abusers do not seek overtly or deliberately to harm the children of their partners, a growing body of research now shows that witnessing domestic violence itself also harms children (Suderman and Jaffe; Bala et al.).

LEGAL PROTECTION AGAINST WOMAN ABUSE

Canada's family and refugee laws are imperfect, but over the past twenty years or so, they have been significantly revised in order to protect against violence against women. Similarly, the laws of other countries, like the United States, have been changed to protect women against domestic violence (Weiner; Leto).

Family Law

In Canada, until relatively recently, wives were their husbands' property and children belonged to their fathers like other chattels, such as farm animals and equipment (Mason). Custody of children, unless it is ancillary to a divorce, is generally in provincial/territorial jurisdiction. As Susan Boyd has documented, struggles for and processes of law reform took place from the mid-twentieth century until the turn of the twenty-first. These processes were different in various Canadian jurisdictions and under the various incarnations of the Federal Divorce Act but resulted in a relatively uniform regime: now children are no longer legally the property of either of their parents. While gender blindness and formal equality remain present in the various legislative regimes in Canada concerning child custody (Boyd, *Child Custody*, "Reforming Custody"), no one now has "rights" to custody of a child under Canadian law. It is the child's right to live in accordance with his or her best interests that is considered in cases where custody of, and access to, children are at issue.

In Canada, custody of children is a separate legal notion apart from the question of where they will live. Custody is a concept relating to legal authority. Whenever custody and access issues arise, the court must determine the application by reference only to the needs of the child. Courts have broad discretion when making custody orders. The sole test to be applied by the Court when it determines custody for a child is the "best interests" of the child(ren) concerned, as is set out in the Divorce Act (s. 16(8), s. 17(5)). The "best interests" test applies both under the Divorce Act to custody disputes ancillary to divorce and to custody disputes in relation to children whose parents are not determining arrangements ancillary to a divorce under provincial statutes like, for example, Ontario's *Children's Law Reform Act* and Alberta's *Family Law Act RSA* 2003. On the one hand, this test has been criticized as notoriously indeterminate; allowing judges almost carte blanche in doing as they see fit (Walker). On the other hand, the indeterminacy of the legal test allows for judges to look at the lives of children in their entirety, and to consider gendered issues of violence against women in making custody determinations.

Section 16(6) of the *Divorce Act* confers this discretion on the court, empowering it to grant custody or access for a definite or indefinite period and subject to any such terms, conditions, or restrictions as the court thinks fit. As Julien and Marilyn Payne note, the "best interests of the child" is a holistic notion encompassing physical, emotional, intellectual, and moral well-being of the child. The court must consider the ramifications of any decision to the child's long term growth and development.

Matrimonial fault, historical problems between the parties, or other aspects of conduct by either party are not relevant to the determination of custody or access in relation to a child. For example, the Ontario's *Children's Law Reform Act* provides that custody and access are to be determined without reference to past misconduct by the spouses against one another (s. 24). Such conduct is only relevant to determinations regarding children if it bears upon a party's parenting ability. This is also set out in the Divorce Act (s. 16(8), s. 17(5)).

As Simon R. Fodden points out, the list of factors that are relevant to custody and access determinations set out in the CLRA is not exhaustive; other considerations can be legitimately within the contemplation of the Court when the custody determination is made. A relatively recent case discussing what factors are to be considered by the Court in determining the child's best interests is the Nova Scotia decision of *Roberts v Roberts*, where it was made clear that custody and access cases require an integrated assessment of all relevant factors and circumstances in order to determine the best interests of the child.[9]

For example, in the Alberta case of *Calahoo v Calahoo*, various factors to be considered in determining the "best interests" of the child were set out in some detail including the following:

> the provision of the necessaries of life, including physical and health care and love; stability and consistency and an environment that fosters good mental and emotional health; the opportunity to learn good cultural, moral, and spiritual values; the necessity of setting realistic boundaries on conduct and fair and consistent discipline in teaching appropriate behaviour and conduct; the opportunity to relate to and love and be loved by immediate and extended family and the opportunity to form relationships; the opportunity to grow and fulfill his or her potential with responsible guidance; to have optimal access to the non-custodial parent in order to encourage and foster a good relationship; to be with the parent best able to fulfill child's needs; and the provision of an environment that is safe, secure, free of strife and conflict, and positively guides the child in development. (*Calahoo v Calahoo* citing *Starko v Starko*)

Where there are no glaring problems with either parent's ability to care for the children, three factors will be important, those being preservation of existing arrangements to afford the children stability in their living arrangements, which parent was the primary caregiver during the parties' marriage, and a disinclination of the courts to split the siblings (see Payne and Payne 2006).

Domestic violence perpetrated by one parent has come to be recognized as a problem with the violent parent's ability to care for children. It has been found in a growing number of cases that domestic violence on the part of a parent negatively impacts children, even where the violence is not directed towards the child. Increasingly, witnessing domestic violence has been understood by Canadian Courts to be harmful to children (see Bala). Domestic violence is even written in to the custody provisions of some provincial and territorial legislation concerning child custody (such as Alberta's *Family Law Act*.) Thus, while domestic violence cannot be considered relevant as "marital fault," it is relevant to the best interests of the child and is considered frequently by Canadian courts as a significant, often determinative factor, in determining with which parent a child will live (see Bala).

Refugee Law

Women fleeing their abusers may become refugees. Refugees are a subgroup of a broader category of displaced persons. A "refugee" is defined under the Geneva Convention as a person outside his or her country of habitual residence who has a well-founded fear of persecution and who is unable to access the protection of that country, or to return there, for fear of persecution.[10] The majority of refugees are women. Like men, these people are vulnerable and need protection. They also face gendered problems in addition to those faced by men. In many countries, legal and governmental regimes either continue to support, or by inaction fail to stop, woman abuse. As a result, their political systems become complicit in the abuse suffered by these women and they must cross international borders to seek protection elsewhere (UNICEF). Or, women may voluntarily flee other forms of political oppression in their countries of origin accompanied by their abusers. Alternatively, women may leave their families and communities in their countries of origin under duress as a result of coercion by the men who have abused them.

Equally, women who cross borders with their children when fleeing abusive intimate partners may not fall within the definition of refugee. For example, if, as Canadian citizens or permanent residents who have been habitually living abroad, they have a right to remain here, they will not be considered refugees.

In its inception the Geneva Convention Relating to the Status of Refugees, 1951, a multilateral international agreement much like The Hague Convention, provides no grounds of sex or gender on which refugees can be granted protection from persecution. Women can be found to be refugees under the Geneva Convention for the same reasons as men. Usual grounds for protection are race, religion, nationality, and political opinion. Being gender-blind, this 1951 international treaty is, like the Hague Convention, also blind to the particular problem of violence against women.

This traditional definition of who is a refugee was designed with men in mind. It does not address problems uniquely faced by women. However, in 1993, long after the Geneva Convention was signed, Canada was first among many countries that began to address the particular needs of woman refugees. The Immigration and Refugee Board prepared Guidelines for woman refugee claims and expanded the particular social group category to cover women as a social group that can be protected (Immigration and Refugee Board of Canada).

So now, in Canada, women can be found to be refugees for reasons relating to their gender, while they still cannot do so in many countries. For example, if a woman fears abuse by an intimate partner from whom her country's government is not able, or is not willing, to protect her, she can make a refugee claim on this basis. Also, women can be found to be refugees if they fear repercussions in their country for breaking rules only applied to women. For example, if women are compelled to wear a certain type of clothing, style their hair a certain way, or participate in an arranged marriage, and they fear punishment for breaking these rules, they could be found to be refugees.

While no system can be perfect, the way Canada has incorporated gender issues into the determination of refugee claims nonetheless provides an example of how concerns about violence against women can be made visible and considered in the context of a determination of rights under an international agreement that, like the Hague Convention, is worded in a way that is gender blind. Further, it is anomalous and disturbing that Canada will accept refugee claims by women in relation to inattention to domestic abuse in countries whose custodial regimes Canadian courts will uphold in Hague Convention cases.

INTERPRETATION OF THE CONVENTION IN CANADA

The drafting of the Hague Convention provides some degree of flexibility to courts in countries deciding applications under it but that discretion has been construed narrowly when domestic violence to a parent is considered.

A detailed discussion of Hague Convention case law from jurisdictions other than Canada is beyond this chapter's scope.[11] Interpretation of the law is similar in the United States to the manner in which it is applied in Canada, although it is at least arguable that the U.S. has been more progressive and holistic in its treatment of allegations of domestic abuse since 2000.[12] Writing by Marisa Leto confirms the importance of the manner in which the Convention is interpreted. Leto finds that interpretation by decision-makers affects the Convention's impact because the wording of the Convention in itself is sufficiently indeterminate so as not to dictate outcomes.

Leto takes the opposite position to Weiner, who argues that the Convention should be amended to address the predicament of abused woman "abductors" and their children (Weiner). Leto, looking at international case law from jurisdictions other than Canada and the United States, argues that, as interpreted in certain other countries, the Convention already relies on a "best interest of the child" standard that is largely subjective and allows judges to make discretionary decisions that may in part be motivated by "gender biases." Leto's criticism makes the flexibility of the treaty's drafting clear. If, in other countries, the Convention is already being read in a manner that makes issues relating to gender and the best interests of children relevant, this means the same perspective could be taken in Canada.

Two aspects of many Canadian decisions under the Hague Convention are particularly problematic. First, the narrow interpretation the courts have often given the exception under Article 13 for "grave risk of harm" prevents the Court from looking at allegations of domestic abuse, and as such flies in the face of how custody is determined under Canadian family law, as discussed above. Second, the negative treatment courts have given to "deception" by the respondent parent in Hague Convention applications presents a further obstacle.

Canadian cases on the Hague Convention are hearings that took place in Canada where an allegation was made by a parent that one or more of their children had been wrongfully retained here or abducted from another jurisdiction to this country. It is difficult to interpret this case law from a gendered perspective for several reasons. By virtue of the formal equality enjoyed by litigants under Canadian law, detailed analysis of cases would have to be made to determine patterns across cases. A detailed statistical analysis of the embodied identity of respondents and petitioners in Canadian Hague Convention proceedings, similar to that conducted in the US by Grief and Hegar, would certainly be useful but is beyond the scope of this paper. This paper presents analysis of "leading" cases, recent Canadian decisions which outline the current state of our common law where allegations of abuse are made.[13]

A salient example of the restrictive meaning given to the "grave risk of harm" defence in Canada is *Medhurst v Markle*. The *Medhurst* decision is important because it is what is known as a "leading" case, meaning the statement of law set out in the decision has been approved of and applied in numerous subsequent decisions. In the *Medhurst* decision, a father sought to have his child returned to Germany under Article 8 of the Hague Convention. The father in *Medhurst* was ultimately successful. At trial, he was unsuccessful, even though it was found that the child's habitual residence was Germany and not Canada. The trial judge found that the proceedings were an abuse of process as the father's real purpose in making the application was to force reconciliation with his wife, who had, in effect, left the country to get away from him. On appeal, it was found that this was an error of law. The Court held that the three conditions determining whether a child is to be returned to Germany were that the appellant had custody "rights" to the child, that the child was wrongfully removed or retained, and that the child was habitually resident in Germany immediately before any breach of custody or access rights. As a result, the child was returned to Germany, leaving the respondent mother with a difficult choice, either to remain in Canada where she herself would be safe from her former partner's abuse and leave the child at risk of harm, or return to Germany to be near her child and seek to ensure the child's protection.

Significantly, the Court in *Medhurst* also indicated that any determination of the fate of a child under the Hague Convention is also subject to a finding on a balance of probabilities that there is a grave risk that the return of the child would expose the child to physical or psychological harm or would otherwise place the child in an intolerable situation. The threshold for this "grave risk of harm" qualification has been very high in Canadian cases. As is shown by *Medhurst*, violence against the child's mother by an abusive spouse seeking the return of his child(ren) to the jurisdiction where he resides is not generally considered.

Some Canadian judges have found domestic violence committed by a petitioner father to be relevant to the appropriateness of the

Hague Convention remedy of return. In a 1999 Ontario Court of Appeal decision authored by Madam Justice Rosalie Abella called *Pollastro v Pollastro*, where a respondent Canadian mother brought substantial evidence of the American petitioner father's alcohol problem and long history of physically abusing and harassing the mother, the Court refused to return the child to him. The Court found that the child would be placed at a "grave risk of harm" if returned to him in the circumstances. The decision allowed that the victimization of the mother by the father was relevant as it impacted on the child's best interests; the physical or psychological harm a return would present to the parent on whom the child was totally dependent would harm the child.

Pollastro can be a useful precedent upon which counsel for mothers in Hague Convention applications can rely. For example, in the 2007 decision of Justice Backhouse in *Rajani v Rajani*, the Court refused to return a child to Tanzania and denied a father's Hague Convention application on the basis of his documented abuse of the child's mother and the effects of the abuse on the child. Still more recently, in *Husid v Daviau* in 2012, the Ontario Court of Appeal followed its decision in *Pollastro* and refused to return a child to Peru where allegations of serious violence and death threats involving guns had been made by the Peruvian father.

However, the risk of harm was unusually clear and well documented in the *Pollastro* case. There was also a great deal of evidence of abuse tendered in *Husid* along with witness testimony by the nanny, grandmother, and others. An abundance of evidence of severe abuse causing injuries over a long period of time was tendered by counsel for the respondent in *Pollastro*. The mother was able to produce documentation of her injuries from a physician in the petitioner's home country. She was able to obtain third party witness reports of the abuse and resulting injuries. In many situations, a woman's abduction of children may be undertaken before years of brutalization take place. A body of evidence of abuse as large as that tendered in *Pollastro* will be difficult to obtain. This is particularly important given that Reesa Pollastro was abused in the United States, where there is some progressive recognition of the problem of domestic violence. Many women's victimization takes place in countries where circumstances prevent a woman from thoroughly documenting abuse she has suffered.

Pollastro has often been distinguished from other cases on its facts. The decision made in *Pollastro* remains exceptional. *Medhurst* continued to be followed after *Pollastro* was decided, and courts in subsequent proceedings continued to interpret the scope of Article 13 (b) narrowly.

An Ontario Court of Appeal case where a mother made spousal abuse allegations against a Hague Convention petitioner father that came shortly after *Pollastro* was *Finizio v Scoppio-Finizio*. *Finizio* provides a good example of the evidentiary difficulty discussed above. In that decision, the Canadian mother contended she had been physically assaulted by the Italian petitioner father by being "punched in the face" on at least one occasion. Here, the Court did not find the domestic assault to meet the threshold of "grave risk of harm" set out in Article 13(b) and as described in *Pollastro*. Despite the evidence of physical assault, the Court found that there was "no evidence that the husband has ever done anything to harm the children" (*Finizio v Scoppio-Finizio*: para 30). The children were ordered returned to Italy over the mother's objections.

A more recent and leading Ontario Court of Appeal case on the question of "grave risk of harm" to children under the Convention is *Jabbaz v Mouammar*. The *Jabbaz* decision makes clear that, even after *Pollastro*, the "grave risk of harm" test is still being given a narrow interpretation by Canadian courts. In *Jabbaz*, a mother resident in the United States allowed her former husband to take their child to Canada on the understanding that the child would be returned to her once her life stabilized. There were no allegations of domestic abuse by the father, but the statement of law provided by the Court as to the scope of the "grave risk of harm" test remains applicable to cases where abuse is alleged. At trial, the Court held that, while the habitual residence of the child was the United States, it would place the child at "grave risk of harm" to be returned there. On appeal, this decision was overturned. In the *Jabbaz* decision, Rosenberg J.A. stated:

> The circumstances in which a court may refuse to order the return of a child under Article 13 are exceptional. The risk of physical or psychological harm or, as alleged in this

> case, an intolerable situation must be, as set out in Article 13, "grave." The use of the term "intolerable" speaks to an extreme situation, a situation that is unbearable; a situation too severe to be endured. (*Jabbaz v Mouammar*: para 23)

At paragraph 24, his Honour went on to say:

> Unlike virtually all other child welfare statutes, the test under The Hague Convention and Article 13 in particular is not framed in terms of the best interests of the child. The court to which the application is made under the Hague Convention is not concerned with determining which parent should have custody of the child using the best interests of the child test.

At paragraph 39 of the *Jabbaz* decision, Justice Rosenberg went on to strongly suggest that decision makers should not import "public policy" notions into their interpretation of the Convention. He wrote as follows:

> I repeat the observations of Chamberland J.A. in F (R) v G (M) at para. 30 that the Hague Convention is "a fragile tool and any interpretation short of a rigorous one of the few exceptions inserted in the Convention would rapidly compromise its efficacy." That means that courts should be very wary of grafting new public policy exceptions on to the Convention in the face of the very clear public policy represented in the Convention itself.

DECEPTION AND ABUSE

Where a mother flees an abuser with her child or children, she will very likely deceive her partner to some degree in doing so. This deception may be necessary for her to safely escape, particularly in the context of a regime that condones or is otherwise complicit in, domestic abuse. This deception, however, may lead to a finding against her in a Hague Convention proceeding. It has been found in Canadian case law that deceptions by a parent that facilitate his or her abduction or retention of a child in violation of the Convention can prevent the country to which they were removed, or where they were falsely retained, from becoming their "habitual residence." It is also arguable that the test for habitual residence calls for consideration of the parents' "purpose" in coming to a country, and should be considered in "all of the circumstances."

Deception has been found by Canadian courts to be an important factor to consider in determining whether a child was wrongfully removed from his or her country of habitual residence under the terms of the Hague Convention. For example, one case where this was found was the Manitoba decision of *Belton v Belton*. In *Belton*, a father removed his daughter from the United States, where they had resided with her mother, on the pretense of visiting his parents in Canada. The mother made an application for return of the child to her under the Hague Convention. She was successful. The Court held that the daughter's habitual residence was Tennessee where she normally resided. She did not lose her place of habitual residence by moving to Manitoba. The wife did not acquiesce in the daughter remaining in Manitoba and took steps as soon as she reasonably could to oppose the husband.

Because of the rules of precedent, and because the Convention is gender blind, the *Belton* case can be used by counsel for abusive petitioners where a female "abductor" has fled domestic violence, to successfully argue that deception by the fleeing parent should prejudice her claim to retain the child with whom she has crossed into Canada.

RECOMMENDATIONS

Amendment of the Convention, changes to how it is interpreted and administered by the courts, advocacy by lawyers on behalf of their clients to effect those changes, and law and policy reform are all ways that the current situation could be remedied.

The Convention should be amended:

To redefine child custody as a question of the child's best interests, not parental rights;

To accord jurisdiction to the petitioned courts to inquire

into the child's best interests if an abducting parent raises the issue of previous spousal abuse;

To set forth detailed uniform standards for courts hearing Convention applications to ensure they address woman abuse and the abuse of children; and

To provide women forced by their abusers to flee another country with an opportunity to have their matters heard in Canada.

Until the Convention is amended, lawyers and judges can better protect vulnerable women and children by working within existing laws. Particularly on the basis of the *Pollastro* decision, there is scope to better protect women using the Convention as written:

Judges should consider domestic violence cases as falling within the scope of the "grave risk of harm" exception under Article 13(b), taking the lead from the Ontario Court of Appeal in the *Pollastro* decision.

Lawyers should advance the "grave risk of harm" argument on their clients' behalf to push the edges of its interpretation.

Government actors could also help remedy the situation: As is shown by the example of the guidelines put in place by the Immigration and Refugee Board with respect to woman refugees, government could set out policy guidance for interpretation of Article 13(b) to ensure the courts interpret the *Convention* appropriately.

And, wherever political action is possible, the public at large can play a role in calling upon government for change.

CONCLUSION

The Hague Convention deals effectively with the sort of international child abductions it was intended to remedy: abductions by parents seeking to gain advantages in litigation, abductions by parents seeking to circumvent lawful custody orders, and third party abductions by parties seeking to exploit children.

However, the Convention fails to adequately address the best interests of children in a majority of cases, because, in most cases where a child is abducted by a parent, there are allegations of domestic violence. There does seem to be some movement in Canada and the United States towards recognizing domestic abuse as harm, as was done in the *Pollastro* case. However, the Convention as currently interpreted in Canada, can still be used as an instrument of violence and harm to women and children when the remedy of return is invoked by a father who has abused the child's mother.

The current gender blindness of the Convention and the Canadian laws that make it enforceable here, together with the preponderance of case law that has been decided under those laws, present a problem. The current approach renders our state complicit in continuing woman abuse. It incorporates and enforces definitions and concepts in relation to child custody that are patriarchal, proprietary, and archaic, and which decades of feminist law reform had largely removed from Canadian child custody law. The Convention sets up double-bind conditions where mothers have to choose between risk of criminalization and risk of harm to themselves and their children.

As currently constructed, the Convention's remedy of return jeopardizes the safety of mothers and the best interests of children while it criminalizes marginalized and vulnerable mothers. Marginalized and vulnerable mothers who have suffered abuse should be protected by—not criminalized—under child custody laws.

ENDNOTES

[1]The Hague Convention of 25 October 1980 on the Civil Aspects of International Child Abduction Can. T.S. 1983, No. 35, 19 I.L.M. 1501 is a multilateral international treaty concluded by the Fourteenth Session of the Hague Conference on Private International Law on 25 October 1980 and entered into force *1 December 1983*. The Convention seeks to protect children from the harmful effects of abduction and retention across international boundaries by providing procedures by which to effect their immediate return. [hereinafter Hague Convention or Convention]

[2] See "A Statistical Analysis of Applications Made in 2008 Under The Hague Convention of 25 October 1980 on the Civil Aspects

of International Child Abduction. Part I – Global Report." Drawn up by Professor Nigel Lowe, Cardiff University Law School. Prel. Doc. No 8 A – update, November 2011. Hague Conference on Private International Law. Web.

[3]Article 3 of the Hague Convention on the Civil Aspects of Child Abduction, 1980, provides as follows: The removal or the retention of a child is to be considered wrongful where a) it is in breach of rights of custody attributed to a person, an institution or any other body, either jointly or alone, under the law of the State in which the child was habitually resident immediately before the removal or retention; and b) at the time of removal or retention those rights were actually exercised, either jointly or alone, or would have been so exercised but for the removal or retention.

[4]Different countries take different approaches to the domestic enforceability of international legal agreements. Discussion of the range of approaches to this is beyond the scope of this paper.

[5]Thorough discussion of these debates is beyond the scope of this paper. For discussion see e.g., Elisa Pez-Vera, Explanatory Report: Hague Conference on Private International Law, in 3 Acts and Documents of the Fourteenth Session 426 (1980) and the U.S. Department of States Legal Analysis of the Hague Convention (51 Fed. Reg. 10494 (1986)) prepared for the Senate Committee on Foreign Relations to which the Convention was referred. These documents confirm that the intention that Article 13 was intended to be afforded a narrow interpretation to avoid re-litigation of custody disputes, and that domestic violence was not given much, if any, consideration, in this determination.

[6]For example, Ecuador is a Hague Convention signatory. If a child was removed to Canada from Ecuador, the question for the Court would be who had custody "rights" to the child in Ecuadorian law.

[7]Guidelines issued by the Chairperson pursuant to Section 65(3) of the Immigration Act -UPDATE- Effective date: November 13, 1996.

[8]For discussion see e.g., Senn.

[9]For discussion of these factors in cases from British Columbia, see for example the decisions in *Rail v. Rail* (1999), 180 DLR (4th) 490 (BCCA), citing *Poole v Poole* (1999), 173 DLR (4th) 299 (BCCA).

[10]More specifically, under the 1951 Geneva Convention, a refugee is "a person who is outside his or her country, who has a well-founded

fear of being persecuted for reasons of race, religion, nationality, membership of a particular social group or political opinion, and whom the state is unwilling or unable to protect."

[11]An excellent collection of international Hague Convention case law is available at www.incadat.com for those who would like to take a look at cases from around the world. A good starting point for review of this case law could be *Re E (Children) (International Abduction)* [2011] UKSC 27 where the UK Court set forth guidelines for interpreting the Convention that severely limit the relevance of domestic violence to determinations under it. It is significant that American courts are increasingly frequently adopting reasoning expressly set out by Weiner and others.

[12]See for example *Brooke v Willis*, 907 F. Supp. 57 (S.D.N.Y. 1995). The father was a citizen of the United Kingdom and the mother was a native of China who had become a naturalized American citizen. *Brooke* is helpful for its articulation of first principles under the Convention. Since 2000, U.S. law concerning grave risk of harm has reflected a growing realization that it is harmful to order that children be sent back to face domestic violence without assessing prior abuse and of the likelihood that the authorities in the country to which the children are being returned will protect them and their mother.

[13]For a more general, earlier statement of the law on the Hague Convention and s. 13(b) where no allegation of abuse was made, see *Thomson* v *Thomson*, 1994 CanLII 26 (S.C.C.), [1994] 3 SCR 551, in which case the Supreme Court of Canada established the interpretative framework for deciding Hague Convention cases in general and Article 13(b) specifically.

WORKS CITED

Law

Divorce Act RSC 1985 (2nd Supp) C 3

Children's Law Reform Act RSO 1990 C 12

Geneva Convention Relating to the Status of Refugees, 1951 Concluded 28 July 1951

Hague Convention of 25 October 1980 on the Civil Aspects of International Child Abduction, concluded by the Fourteenth

Session of the Hague Conference on Private International Law on 25 October 1980 and entered into force 1 December 1983 Can. TS 1983, No 35, 19 ILM 1501

Immigration and Refugee Board "Guidelines on Women Refugee Claimants Fearing Gender-Related Persecution." March 1993

Belton v Belton (1998) MJ No 562 (Man QB)

Calahoo v Calahoo (2000) AJ No 815 (Alta QB)

Finizio v Scoppio-Finizio (1999) 46 OR (3d) 226 (Ont CA)

Husid v Daviau (2012) ONCA 655 (CanLII)

Jabbaz v Mouammar (2003) OJ No 1616 (Ont. CA)

Medhurst v Markle (1995) OJ No 3085 (Gen Div)

Pollastro v Pollastro (1999) 45 RFL (4th) 404 (Ont CA)

Rajani v Rajani (2007) CarswellOnt 5834 (Ont. SCJ)

Re E (Children) (International Abduction) (2011) UKSC27

Roberts v Roberts (2000) NSJ No 218 (Fam Ct)

Starko v Starko (1990) 74 Alta LR (2d) 168 (Alta QB)

Literature

Bala, Nicholas. "A Differential Legal Approach to the Effects of Spousal Abuse on Children: A Canadian Context." *Children Exposed to Domestic Violence: Current Issues in Research, Intervention, Prevention, and Policy Development.* Ed. R. A. Geffner, P. G. Jaffe, and M. Sudermann. New York: Haworth Press, 2000. 301-328. Print.

Bala, Nicholas, Lorne D. Bertrand, Joanne J. Paetsch, Bartha Maria Knoppers, Joseph P. Hornick, Jean-François Noel, Lorraine Boudreau, Susan W. Miklas. *Spousal Violence in Custody and Access Disputes: Recommendations for Reform.* Ottawa: Status of Women Canada, 1998. Print.

Boyd, Susan. *Child Custody, Law and Women's Work.* Oxford: Oxford University Press, 2002. Print.

Boyd, Susan. "Reforming Custody Laws: A Comparative Study." *International Journal of Law, Policy and the Family* 18 (2004): 119-146. Print.

Canadian Center for Justice Statistics. *Family Violence in Canada: A Statistical Profile 2005.* 85-224-XIE.Web. January 25, 2014.

Crawford, Maria and Rosemary Gartner. *Woman Killing: Intimate Femicide in Ontario 1974-1990.* Toronto: The Women

We Honour Action Committee, 1992. Print.
Domestic Abuse Intervention Project. "The Power and Control Wheel." 1984. Web. January 25, 2014.
Fodden, Simon R. *Canadian Family Law* Toronto: Irwin Law, 1999. Print.
Greif, Geoffrey and Rebecca L. Hegar. *When Parents Kidnap: The Families Behind the Headlines*. New York: The Free Press, 1993 Print.
Leto, Marisa. "Whose Best Interest? International Child Abduction Under the Hague Convention." *Chicago Journal of International Law* 3.1(2002): 247-254. Print.
Lowe, Nigel. "A Statistical Analysis of Applications Made Under the Hague Convention 1980 on the Civil Aspects of International Child Abduction." Hague Conference on Private International Law, November 2011. Web. January 25, 2014.
Mason, Mary Ann. *From Father's Property to Children's Rights: A History of Child Custody.* New York: Columbia University Press, 1994. Print.
Payne, Julien and Marilyn Payne. *Canadian Family Law (In A Nutshell)*. Toronto: Irwin Law, 2006. Print.
Razack, Sherene. "What Is to Be Gained by Looking White People in the Eye? Culture, Race, and Gender in Cases of Sexual Violence" *Signs* 19.4 (Summer 1994) 894-923. Print.
Ruddick, Sara. *Maternal Thinking: Towards a Politics of Peace.* Boston: Beacon Press, 1989. Print.
Senn, Charlene. "Violence against Women and Girls: What Feminist Counsellors Need to Know to Begin their Work with Women." *Feminist Counselling: Theory, Issues, and Practice*. Ed. Lynda Ross. Toronto: Canadian Scholars/Women's Press, 2010. 77-99. Print.
Statistics Canada. *Family Violence in Canada: A Statistical Profile 2010*. Statistics Canada, May 31, 2013. Web. January 25, 2014.
Status of Women Canada. "Fact Sheets on Violence Against Women for the National Day of Remembrance." Government of Canada. 2004. Print.
Sudermann, M. and Jaffe, P. *A Handbook for Health and Social Service Providers and Educators on Children Exposed to Women Abuse/Family Violence*. Family Violence Prevention Unit, Health

Canada, 1999. Web. January 25, 2014.

UNICEF, United Nations Children's Fund. "Domestic Violence Against Women and Girls." *Innocenti Digest* 6 (2000). Web. January 25, 2014.

United States Department of Justice. "Violence Against Women: Estimates from the Redesigned Survey August 1995." Special Report, NCJ-154348. 1995. Print.

Walker, Keith. "Jurisprudential and Ethical Perspectives on the Best Interests of Children." *Interchange* 29.3(1998): 309-316. Print.

Weiner, M. "International Child Abduction and the Escape from Domestic Violence." *Fordham Law Review* 69 (2000): 593-706. Web. January 25, 2014.

7. Race, Nation and Citizenship in "Mothers Who Kill Their Children"

The Case of Rie Fujii

HIJIN PARK

IN MAY 2001, RIE FUJII, a 23-year-old Japanese national living in Calgary, Alberta, left her two infant children—aged 15 months and three months—alone in her apartment for ten days while visiting her new, out-of-town boyfriend. The children, Domenic and Gemini, died of dehydration and starvation. Estranged from the children's father, who is represented in media and judicial documents as an abusive white Canadian, Fujii was financially destitute and living alone with her infant children. Fujii was unable to seek adequate support from women's and immigrant service agencies and the criminal justice system in part because she had overstayed her visitor visa, and did not have status in Canada. Charged with two counts of second-degree homicide, Fujii pled guilty to manslaughter and received an eight-year sentence (*R. v. Fujii*). Upon serving two-thirds of her sentence, Fujii was paroled and deported to Japan in 2006.

This chapter explores how constructions of race, nation, and citizenship intersect with gender and class in media representations of the Rie Fujii case. In line with recent postcolonial feminist and anti-racist feminist scholarship, I contend that an examination of Fujii's crimes and criminalization requires an analysis that accounts for how race, gender, class, and nation intersect in the context of Canadian white settler nationalism (Dua and Robertson; Jiwani; Thobani).

While there is research on violent women and on mothers who kill their children, there is almost no research on how race, gender, class, nation, and economy shape the violence or conceptualizations of the violence of non-Indigenous racialized mothers in Canada (see Braunmühl; Burfoot and Lord; Morrissey; Oberman and Meyer; Sheehy; Sjoberg and Gentry).[1] Racialized women are the fastest growing sector of the prison population in North America (Wortley 107; Balfour 735), yet racialized women are largely absent in legal and media formulations of crime and violence. The normative criminal remains constructed as a (racialized) man and the normative victim as a white, middle-class, heterosexual woman (Vandenberg, Brennan and Chesney-Lind 51). The crimes deemed most objectionable and in need of punishment often conform to racialized, gendered, and heterosexualized scripts involving criminal men of colour, victimized middle-class white women and children, and heroic white males who take up the cause of protecting "their" women, children and nation (Irving 11).

Violent crimes committed by women constitute another category of crime deemed most objectionable in mainstream North American culture, particularly the crimes of mothers who kill their children. Most scholarship on mothers who murder their children does not include an analysis of race and how constructions of motherhood are racialized (as well as gendered, classed, and heterosexualized), rendering racialized women invisible. For example, Michelle Oberman and Cheryl Meyer in their text *When Mothers Kill: Interviews from Prison*, acknowledge that approximately 40 percent of the 40 imprisoned women they interviewed were women of colour. However they did not ask the mothers about their race or incorporate race as an analytical category. The authors believe that "class, or socioeconomic status, was a far more salient factor in contributing to our understanding of this crime than factors such as race, ethnicity, or culture" (11) (see Minaker "Review of When Mothers Kill" 276). Barbara Barnett, in her influential research on media representations of cases involving mothers in the U.S. who murder their children, does not examine issues of race because the news stories did not identify the women by race, even though many of the mothers were racialized women (415-416).

In media representations of Rie Fujii's crimes, Fujii is continually identified as Japanese, but not as Asian. Nonetheless, I contend that Fujii's crimes are heavily racialized (as well as gendered, classed, and heterosexualized). Racialization must be a central analytic through which her crimes have been understood and punished. In examining the specificities of non-Indigenous racialized mothers, I aim to explore how individualized and de-racialized conceptualizations of the violence of mothers who kill their children can mask the systemic violence of white settler nationalism, global migration, capitalism, and everyday structural forms of gendered racism. This systemic violence, I surmise, informs the violence of racialized mothers and their criminalization. In analyzing media representations of the case of Rie Fujii, I seek to reveal some of the ways that social constructions of race, gender, class, violence, and crime shape and legitimize white settler practices of surveillance, punishment, reward, and regulation.

I begin by describing my research methodology and the role the media may play in producing criminalized subjects. This is followed by a brief overview of the literature on race and violent women, particularly mothers charged with murdering their children. Paying attention to the intersections of race, gender, class, nation, and citizenship, I then explore some of the ways mainstream Canadian newspapers represented Rie Fujii. In keeping with a postcolonial feminist and anti-racist feminist analytic, I address the broader socio-historical context in which the violence is produced and defined as well as a microstructural analysis of the language and composition of media coverage.

Stuart Hall utilized the term "narratives of nationhood" to describe how the media contribute to constructing the boundaries of acceptable citizenship (Mackey citing Hall 71). This research focusses primarily on the assumptions about gender, race, class, nation, and mothering that informed how Fujii and her crimes were defined. My interest is not in proposing causes and solutions for maternal filicide. Rather, I focus on the availability and construction of certain narratives as truths, and as a corollary, I look at how the negation of historical and contextual elements can prevent some questions from being considered (see Carney 191).

MEDIA AND REPRESENTATIONS OF RACE, GENDER AND CRIME

This research draws on a critical discourse analysis of 146 newspaper articles from five mainstream Canadian English-language newspapers, the *Calgary Herald* (local), the *Toronto Star* (central Canada), the *Vancouver Sun* (west coast), *The Globe and Mail* (national), and *The National Post* (national). The newspapers were chosen to reflect local, regional, and national coverage. All media documents were obtained through electronic databases such as *Canadian Newsstand* and *LexisNexis*. The searched time period was from June 2001, when Fujii was charged, to May 2006 when she was deported. Although the case of Rie Fujii received significant national attention, sustained coverage was largely local and the majority of media texts were from the *Calgary Herald*.

There is much that has been written about how the media and the criminal justice system have a symbiotic relationship in producing and supporting narratives of respectable citizenship (Vandenberg, Brennan and Chesney-Lind 48-49; Surette). The media and the criminal justice system contribute to the production of fictions that enforce the gendered, racialized, and classed order through the criminal justice system's administrative and punishing regimes. Both are central to the regulation of minorities (Chesney-Lind and Eliason 43). In the case of Rie Fujii, as with most "newsworthy" crimes, the media played a central role in presenting the select views of "the public," including social service workers, members of relevant advocacy organizations, medical professionals, and in particular, law enforcement officers (Doyle and Ericson; Surette).

Carney argues that in the United States context, it is an axiom that people of colour and white people are treated differently in both the criminal justice system and news reporting, with Blacks in particular heavily criminalized (187). Studies show that defendants who receive negative pre-trial publicity are more likely to be found guilty than defendants who receive minimal or no negative publicity (Clow, Lant and Cutler 1). Similar research results exist in the Canadian context although the amount of research on race and media representations and their effect on the criminal justice system is minimal in comparison to the United States (Clow, Lant and Cutler 2; Pieters and Wortley). Little research exists on the criminalization of non-Indigenous, racialized female offenders, which is where we will now turn.

RACE, GENDER, VIOLENCE, AND MOTHERING

Most scholarship on violent women argues that the public is particularly fascinated with murderous women because they have violated both the law of the land and more importantly, nature's law, which defines women as the passive, non-aggressive, and virtuous gender (Comack and Brickey 1). Cases of fathers who murder their children do not become media spectacles in similar quantity and quality as cases of mothers killing their children, as the crimes of mothers more violently transgress societal norms regarding motherhood, femininity, and family (see Carney 186). In arguments about violent women violating gendered constructs of femininity and motherhood, the implied and unnamed subject is a white heterosexual able-bodied, middle-to-upper-class woman. This is because marginalized women, women who are racialized, queer, working-class, and disabled, have often been constructed in dominant media and judicial discourse as aggressive and/or cunning, monstrous, violent, licentious, and in need of control, both historically and in the contemporary context (see Vandenberg, Brennan and Chesney-Lind 50-51; Chesney-Lind and Eliason; Minaker "Sluts and Slags"). Studies show that battered woman syndrome, for example, is a defence less available to Black women than white women in the United States, since Black women are stereotyped as aggressive and white women epitomize representations of the kinder, gentler sex (Kruttschnitt and Carbone-Lopez 325). While Asian women are represented as more passive than white women, their passivity is framed within gendered Orientalist constructions of Asianness as a deceitful, not fully human, robotic, immoral, and culturally backward foreignness that threatens the white, civilized nation (Park).

Wilcox explains that criminal justice and media systems criminalize women in relation to the extent of their deviance from what she refers to as the "Benchmark Man" and the "Benchmark Woman." The "'Benchmark Man' is the white, heterosexual, able-bodied, middle class, and above all *rational*, sexed-male body, which remains the assumed subject of legal and other public discourses" (521, emphasis in original). The Benchmark Woman is "the white, heterosexual, able-bodied, irrational or arational, middle-class, sexed-female body, which has been a metaphor for 'innocence'" (521). An aberration from Benchmark Woman as well as Benchmark Man, racialized mothers like Rie Fujii are demonized not only by what they do, but also by who they are thought to be. In other words, as Black, Indigenous, or Asian women, they can never be the ideal mother who is deserving of sympathy, since purity, benevolence, and selfless-care are racialized as white.

Scholars such as Huckerby and Rudrappa contend that middle-class white women who murder or attempt to murder their children tend to receive lighter sentences and are seen as more redeemable than racialized women. This accords with judicial and media constructions of murderous women as either mad or bad. Middle-class white women are more likely to be deemed mad and thus less or not criminally responsible, whereas racialized women are more likely to be deemed bad, inhuman, or simply evil and thus fully responsible. As Huckerby states:

> ... the "double jeopardy" (in breaking both the criminal law and societal expectations) to which women offenders are subject, becomes a "triple jeopardy" for poor women of color because their precrime status already constitutes an inherent offense to societal norms (157).

By precrime status Huckerby is referring to their race and class. Importantly, these constructions of "white female purity"—she must be *mad* in order to do what she did—and of the "irredeemable *bad* women of colour"—she must be *bad*—maintain white heteropatriarchal supremacy.

When white middle-class women are defined as mad this preserves white heterosexual femininity by constructing women's deviance as a biological abnormality rather than a sign of problematic constructions of motherhood and its material realities (Brennan and Vandenberg 146). Constructing poor women of colour as bad people as well as bad mothers preserves a particular kind of ideal normative motherhood. These constructs of good and bad mothers are arguably racialized, heterosexualized, classed, and ableist as well as misogynist. It is, as Fine cites Van Denend, "a divide between a patronistic protection of the good mother and retaliatory persecution of the bad mother" (24). Both constructs of mad white women and bad women of colour support disparate but continued surveillance of racialized and non-racialized mothers by husbands, lawmakers, medical professionals and institutions, and criminal justice systems (Huckerby 172).

Narratives of mad and bad mothers tend to negate the social relations and structural realities that shape the violence committed by murderous women, as well as the various forms of systemic and interpersonal violence experienced by many mothers who harm their children. Scrutinizing individual mothers as mad or bad, Carney states, "ignores (or erases) other particular kinds of historical context, in particular, long histories of oppression and racism as well as the day-to-day struggles of living in conditions of poverty" (191). Speaking specifically about child neglect and failure to protect cases in the United States, Carney argues that the number of these cases has increased dramatically in the twenty-first century, and is a reflection of the process of personal responsibilization that legitimates the dismantling of the welfare state. Media and legal discourse construct mothers, more than fathers, as responsible for ensuring the welfare of families and communities (see also Vandenbeld Giles 123). The extent of this responsibilization is evident in the fact that mothers are also often charged with failure to protect along with the father or another male who is the sole-person who has committed the act. On the other hand, fathers are not charged along with mothers with failure to protect or child neglect when the mother alone committed such acts. Those charged with "bad mothering" tend to be heavily racialized and classed as well as gendered: they are racialized and poor mothers who stray from social constructions of acceptable and respectable motherhood (Carney 186-187; Strega, Krane and Carlton 16 and 20-22). Writing about Canadian infanticide law, Kramar concurs that the contemporary neoliberal retributive and criminalizing climate regarding child abuse and murder has produced the subject of the rights-bearing, fully innocent child and the wholly responsibilized mother (13-16). These constructed subjects obscure the conditions of poverty and exclusion that shape the violence of mothers, particularly marginalized mothers. The next section examines narratives of race, gender, mothering and responsibilization by focussing on the case of Rie Fujii.

B/ORDERING RIE FUJII AS "NOT LIKE US"

In their research of front page *New York Times* and *Los Angeles Times* news stories of female offenders, Brennan and Vandenberg found that news stories about white female offenders were three times more favourable than news stories about women of colour female offenders. White female offenders were much more likely to be presented as flawed but still human, as redeemable, and as possibly not responsible. Stories were more likely to contain excuses for their crimes. In contrast, reporting about women of colour female offenders contained elements of what Razack terms "race thinking": "they are not like us" ("Abandonment" 90); they are "incapable of reform" (Brennan and Vandenberg 164-165). Brennan and Vandenberg surmise that similar scripts operate throughout the criminal justice system.

In a more recent larger study that expanded on this earlier work, Vandenberg, Brennan and Chesney-Lind confirm that race and ethnicity are the strongest predictors of a story's general tone. News stories about white female offenders were 83.1 *percent* less likely to have a negative tone compared with stories about women of colour offenders. This largely held true irrespective of the type of offense (violent, white-collar, and non-violent crimes) and the amount of attention a case received (59). Vandenberg, Brennan and Chesney-Lind conclude, citing Gilliam, that "it is race and not violence that is the more important element of crime news coverage" (67). Stories about white women killing their children and women of colour killing their children contained "vastly different" (64) narratives that drew on and reinforced racial stereotypes about racialized minorities (53 and 67).

In all five newspapers, media representations of Rie Fujii and her crimes overwhelmingly describe her as an unsympathetic, foreign, and perhaps evil in character. Headlines include, "Mom on sex, drug binge 'left babies to die'" (*Vancouver Sun* A4), and "Japanese mother who left children to die is deported" (*The Globe and Mail* A12). The editor of the *Calgary Herald* writes:

> In our quest to be a just and compassionate society, it has become fashionable to avoid the words bad or evil when we talk about criminals. When a crime is particularly heinous, we impulsively say someone is "insane" to have done it. But no one—not the psychologist, nor the psychiatrist, not even the defence counsel—tried to argue that Fujii was insane. This was an act of staggering evil that was allowed to play itself slowly, cruelly, over 10 days. ("Nature of the crime" A18)

Similarly columnist Don Braid defines Fujii as depraved—a "child killer"—rather than ill.

> The most infamous local child killer is surely Rie Fujii, who was sentenced last year to eight years in prison after she left her two children, aged 15 months and three months, alone in her apartment for several days while she went off to party with her new boyfriend. The children died in circumstances too horrible to imagine. Fujii disposed of one corpse, which was never found. Evidence that she was depressed and suffered a personality disorder cut no ice with the public or the judge. That case strained our notions of depravity.... (A3)

Almost all news stories mention that Fujii is Japanese and refer to her expired visa. Race is not mentioned, but Fujii's Japanese nationality and her non-status in Canada, as well as her possible deportation are almost always key elements of the story that mark her clearly as Other. In the Canadian context, race is commonly subsumed under talk of culture, cultural difference, and immigration. This is how race thinking that says "they are not like us" operates and yet is obscured (Thobani). Fujii's non-status follows her even when the story is not about her. A *Calgary Herald* report of a body found in the same apartment building as Domenic's body states:

> The same building was home to child killer Rie Fujii, who let her 15-month-old son Domenic and infant daughter Gemini starve to death in her second-floor suite while she

> partied with a boyfriend in Cochrane for 10 days in May 2001. Fujii, a Japanese citizen who was in Canada illegally after her visa expired, is now serving an eight-year sentence for manslaughter. (van Rassel "Witness Sought")

I propose that the terms "Japanese," "illegal," and "deportation," are racialized constructs and these also have nationalist overtones. They are code words for race and, although race is not named, the continual reference to Fujii's Japanese nationality, illegal presence and expected deportation feed into and may summon histories of anti-Asian racism that define Asianness as foreignness that threatens Canadian economic, political, and social stability (Heer). It may also tap into more recent xenophobic debates about illegal migration and the need to deport foreign criminal elements, a narrative that is central to Canadian white settler nationalism (Pratt; Chan).

Hypersexuality also appears to be central to Fujii's heightened vilification. This is in keeping with western constructions of the Madonna/whore complex in which hypersexuality is a key definer of inappropriate femininity, bad womanhood and bad motherhood. Racialized women, both in general and in particular, are stereotyped as hypersexed (Brennan and Vandenberg 147). Bond-Maupin argues that while white female offenders are often represented by US media through discourses of sexual manipulation, race adds an element of ruthlessness, particularly for Russian and Asian women (43). They are hyper-hypersexed, even more dangerous and depraved. In the case of Fujii, the death of her children is often framed as Fujii putting her sexual needs and desires ahead of her children's welfare. The article "Mother partied while babies died" begins with the words:

> Rie Fujii put her selfish sexual cravings ahead of her two young children when she fled to Cochrane, only to return 10 days later to find her young children had starved to death. The 24-year-old Japanese woman, living illegally in Calgary on an expired visitor's visa last year, lied to new boyfriend Chris Knowler about having left 15-month-old son Domenic and three-month-old daughter Gemini with a babysitter. (Slade "Mother Partied")

The first line of a *National Post* article reporting on Fujii's guilty plea reads, "Rie Fujii abandoned her two young children to have sex with her new boyfriend, returning 10 days later to find the toddlers had starved to death, court heard yesterday" (Slade "Mother Left"). Her abuse at the hands of the children's father, Peter Brown, is mentioned at the end of the article. However prior to this, the emphasis is on Fujii's awareness of social services and women's shelters and the fact that she did not use them. Psychiatrist George Duska is cited as saying that "the tragedy of this situation was she wanted to meet her own needs and those children were left at home to die" and that "she went to Cochrane with this guy clearly to have a good time" (Slade "Mother Left").

Reports on her first parole hearing emphasize Board members' uncertainty about whether Fujii had adequately vanquished her "apparent need to respond to men" (van Rassel "Child Killer"). Rather than naming some of the structural causes of her crimes, media coverage portrays her as a hypersexual yet naïve and irresponsible young Japanese woman who excelled at deception. Bob Weber of the *Toronto Star* reports:

> A Japanese citizen, Fujii was in Canada on an expired student visa [sic]. Her parents thought she was attending college classes and didn't even know about their grandchildren until after they were dead. Fujii financially supported the father of her children. But when the two broke up and Fujii found a new boyfriend, she decided it was time for some fun. "I left my kids by themselves a few times. I thought maybe I can do that again. I was just thinking about myself."

Economically impoverished and alone in a barren apartment with her two infant children, Fujii could not work or seek adequate support from social service agencies due to her expired visa. The only child to parents whom she described as "strict" (van Rassel "Child Killer"), she hid her pregnancies from her family. Her parents were unaware of her children until contacted by police after their death and her arrest.

In addition to constructions of Fujii, representations of the men in her life are of particular relevance to her criminalization. Huckerby explains that "... there are essentially three main variables which determine the value that attaches to motherhood: race, class, and the role that the father has in relation to both the child(ren) and mother" (152). Fujii was estranged from the father of her two children, Peter Brown—described as a physically abusive Canadian male, an often-homeless drug addict and petty criminal. Media documents highlight the criminal records of both the father of Fujii's children and the new boyfriend with whom Fujii had her "sex, drug binge" (see van Rassel "Ex-beau Charged"; Semmens B8). The men in her life diminish her claim to good motherhood and good personhood. Fujii strays from the "good mother ideal" in that she is racialized, destitute, non-status, and a single-mother estranged from the father of her children, a father who is a member of the white underclass. Fujii departs from the norm. She is not the "ideal mother" or part of an ideal Canadian family. In a white settler society defined by a racial hierarchy of citizenship (see Razack "When Place" 1-2), Fujii is also not an ideal citizen or an ideal migrant.

All of these elements may have influenced Fujii's relatively harsh eight-year sentence for her conviction in the death of her two children. In contrast, in 2003, 23-year-old Sabrina Milne, a white woman, received a nine-month conditional sentence for the death of her 18-month-old daughter, to be spent at her mother's house. This sentence also came from an Alberta court. The year after Fujii had left her two children alone for ten days, Sabrina Milne performed chores and talked with friends on the telephone while her daughter cried and starved to death (Simons). More recently, also in the province of Alberta, Allyson McConnell was found guilty of two counts of manslaughter in the drowning deaths of her two boys, aged two-and-a-half years and ten months. After serving a ten-month sentence, McConnell, a white Australian citizen who had married a white Canadian, was deported to Australia (Zabjek). Subsequently McConnell was found dead under a bridge near her home north of Sydney from an apparent suicide (Ibrahim). Prior to the killing of the children, both the Milne and McConnell families conformed to constructions of ideal white heterosexual Canadian families.

There is almost no news reporting on the Sabrina Milne case[2] whereas the Rie Fujii case was a spectacle of national proportions. The Allyson McConnell case received a great deal of interest perhaps because McConnell tried to commit suicide by jumping off a bridge onto a highway after she had drowned her two children, and also because of recent public and government interest and parliamentary debates about mental illness and criminal responsibility (Rimke). The McConnell case appears to conform to research that reveals that white heterosexual femininity can more easily mobilize narratives of madness rather than badness, a narrative that can lead to more favourable, neutralizing or at minimum more complex and varied representations and a more lenient sentence.

Prevalent in constructions of the crimes of Rie Fujii is a morality tale of unspeakable evil that was deported and had little to do with us. The dismantling of the welfare state, increased immigration control that places people in vulnerable and exploitable positions, the push and pull factors of global migration, violence against women, and patriarchy in Japan and Canada are issues that are marginalized and privatized. Under a neoliberal framing, violence against women has been privatized and individualized as a victim's rights/or service provision issue, rather than a structural and political issue of concern to all members of society (Beres, Crow and Gottell). In the context of increasing numbers of white economically poor in North America, the continual move toward criminalizing migration and migrants can heighten anti-immigrant/anti-people-of-colour sentiments that are arguably foundational to white settler societies such as Canada (Arat-Koc). The representation of Fujii's crimes as those of a depraved, foreign woman can mask how, as Richie argues, economically susceptible women of colour are "most likely to be in both dangerous intimate relationships and dangerous social positions" (1136). While the vast majority of crimes committed by mothers against their children are individualized, the violence for women of colour is framed in significantly different ways reinforcing racialized, heterosexualized, classed, and misogynist constructions of women, mothers, and citizens.

CONCLUSION

Racialized women in Canada are largely invisible in legal and media formulations of crime and violence. In part, this is due to the dominance of single-cause explanations of violence in legal and public discourse (for example race *or* gender) that can obscure the context in which racialized women experience, perpetrate, respond, and are susceptible to violence (Volpp 1200-1201). The majority of scholarship on racialized women and violence in Canada is limited to examinations of heterosexual violence within racialized communities, or on what racialized men and boys do to racialized women and girls (Jiwani *Discourses* chapter 5). In western judicial and public discourse, the cause of the violence of the Other is the collective cultural and religious difference of their communities and nations (Volpp 1187; Mohanty; Jiwani *Discourses* 205-206). Absent in these formulations where violence is seen as resulting from the misogyny of "traditional," non-western, less democratic men, cultures, and nation-states are structural considerations regarding the violence systemic to white settler nation-building, global migration, capitalism, and everyday and structural forms of racism and sexism (Jiwani "Walking a Tightrope" 852).

By analyzing the criminalization of Rie Fujii, this chapter has explored how conditions for violence against and by racialized mothers are facilitated by gendered racism, the dismantling of the welfare state, and nationalist and neoliberal sentiments justifying the criminalization of Others. Feminist criminology is credited with revealing how women's pathways to crime differ from those of men: incarcerated women and girls have significantly higher rates of physical and sexual abuse than incarcerated men (Comack). The framing of the victimization/criminalization nexus as limited to histories of physical and sexual abuse, however, may reduce our understanding of how gendered racism and the neoliberal dismantling of the welfare state facilitate the conditions for violence against and by racialized women. According to Wortley, evidence suggests that racialized women in North America experience higher rates of hate crimes than racialized men, as well as higher rates of domestic violence and sexual assault than middle and upper-class white women (108). The relations of power that inform Wortley's statement cannot be adequately examined unless one accounts for a more intersectional and structural analysis of crime and criminalization. Adding to this work, this chapter highlighted how race, gender, class, sexuality, nation, and economy shaped criminalizing motherhood in the case of Rie Fujii.

ENDNOTES

[1]Vandenberg, Brennan and Chesney-Lind contend that there are only five studies that examine the disparate ways that white female offenders and women of colour female offenders are represented in mainstream media. All of the studies focus on United States newspapers and television shows (48-49). In the Canadian context the vast majority of work that examines non-white female offenders focuses exclusively on Indigenous women (see McGill; Fontaine). Since Indigenous women have a unique colonial relationship to the state and white settler colonialism, this paper examines issues specific to racialized non-Indigenous women.
[2]A *LexisNexis* search revealed a total of ten newspaper articles on Sabrina Milne.

WORK CITED

Arat-Koc, Sedef. "New Whiteness(es), Beyond the Colour Line?: Assessing the Contradictions and Complexities of "Whiteness" in the (Geo)political Economy of Capitalist Globalism." *States of Race: Critical Race Feminism for the 21st Century*. Ed. Sherene Razack, Malinda Smith and Sunera Thobani. Toronto: Between the Lines, 2010. 147-168. Print.

Balfour, Gillian. "Re-imagining a Feminist Criminology." *Canadian Journal of Criminology and Criminal Justice* 48.5 (2006): 735-752. Print.

Barnett, Barbara. "Medea in the Media: Narrative and Myth in Newspaper Coverage of Women Who Kill their Children." *Journalism* 7.4 (2006): 411-432. Print.

Beres, Melanie A., Barbara Crow, and Lise Gotell. "The Perils of Institutionalization in Neoliberal Times: Results of a National

Survey of Canadian Sexual Assault and Rape Crisis Centres." *Canadian Journal of Sociology* 34.1 (2009): 135-163. Print.

Bond-Maupin, Lisa. "'That Wasn't Even Me They Showed': Women as Criminals on America's Most Wanted." *Violence Against Women* 4.1 (1998): 30-44. Print.

Braid, Don. "Troubled Mother Given Second Chance to Turn Life Around." *Calgary Herald* 22 Aug. 2003: A3. Print.

Braunmühl, Caroline. *Colonial Discourse and Gender in U.S. Criminal Courts: Cultural Defenses and Prosecutions.* New York: Routledge, 2012. Print.

Brennan, Pauline K. and Vandenberg, Abby L. "Depictions of Female Offenders in Front-Page Newspaper Stories: The Importance of Race/Ethnicity." *International Journal of Social Inquiry* 2.2 (2009): 141-175. Print.

Burfoot, Annette and Susan Lord, ed. *Killing Women: The Visual Culture of Gender and Violence.* Waterloo: Wilfrid Laurier University Press, 2006. Print.

Carney, Sarah. "Representations of Race and Social Responsibility: News Stories about Neglect and Failure to Protect." *Off White: Readings on Power, Privilege and Resistance.* 2nd ed. Ed. Michelle Fine, Loise Weis, Linda Powell Pruitt and April Burns. New York: Routledge, 2004. 186-205. Print.

Chan, Wendy. "Crime, Deportation and the Regulation of Immigrants." *Crime, Law and Social Change* 44.2 (2005): 153-180. Print.

Chesney-Lind, Meda and Michele Eliason. "From Invisible to Incorrigible: The Demonization of Marginalized Women and Girls." *Crime, Media, Culture* 2.1 (2006): 29-47. Print.

Clow, Kimberley A., James M. Lant and Brian L. Cutler. "Perceptions of Defendant Culpability in Pretrial Publicity: The Effects of Defendant Ethnicity and Participant Gender." *Race and Social Problems* 5.4 (2013): 250-261. Print.

Comack, Elizabeth. "The Feminist Engagement with Criminology." *Criminalizing Women.* Ed. Gillian Balfour and Elizabeth Comack. Halifax: Fernwood, 2014. 12-46. Print.

Comack, Elizabeth and Salena Brickey. "Constituting the Violence of Criminalized Women." *Canadian Journal of Criminology and Criminal Justice* 48.5 (2007): 1-36. Print.

Doyle, Aaron and Richard V. Ericson. "Breaking in Prison: News Sources and Correctional Institutions." *Canadian Journal of Criminology* 38.2 (1996): 155-190. Print.

Dua, Enakshi and Angela Robertson, ed. *Scratching the Surface: Canadian Anti-Racist Feminist Thought*. Toronto: Women's Press, 1999. Print.

Fine, Michelle. "The Breast and the State: An Analysis of Good and Bad Nipples by Gender, Race, and Class." *Studies in Gender and Sexuality* 11.1 (2010): 24-32. Print.

Fontaine, Nahanni. "Surviving Colonization: Anishinaabe Ikwe Gang Participation." *Criminalizing Women*. Ed. Gillian Balfour and Elizabeth Comack. Halifax: Fernwood, 2014. 113-129. Print.

Heer, Jeet. "Introduction." *"Too Asian?" Racism, Privilege and Post-secondary Education*. Ed. R. J. Gilmour, Davina Bhandar, Jeet Heer and Michael C. K. Ma. Toronto: Between the Lines, 2012. 1-13. Print.

Huckerby, Jayne. "Women Who Will Their Children: Case Study and Conclusions Concerning the Differences in the Fall from Maternal Grace by Khoua Her and Andrea Yates." *Duke Journal of Gender Law & Policy* 10 (2003): 149-172. Print.

Ibrahim, Mariam. "Mother Who Killed Sons Takes Own Life." *National Post* 19 Sept. 2013: A7. Print.

Irving, Toni. "Decoding Black Women: Policing Practices and Rape Prosecution on the Streets of Philadelphia." *NWSA Journal* 20.2(2008): 100-20. Print.

"Japanese mother who left children to die is deported." *The Globe and Mail* 11 May 2006: A12. Print.

Jiwani, Yasmin. *Discourses of Denial: Mediations of Race, Gender and Violence*. Vancouver: University of British Columbia Press, 2007. Print.

Jiwani, Yasmin. "Walking a Tightrope: The Many Faces of Violence in the Lives of Racialized Immigrant Girls and Young Women," *Violence Against Women* 11.7 (2005): 846-887. Print.

Kramar, Kirsten Johnson. *Unwilling Mothers, Unwanted Babies: Infanticide in Canada*. Vancouver: University of British Columbia Press, 2005. Print.

Kruttschnitt, Candace and Carbone-Lopez, Kristin. "Moving Beyond the Stereotypes: Women's Subjective Accounts of their

Violent Crime." *Criminology* 44.2 (2006): 321-351. Print.

Mackey, Eva. *The House of Difference: Cultural Politics and National Identity in Canada.* New York: Routledge, 1999. Print.

McGill, Jena. "An Institutional Suicide Machine: Discrimination against Federally Sentenced Aboriginal Women in Canada." *Race/Ethnicity: Multidisciplinary Global Contexts* 2.1 (2008): 89-119. Print.

Minaker, Joanne C. "Review of When Mothers Kill: Interviews From Prison." *Journal of the Motherhood Initiative* 3.1 (2012): 275-276. Print.

Minaker, Joanne C. "Sluts and Slags: The Censuring of the Erring Female." *Criminalizing Women: Gender and (In)justice in Neo-Liberal Times*. Ed. Gillian Balfour and Elizabeth Comack. Halifax: Fernwood, 2014. 73-91. Print.

Mohanty Chandra Talpade. "'Under Western Eyes' Revisited: Feminist Solidarity Through Anticapitalist Struggles." *Signs* 28.2(2002): 499-535. Print.

"Mom on sex, drug binge 'left babies to die.'" *Vancouver Sun* 21 Jun. 2002: A4. Print.

Morrissey, Belinda. *When Women Kill: Questions of Agency and Subjectivity*. New York: Routledge, 2003. Print.

"Nature of the crime: A mother who allows her children to die is not necessarily insane." *Calgary Herald* September 10, 2002: A18. Print.

Oberman, Michelle and Cheryl L. Meyer. *When Mothers Kill: Interviews from Prison*. New York: New York University Press, 2008. Print.

Park, Hijin. "Interracial Violence, Western Racialized Masculinities and the Geopolitics of Violence against Women." *Social & Legal Studies* 21.4 (2012): 491-509. Print.

Pieters, Gary and Scot Wortley. *Race and Justice in Toronto. 2013-2014 Justice in Toronto Lecture Series*. Sponsored by the Global Cities Institute, University of Toronto. January 30, 2014. Public Lecture.

Pratt, Anna. *Securing Borders: Detention and Deportation in Canada*. Vancouver: University of British Columbia Press, 2005. Print.

R. v. Fujii. Court of Queen's Bench of Alberta 805. Judicial District of Calgary, 016819476Q1, 2002.

Razack, Sherene. "Abandonment and the Dance of Race and Bureaucracy in Spaces of Exception." *States of Race: Critical Race Feminism for the 21st Century*. Ed. Sherene Razack, Malinda Smith and Sunera Thobani. Toronto: Between the Lines, 2010. 87-107. Print.

Razack, Sherene. "When Place Becomes Race." *Race, Space and the Law: Unmapping a White Settler Society*. Ed. Sherene H. Razack. Toronto: Between the Lines, 2002. 1-20. Print.

Richie, Beth. "A Black Feminist Reflection on the Antiviolence Movement. *Signs* 25 (2000): 1133-1137. Print.

Rimke, Heidi. "Beheading Aboard a Greyhound Bus: Security Politics, Bloodlust Justice, and the Mass Consumption of Criminalized Cannibalism." *The Annual Review of Interdisciplinary Justice Research* 1 (2010): 172-192. Print.

Rudrappa, Sharmila. "Madness, Diasporic Difference, and State Violence: Explaining Filicide in American Courts." *Cultural Dynamics* 19.2/3 (2007): 257–277. Print.

Semmens, Grady. "Dead Children's Dad Heads Back to Jail." *Calgary Herald* 8 Sept. 2001: B8. Print.

Sheehy, Elizabeth A. *Defending Battered Women on Trial: Lessons from the Transcripts*. Vancouver: University of British Columbia Press, 2014. Print.

Simons, Paula. "Mikado Could Teach us About Punishments that Fit the Crime." *Edmonton Journal* 8 Feb. 2003: B1. Print.

Sjoberg, Laura and Caron E. Gentry. *Mothers, Monsters, Whores: Women's Violence in Global Politics*. New York: Zed Books, 2007. Print.

Slade, Daryl. "Mother Partied While Babies Died." *Calgary Herald* 21 Jun. 2002: A1. Print.

Slade, Daryl. "Mother Left Children to Starve: Babies Alone for 10 days While Woman Spent Time with Boyfriend." *The National Post* 21 Jun. 2002: A7. Print.

Strega, Susan, Julia Krane and Rosemary Carlton. "G-d Couldn't be Everywhere so he Created Mothers: The Impossible Mandate of Maternal Protection in Child Welfare." *Failure to Protect: Moving Beyond Gendered Responses*. Eds. Susan Strega, Julia Krane, Simon Lapierre, Cathy Richardson, and Rosemary Carlton Halifax: Fernwood Press, 2013. 11-29. Print.

Surette, Ray. *Media, Crime and Criminal Justice*. 4th edition. Belmont, CA: Wadsworth Publishing, 2010. Print.

Thobani, Sunera. *Exalted Subjects: Studies in the Making of Race and Nation in Canada*. Toronto: University of Toronto Press, 2007. Print.

van Rassel, Jason. "Child Killer Denied Parole." *Calgary Herald*. 4, Jun. 2004: B1. Print.

van Rassel, Jason. "Child Killer's Ex-beau Charged with Robbery." *Calgary Herald*. 9 Apr. 2003: B1. Print.

van Rassel, Jason. "Witness Sought in Woman's Death." *Calgary Herald*. 26 Feb. 2004: B13. Print.

Vandenbeld Giles, Melinda. "From 'Need' to 'Risk': The Neoliberal Construction of the 'Bad' Mother." *Journal of the Motherhood Initiative* 3.1 (2012): 112-133. Print.

Vandenberg, Abby L., Pauline K. Brennan and Meda Chesney-Lind. "What's the Story? The Impact of Race/Ethnicity on Crime Story Tone for Female Offenders." *Perceptions of Female Offenders: How Stereotypes and Social Norms Affect Criminal Justice Responses*. Ed. Brenda L. Russell. New York: Springer: New York, 2013. 47-75. Print.

Volpp Leti. "Feminism versus Multiculturalism." *Colombia Law Review* 101 (2001): 1181-1218. Print.

Weber, Bob. "Mother's parole plea refused." *Toronto Star* 4 Jun. 2004: A21. Print.

Wilcox, Paula. "Beauty and the Beast: Gendered and Raced Discourse in the News." *Social & Legal Studies* 14.4 (2005): 515–532. Print.

Wortley, Scott. "Hidden Intersections: Research on Race, Crime, and Criminal Justice in Canada." *Canadian Ethnic Studies* 35.3 (2003): 99-117. Print.

Zabjek, Alexandra. "'I Was Actually a Very Loving Mother'; Killer Allyson McConnell Won't Rule Out Having More Children." *Edmonton Journal* 29 Apr. 2013: A3. Print.

8.
Legal and Medical Maneuvers

The Attitude of the Legal and Medical Systems to Ellen Harper Who Murdered her Infant Daughter in 1878

TAMAR HAGER

> Ellen Harper stands charged before the undersigned one of Her Majesty's justices of the Peace for the said County of Somerset, this thirtieth day of October in the year of our Lord one thousand eight hundred and seventy seven for that the said Ellen Harper on Wiveliscombe in the County of Somerset aforesaid feloniously willfully and of her malice aforethought did kill and murder a certain infant female child born of her body of the said Ellen Harper and of tender age, to wit, of the age of twelve hours or thereabout and not named. (National Archives, Harper)

I DISCOVERED THIS INDICTMENT at the British National Archives in Kew Gardens, London. I was there to search for stories of mothers who had murdered their children in Victorian England as part of the research for a book I was writing. The book dealt with the complex and changing image of "bad mothers" and the interests of the social institutions that created, transformed, or maintained this image.

The research originated from the time my twin daughters, Naomi and Shira, were born and I confronted what Adrienne Rich has termed "the institution of motherhood," the range of societal expectations which restrict women's movements and freedom, and ensure male control over their attitudes towards reproduction and towards their children (Rich 13, 14). Rich called for the abolition of patriarchal motherhood, which will lead to anti-sexist childrearing, challenging the traditional practices of gender socialization for sons and daughters. However, Andrea O'Reilly rightfully claims that Rich's descriptions and the depictions of most feminist activists and scholars of alternative, feminist-empowered models of motherhood are centered on the assumption that new maternal ways will first and foremost benefit the children, while the mothers' benefits are not taken into account (O'Reilly 327). O'Reilly argues that, based on the assumption that patriarchal culture will accord mothers resources if they use them on behalf of children, most feminist campaigns and research are still trapped in the patriarchal logic in which mothers are not free agents, but exist for the sake of their own children. My research intended to explore this patriarchal trap by looking into how the legal and medical systems contributed to its formation in a certain historical and cultural context.

Rich and other feminist researchers have pointed to the Victorian era as a significant period in the characterization of the role of motherhood that controls our mindset so effectively even today (see for example Forna 34-42; Gillis 152-178; Silva Bortolaia 10-36; Shuttleworth 31-51; O'Reilly 323-330). I hoped that in the legal documents about the murder of children, I would find echoes of the evolvement of this social role. The story of Ellen indeed reflects the change in the perception of motherhood. It exposes the contradiction between the written law, which perpetuated the past, and the actual attitude of the courts and of the medical establishment towards mothers who had murdered their children.

Until 1803, the crime of infanticide was tried in England under an act of 1624 that defined the offense as one committed specifically by an unmarried woman (Jackson 5-6; Emsley 156-157). It placed the responsibility on the accused, with the support of at least one witness, to prove that a dead infant had been born dead. Concealment of death was taken as evidence of murder and resulted in conviction and hanging. By the middle of the eighteenth century, the act was increasingly perceived as cruel, and trials of infanticide were turned by juries into murder trials in which the prosecution was required to prove that an offence had been committed rather than the other way around.

The *Act of Lord Ellenborough* in 1803 formalized this state of affairs, henceforth considering infanticide like any other murder, a criminal charge punishable by the death penalty (Marland, "Getting Away" 170). However, during the Victorian era, the courts avoided convicting mothers who committed infanticide. Several witnesses before the 1866 Royal Commission on Capital Punishment testified that juries were reluctant to convict as long as the death sentence remained. Court records show that counsellors, juries, and judges developed ways to bypass the law, cooperating with medical institutions when physicians and alienists were willing to collaborate (Smith 146-147; Ross 187; Oberman 10-11; Jackson 1-17; Marland, "Getting Away" 170). In this paper, I will analyze how the legal and medical systems behaved in the case of Ellen Harper, a mother who confessed to killing her child. What legal and medical maneuverings were used to save her from the hangman's noose?

MICROHISTORY AS A FORM OF ANALYSIS

Historians like Carlo Ginzburg, Natalie Zemon Davis, Giovanni Levi and Margaret Arnot have already demonstrated the value of microhistory (Ginzburg xx-xxiv; Zemon Davis VIII; Levi 95 and 106; Arnot, "The Murder" 149). Microhistory reduces the scale of observation to the microscopic analysis and intensive study of documentary material (Levi 95). Departing from a particular case, it proceeds to identify the meaning of this case in light of its specific context.

Employing a reflexive narrative, the historian incorporates the procedures, limits, and uncertainty of research itself into the story, making her (in this case my) point of view an intrinsic part of the account. "The research process is explicitly described and the limitations of documentary evidence, the formulations of hypotheses and the lines of thought followed are no longer hidden away.... The reader is involved in a sort of dialogue and participates in the whole process of constructing the historical argument" (Levi 106).

As most microhistorians, I start my reading and interpretation of Ellen's Harper depositions with details that don't fit either in the stories the witnesses tell or in the sequence of their narrative. These concrete details, personal experiences, or events—the micro level—are analyzed and interpreted by using data accumulated by social, legal, and medical histories—the macro level (Peltonen 359).

This way of history-writing breaks with the traditional assertive, authoritarian form of discourse adopted by many historians (for the traditional form of histories on infanticide see Jackson; Rose; Higginbotham; Chadwick). In addition, in so doing, microhistory breaks with the traditional dichotomy between factual history and fiction, foregrounding the view that every recreation of history is a form of factually based fiction. Following Michel Foucault I am aware that a historical text is a construct, a fiction, but I agree with him that, "the possibility exists for fiction to function in truth" (Foucault, 193).

My intention in writing microhistory, however, extends beyond the aim of microhistorians of crime, to uncover a possible "piece of social history" (Arnot, "The Murder" 149, 167). For me, this is also a political choice. Being a feminist writer, I follow the anthropologist Ruth Behar who declares "that how we plot ourselves into our fictions has everything to do with how we plot ourselves into our lives" (Behar 15). Living in a world where women's lives, their histories, their struggles, their ideas constitute no part of dominant science, I find it difficult to identify an adequate model for writing the story of Ellen Harper who committed infanticide (Mies 66). It seems inappropriate to me to recover Ellen's story using the traditional model of history writing. Attempting to take part in the project of feminist history, I follow Joan W. Scott who declared that just adding women to an existing body of stories is not sufficient. As a feminist historian I wanted to change "the way the stories would be told" (Scott 10). Microhistory accordingly lends itself as the correct form for political and ideological reasons.

My detailed analysis of Ellen's legal and medical documents in the context of social and legal histories that cite other cases of infanticide suggests that gender, class, personal status, and position in the community all combined to determine the conduct of the police, the medical court, and the medical profession towards the accused. It also reveals the way social agents distributed, circulated and maintained the mind-sets that supported their intricate interests and agenda.

Moreover, whereas most histories of infanticide attempt at generalizing legal and medical norms and conventions concerning infanticide, my micro-analysis shows how these norms came into practice in one specific case, thus illuminating specific methods used by particular counsellors, juries, judges, physicians, and alienists. I do not intend to argue however, that Ellen Harper's story is proof of the attitudes of the legal and medical systems in England towards the murder of children. What I do present here is a possible social and political reading of the legal and medical events.

However like most microhistories, my reading of these events illustrates the function of the formal institutions in power and how they handle people's affairs. The detailed analysis of a particular story provides a comprehensive description of social and political procedures of control and oppression exerted on mothers living on the social margin. Thus, this story "has much wider application, going well beyond the specific case under examination" (Magnusson 710). At the end of the chapter, I apply some essential conclusions that can be drawn from Ellen's story to the way contemporary legal and medical institutions treat mothers who have committed infanticide.

ELLEN HARPER'S STORY

Ellen Harper was 17 when she murdered her infant daughter. She was the wife of George Harper and resided with her husband in the city of Weston-super-Mare in Somerset, England. The Civil Registration Index, the UK censuses, and the legal depositions disclose that in September, the month she married, already in an advanced stage of pregnancy, she returned to the town of Langley Marsh, to the home of her grandparents, James and Sarah Quick, in order to bear her child there.[1] She had formerly lived in that poverty-stricken home (her grandfather was an unskilled worker) until the age of eight or nine, when she had left to become a servant. She gave birth on 13 October 1877 between seven and eight in the morning. After being present at the birth, her grandmother hurried to call the midwife, Elizabeth Treble, who cut the umbilical cord, and treated the infant and mother. Twelve hours later the infant was dead (National Archives, Harper).

At first, Ellen tried to deny responsibility for the murder. She told the midwife, her aunt, Elizabeth Quick, and her grandmother,

Sarah Quick, who were at her bedside, that perhaps she had unintentionally done it with her arms. However, they quickly rejected this possibility. She tried to prevent the midwife from calling for a doctor. When this failed as well, she tried to convince them to use powder to hide the three red marks that could be seen on the baby's neck. In her testimony the midwife reported that when the doctor, John Watt Pratt, arrived, Ellen complained to him that the baby had died because no doctor had been there.[2] Dr. Pratt examined the body of the infant and determined that it died of strangling, but not Ellen, nor anyone else was charged with murder.

Eight days later, Ellen wrote to Dr. Pratt, asking him to come to her grandfather's home. When he arrived, she insisted on telling him how the signs had appeared on the infant's neck.

> I told you in that the child seemed choked, didn't I Sir, but I didn't tell you what I did to it. I had the child Sir in my arms.... Then Sir I took it up something came across me. It was a horrible thought. Then sir I wrapped the cloths around it quite tight ... and I laid it back in bed. I don't know what made me do it and I turned round on my side sir ... and then I turned round again and looked at the child and I saw its lips are purple.... I unwrapped it—then it had something making a noise in its throat.... Then sir it was quiet.... Then ... I heard a noise in its throat again and then I called [mother] and then sir when she came up the baby was gone. That's all Sir. It seemed as if it wanted to cry and couldn't sir.[3] (National Archives, Harper)

The investigation of the death by the police of Wiveliscombe, the town adjacent to Langley Marsh, apparently took three days, and was partially conducted in the presence of the dead baby's body. The inquest included jurors and witnesses and was administered by the regional coroner William Weber Munckton Esq. and the magistrate Arthur Capel Esq. who collected the evidence.[4] Five statements were assembled, all by the prosecution: from the midwife, Elizabeth Treble; from Ellen's grandmother, Sarah Quick; from Ellen's aunt, Elizabeth Quick; from the doctor, and birth and death registrar, John Watt Pratt; and from the police inspector,

John Ross. The process ended with the following words written on the back of the statements: "Verdict: Willful murder against Ellen Harper." The indictment was then written and Ellen was remanded until trial (National Archives, Harper).

REFUSAL TO CONVICT

Ellen Harper's act was not out of the ordinary. Infanticide was well-known in England during the nineteenth century. "Contemporary authors ... between 1840 and 1880 ... almost unanimously agreed that there had been a considerable increase in infanticide, and limited statistical evidence further suggests a rise at mid-century (Sauer quoted in Robinson 166). In the 1860s and 1870s, panic was aroused when two coroners in London joined forces with journalists to call attention to the widespread murder of children. The argument was that infant death statistics proved that murder was a common event. This was reinforced by the rise in the number of reports of infant bodies found in alleyways and in forests. According to one of the estimations, infants under the age of one, who constituted three percent of the English population between 1863 and 1887, comprised sixty percent of the murder victims (Robinson 166; Ross 187; Higginbotham 319-37; Smart 16; Ward "Legistlating" 253-255).

Elaine Showalter and Roger Chadwick point out that infanticides were rare in middle class homes, where nursemaids and servants helped mothers care for their offspring, and the frequency of these cases increased among mothers from the lower classes who suffered from poverty, violence, and oppression (Showalter 59; Chadwick 299). Under these conditions, the tensions aroused by childcare were at times unbearable (Oberman 14). Policy-makers, the legal establishment and social reformers represented infanticide as a sign of social breakdown and a threat to the social order (Robinson 166; Smart 16-17; Oberman 13-14). It came to be identified with the practice of female infanticide in the Indian subcontinent discovered by the British some years earlier (Oberman 13; Smart 16). Benjamin Disraeli wrote ironically in his novel *Sybil* in 1845 that "infanticide is practiced as extensively and legally in England as it is on the banks of the Ganges" (Quoted in Rose 36). This comparison, drawn throughout the nineteenth century by policy-makers, legal authorities, and social reformists, was intended to represent the act as heathen and the perpetrator as immoral and un-British (Robinson 166; Smart 16-17).

But it appears that the campaign against child murder was blocked at the gates of the court. Judges and juries refused to cooperate and to show severity when it came to mothers who committed infanticide. Women who had killed their small children were only rarely convicted, and from 1849 onwards the courts refused to convict women who had murdered babies of less than a year old. According to historian Ellen Ross, some of the verdicts from Old Bailey at the end of the nineteenth century freeing mother murderers are striking in their level of disregard for the crime (Ross 187). The courts tended to present these deeds as mishaps, and deaths that took place at home were explained as accidental, or as the will of God. Most of the murder cases did not even reach trial (Rose 70-78; Smith, 146-47; Jackson, 1-17; Chadwick, 292; Arnot "Understanding Women" 56-57; Higginbotham 323; Ward, "Legislating" 255-257).

Historians maintain that what created this policy was the draconian law that determined that conviction meant death (Emsley 157; Ross 187; Marland, "Getting Away" 169; Oberman 14). This penalty did not match social agents' opinions about the act of child murder for a number of reasons. The birthrate was high and there were not enough resources to feed all of the infants who were born (Arnot, "Understanding Women" 59-60). The courts felt that the murdering mothers had done the right thing in saving their infants from dying of hunger or disease later on (Knelman 153). In 1834, the old Poor Law, which had forced the district to assist unwed mothers and which enabled relief to large families with many children, was revoked. The judges and juries thus understood that a significantly worsening economic situation might lead some mothers to murder their children (Smart 17; Rose 70-78).

In addition, the motherhood myth, which was gaining momentum during the nineteenth century among the upper and middle classes, determined that maternal feelings were natural and biological impulses shared by all females. Mothers' sacred mission was to breastfeed and rear children, "to ensure, physically, the healthy reproduction of the race, as well as the spiritual superiority of the middle class" (Shuttleworth 32). Mother's voice, mother's smile and mother's love, her spiritual grace that filled the domestic sphere, became central symbols in Victorian society (Gillis 175). She was presented as the "hearth angel" who created a nest for her children and a refuge for her husband (Forna 37). The maternal instinct, it was believed, would lead a mother to protect her children and even sacrifice herself for them. This affected the attitude of the justice system toward mothers who murdered their infants. Doctors, lawyers, judges and juries, all of whom belonged to the middle class, had internalized the motherhood myth as part of their bourgeois ideology, viewing the child-murdering mother as a deviant creature, a victim of the biology and the psychology of her unstable female nature, a madwoman whose place was in a mental institution rather than in a prison or at the gallows (Marland, "Dangerous Motherhood" 167-182; Smart 16-17; Showalter, 57-59 and 71-72; Smith 150-154; Jackson 10; Chadwick 293-295).

Therefore, when the bills of indictment reached the courts, as in the case of Ellen Harper, the judges and juries preferred to either convict the mothers of concealing the birth, a lesser crime punishable by two years in prison (Jackson 7; Emsley 157; Ross 187; Rose 70-71; Ward, "Legislating" 256), or to acquit them on grounds of insanity (Andrews 216-223; Baker 14; Marland, "Dangerous Motherhood" 178-182). In 1864, the Home Office adopted the policy of advising commutation of the death penalty to imprisonment for all cases in which women were convicted of murdering infants under a year old (Ross 187; Smith 147). Only in rare cases were women who had killed children of any age punished by hanging (Chadwick 292; Arnot, "The Murder" 170).

Considering these legal proceedings, the case of Ellen Harper proved problematic. Her profile—a young woman who had just gotten married, who had not concealed her pregnancy or the coming birth of a child and who had murdered her first child immediately after birth, did not fit the accepted profile of mothers who had been indicted. Historians such as Margaret Arnot, Ann R. Higginbotham, and Lionel Rose have found that women who had reached the courts had generally been unwed mothers who wanted to hide their pregnancy because of the impossible economic realities of unmarried parenthood; poor mothers who had to care for large families and for whom another mouth to feed meant economic disaster; and especially mothers who had murdered children of more than a year old (Andrews 219-223; Higginbotham 320-324; Knelman 124-138 and 150-151). None of these matched Ellen's story.

Moreover, Ellen had given birth in the community where she belonged, in Langley Marsh. Historians indicate the fact that, very often, the family, the midwives, the doctors, and the police cooperated in order to hide the death of an infant and to prevent the mother from going to trial (Perkin 181; Rose 85-92; Chadwick 292). Further, in the case of Ellen, an indictment would not have been submitted if she had not confessed. Examining the two instances—the inquest and the trial—indicates that the representatives of the legal system actually made every effort to acquit Ellen.

THE INQUEST: "WILLFUL MURDER"

Already during the inquest there were reports of continuing unsuccessful attempts by the participants to prevent an indictment.[5] The doctor told the clerk of the peace that he had made three attempts to convince Ellen not to confess to him. "I told her she would be very unwise to state anything to me that would be injurious to her and that if she had anything on her mind that she wished to have advance upon I would request the clergyman of the parish to meet her" (National Archives, Harper). Ellen insisted on telling him the story and Dr. Pratt tried again to stop her. This time he stated that whatever she said to him, he would be compelled to report further. And when she continued: "I then again begged her not to say anything that would be injurious to her" (National Archives, Harper).

The doctor was surprisingly candid when describing his attempt to help a murderer avoid punishment and the clerk of the peace did not see anything wrong with that. The opposite was true; he reported this to the court. It appears that Dr. Pratt intended to show the clerk that he had been trying to prevent any discomfort to the court which might be created by Ellen's confession. The clerk presented this testimony for the same reason—to show that efforts had been made to prevent the case from reaching trial.

The clerk himself initiated such an attempt. In Ellen's grandmother's deposition, the following report appears: "The prisoner came to me a month before she was confined. She brought with her a quantity of very good baby linen.... I had [indecipherable word] to Mrs. Treble the midwife from a fortnight to three weeks before the prisoner was confined" (National Archives, Harper). These sentences, which stray from the chronological story, were certainly answers to questions which had been posed by the clerk. Historian Olwen Hufton argues that juries tended to acquit women who proved that they had been preparing for the birth (Hufton 273). Perhaps these sentences answered the standard question of whether Ellen had been planning for a birth, a question which stemmed from the court's obligation to acquit women who had been behaving normally when the baby was born.

The fact that Dr. Pratt related to the possibility that Ellen had killed her baby as a result of insanity, puerperal mania, apparently resulted from the same obligation. In those years, insanity was the common and preferred interpretation by the courts in cases of child murder. It was described as a mental aberration caused by giving birth. "A woman suffering from puerperal mania" explained Dr. Pratt, "would not be accountable for what she did" (National Archives, Harper). However, the doctor concluded that Ellen was not suffering from insanity.

> When I saw the prisoner on the evening of the day in which she was confined, I asked her how she was—she said she was very well. I next saw the Prisoner with the coroner on the following Wednesday. I enquired after her health she said she was very well.... When the prisoner made the statement to me on the 21st she appeared calm. There were no symptoms at all of puerperal mania. Her making the statement did not appear to me as a symptom that she was not a sane person. (National Archives, Harper)

The way Ellen had acted did not fit the accepted description of puerperal mania. In the eyes of contemporaries, women with puerperal mania were indifferent to the usual conventions of politeness and decorum in speech, dress, and behaviour. Sometimes, their behaviour was described as explicitly sexual, and in other cases, they were characterized as severely depressed and often suicidal. Ellen was not indifferent to the accepted norms of behaviour, speech and dress, and she did not act in a very sexual way nor was she severely depressed (Showalter 58-29; Marland, "Dangerous Motherhood" 9-64). The opposite was true; her polite answers to the concerned questions of the doctor proved that she was aware of the social codes of her status and her gender.

Doctor Pratt's conclusion could be explained in one of two ways. First he suspected that Ellen had murdered the infant in a state of temporary insanity, but chose to hide this from the clerk in order to save her from being committed to a mental asylum. In 1865, Alfred Swaine Taylor wrote about Broadmoor, the institution Ellen Harper was ultimately sent to: "Those who have been acquitted of murder on the ground of insanity, after having once entered this establishment, are as dead to the world as if the earth had closed over them" (1098). Second, which seems to me more reasonable, Dr. Pratt was willing to prevent Ellen's conviction as long as he was not required to breach his professional ethics. Just as he reported Ellen's confession, (because as a doctor he was obligated to do so even if it would cause embarrassment to the court) so too was he unwilling to present a diagnosis in contradiction to his professional judgment. His decision against insanity could be supported by the fact that puerperal insanity was an elusive disorder (Marland, "Dangerous Motherhood" 28-64).

But it was not only the testimony of the doctor that determined Ellen's guilt in the first proceedings but also the deposition of the midwife, Elizabeth Treble. In order to remove any suspicion from her, the midwife stressed Ellen's responsibility for the infant's death.[6] She cited the fact that Ellen had feared the child's death, but because she had shown affection for her daughter, there had been no previous sign that she might behave violently. Treble also reported that after the death of the infant, Ellen had asked her to conceal the marks with a bit of powder, but she had refused to comply. The inquest ended with the verdict: "Willful murder against Ellen Harper" (National Archives, Harper).

THE TRIAL: "ACQUITTAL ON THE GROUNDS OF INSANITY"

At the trial, which took place at Exeter Castle in Devon on 15 January 1878, Ellen was acquitted on the grounds of insanity. This verdict was contrary to the inquest decision of premeditated murder while contradicting Dr. Pratt's assessment of her sanity.[7]

The trial took place before the judge, Sir John Mellor.[8] The prosecutors were Mr. Spike and Mr. Broadmede and the defence counsel was Mr. Bailey who was probably appointed by the judge on the day of the trial from among the young lawyers sitting in the courtroom, as in other cases of poor defendants (Bentley 105-130). Bailey examined the witnesses according to the depositions collected for the coroner's inquest and thus, no new details were added. Nevertheless, the defence attorney and the judge created a new reading of the facts of the case and offered a different explanation than the one given by the inquest report. Their interpretation better-suited the judicial policy of acquitting mothers who had murdered their children.

In his closing speech, Bailey reminded the jurors that a guilty verdict would mean the death penalty for Ellen and he requested that they take that into consideration. He stressed that Ellen's behavior—the return home to give birth, bringing undergarments for the infant, the announcement to the midwife of the impending birth, her fondness for the infant, and more—showed that she did not want to murder her daughter. But, argued Bailey, following the hasty birth, she had been carried away in an attack of hallucinations known as puerperal mania and had harmed her child. The local newspaper reported that this medical diagnosis, which had contradicted the assessment of Dr. Pratt, who was present in the courtroom, was put forward unequivocally, despite the fact that Ellen's behaviour had not been consistent with any of the definitions of insanity.

Bailey's act was not uncommon. Doctor John Baker, Deputy Superintendent of Broadmoor, who in 1902 published a report on the conditions of female patients in Broadmoor relates to a similar phenomenon: "...the lawyers are more than ready to accept a plea of insanity, pity inspires both judge and jury, and the opinion of the expert is not often required in evidence" (Baker 15). Smith and Marland claim that testimonies of friends, neighbours, and passers-by as to the women's state of mind were considered as valid as the evidence of a medical expert (Smith 148-149; Marland, "Getting Away" 181).

Bailey maintained that the murder had not been a logical act, considering the fact that Ellen was young and was married, and therefore had no reason to feel guilty or ashamed at the birth of her first born child. Her quick confession, he claimed, was another proof that she had committed the murder due to an uncontrollable urge. Bailey claimed that the midwife had acted irresponsibly when leaving Ellen for such a long period after the birth without the professional care she had needed. The *Devon Weekly Times* conveyed that at this stage, members of the jury applauded him by crying "Hear, hear" ("The Alleged Child Murder"). When requesting that she be acquitted on the grounds of insanity, "his speech was greeted with loud applause from the body of the Court. It was, however, speedily suppressed, and His Lordship threatened if a repetition occurred to clear the Court" ("The Alleged Child Murder").

Bailey had done several things in his speech: he had aroused the sympathy of the jurors for Ellen who would have had to die if she had been convicted. He had drawn a portrait of a devoted mother who had been stricken, and he had determined indisputably and in contradiction to the decision of an expert that here was a case of insanity. He also pointed an accusatory finger at the midwife when he declared that such a young woman should not have been left alone on the day she had given birth.

But what also helped the jurors to decide was the apparent agreement of the judge with Bailey's line of defence. In accordance with research of historian Hilary Marland, Mellor's position was common, as judges usually preferred verdicts of insanity in cases in which mothers had killed their children ("Getting Away" 178-182). Expressing "his disapprobation" of Bailey's effort to influence the jury's verdict by asking its members to consider the consequences of a conviction, Mellor made a similar attempt. He declared that, in his experience, no mother who had murdered her child in similar circumstances had been executed for many years. His statement, which determined indirectly that even if

Ellen was convicted, she would not be hung, clearly presented the court policy of being lenient with crimes of this sort (Ross, 187; Rose 70-78; Smith 146-47; Jackson 1-17; Chadwick, 292; Arnot, "Understanding Women" 56-57).

The Western Times declared that Mellor had also affirmed the sympathetic attitude towards Ellen—"an unfortunate woman with whom everyone must sympathize on at such an age in such circumstances"—and avoided objecting when Bailey boldly declared that Ellen was insane, in contradiction to the expert's medical diagnosis ("The Alleged Child Murder"). Furthermore, he supported Bailey's interpretation of insanity by determining that the murder was illogical considering Ellen's circumstances. He also partially affirmed the accusation of the midwife when asserting that she should have visited Ellen during the afternoon.

Mellor, who indirectly supported the points made by the defence counsel, described Ellen as a woman worthy of pity who was not responsible for her deeds: She was young; she was an unfortunate; someone should have taken care of her, the midwife or her grandmother. This image of Ellen corresponded to the common view of Victorian womanhood. The historians Tony Ward, Sally Shuttleworth and Hilary Marland claim that women were seen as frail creatures, dominated by their reproductive systems, which were a source of anarchic disruption and potential violence (Ward, "The Sad Subject" 165, Shuttleworth 37, Marland, "Dangerous Motherhood" 20). Childbirth was viewed as a traumatic experience and a woman giving birth was generally considered "hysterical" and prone to "what amounts almost to temporary madness" (Royal Commission, 1866 Q. 2193 quoted in Ward, "The Sad Subject" 165-166). The Home Office in deciding how long those reprieved from execution should stay in prison accepted that immediately after birth, a woman was "hardly to be said to be in her right senses" (quoted by Ward, "The Sad Subject" 166). Socio-economic pressures were also considered relevant to infanticide and were perceived as another source of overwhelming tension and stress (Andrews 222, Ward, "The Sad Subject" 176). According to Ward the boundaries between psychological and social pressures were not clear cut ("The Sad Subject" 165). In fact, the portrait woven by Mellor and Bailey and presented to the jury, and which led to

Ellen's acquittal on the grounds of insanity, fits the accepted image of this type of criminality in the courts from the Victorian era until the present. It has been defined by sociologist Rose Pearson as "neither mad nor bad but 'sad'" (Pearson quoted in Ward, "The Sad Subject" 176).

Various agents of the legal system whose Victorian sentiments obliged them to be merciful in their punishment of women who had murdered their children, made every effort to save her from conviction. The line of defence created a positive profile of Ellen, contradicting a medical opinion of her mental condition, and it pointed an accusatory finger towards the midwife. The jurors supported Treble's vilification seemingly because it was easier to identify with Ellen, a young suffering woman who according to *The Devon Weekly Times* sat without moving, her face buried in a handkerchief, rather than with a woman who only wanted to save her professional reputation ("The Alleged Child Murder").

HOSPITALIZATION: AN IRRATIONAL KILLER

Ellen's assumed insanity in the judicial maneuvering turned into a positive medical fact when she arrived at Broadmoor, an asylum for the criminally insane, on 13 March 1878. The report of her story and her condition in the casebook and case file records show that it became the medical justification to hospitalize her in the asylum for two years, despite the fact that she had never revealed any obvious sign of mental illness.[9] In a 1901 lecture he gave in Bath, Doctor John Baker clarified that many mothers sent to Broadmoor after committing infanticide were not insane. "The gravity of the mental symptoms may be gauged from the fact that twelve out of twenty Broadmoor cases were discharged after comparatively short detention" (Baker 19). It was common knowledge among the physicians and alienists that acquittal on the grounds of insanity was the last resort of the court to save these mothers from execution (Baker 15, 27). The Broadmoor report of Ellen's case on the day of her admission tells the following story:

> Felt nothing particular until four in the afternoon when she observed sharp pains as if from the pricking of needles

> in both breasts but more specially in the left. And soon after she felt something rise up as from her breasts into her head: and she experienced an indescribable feeling in her head together with a diminished clearness of vision: so that she hardly knew what she was doing. About 7 in the evening the feeling first came upon her that she must do 'something' to the child but she did not know clearly what she was to do. Yet she called out six or seven times to her grandmother, who being deaf and in another room, did not hear her. She felt blackness & pressure & an entire want of control over herself & she took the child, which was in her arms & wrapped the bedclothes round its neck tightly & strangled it & then turned on her side away from it ... on being questioned, she says that if her grandmother had not come into the room, she had so little power over herself (indeed she felt she had no power) & the "feeling" continued to "press hard" upon her, that she might have gone on to do something to herself ... she makes not demonstration of sorrow nor does she express any regret. (Berkshire Record Office D/H14)

This story contains elements that did not appear in the story told to Dr. Pratt. Ellen did not tell the doctor about shooting pains in her breasts or about pressure in her head and blurred vision, or about a feeling that she had to do something to the infant or about her calls to her grandmother that went unanswered. She also did not tell him that she had used the sheet or blanket to strangle her infant nor did she mention the desire to commit suicide. If these facts were true, why had none of them appeared in Ellen's detailed account of her infant's death to Dr. Pratt five months earlier? What had led to the transformation of a half-conscious killing, which ended in Ellen's regret and was reflected in her insistence on confessing and being punished, into an irrational yet deliberate murder?

There is no way to determine which version better corresponded to Ellen's act of infanticide. However, the story told at Broadmoor seems to me uncertain for two reasons. First, I doubt whether Ellen could remember most of the physical and emotional details provided by the report (for example, which breast hurt more) after five months. Second, the facts recounted by the report fit too well with one of the accepted descriptions of puerperal mania.

Harriet Nowell-Smith suggests that nineteenth century case notes could be less than objective, as the recorders "transformed individuals' bodies into something statistically regular and understandable" (48). Hilary Marland argues that medical descriptions of women who had reached mental asylums reflected the realms of interest, the expectations and the perceptions of the doctors who treated them, and were often fitted into diagnoses, which were known in advance ("Dangerous Motherhood" 99-105).

Thus, the account of Ellen's violent impulse to kill her child and herself, and her struggle against it by calling her grandmother, which had been absent from her original report to Doctor Pratt, corresponded to common contemporary medical descriptions of puerperal mania. James Reid, a famous physician and an author on puerperal insanity who was much cited in forensic texts, described in 1848 how "the mother is urged on by some unaccountable impulse to commit violence on herself or on her offspring" while at the same time struggling against it imploring "that the infant may be removed from her…" (Reid quoted in Marland, "Getting Away" 175-176). Moreover Ellen's report that "she felt something rise up as from her breasts into her head" reflected another accepted notion that female mental illness could break out due to the creation of milk (Berkshire Record Office D/H14). This medical interpretation was quite common at the time as explained by Baker in 1902: "The infanticide occurs much more frequently in connection with the insanity of lactation" (16). The lack of remorse the doctor ascribed to Ellen was also a well-known symptom of puerperal insanity at the time (Baker 22).

There is no way to know if Ellen tried to tell the physician who interviewed her on admission the version she had delivered Dr. Pratt. Yet even if she did, his attempt to appropriate her story into the accepted paradigm of puerperal insanity does not come as a surprise. Elain Showalter claims that the voices of female lunatic patients were absent from nineteenth century asylum case histories. Victorian asylum superintendents were reluctant to listen to their patients or to find out how they felt and why. Their treatment involved refusing to discuss the lunatic's feelings, ignoring her demands and observations and instead, diverting her mind to physical activity and communal work (Showalter 60-61). The historian Roy Porter maintains that the medical encounter between a psychiatrist and a patient was frequently a monologue that impersonated a dialogue with the patient (175). Case histories, along with other asylum records were frequently "dialogues of the deaf; too often those who have been shut up have indeed been shut up, or at least nobody has attended to what they have said..." (Porter quoted in Marland "Dangerous Motherhood" 100). In such a medical context, no one expected a woman who had reached the institution after being suspected of insanity, and in the case of Ellen, who had also committed a criminal act, to transmit a reliable version of what had happened to her. Cath Quinn suggests that the construction of puerperal mania as a consequence of the maternal state served to emphasize the disruptive potential and unstable nature of all women (Quinn 195). In the case of Ellen, this potential turned into reality. So even if she insisted on speaking, the odds were that no one really listened, and in rare cases, when a doctor who listened was in the room, he was only searching for proof of her insanity (Porter 175).

I assume that Ellen was led by the doctor to tell a story that fitted his idea of her illness while her own voice and her original story told to Dr. Pratt were silenced. Her image as the insane mother who had murdered her daughter as a result of an abnormal violent impulse, which had erupted as result of her unstable feminine nature following the birth, was thus consolidated.

A year after her admission, one of the doctors wrote another report recommending Ellen's release: "We consider that she is now restored to her normal state of mind. We do not see that any further benefit in this respect is to be looked for by prolonging her detention here" (Berkshire Record Office D/H14). However, the image of the insane mother constructed when she had been admitted to Broadmoor a year earlier led the hospital's authorities to reject this medical recommendation and to extend her detention for another year. Ellen was conditionally discharged on 15 April 1880 into the custody of her family—her mother, Jane, and her husband, Charles Gilling—like other criminal lunatics who were considered recovered enough to be safely looked after by others.

CONCLUSION: SAVING THE MOTHERHOOD MYTH

The case of Ellen shows how Victorian legal and medical systems avoided executing mothers who committed infanticide. These endeavours reflected popular sentiment that was also echoed by Queen Victoria's call to abolish capital punishment for infanticide (Smith 148, Rich 261). For the leading criminal jurist of the period, Sir James Fitzjames Stephen, the function of criminal law was to reinforce public morality and this made it important to avoid too sharp a conflict with public sentiments (Ward "Legislating" 257). It seems that even when juries and judges were left in little doubt as to whether a murder had taken place, as in the case of Ellen, they were keen to consider acquitting mothers on the grounds of insanity. This tendency was reflected in Bailey's line of defence, which turned aside a professional assessment as to Ellen's mental condition thereby winning the full support of the jury and the judge, John Mellor.

This lenient attitude towards infanticide was expressed again by the readiness of the alienists in Broadmoor, where Ellen was hospitalized after the trial, to cooperate with the verdict—acquittal on grounds of insanity—by diagnosing and treating her as a typical case of puerperal mania.

This legal and medical maneuvering saved Ellen's life. However, neither Ellen nor any other individual mother in similar circumstances was the focus of these institutional manipulations. At stake was the inclination to protect and cherish the good motherhood myth being developed, distributed, and circulated among the upper and middle classes during Victorian times. In the face of mothers' deviation from what had been considered as normal feminine and maternal instincts and behaviour, legal and medical agents used professional mechanisms to turn these women into miserable outcasts, sociological, psychological and pathological exceptions, thus preserving and consolidating the ruling maternal norm.

In this vein I would suggest interpreting the transformation of Ellen's image by the legal and medical procedures from a sane murderer into an insane miserable mother as an example of how both institutions acted in cases of infanticide. The legal and medical systems not only reflected Victorian accepted maternal norms but were also committed to actively maintaining them as such.

Surveys of research on contemporary cases of infanticide in England and the US reveal that similar legal and medical narratives are still in use and echo similar accepted maternal norms that see women's violence towards their offspring as a pathological or sociological deviation from a severe social expectation. Ania Wilczynski found for example that women are predominantly viewed as "sad"—"social casualties" who act irrationally in response to their difficult circumstances and/or inadequacy—or "mad" (mentally disturbed); consequently, their killings tend to be viewed as aberrant "tragedies" for which they are not responsible (Wilczynski 424). Bronwyn Naylor located in the press an emphasis on excusatory explanations based on hormones and depressive conditions (172). Cheryl L. Meyer and Michelle Oberman also pointed to a general social inclination to see mothers who committed infanticide as irresponsible for their deeds, either as a result of mental health problems or for social reasons (70).

In light of these findings, Ellen's evolving narrative seems still relevant in the twentieth and twenty-first centuries. It shows how certain legal and medical agents at a particular historical moment in a distinct culture translate their cultural and social responsibility to preserve and protect the myth of good mothering into practice. In Ellen's case and often in contemporary cases as well, the result of the manipulation and the cooperation between the legal and medical establishments turned women who commit infanticide into an insane women, thus preserving the social assumptions, true in our times as well, regarding the maternal instinct, which only an attack of madness can defeat.

ENDNOTES

[1]Apart from the legal documents and the reporting newspapers, data about Ellen Harper was drawn from England and Wales, Civil Registration Index; UK Census 1861; UK Census 1871; UK-Census 1881.

[2]At the end of the nineteenth century, delivery of a child by a doctor was considered a safer yet more expensive option and was thus inaccessible for rural lower-class people such as the Quicks. See Knibiehler,

[3]In her confession Ellen named her grandmother "mother," since terms like mother, grandmother, aunt, etc. were fluid, implying that family was still a flexible concept among the English lower classes even at the end of nineteenth century. Mother was a woman that took care of children and could be almost anybody. See Gillis 152-178.

[4]The inquest system, a quasi-judicial inquiry that was held by a coroner, elected by the county ratepayers, with jury and witnesses to determine the cause of death, is peculiar to England and Wales and the United States. See Rose 57-62 and Bentley 51-54.

[5]Information on the inquest was taken from National Archives, Harper and "The Charge of Murder."

[6]See the midwife's testimony in "The Charge of Murder." The declining status of midwives in the nineteenth century was probably one of the reasons which forced Treble to report on Ellen. See Knibiehler 334; Donnison 21-61.

[7]For the verdict, see National Archives, Criminal Register; National Archives, Calendar of Prisoners; National Archives, Ellen Harper

[8]The information on Ellen Harper's trial was taken from "Charge of Willful Murder," "The Alleged Child Murder at Wiveliscombe" (*The Western Times),* "The Alleged Child Murder at Wiveliscombe" (*The Devon Weekly Times.*)

[9]For the casebook, see Berkshire Record Office D/M14/D2/1/2/1; for the case file records see Berskhire Record Office D/H14 acc 7973.12 file 271.

WORKS CITED

Primary Sources

"The Alleged Child Murder at Wiveliscombe." *The Western Times,* Wednesday, January 16, 1878: 3.

"The Alleged Child Murder at Wiveliscombe." *The Devon Weekly Times.* Friday January 18, 1878.

Berkshire Record Office, Broadmoor Lunatic Asylum, Case Book

D/M14/D2/1/2/1 13 March 1878
Berkshire Record Office, Broadmoor Lunatic Asylum, Case File Records D/H14 acc 7973.12 file 27, March 1878 – April 1880.
"The Charge of Murder." *(Taunton, UK) Somerset County Gazette: Bristol Express and Devonshire News*, Saturday, 3 November. 1877.
"Charge of Willful Murder at Wiveliscombe (Somerset)." *The Exeter and Plymouth Daily Telegram*, Wednesday, January 16, 1878
England and Wales, Civil Registration Index: 1837-1983. Ancestry.com. N.d.. Web. November 20, 2005.
National Archives, Public Record Office. Ellen Harper. 1877. ASSI 26/14, October 1877. London: National Archives.
National Archives, Public Record Office. Calendar of Prisoners. HO 140/41. 11 January 1878. London: National Archives.
National Archives, Public Record Office. Criminal Register HO 27/179. Bedford to Kent Vol 1.
UK Census. 1861 England Census. Web. April 2, 2013.
National Archives, Public Record Office. 1871 England Census. Web. April 2, 2013.
National Archives, Public Record Office. 1881 England Census. Web. April 2, 2013.

Secondary Sources

Andrews, Jonathan. "The Boundaries of Her Majesty's Pleasure: Discharging Child Murderers from Broadmoor and Perth Criminal Lunatic Department, c.1860-1920." *Infanticide: Historical Perspectives on Child Murder and Concealment, 1550-2000*. Ed. Mark Jackson. Hants, UK: Ashgate, 2002. 216-48. Print.
Arnot, Margaret. "Understanding Women Committing Newborn Child Murder in Victorian England." *Everyday Violence in Britain 1850-1950*. Ed. Shani D'Cruze. Harlow, UK: Longman, 2000. 55-69. Print.
Arnot, Margaret. "The Murder of Thomas Sandles: Meanings of a Mid-nineteenth-Century Infanticide." *Infanticide: Historical Perspectives on Child Murder and Concealment, 1550- 2000*. Ed. Mark Jackson. Hants, UK: Ashgate, 2002. 149-167. Print.
Baker, John. "Female Criminal Lunatics: A Sketch." *Journal of Mental Science* 47 (1902): 13-26. Print.

Behar, Ruth. "Introduction: Out of Exile." *Women Writing Culture*. Ed. Ruth Behar and Deborah A. Gordon. Berkeley: University of California. 1-32. Print.

Bentley, David. *English Criminal Justice in the Nineteenth Century*. London: Hambledon, 1998. Print.

Chadwick, Roger. *Bureaucratic Mercy: The Home Office and the Treatment of Capital Cases in Victorian Britain*. New York: Garland, 1992. Print.

Donnison, Jean. *Midwives and Medical Men: A History of Inter-Professional Rivalries and Women's Rights*. London: Heinemann. Print.

Emsley, Clive. *Crime and Society in England 1750-1900*. London: Longman, 1996. Print.

Forna, Aminata. *Mother of All Myths: How Society Moulds and Constrains Mothers*. London: HarperCollins, 1999. Print.

Foucault, Michel and Colin Gordon. *Power/Knowledge*. New York: Knopf Doubleday Publishing Group, 1980. Print.

Gillis, John, R. *A World of Their Own Making: Myth, Ritual, and the Quest for Family Values*. Cambridge, MA: Harvard University P. 1996. Print.

Ginzburg, Carlo. *The Cheese and the Worms: The Cosmos of the Sixteenth-Century Miller.* Trans. John and Anne Tedschi. Baltimore: The John Hopkins University Press, 1992. Print.

Higginbotham, Ann R. "'Sin of the Age': Infanticide and Illegitimacy in Victorian London." *Victorian Studies* 32.3 (1989): 319-37. Print.

Hufton, Olwen. *1500-1800. The Prospect Before Her: A History of Women in Western Europe Vol 1*. London: HarperCollins, 1996. Print.

Jackson, Mark. "The trial of Harriet Vooght: Continuity and Change in The History of Infanticide." *Infanticide: Historical Perspectives on Child Murder and Concealment, 1550-2000*. Ed. Mark Jackson. Hants, UK: Ashgate, 2000. 1-17. Print.

Knelman, Judith. *Twisting in the Wind: The Murderess and the English Press*. Toronto: University of Toronto Press, 1998. Print.

Knibiehler, Yvonne. "Bodies and Hearts." *A History of Women in the West: Emerging Feminism from Revolution to World War*. Ed. Genevieve Fraisse and Michelle Perrot. Cambridge, MA:

Harvard University Press, 1995. Print.
Levi, Giovanni. "On Microhistory." *New Perspectives on Historical Writing*. Ed.Peter Bruke. University Park: Pennsylvania State University Press, 1992. 97-119. Print.
Magnusson, Sigurdur G. "The Singularization of History: Social History and Microhistory within the Postmodern State of Knowledge." *Journal of Social History* 36.3 (2003): 701-735. Print
Marland, Hilary. "Getting Away With Murder? Puerperal Insanity, Infanticide and the Defence Plea." *Infanticide: Historical Perspectives on Child Murder and Concealment, 1550-2000*. Ed. Mark Jackson. Hants, UK: Ashgate, 2002. 168-92. Print.
Marland, Hilary. *Dangerous Motherhood: Insanity and Childbirth in Victorian Britain*. New York: Palgrave Macmillan, 2004. Print.
Meyer Cheryl and Michelle Oberman. *Mothers Who Kill their Children: Understanding the Acts of Moms from Susan Smith to the "Prom Mom."* New York: New York University Press. 2001. Print.
Mies, Maria. "Women Research or Feminist Research: The Debate Surrounding Feminist Science and Methodology. "*Beyond Methodology: Feminist Scholarship and Lived Research*. Ed. Mary Margaret Fonow and Judith A. Cook. Bloomington: Indiana University Press, 1991. 60-84. Print.
Naylor, Bronwyn. "The 'Bad Mother' in Media and Legal Texts." *Social Semiotics* 11.2 (2001): 155-176. Print.
Nowell-Smith, Harriet. "Nineteenth-Century Narrative Case Histories: An Inquiry into Stylistics and History." *Canadian Bulletin of Medical History* 12 (1995): 47-67. Print
Oberman Michelle 1996. "Mothers Who Kill: Coming to Terms with Modern American Infanticide." *American Criminal Law Review* 34.1 (1996-1997): 2-110. Print.
O'Reilly, Andrea. "Between the Baby and the Bathwater: Some thoughts on a Mother-Centers Theory and Practice of Feminist Mothering." *Journal of the Association for Research on Mothering* 8.1/2 (2006): 323-330.
Peltonen, Matti. "Clues, Margins, and Monads: The Micro-Macro Link in Historical Research." *History and Theory* 40 (2001): 347-59. Print.

Perkin, Joan. 1993. *Victorian Women.* New York: New York University Press. Print.

Porter, Roy. "The Patient View: Doing Medical History from Below." *Theory and Society* 14 (1985): 175-198. Print.

Quinn, Cath. "Images and Impulses: Representations of Puerperal Insanity and Infanticide in Late Victorian England" *Infanticide: Historical Perspectives on Child Murder and Concealment, 1550-2000*. Ed. Mark Jackson. Hants, UK: Ashgate, 2002. 193-215. Print.

Rich, Adrienne. *Of Women Born: Motherhood as Experience and Institution.* London: Virago Press, 1986. Print.

Robinson, Warren C. "Population Policy in Early Victorian England." *European Journal of Population* 18.2 (2002): 153-73. Print.

Rose, Lionel. *The Massacre of the Innocents: Infanticide in Britain 1800-1939*. London: Routledge, 1986. Print.

Ross, Ellen. *Love and Toil: Motherhood in Outcast London 1870-1918.* New York: Oxford University Press, 1993. Print.

Scott, Joan, W. "Feminism's History." *Journal of Women's History* 16.2 (2004): 10-29. Print.

Showalter, Elaine. *The Female Malady: Women Madness and English Culture, 1830-1980.* New York: Penguin, 1985. Print.

Shuttleworth, Sally. "Demonic Mothers: Ideologies of Bourgeois Motherhood in the Mid-Victorian Era." *Rewriting the Victorians: Theory History and the Politics of Gender.* Ed. Linda M. Shire. New York: Routledge, 1992. 31-51. Print.

Silva Bortolaia, Elizabeth. "The Transformation of Mothering." *Good Enough Mothering? Feminist Perspectives on Lone Motherhood.* Ed. Elizabeth Silva Bortolaia. London: Routledge, 1996. 10-36. Print.

Smart, Carol. "Disruptive Bodies and Unruly Sex: The Regulation of Reproduction and Sexuality in the Nineteenth Century." *Regulating Womanhood: Historical Essays on Marriage, Motherhood and Sexuality.* Ed. Carol Smart. London: Routledge, 1992. 7-32. Print.

Smith, Roger. *Trial by Medicine: Insanity and Responsibility in Victorian Trials.* Edinburgh: Edinburgh University Press, 1981. Print.

Taylor, Alfred Swaine. *The Principles and Practices of Medical Jurisprudence*. Vol. 2. London, 1865. Print.

Ward, Tony. "The Sad Subject of Infanticide: Law, Medicine and Child Murder 1860-1938." *Social and Legal Studies* 8.163 (1999). 163-180. Print.

Ward, Tony. "Legislating for Human Nature: Legal Responses to Infanticide, 1860-1938." *Infanticide: Historical Perspectives on Child murder and Concealment, 1550-2000*. Ed. Mark Jackson. Hants, UK: Ashgate, 2000. 249-269. Print.

Wilczynski, Ania. "Mad or Bad? Child Killers, Gender and the Courts." *British Journal of Criminology* 37.2 (1997). 419-436. Print.

Zemon Davis, Natalie. *The Return of Martin Guerre*. Cambridge, MA: Harvard University Press, 1983. Print.

9. Pregnant, Incarcerated and Overlooked

Shedding Light on Pregnancy in Juvenile Detention Centers

KERI K. O'NEAL AND WENDY K. WATSON

ALTHOUGH THOUSANDS of pregnant teenagers find themselves in correctional facilities each year in the United States, insufficient scholarly, policy, and criminal justice attention has been paid to this population. Diana Royal refers to pregnant incarcerated adolescents as "Detained, Pregnant and at Risk" and argues that "[t]he lack of research related to the health needs of female detainees shows an already marginalized population being subjected to further marginalization" (1). Pregnant adolescent detainees are, in Linda Acoca's words, "dangerously invisible from a research perspective" (55). Since a significant number of teenagers find themselves in this very situation, questions then arise as to why they receive such little consideration in the literature. Is this specific to pregnant incarcerated teens? Does it point to broader concerns about girls and risk taking behaviours in general? In practical terms, if the body of work continues to be scant what are the consequences of relying on misperceptions about these girls, their choices, and their lives?

The psychological and social issues surrounding pregnancy during adolescence are complex. Pregnant youth frequently lack the resources to obtain quality prenatal care, which can lead to various complications during the pregnancy. The adolescent's mental and emotional state and her surrounding support network (or lack of supports) can exacerbate her situation. Pregnant teenagers housed in correctional detention facilities are faced with unique challenges physically, emotionally, and socially, which are often overlooked in mainstream society and academic discourse.

These institutions are frequently ill-equipped to offer adequate and appropriate prenatal and postnatal care. And given such environments, an adolescent's ability to cope with the stressors of pregnancy is likely aggravated by the increased pressure of confinement. In their analysis of criminalized adult mothers, Ferraro and Moe reached the conclusion that parenthood behind bars was valued *and* devalued. Suzanne Allen, Chris Flaherty and Gretchen Ely claim that maternal incarceration is related to the criminalization of female poverty and call attention to the betrayal these mothers felt by a system that treated them as "throwaway moms" (160).

We argue that viewing the lack of attention to incarcerated pregnant adolescents and resource allocation through a feminist lens may help to shed light on why this population continues to be marginalized, overlooked, and underserved. A feminist understanding of pregnancy and childbirth underscores that healthy environments involve the pregnant individual having the right to make informed decisions regarding the birth and care of the newborn. The prohibitive and restrictive nature of the environment for those in correctional detention facilities challenges the assumption that mothers to be can or should be empowered. Further complicating matters is the juvenile status of adolescents in the United States, who may not have the same rights regarding health and freedom of choice as their adult counterparts.

To date, there has not been a comprehensive compilation of available research discussing this important topic. Nor has there been a concerted effort to make connections between research and practice to understand the issues facing pregnant incarcerated young women from a feminist theoretical perspective that recognizes diversity.

Our synthesis of the literature seeks to add to the larger conversation of what is currently known and aims to heed the call for a "renewed effort to access and better understand this vulnerable group" (Royal 2). In this chapter we use a multiracial feminist framework to examine social and cultural contextual factors surrounding pregnant incarcerated adolescents. This feminist lens allows us to address the intersectionality of race, class, age, and gender.

FEMINIST PERSPECTIVE

Feminist theories of criminology provide the means to examine pregnant incarcerated teen's experiences within the contexts of not only gender, but also race and class (Burgess-Proctor 28; Miller and Mullins 217; Dohrn 305; Daly 207; Ocen 1243; Allen, Flaherty and Ely 162). Feminist perspectives in criminology emphasize different aspects of the gender inequities within a larger system (Burgess-Proctor 29). Sometimes referred to as intersectionality theory or multicultural feminism, multiracial feminism provides us a lens through which to examine "gender as being socially constructed through interlocking systems of race, class, gender, and other sources of inequality" (Burgess-Proctor 36). It is through this perspective that one can explore the intersectionality of identities that serve collectively to deprive these young, pregnant, often poor, often non-white teens of power (Daly 207).

In her analysis of the juvenile justice system and its relationship with young women, activist, academic, and child advocate Bernadine Dohrn sheds light on the private and public systems that serve very different populations and how class plays a role in how punishment is exacted (315). She demonstrates how family resources play a major role here in that if a girl who is in trouble with the law has adequate funds, she is often sheltered from the court system and instead allowed to go to a private boarding school or sent for treatment to a private hospital or rehab facility. A young woman without these resources is more likely to find herself arrested and put into the court system for punishment within a public facility (e.g., detention centers, reformatories).

Using a multiracial feminist perspective to understand the experiences of young women who are incarcerated means looking at the overlap of gender, race, and class. As Dohrn states, "[g] ender and racial disparity overlap and intersect, putting girls of color into secure detention and correctional facilities at far greater proportions. African American girls are almost half of those in public detention centers, and Latinas are about 13 percent" (309). Ocen provides a provocative exploration of how incarceration and treatment of women, particularly pregnant women, reproduces behaviors and images of slavery (1259). When we shackle women who are pregnant throughout delivery, we are engaging in a practice of punishment with strong historical ties. This also represents an attempt to control women's sexuality as Black slave women were seen as dangerous with their uncontrolled sexuality (Ocen 1258). These traditions of control historically perpetrated upon Black women have extended to women of other races in the prison system (Ocen 1245).

"When framed in this manner, the shackling of pregnant prisoners appears as a manifestation of the punishment of 'unfit' or 'undesirable' women for exercising the choice to become mothers" (Ocen 1243-4). Although largely analyzing adult women's experiences, this same argument can be extended to young pregnant women. Having children is certainly a gender appropriate task, a way of "doing gender" (West and Zimmerman), but these young women are not seen as "fit" or "desirable" mothers, largely because of their age, but also because of their race and class (Ocen 1243; Allen, Flaherty and Ely 162). "Women incarcerated in institutions are unable to adhere to white middleclass normative standards of 'womanhood' and are therefore deemed unfit to be mothers as a result of the intersection of their race, gender, class, and incarcerated status" (Ocen 1254). They do not fit society's views of a "good" mother and while being denied rights as deemed appropriate by the judicial system, they are also stripped of their decision-making rights as mothers. A startling contradiction appears in that these women are denied power in areas in which women are often deemed powerful, namely, pregnancy, childbirth, and mothering. These young women's status as "criminal" and "deviant mothers" may serve to exclude them and justify attempts on the part of correctional staff to make decisions *for her own good.*

INCARCERATED GIRLS AND THE IMPACT OF TEEN PREGNANCY

When we examine the experiences of incarcerated young women, we find a variety of reasons for incarceration. As has traditionally been the case, girls continue to be held in custody for more minor offenses when compared to boys. Specifically, female juveniles are more often held for "status offenses," which are offenses that only juveniles can be taken into custody for and include behaviours such as running away from home, curfew violations, and truancy (Chesney-Lind and Shelden, 7). In 2010, status offenses accounted for 11 percent of girls in custody versus 3 percent for boys in custody (OJJDP Statistical Briefing Book).

The matter of status offenses and the discrepancy in arrest rates by sex has long been an issue for the juvenile female offender (Chesney-Lind "Are Girls Closing" 1-2; Chesney-Lind and Sheldon *Girls* 33-36). Chesney-Lind and Sheldon (1998) contend that the explanations for these differences are not entirely clear. For example, the runaway rates of adolescents tend to be comparable across females and males while the arrests rates are higher for female juveniles. They posit that parents may be more likely to report a daughter who does not return home, additionally police officers may be more likely to arrest a female runaway compared to a male runaway. As a number of these young women are victims of sexual abuse, feminist scholars note that incarcerating these women serves to control them (Dohrn 306). Instead of providing support for victims of abuse, the system attempts to control these women and lock them away in facilities often deficient in services or healthcare. This type of incarceration further victimizes these women with punishments such as strip searches while providing no support for many who suffer from post-traumatic stress disorder (PTSD) as a result of many years of abuse (Dohrn 307).

When considering the number of female adolescents that are incarcerated each year it is only logical to expect that some of these individuals will be pregnant. Although quite limited, some studies have attempted to estimate the number of pregnant teenagers in correctional facilities. Breuner and Farrow (1995) surveyed 261 detention and long-term correctional facilities in the United States housing incarcerated juvenile females. Of these institutions, 68 percent reported holding one to five pregnant adolescents on a given day and estimated holding 2,000 pregnant girls per year. The authors extrapolated from these data and suggest that nationally an estimated 24,000 pregnant adolescents are incarcerated yearly or 670 individuals on a given day.

More recently an overview of 1255 nationwide juvenile residential facilities examining pregnant adolescent residents found 346 facilities reporting at least one pregnant teen within the referent month (Gallagher, Dobrin, and Douds 222). This translates into at least 2.1 percent of incarcerated juvenile females being pregnant. Further, findings from the Survey of Youth in Residential Placement (Sedlak and Bruce 6), a self-reported survey in conjunction with the Office of Juvenile Justice and Delinquency Prevention, indicates that 14 percent of youth in custody report having children (15 percent for males and 9 percent for females). While 12 percent of both males and female juveniles reported currently expecting a child, the breakdown by sex has not yet been released. It is also important to note that these numbers are likely to be underestimates as this does not take into consideration the number of adolescents under 18 years nor those 18 and 19 years old who are being housed in adult facilities nationwide (Acoca 68). This particular subset of girls is largely overlooked statistically and in program implementation. To date, there are no available statistics that further break down the demographics of the pregnant adolescent incarcerated community. It is reasonable to assume that it follows the general population housed throughout the United States with a minority to Caucasian ration of 2.8 to 1 (OJJDP Statistical Briefing Book).

The implications of pregnancy during adolescence are far reaching. Compared to older women, our literature synthesis reveals that pregnant adolescents have limited access to resources and quality prenatal care. For example, the youngest teens, aged 10-14, are less likely to obtain early prenatal care with less than half of this population starting prenatal care in the first trimester (Savio Beers and Hollo 218). As a result, teens are at an increased risk of experiencing myriad physical and psycho-social issues associated with their pregnancies. Discussing the challenges that pregnant adolescents face provides a foundational understanding for their experiences with an eye to how they are further impacted when they find themselves not only pregnant, but also incarcerated.

MEDICAL AND PSYCHO-SOCIAL IMPLICATIONS OF ADOLESCENT PREGNANCY

Frequently the foci of teen pregnancy are the medical concerns that arise while being pregnant at a young age. Although pregnant adolescents are at an increased risk of having some medical complications, most teens go on to have pregnancies that are without major medical incidents (Jolly et al. 962). For instance, as compared to women 20 years and older, juveniles are less likely to experience age-related chronic diseases that might affect pregnancy outcomes like diabetes, and endure childbirth with less need for operative interventions.

The highest rates of negative outcomes are found in the youngest and most economically disadvantaged mothers. Many of these outcomes are strongly correlated not with the age of the mother, but with the late commencement and improper application of prenatal care for mothers in marginalized circumstances (Savio Beers and Hollo 218). The issues pregnant adolescents are most likely to experience include: anemia, pregnancy-associated hypertension, toxemia, poor maternal weight gain, and preterm labour (Klein 283). The probability of having a low birth weight infant is more than twice that for a young mother relative to adult mothers and neonatal deaths are almost 3 times higher. And, while low, the mortality rate for teen mothers is twice that when compared to adult mothers (Forrest 108). Adolescent mothers are also at risk for experiencing postpartum depression (Birkeland, Thompson, and Phares 297). These physical complications are likely either ameliorated or compounded by the contextual variables surrounding the adolescent.

Research involving the psychosocial complications of early pregnancy has evolved over the years. Previously the foregone conclusion was that detrimental effects would follow the adolescent into adulthood. Studies reported that these individuals were at an increased risk for issues such as: school interruption, lower educational attainment, socioeconomic disadvantages, separation from the child's father, and divorce (Coley and Chase-Lansdale 155-156; Corcoran 54-61). Further, results of early pregnancy may hinder the completion of normative psychological tasks presented in adolescence. These tasks include identity development and autonomy formation (Chase-Lansdale, Wakschlag, and Brooks-Gunn 524-526). And although all of these outcomes have the potential to be realized there are key factors that are likely to lessen their inevitability. Specifically, for those communities where teen pregnancy is seen as a normative or even positive life event the adolescent experience may not be that much different when comparing nonpregnant and pregnant teens (Savio Beers and Hollo 217). Research suggests that it is the contextual factors surrounding the individual, such as strong social and functional supports, that have a higher probability of determining outcomes (Klein, 2005). Quite simply, context matters. An important research question follows: to what extent do young mothers experience relationships of support in the context in which they live in prison and within their home communities?

CARE FOR INCARCERATED ADOLESCENTS

Given the number of youth moving through these various facilities, national medical organizations including the American Academy of Pediatrics, the National Commission on Correctional Health Care, and the Society for Adolescent Medicine have provided minimal standards of care (e.g., health screenings; timeliness of medical and dental care for emergent, acute, and chronic conditions; access to mental health services) as they relate to juveniles in custody (Gallagher, Dobrin, and Douds 225). As indicated in the "Position Paper of the Society for Adolescent Medicine" (73), "The time in custody presents a unique opportunity to address the basic health concerns of this population and provide health education." Unfortunately this opportunity is often not realized as under current federal regulations, incarcerated teens in public institutions are ineligible for Medicaid benefits. As such, the pathway to needed healthcare is frequently hindered. And when health testing and services are being provided many juvenile justice residential facilities are not following the recommendations laid out by the medical organizations but rather are operating on an as-needed basis centered on self-reports (Gallagher et al. 225). An inherent problem with this strategy is the underreporting done by the juveniles. Therefore, many individuals needing services are often overlooked.

To date, there has been one national overview of reproductive health care services for girls in juvenile justice residential facilities (Gallagher, Dobrin and Douds 217-226). The study found that testing of the entire population for pregnancy and sexually transmitted diseases transpires in less than 18 percent of the facilities with 85 percent reporting that only some girls receive care from a gynecologist. As previously stated, many of the tests and services are completed on an ad hoc basis contingent upon self-reporting by the adolescent, proving problematic since many conditions are asymptomatic. Further, although roughly 25 percent of facilities report housing at least one pregnant resident, the same percentage provide no obstetric services. The type of facility plays a role in the level of care received as well. All-female, state-owned, large population, and longer stay facilities, as compared to short stay, mixed-gender, crowded, and locally and privately owned facilities, are significantly more likely to provide gynecologic services to all residents.

Beyond the medical treatment administered to the adolescents is the interaction they have with medical professionals. The attitudes of the facility's staff may play a role in the care received. Hufft and Peternelj-Taylor (94-95) discuss the various issues nurses face when dealing with pregnant incarcerated teens and how the residents' behaviours associated with their crime may divert attention away from their general healthcare requirements. Specifically, nurses may find they are conflicted by the values and behaviours of the girls in terms of their attitudes about teenage pregnancy and abortion. Moreover, there may be the tendency to pass further judgment if the adolescent has engaged in activities that potentially harm the fetus or has additional common health issues such as drug use and sexually transmitted diseases (Acoca 67). These behaviours may be seen by medical staff as further proof of the adolescent's deviant behaviour and impact the treatment received.

The issue of minors in custody and consent to medical services is complex. Legal considerations must be taken into account when assessing the rights afforded to adolescents. When an incarcerated teen is pregnant, counselling regarding options for termination, adoption, and keeping the child need to be administered (Cohen, Burd, and Beyer 134). However, rights to minors for counselling related to abortion and the right of the adolescent to make her own decision varies by state. In most states, informed consent must be granted by the parents or legal guardians. Provided that many of these girls come from untenable home situations, parental involvement may equate to additional challenges for the adolescent. Although counselling regarding options should be provided, given the ad hoc basis in which most services are provided to these girls, it is reasonable to assume that such services are often either not provided or are lacking in developmental appropriateness and comprehensiveness (Acoca 68).

Furthermore, the attitudes of the staff members within detention facilities may once again impact the type of medical treatment received. Specifically, if ethical dilemmas regarding choice exist among staff, abortion options may be pushed back until it is too late to have one (Hufft and Peternelj-Taylor 95). Standard practices and procedures need to be instilled so that counselling and any necessary procedures are handled within a specified timeframe.

Although it has been estimated that thousands of pregnant adolescents will be incarcerated each year (Breuner and Farrow 329; Gallagher, Dobrin, and Douds 217), there is scant descriptive information regarding the challenges and outcomes for these individuals. However Acoca (66-68), working in conjunction with the Juvenile Law Center of Philadelphia and In Our Daughters' Hands, Inc. of Fairfax, California, has worked to develop a screening instrument that attempts to identify health needs of incarcerated girls in various regions within the United States. In doing so, a portrait of what is experienced by pregnant teens in detention facilities begins to emerge. Residents reported frequently being hungry and that they had not been offered prenatal vitamins. Interviewer observations revealed the girls having to wear improperly fitting uniforms, sleeping on thin mattresses placed either on cell floors or cement slabs, no prenatal or parenting classes, experiences of physical restraints at the wrists and ankles, that miscarriage was common, and upon delivery being separated from the baby (i.e. hours to days) and returned to the general population of the facility with little to no medical or psychological support services.

And while this only provides the slightest glimpse into the world of a pregnant incarcerated teen, it begins to elucidate the experiences and challenges they face. At least in the environment described above, we can see how ill-equipped a detention facility can be when housing this unique population. For example, of those interviewed 83 percent of incarcerated adolescents reported being separated from their infant for three months (Acoca 68). The implications for the children being removed from their mother so soon after birth are far reaching for the overall health and development of the child. Moreover, the lack of counselling services provided to the adolescent upon reentry into the general population of the detention center, compounded by her susceptibility towards experiencing postpartum depression (Birkeland, Thompson, and Phares), may further prove detrimental and damaging to the juvenile. More in depth research is needed that examines the lived experiences of these girls. Their voices deserve to be heard and the voices of the professionals to whom their care is entrusted recognized.

The extent of the problems these girls will experience are unknown as follow-up studies are currently non-existent. However, it is possible to glean some insight by understanding what proves successful for adolescents upon reentry into the general population after a period of confinement. As indicated by the Office of Juvenile Justice and Delinquency Prevention (OJJDP Statistical Briefing Book) youth are more likely to succeed if they have access to high-quality reentry and aftercare services. The authors stressed that these services need to begin prior to the youth leaving the facility and involve both the family and wider community (e.g., social workers, etc.) in which the youth will reenter. It is reasonable then to conclude that specific quality services are required for the unique population of pregnant incarcerated teens during pregnancy and after the child is born. And if such services are not provided it is realistic to assume that these individuals are likely to experience complications as well.

Given that thousands of young pregnant females are housed in correctional institutions each year an expectation of preparedness and prenatal and postnatal care within these facilities does not seem unreasonable. However, the limited available evidence does not support the claim that the needs of pregnant adolescent girls are being met. Looking to the feminist literature, specifically utilizing a multiracial perspective helps to elucidate why the gap between need for services and appropriate care continues.

DISCUSSION

The "problem" of teen pregnancy for females in conflict with the law is complex. As we have seen in this chapter, myriad factors in the adolescent's physical, emotional, and social world serve to impact her pregnancy. As such, the more chaotic the situation surrounding the individual, the more likely she is to experience detrimental consequences to herself and her unborn child. Pregnant girls housed in juvenile detention facilities with limited resources and services are prime candidates for suffering these ill effects. Given the implications for this population, it is essential that research is done, which lends itself to meaningful strategies to assist young female detainees.

Regardless of the fact that these young women do not make up a majority of teens housed in detention facilities, this chapter has pointed out many factors of importance that need to be taken into consideration when incarcerating and caring for young, pregnant teens. Many young women come to detention facilities having suffered years of abuse. Therefore, healthcare must not only take into account their physical needs as young, pregnant women, but also their psychological needs as victims of abuse. There is more work to be done to understand the experiences of young, incarcerated adolescents.

A multiracial feminist perspective calls for inclusion of the voices of these young women as we learn more about their situations, lives, and needs (Allen, Flaherty and Ely 161; Dohrn 303). "[T]he lack of definitive clinical research regarding the care of pregnant adolescents confined to correctional settings further exposes them to stereotypical care based on nonincarcerated pregnant youth and/or incarcerated adults, neither of which is appropriate" (Hufft and Peternelj-Taylor 95). As mentioned earlier, at least one quarter of juvenile justice residential facilities have no obstetric services. Regardless of whether they are incarcerated for a violent crime or a status offense, these young women may not receive proper prenatal care and not have a say in the circumstances of delivery. Taken together, there is insufficient research regarding young, pregnant, incarcerated women, but one can look across these studies to surmise that young women are not left in a position of power.

As feminist poet Audre Lorde states, "The master's tools will never dismantle the master's house" (110). Her words reinforce the notion that using traditional theories to understand the experiences of these girls is insufficient. It is through a feminist lens that we can have a better understanding of their experiences. Multiple identities serve to deny power to these young women, identities experienced due to race, gender, class, age, and situation. Young, often African American or Latina, poor, and incarcerated females, are marginalized in society and are more likely to be criminalized (as the other chapters in this collection demonstrate). These young women are not viewed by society as "fit mothers." Within their circumstances of incarceration, agency in their choices about the pregnancy and childbirth is often denied. As Allen, Flaherty and Ely explain,

> Poor and marginalized women...do not fit the idealized portrayal of motherhood. Consequently, they may be perceived as not only inadequate mothers but as inadequate women. They are also, by virtue of their poverty status and marginalization, the most likely to become involved in the criminal justice system and, therefore, more susceptible to having their maternal rights impinged upon. (162)

To provide thoughtful care, as well as fair incarceration, attention should be paid not only to their pathway to detention, but also to the intersectionality of race, class, gender, and age, and how these factors play a role in young women's experiences before, during, and after incarceration.

FUTURE DIRECTIONS

We may be remiss in discussing future directions related to pregnant incarcerated adolescents to not first address the issues of prevention. Ideally, programming initiatives would be in place that prevents (a) unplanned or unwanted pregnancies and (b) becoming incarcerated. Pregnancy prevention efforts are often hindered by what is frequently defined as "problem definition," meaning "what is the problem we are trying to fix?" Conflict arises with those arguing that prevention should focus on abstaining from sexual intercourse while others argue that programming should provide a combination of sex education while reinforcing the option of abstinence. This controversy attends to the value judgments frequently tied to female sexuality. Unfortunately, and as a result, this often leads to abstinence-only programs being put into place that have a lower likelihood of being beneficial when compared to programs that combine sex education with discussions of abstaining (Chin 290). Researchers, clinicians, and educators need to continue disseminating prevention endeavours that have the greatest chance for a reduction in unplanned pregnancies. One place to start is to listen to the girls themselves.

As with pregnancy, the issues of delinquency and crime prevention offer unique challenges for a teenage girl. We have discussed the discrepancies between detention and types of offenses between males and females. This has led Chesney-Lind to conclude "...girls are now arguably the recipients of the worst of both worlds in the current juvenile justice system. That is to say girls in the new millennium are enduring the effects of a juvenile justice system that is becoming more punitive toward youth while also not shedding its more historic role of being deeply involved in the moral and social policing of girls" (*Fighting for Girls* 71). Until and unless this changes, girls will be hard pressed to receive fair and just treatment. Exploring *how* and *why* girls are incarcerated provides a deeper understanding of their lived experiences.

Of equal value to prevention efforts are the motivations for enacting and engaging in risky behaviours (such as unprotected sex, involvement in prostitution). Boys and girls define and take risks for different reasons (Christopherson and Conner 519). The policy implications for this are far reaching and render inadequate the "one size fits all" programming so often employed. Thus, only through understanding these differences can programs be tailored to specific populations and provide a better chance for meaningful and lasting success.

As Hufft and Peternelj-Taylor (96) so aptly concluded: "The experiences of imprisoned girls serve as a harsh reminder that there is no such thing as having a right or a choice without access to the resources needed to carry out that choice. When judges and juries send girls to prison, they do not sentence them to a term of medical neglect or to continue a pregnancy against their will, but unfortunately these are often the consequences of incarceration." To help them, we must understand them and the lives they have led. Efforts are needed to examine their experiences both prior to engaging the system and within the system. Doing so will provide the foundation for policy and supportive programming that represents the actual needs of this marginalized population. With this knowledge we will have greater insight into what steps to take to divert girls' entrance into the juvenile justice system.

To this end, we must too be cognizant of the developmental stage in which we find these adolescents. They are not adults and, as such, programming efforts that are efficacious for older women may not translate successfully to teens. Further research is needed to fully understand the complexity of the issues surrounding pregnant incarcerated teens, specifically looking at and giving voice to: their personal experiences while being detained, the types and variations in services provided, compliance and implementation of medical standards, and proposals for successful interventions. Only after these issues are given the attention they deserve will policies and procedures be created that are most likely to impact these girls in a positive, meaningful way. Not doing so will simply perpetuate the lack of understanding and marginalization of this vulnerable population. Perhaps, in doing so, this group will no longer be overlooked.

WORKS CITED

Acoca, Leslie. "Are Those Cookies for Me or My Baby? Understanding Detained and Incarcerated Teen Mothers and Their Children." *Juvenile and Family Court Journal.* 55.2 (2004): 64-80. Print.

Allen, Suzanna, Chris Flaherty and Gretchen Ely. "Throwaway Moms: Maternal Incarcerations and the Criminalization of Female Poverty." *Journal of Women and Social Work* 25.2 (2010): 160-172. Print.

Birkeland, Robyn, Kevin J. Thompson and Vicky Phares. "Adolescent Motherhood and Postpartum Depression." *Journal of Clinical Child and Adolescent Psychology* 34.2 (2005): 292-300.

Breuner, Cora Collette and James A. Farrow. "Pregnant Teens in Prison: Prevalence, Management, and Consequences." *Western Journal of Medicine* 162 (1995): 328-330. Print.

Burgess-Proctor, A. "Intersections of Race, Class, Gender, and Crime. Future Directions for Feminist Criminology." *Feminist Criminology* 1 (2006): 27-47. Print.

Chase-Landsdale, P. Lindsay, Lauren S. Wakschlag, and Jeanne Brooks-Gunn. "A Psychological Perspective on the Development of Caring in Children and Youth: The Role of the Family." *Journal of Adolescence* 18 (1995): 515-556. Print.

Chesney-Lind, Meda. "Imprisoning Women: The Unintended Victims of Mass Imprisonment." *Invisible Punishment.* Ed. Marc Mauer and Meda Chesney-Lind. New York: The New Press, 2002. 79-94. Print

Chesney-Lind, Meda. "Are Girls Closing the Gender Gap in Violence? *Criminal Justice Magazine* 16.1 (2001): 1-9.

Chesney-Lind, Meda and Nikki Jones. *Fighting for Girls: New Perspectives on Gender and Violence.* Albany, New York: State University of New York Press, 2010. Print.

Chesney-Lind, Meda and Randall G. Shelden. *Girls, Delinquency, and Juvenile Justice.* 2nd ed. Belmont, California: West/Wadsworth, 1998. Print.

Chesney-Lind, Meda and Randall G. Shelden. *Girls, Delinquency, and Juvenile Justice.* 3rd ed. Belmont, California: West/Wadsworth, 2004. Print.

Chin, Helen B., Theresa A. Sipe, Randy Elder, Shawna L. Mercer, Sajal K. Chattopadhyay, Jacob Verughese, Holly R. Wethington, Doug Kirby, Donna B. Elliston, Matt Griffith, Stella O. Chuke, Susan C. Briss, Irene Ericksen, Jennifer S. Galbraith, Jeffrey H. Herbst, Robert L. Johnson, Joan M. Kraft, Seth M. Noar, Lisa M. Romero and John Santellie. "The Effectiveness of Group-Based Comprehensive Risk-Reduction and Abstinence Education interventions to Prevent or Reduce the Risk of Adolescent Pregnancy, Human Immunodeficiency Virus, and Sexually transmitted Infections: Two Systemic Reviews for the Guide to Community Preventive Services." *American Journal of Preventive Medicine*

42.3 (2012): 272-294. Print.

Christopherson, Toni M. and Bradley T. Conner. "Mediation of Late Adolescent Health-Risk Behaviors and Gender Influences." *Public Health Nursing* 29.6 (2012): 510-524. Print.

Cohen, Michael D., Larry Burd, and Marty Beyer. "Health Services for Youth in Juvenile Justice Programs." *Clinical Practice in Correctional Medicine*. Ed. Michael Puisis. Philadelphia: Mosby Elsevier, 2006. 144-163. Print.

Coley, Rebekah L and Lindsay P. Chase-Lansdale. "Adolescent Pregnancy and Parenthood: Recent Evidence and Future Directions." *American Psychologist* 53.2 (1998): 152-166. Print.

Corcoran, Jacqueline. "Consequences of Adolescent Pregnancy." *Social Work in Health Care* 27.2 (1998): 49-67. Print

Daly, Kathleen. "Feminist Thinking about Crime." *The Essential Criminology Reader*. Ed. Stuart Henry and Mark M. Lanier. Boulder: Westview Press, 2006. 205-13. Print.

Dohrn, Bernardine. "All Ellas: Girls Locked Up." *Feminist Studies* 30.2 (2004): 302-24. Print.

Ferraro, Kathleen J., and Angela M. Moe. "Mothering, Crime, and Incarceration." *Journal of Contemporary Ethnography* 32.1 (2003): 9-40. Print.

Forrest, Jacqueline D. "Timing of Reproductive Life Stages." *Obstetrics & Gynecology* 82.1 (1993): 105-111. Print.

Gallagher, Catherine A., Adam Dobrin and Anne S. Douds. "A National Overview of Reproductive Health Care Services for Girls in Juvenile Justice Residential Facilities." *Women's Health Issues* 17 (2007): 217-226. Print.

Hufft, Anita. "Supporting Psychological Adaption for the Pregnant Adolescent in Corrections." *The American Journal of Maternal Child Nursing* 29.2 (2004): 122-127. Print.

Hufft, Anita G. and Cindy Peternelj-Taylor. "Ethical Care of Pregnant Adolescents in Correctional Settings." *Journal of Forensic Nursing* 4 (2008): 94-96. Print.

Jolly, M. C., N. Sebire, J. Harris, S. Robinson and L. Regan. "Obstetric Risks of Pregnancy in Women Less Than 18 Years Old." *Obstetrics & Gynecology* 96.6 (2000): 962-966. Print.

Klein, Jonathan D. "Adolescent Pregnancy: Current Trends and Issues." *Pediatrics* 116 (2005); 281-286. Print.

Lorde, Audre. "The Master's Tools Will Never Dismantle the Master's House." 1984. *Sister Outsider: Essays and Speeches*. Berkeley, CA: Crossing Press, 2007. 110-114. Print

Miller, J. and C. W. Mullins. "The Status of Feminist Theories in Criminology." *Taking Stock: The Status of Criminological Theory*. Ed. Francis Cullen, John Wright, and Kristie Blevins. New Jersey: Transaction Publishers, 2006. 217-249. Print.

Ocen, Priscilla A. "Punishing Pregnancy: Race, Incarcerations, and the Shackling of Pregnant Prisoners." *California Law Review* 100.1239 (2012): 1239-1311. Print.

Office of Juvenile Justice and Delinquency Prevention (OJJDP). Statistical Briefing Book. "Juveniles in Corrections." OJJDP, 2010. Web. 3 March 2013.

Royal, Diane. "Detained, Pregnant and at Risk: A Call for National Pregnancy Care Standards in Juvenile Detention Centers." *UCSF Global Health Sciences Student Policy Brief*. July (2012): 1-2. Web. 3 March 2013.

Savio Beers, Lee A. and Ruth E. Hollo."Approaching the Adolescent-Headed Family: A Review of Teen Parenting." *Current Problems in Pediatric and Adolescent Health Care* 39.9 (2009): 216-229. Print.

Sedlak, Andrea J and Carol Bruce. "Youth's Characteristics and Backgrounds: Findings from the Survey of Youth in Residential Placement." *Juvenile Justice Bulletin* December (2010): 1-10. Web. 3 March 2013.

Society for Adolescent Medicine. "Health Care for Incarcerated Youth: Position Paper of the Society for Adolescent Medicine." *Journal of Adolescent Health* 27 (2000): 73-75. Print.

West, Candace and Don H. Zimmerman. "Doing Gender." *Gender and Society* 1.2 (1987): 125-151. Print.

Part II:
Maternal Narratives/
Beyond Criminalization

10. (M)othering with HIV

Resisting and Reconstructing Experiences of Health and Social Surveillance

SAARA GREENE, ALLYSON ION, DAWN ELSTON, GLADYS KWARAMBA, STEPHANIE SMITH AND MONA LOUTFY

SINCE THE EARLY 2000s, women have represented about 25 percent of positive HIV tests in Canada and women of childbearing years are the fastest growing group of persons to be infected with HIV (Public Health Agency of Canada, "HIV/AIDS"). With the success of combination antiretroviral therapy (cART), decreased perinatal HIV transmission rates, and a normalization of pregnancy, rates of pregnancy amongst women living with HIV will continue to rise (Chen et al.; Loutfy et al.)

The decline in vertical transmission of HIV is most attributable to the success of cART. Vertical transmission can occur in three main ways: during fetal gestation and maternal-fetal blood exchange, accounting for 25 percent of all transmissions; during labour and delivery, which is most common, and accounts for 75 percent of reported vertical transmissions; and finally, babies may be infected postpartum vis-à-vis breastfeeding (WHO "HIV Transmission"). Without cART or any perinatal intervention, including Caesarian section, the risk of perinatal or vertical transmission is 15 to 25 *percent* in Europe and North America and 25 to 45 percent in developing areas (Cooper et al.; Public Health Agency of Canada, "At a Glance"; WHO "HIV Transmission"). Breastfeeding presents an additional risk of transmission of 15 to 20 percent without cART (WHO "HIV Transmission"). The discovery and use of cART has resulted in a dramatic decrease in perinatal HIV transmission in Canada from greater than 20 percent in the 1980s to early 1990s to 1.6 percent in 2011 (Public Health Agency of Canada, "At a Glance"). Using cART in the context of pregnancy reduces the risk of vertical transmission to less than 2 percent (Cooper et al.) and this can be further reduced to 0.4 percent when cART is initiated more than four weeks prior to delivery (Forbes et al.).

Despite advances in medical interventions to support mothers living with HIV during the fertility, pregnancy, and birthing trajectory, these interventions have yet to shift social constructions of HIV-positive mothers. While mothers living with HIV are planning pregnancies and becoming mothers, they continue to come up against HIV-related stigma and social exclusion (Elston and Ion; Ion and Elston; Sandelowski, Lambe, and Barroso). The social construction of "ideal" motherhood impacts all women to some degree, yet the gaze upon mothers living with HIV brings with it stigmatizing healthcare experiences that women living with HIV-describe as compromising their emotional and psychological safety (Elston and Ion; Ion and Elston).

In this chapter, the narratives of mothers living with HIV in Ontario expose the spaces where they are "policed by ... the gaze of others" (Ruddick 111) as they encounter multiple modes of surveillance through their interaction with health and social care professionals. Of equal importance are the ways that mothers living with HIV respond to experiences of surveillance throughout pregnancy and motherhood. Drawing on Foucault's notion of resistance, this chapter will illuminate the ways that mothers living with HIV attempt to challenge dominant discourses about pregnancy and motherhood in the context of HIV. As a result, we will see how mothers living with HIV engage in acts of resistance against practices of surveillance.

MOTHERING WITH HIV STUDY

The Mothering with HIV Study is a mixed method, observational study that aimed to explore the psychosocial experiences and needs of mothers with HIV during their pregnancy and the first year of motherhood. Seventy-seven pregnant women living with HIV from across Ontario enrolled in the Mothering with HIV Study where they accessed HIV or obstetrical care from March 2011 to December 2012. A critical component of our methodology was to listen to women's stories vis-à-vis narrative interviews during pregnancy as well as three and twelve months post-partum. We asked the women to share with us their experience of living with HIV throughout their pregnancy /birthing /mothering trajectory. This chapter is based on these narrative interviews and the stories about surveillance that subsequently emerged. First, we situate the current judicial context under which mothers living with HIV experience health and social surveillance and then discuss our theoretical and methodological approach to understanding these experiences. Next, we explore the stories that shaped our analysis of the ways in which mothers living with HIV bump up against methods of surveillance in their daily lives, and the ways in which they attempt to resist and reconstruct these experiences.

SETTING THE CONTEXT: CRIMINALIZATION OF MOTHERS LIVING WITH HIV

The criminalization debate in Canada is mainly focussed on issues of disclosure of HIV to sexual partners in situations where sex would pose a "significant risk" of HIV transmission (Canadian HIV/AIDS Legal Network). For vaginal sex, the court states that a realistic possibility of transmission would be negated if a person had a low or undetectable viral load and condoms were used (Allard, Katatchkine, and Symington). Curiously, "criminalization is often described and perceived as a tool to protect heterosexual women from HIV infection" (Canadian HIV/AIDS Legal Network 1). However, a gendered analysis of the current law in Canada suggests that the law does little to protect women from HIV infection and, due to HIV-related stigma and discrimination and the complexity surrounding HIV disclosure to family and friends, has particularly negative consequences for women who face poverty, racism, the historical impact of colonization of Aboriginal people in Canada, and a precarious immigration status (Allard, Katatchkine, and Symington). HIV-related criminalization is further complicated for mothers living with HIV. At the most extreme end of the continuum are places like Mongolia where women with HIV are legally required to terminate any pregnancy (Worth, Patton, and Goldstein 7), while in some countries legislation specifically targets vertical transmission of HIV (Ahmed). Moreover, the language used in HIV-specific laws is often broad and leaves open the possibility of prosecuting vertical transmission of HIV whether through pregnancy, childbirth, breastfeeding, or another route. Strict interpretations of these laws contribute to the social construction of mothers living with HIV as criminal or having the potential to engage in criminal acts, such as not taking antiretroviral therapy during pregnancy or breastfeeding once the baby is born (Ahmed; Csete, Pearshouse, and Symington; Little, Hu, and Dominguez). Moreover, this situates women living with HIV in the position of *feeling* criminalized as they navigate a web of health, social, and legal spaces and demonstrates how criminalization can operate both formally and informally. Brant and Brant distinguish between formal and informal criminalization stating that:

> Informal criminalization is the societal or social construction of certain behavior as criminal. Formal criminalization is the legal definition of certain behavior as criminal, expressed by ways of statutes, and sanctioning by judicial authorities. These definitions do not necessarily overlap. Not everything that is legally criminal is also considered criminal by society and vice versa. (qtd. in Huisman 114)

While it is not considered "criminal" for a woman with HIV to become pregnant, her pregnant body may raise questions about her method of conception and the possibility of vertical transmission. Consequently, the policing of women's bodies during pregnancy and child birth and in their role as mothers puts women with HIV in the position of having to defend the choices they make to have sex, to become pregnant, and to mother. This is perhaps most clearly understood within the criminalization of HIV discourse, which highlights:

> The widening social gap between seropositive and seronegative members of affected communities; gender and race as they shape the experience of AIDS … and the impact of culture on health decision making, moral regulation, and the policing of sexuality, public health, and judicial delineation of specific populations. (Worth, Patton, and Goldstein 3)

These constructions of people living with HIV are woven through HIV/AIDS criminalization cases in which various legal approaches have been used (Worth, Patton, and Goldstein). Some approaches include HIV-specific laws, while other jurisdictions (including Canada and parts of the United States) use existing laws to prosecute HIV exposure and/or transmission. Charges related to non-disclosure of HIV status are further complicated for mothers with HIV (Ahmed; Weait). During the first decade of the HIV epidemic, Miller and Carlton suggested that vertical HIV transmission be included in definitions of child abuse and neglect (qtd. in Gilbert 100). Although this policy was never widely adopted, there have been cases where non-HIV specific laws have been used to prosecute mothers living with HIV. For example, in Canada, section 215 of the Criminal Code of Canada states that a parent, guardian, or head of a family who has legal duty to provide the "necessaries of life for a child under the age of 16 years" and who fails to do so without a legitimate excuse, commits an offence (Criminal Code).

In these cases, mothers can be charged with child neglect for vertical transmission of HIV. Such was the case in 2006 when Canada became the first country to prosecute vertical transmission of HIV when an Ontario woman was convicted of child neglect as a result of the vertical transmission of HIV to one of her children. In the judge's decision, he cited her "lack of remorse" as driving his decision to remove her children from her care, and included her ongoing HIV management in the conditions of her sentence (Catholic Children's Aid Society of Hamilton). This case is reminiscent of the ways in which the female criminal was historically cast as "excessively vile and cruel in their crimes ... [and] combined the qualities of the criminal male with the worst characteristics of the female ... lacking 'maternal instinct'" (Balfour and Comack 25), thus serving to further the othering of women when they depart from what is deemed "appropriate" mothering behaviour.

Regardless of the numbers of mothers with HIV being formally prosecuted under the law for HIV-related issues, women living with HIV remain under the constant surveillance of health and social care professionals partly to support them in their care, and partly to ensure that they do not put their babies or children "at risk." It is here that we question the ways in which criminality is also a social construction and consider the ways in which this subjects mothers living with HIV to becoming informally criminalized. We argue that while the formal criminalization of HIV is troublesome and continues to subject women and mothers to being viewed as "vectors of transmission," it is the social construction of informal criminalization that is most disruptive in the daily lives of mothers living with HIV. Mothers living with HIV "are routinely sanctioned not only for violating legal codes, but also for violating codes of conduct that regulate and patrol the boundaries of 'appropriate' female behaviour" (Balfour and Comack 74-75). Along the preconception, pregnancy, and motherhood trajectory some women face more surveillance and are more vulnerable to formal criminalization, as we will learn from participants in the Mothering with HIV Study.

Finally, impending motherhood may be complicated by external and internalized manifestations of HIV-related stigma within clinical, community, and personal spaces. Where HIV-related stigma and socially constructed ideals of motherhood collide, the consequences may be detrimental to both women and children (Breitbart et al.). For example, the belief that children who are born to women living with HIV or women who use drugs are "innocent" victims of "bad mothers" can be devastating for mothers and their children (Breitbart et al.). If health and social care professionals continue to uphold biased views about the "face" of HIV, women with HIV may perceive themselves as vulnerable targets of healthcare providers like nurses or physicians and social service agencies. This could be exacerbated for women during pregnancy and postpartum when there is an increase in the surveillance and monitoring of their health and the health of the fetus/baby. What follows is an analysis of the ways in which women living with HIV are *informally criminalized* through this ongoing process of surveillance and the impact this has on their experience of pregnancy and motherhood.

THEORETICAL LENS: THE SOCIAL CONSTRUCTION OF MOTHERS WITH HIV

When people hear that you are HIV-positive they auto-

matically think, ok, you shouldn't be having babies and then it's defending my right to have children, you know?
—(Mother of three)[1]

Identities of mothers with HIV are socially constructed long before they become pregnant and give birth. These constructions are influenced by conventional and long-established perceptions about women living with HIV that are embedded in the very institutions and systems where they receive their health and social care and, in some places, in the way this care is provided (Elston and Ion; Ion and Elston; Krentz, Dean, and Gill; Wingood et al.). The misconception that the route of HIV infection for women is through illicit and/or promiscuous behaviour (Sandelowski, Lambe, and Barroso; Webel and Higgins) exacerbates stereotypes about, and stigma toward, women with HIV. This focus on women's sexuality and reproductive social role reinforces essentialized notions of sex and gender that obscure the structural determinants of HIV vulnerability and perpetuate notions of women as vectors of transmission (Lekas, Siegel, and Schrimshaw; Wingood et al.). These stereotypical assumptions continue during pregnancy and motherhood. As Sandelowski, Barroso and Voils argue, "in the case of HIV-positive women who are or want to be mothers, motherhood places them in a 'double-bind' as they are following the cultural script for normal womanhood while violating the script that 'good' mothers do not expose children to the risk of illness and death" (4). Consequently, during pregnancy and motherhood women with HIV often find themselves being policed by doctors, nurses, and social workers attempting to ensure that they engage in 'good' mothering. Within these systems they access for care and support, mothers with HIV confront HIV-related stigma.

Our analysis of the social construction of mothers living with HIV echoes a feminist argument that explores the complexities and nuances of motherhood, which we place at the intersection with various social, political, and economic tensions. The women in our study were "mothering under duress" (Greaves et al. 1). This occurs through a process of being "routinely subjected to high expectations and idealistic standards of behaviour and nurturance in relation to their children" (Greaves et al. 3). These standards play themselves out through regulatory practices and "disciplinary machinations" (Campbell 921) that govern through and are embedded in social and legal policies.

Adrienne Rich posits two features of modern patriarchal motherhood that are particularly harmful to mothers. First, is the assumption that mothering is natural to women and that child rearing is the sole responsibility of the biological mother (qtd. in O'Reilly 5). Second, mothers are assigned sole responsibility for "motherwork," but are given no power to determine the conditions under which they mother (qtd. in O'Reilly 5). Consequently, as Ruddick argues, "mothers are policed by ... the 'gaze of others' ... teachers, grandparents, mates, friends, employers, even an anonymous passerby can judge a mother" (Ruddick 111) and, as a result, "relinquish authority to others [and] lose confidence in their own values" (Ruddick 111). We take this argument in a different direction. We suggest that rather than "relinquish" their authority, "the gaze of others" that mothers with HIV experience leads to undermining, challenging and, at times, appropriating their authority, through formal and informal governance. Mothers are policed both formally vis-à-vis the HIV criminalization law and informally by being under the constant surveillance of health and social care professionals and society, which places them in a more complex and difficult situation than a "double bind." Fundamentally, m/othering with HIV occurs whilst her right to mother is called into question.

METHODOLOGY: TELLING STORIES

We completed 77 narrative interviews with Mothering with HIV Study participants in their third trimester of pregnancy and again at three and twelve months post-partum between March 2011 and June 2013. We used a narrative methodological approach to listen to and represent storied interpretations of life experiences and events of a marginalized and traditionally silenced population (Hendry). This approach was chosen to reflect our commitment to community-based research and positioning women's voices at the centre of the research process. As participants shared stories, we listened, seeking clarification or an expansion of the stories they shared within the larger narrative. The interviews were audio recorded and transcribed verbatim.

Our approach to narrative analysis most closely reflects Riessman's process of unpacking, interpreting, and analyzing the story with close attention paid to the uniqueness of time and environment in which the story was told. We engaged in this process through hiring and training Peer Research Associates (PRAs) who were mothers living with HIV to engage in narrative interviews with participants and be involved in the narrative analysis. Narrative informed content analysis was conducted to fully unpack and reflect on the stories within the narrative interviews. Research team members including the PRAs participated in a process of reflexivity that incorporated the PRAs' reflections of their experience of the narrative interview and their interpretation of the stories that were being told.

In order to share and highlight stories associated with health and social surveillance during pregnancy and/or the early stages of motherhood, we focus on four vignettes that reflect the range of experiences shared by Mothering with HIV Study participants and that highlight both the differences and similarities of becoming and being a mother living with HIV. Moreover, these stories highlight common themes expressed by the majority of women who participated in our study: that mothers living with HIV often engage in myriad coping strategies such as "passing" in order to resist the cultural scripts ascribed to them (Ingram and Hutchinson "Double Binds") while at the same time navigating the multiple spaces in which mothers living with HIV come up against stigma.

THE STORIES

Pamela's Story: "As a patient you're always thinking in your head, what are they thinking?"

Pamela was diagnosed with HIV early in her first pregnancy as part of prenatal testing efforts across Ontario. When expecting her second child, Pamela reflected on her experience as a mother living with HIV in a small, rural town in Ontario with one child under the age of five. Her anxiety was instantly heightened when she recounted her awareness of and concern for privacy and confidentiality throughout pregnancy and early postpartum, predominantly because of her HIV diagnosis:

> *Finding everything out ... it changed my whole pregnancy cause I had to get monitored more and then, you know ... when you go into the hospital there's always a random person that's checking your file so it's like every day you are, like, melting cause you're like, Oh God!, One more person has seen that.*

Pamela talked about having her pregnant body being subject to the constant surveillance of healthcare providers. This made Pamela feel "different" from other mothers in her community and, as a result, she decided to limit her movements to conceal her HIV status:

> *It was a lot of, like, just unsettledness...not knowing who you are going to run in to, who's going to see you there, who's going to say something, when you're constantly meeting new people ... or having to go to the hospital ... the less places that I am, where they don't know ... just doing those things made it so I had to be there more.*

Pamela also employed a process of concealment in response to the lack of health education and sensitivity toward women with HIV during the birthing process. Recalling how the moments following the birth of her child made her feel particularly vulnerable, Pamela shared:

> *I remember after the baby was born ... the nurses were there for the clean-up process.... I remember them saying, "So what are we supposed to do now with the placenta and blood and stuff?" I remember them talking to each other and me being listening and thinking, "what the heck?" ...Thinking in my head, "I know why they are saying this, do they know that I know why they are saying this?" ...I'll never forget that moment ... it's just burned into me.*

Pamela's experience of being under medical surveillance and constantly feeling "othered" by healthcare providers continued after her baby was born. To protect herself from being "burned" again, Pamela and her partner planned for the ongoing surveillance of her birthing and mothering "choices." Pamela recounts:

> *We had to lie to everyone why I am having a caesarian... researching different diagnoses that I could have because you don't want to tell anyone the truth, and then it's like, why aren't you breastfeeding? So you are making up all these lies ... no one knew ... the hospital staff knew, but my family didn't know, his family didn't know, our friends didn't know, nobody knew.*

Like other mothers with HIV Pamela took cART to prevent vertical transmission of HIV to the fetus. Once the baby is born, the mother can stop taking cART if it is clinically indicated and appropriate, but must administer antiretroviral medication to the baby until they are six weeks old (Bitnun et al.; Burdge et al). Eventually, all of the prenatal and postpartum appointments, infant HIV testing, and other modes of surveillance and control that Pamela experienced during pregnancy, birth, and postpartum ended. Pamela's body went from being a site of constant surveillance to a body left alone. Yet, this process continues to resound deeply for Pamela as she considers the possibility of having another baby:

> *It definitely makes you reflect on whether you would do it again.... I would like to, but when I think about the whole process.... It's nice to have that all done and not have to keep going to doctors and getting on with your life.... Now we can just have a normal life because I just have to go for my four checks a year and my blood work and as long as everything keeps coming back and my drugs are working, then it's like, it's non-existent...the making baby part, the whole thing brings it back to the forefront.*

Hence, for some women living with HIV, the decision to become a mother includes deep consideration and anticipation of how HIV will impact their overall experience of pregnancy and the first few months of motherhood. For Pamela, her experience of pregnancy and motherhood were constant reminders of her HIV status and the deep-seeded concerns she carried about HIV-related stigma in both her personal life and with her interactions with healthcare professionals. As the following vignettes will detail, the reality of, and concerns about HIV-related stigma persists once the baby is born.

Elizabeth and Lydia's Stories: "Why aren't you breastfeeding?"

Echoing the voices of many mothers who participated in the Mothering with HIV Study, Elizabeth and Lydia expressed multiple moments of surveillance with regard to their infant feeding practice. Elizabeth had been diagnosed with HIV when she gave birth to her first child five years ago. At that time, she lived in the Caribbean via West Africa and has since settled with her husband and child in a mid-sized city in Ontario. Elizabeth's experiences of HIV stigma in the Caribbean resulted in her decision not to disclose her HIV status to anyone, including very close family and friends. Early on in her story she shared, "I have refused to tell anybody here (in Canada), nobody except the clinic.... I don't want to be identified with HIV, like, I'm sorry, but it's that's how I feel, like it's something I don't want to be associated with."

However, Elizabeth's need to protect herself from being identified as HIV positive coupled with her desire to detach herself from being linked with other women with HIV became increasingly challenging upon becoming pregnant and giving birth. This was perhaps most salient for Elizabeth in the context of her desire to breastfeed. Elizabeth stated: "Before this situation, I planned that I was going to breastfeed for two years, now I can't do it at all." This disappointment resulted in her feeling torn between the desire to breastfeed and the fear of exposing her baby to HIV. Lydia, who was diagnosed during pregnancy, recalled similar memories: "It was the first thing I asked when the doctor told me and I was the first patient he ever had that was HIV positive which made it worse, and he goes 'ya your test came back (positive),' and the first thing I said was, can I breastfeed? I remember that."

In Canada, mothers living with HIV are recommended to not breastfeed in order to prevent the risk of HIV transmission through the consumption of breast milk (Bitnun et al.). Both Elizabeth and Lydia were devastated upon being advised against breastfeeding and their stories highlight the multiple ways in which women are socialized to equate good mothering with breastfeeding. Elizabeth shared:

> *The heartbreaking side of it, I feel like when I had him I was almost getting into depression 'cause I couldn't breastfeed him. I love him so much that I want to breastfeed him.... I know how they love breasts and all that, so not being able to breastfeed is emotionally dramatic for me.*

These feelings were echoed by Lydia when she spoke about both the personal and societal value put on breastfeeding and how this contributed to her feelings about good mothering:

> *It was important, it is important. I mean, that is what we are equipped to do you know, it's just part of mothering so, that's why I feel bad that I am pregnant; like I knew all this stuff you know? And all those books that I read, the pregnancy books they always say breastfeeding is way better than bottle-fed babies, I wish they would just split it in half to make us feel better you know.*

When Elizabeth's second child arrived, she continued to struggle with her feelings about not breastfeeding. This time however, she was equally challenged by the surveillance of her infant feeding practices and ultimate pressure to breastfeed from her sister-in-law who was unaware of her HIV status:

> *She kept asking me, she had asked me on the phone if I'm breastfeeding, I told her, yes, I was breastfeeding.... She came and asked me again, I was going to get upset, but I just didn't want any misunderstanding, like, why will you keep asking me this same question? ... My brother was telling me that he already told her not to bother me with*

> *personal questions...she's a doctor so she...really knows how to ask the questions.*

Lydia's concerns about the future echoes Elizabeth's current experience as she disclosed her anxiety at how she would manage the onslaught of infant feeding surveillance and questions by friends:

> *That's also why I don't want my friends to come to the hospital to visit me because they are going to be why are you, how do you know you can't breastfeed, why are you just bottle feeding right away, I can't say oh well the baby wouldn't latch on like I can't say those things 'cause you can see I haven't even tried. It's a big thing for me to come up with us something to say.*

Elizabeth's infant feeding practices continued to be under the surveillance of friends and family in the very spaces where she sought social and faith-based support:

> *I go to church every Sunday.... If I go now and she's struggling with the bottle... [t]hey will be asking me to breastfeed her and I don't want to be lying.... I'll tell them that I don't breastfeed in the day.... God forgive me, I don't like lying, but I don't want to start explaining too many things.*

Serena's Story: "I've been doing everything I'm supposed to"

For over a quarter of Mothering with HIV Study participants, experiences of social surveillance and the policing of their mothering started as a result of their involvement with the Children's AIDS Society (CAS). This was the case for Serena, a young Aboriginal woman living in rural Ontario. Serena was eight months pregnant with her seventh child when she shared with us her history of CAS involvement. Her six other children were placed into the care of her parents because of a concern regarding domestic violence with a previous partner. Prior to her seventh pregnancy, Serena became aware of her HIV status and engaged in HIV care in her community. One year later, under the care of a supportive HIV care team, Serena and her new partner were expecting a baby. This support gave Serena the confidence to be open about her HIV status with the CAS workers managing her case:

> *I'm open with people, like other professionals ... 'cause I expect that respect and being professional, right? ... I did everything, I've got all my appointments, I've been doing everything I'm supposed to ... . I have to get a letter and kind of, you know, cover my back that way I guess 'cause I know once this baby comes ... it could become a big issue, so I need to be prepared.*

However, after disclosing her HIV status to her child protection worker, Serena witnessed a lack of knowledge about and sensitivity toward her as a mother living with HIV: "She [CAS worker] ended up turning it against me saying, well, you know, you could drop dead any minute and ... you shouldn't be around the kids, you shouldn't risk them ... they are not very knowledgeable about that."

It appeared to Serena that her decision to disclose her status resulted in a shift from being supported to being policed by the CAS. Although Serena was "doing everything she was supposed to" regarding medical care for herself and the fetus, she was now under the constant surveillance of her child protection worker to ensure the protection of her baby while in utero:

> *They said I knew I was pregnant ... and I should have started my medication right then but ... there was no possible way I could have known.... I went right away to the doctor and got referred and went through the whole process, everything was fine, the doctor was completely happy I did everything on time and started my medication on time and my virals were low and just to be safe for the baby, you know, I have to take the medication so I've done everything I had to, but CAS is, like, you should have started it in December ... so I gave them all of the dates ... and they are still using it against me.*

Even though Serena was receiving support and validation by her physician, she continued to be policed by the CAS regarding her

HIV care. It was unclear to Serena how her "mothering" capacity to care for her baby would be assessed:

> *I know I'm gonna have to fight for this baby and I'm ... scared what's going to happen and especially with the medicine and the treatments and I don't want them to think I'm not doing what I can for this baby ... with the* CAS *they think I shouldn't have a baby, I shouldn't be pregnant.*

Corresponding with the experiences that Pamela, Elizabeth and Lydia shared, Serena's story highlights the gravity of HIV-related stigma and discrimination in the lives of pregnant women and mothers living with HIV. However, Serena's story amplifies, through her interactions with the CAS and her worry about having to "fight" for her baby, the intersecting of HIV-related stigma and the policing of mothers living with HIV. This is a critical point that exposes the centrality of surveillance in the lives of women living with HIV.

(M)OTHERING UNDER SURVEILLANCE: INTERROGATING PRACTICES

The social positioning of mothering has been both "revered and denigrated over the centuries" (Greaves et al. 3), and this has meant that, at times, motherhood has also been viewed as requiring some form of regulation and surveillance (Smart). Today, academic literature documents how health and social care professionals continue the practice of "othering" of mothers through their surveillance of women from socially marginalized groups (Van Den Tillaart, Kurtz, and Cash; Vasas). The concept of surveillance that denotes the process of exercising disciplinary power (Foucault) is particularly useful as it acknowledges both the "medical gaze" and social control function of social work and allied health care providers (Burton-Jeangros; Davies and Allen; Greene). For example, Robinson's report on health visiting in the United Kingdom illustrates how health visitors shifted their practice from a position of providing support to the practice of policing new mothers vis-à-vis assessment for the risk of child abuse (Robinson). Further along this trajectory of new motherhood is Greene's research, which argues that pregnant teenagers and young mothers are subject to surveillance and control by social workers, educators, and healthcare providers, and that the "policing" of poor and working class young women in particular, is a "process that begins from the time she is viewed as possessing a sexual body and continues throughout her pregnancy and maternity" (Greene 128). More recently, Burton-Jeangros identified how the prevalence of risk management with regard to the health of pregnant women in general has increased through the medicalization of pregnancy, birth, and breastfeeding, which has resulted in defining "legitimate and illegitimate maternal practices" (421). Consequently, these deep-seeded and formalized modes of surveillance result in socially and culturally "acceptable" ways of doing pregnancy and motherhood and, in turn, are out of reach for mothers living with HIV. As we have demonstrated throughout this chapter, women living with HIV during pregnancy, birth, and motherhood must navigate both cultural constructions of good mothering and misconceptions about their capacity to mother because of their HIV status.

The policing of women's bodies is not a new phenomenon. For example, scholars have argued that young, working-class, poor, and racialized women before, during, and after pregnancy are under the intense surveillance of health and social service providers and that the policing of their sexuality is a process that continues throughout pregnancy and maternity (Greene; Greene, O'Brien-Teengs, et al.; O'Brien-Teengs et al.; Walkerdine, Lucey, and Melody). The consequences of this are feelings of alienation and stigma as a result of their interactions with health and social care professionals (Greene, Chambers, et al.; Ion et al.). These arguments are echoed by the women in our study and are reflected in the vignettes above.

The vignettes delineate three moments in time when mothers living with HIV are particularly subject to both formal and informal modes of surveillance by health and social care providers, family, and friends. This increased surveillance occurs during pregnancy, immediately following birth, and in the early stages of motherhood. These stories also demonstrate that although the mothers we interviewed did not engage in "criminal" acts under the law, by virtue of being HIV-positive, the acts they did engage in were treated as such by the very people who would normally provide support. Moreover, these stories highlight the ways that mothers with HIV are portrayed as women who have the potential to engage in criminal acts under the law or whose life choices are viewed as criminal, albeit informally by virtue of being HIV-positive. This emerged through expressing their feeling that their sexuality and ability to "do" pregnancy and motherhood was called into question.

Many mothers living with HIV found receiving care and support within health and social care systems and institutions difficult, given the inherent power imbalances within the service provider-client relationship. This was salient for women who were pregnant or had just given birth, who experienced a unique form of surveillance and monitoring by a range of health and social care professionals. Moreover, in situations where the prevention of vertical transmission of HIV from mother to child is the primary goal of their care, "the patient-professional interaction is organized as an interrogation" (Kleinmann 16). Interrogation in the lives of the mothers who participated in our study emerged through being questioned about their mothering abilities and responsibilities in the context of living with HIV. It is critical that we acknowledge this is not always the case, and that some HIV clinicians are committed to providing respectful and supportive care. However, when it is not, the marriage between surveillance and interrogation is consummated. It is within these situations that we agree with Pryce who argues that the encounter in the clinic between lay person and service provider may be especially intense because of constructions of disciplinary power and forms of lay knowledge and experience. This was palpable in the stories were heard from Pamela and Lydia, both diagnosed with HIV during pregnancy. In their cases, power, knowledge, and experience became elusive insofar as a patient they became "disembodied." Their maternal bodies were "sites of governmentality" where tensions arise between a "disciplinary regime of surveillance and discretion through self-monitoring" (Pryce 109).

The marriage between surveillance and interrogation is a strong one, and continues throughout pregnancy and after birth. As mothers with HIV are caught in the middle of this relationship, the tension they experience occurs within formal and informal settings. Here, we recall Pamela's statement that being diagnosed with HIV during pregnancy "changes everything." Yet, the changes that Pamela focussed on when she told her story related to her experience of being under surveillance. Suddenly her body was monitored in ways she did not anticipate. She felt vulnerable to a range of people who had access to her personal information and HIV diagnosis, including people outside the medical profession. Medical surveillance during pregnancy and birth overlapped and then shifted to the hands of family and friends. She anticipated being interrogated about her birthing decisions and prepared to "lie" to ensure her HIV status was not disclosed. Pamela engaged in "defensive mothering" (Ingram and Hutchinson, "Defensive mothering" 246). For Pamela, the fear of being exposed and stigmatized as a woman living with HIV led her to guard herself against "being caught." Pamela did the "mental work" of planning and assessing her every move, fearing the potential consequences of her HIV status being disclosed for her partner, her children, and herself.

Experiences of infant feeding is perhaps one of the most clearly defined moments where the relationship between surveillance, interrogation, and "defensive mothering" plays out for women living with HIV. Formally, this occurs through infant feeding policy discourses in the context of HIV. In Canada, women with HIV are recommended to avoid breastfeeding. This is irrespective of whether they are taking cART, as well as how much HIV is in their blood (which can be determined by a blood test) or how much HIV is in their breast milk (testing that is not conducted in routine clinical practice) (Bitnun et al.; Burdge et al.). Around the globe, however, there exists a range of clinical practice guidelines recommending how mothers living with HIV should (or should not) feed their infant (Bitnun et al.; Burdge et al.; Department of Health; World Health Organization, "Guidelines"), as well as how mothers' infant feeding practices should be monitored by health and social care professionals in both clinical and community settings. Elizabeth and Lydia's experiences with "well-intentioned" family and friends reveal tensions between surveillance and women's agency, particularly "defensive mothering." Most distressing here is the social and political context in which modes of surveillance arise and how mothers living with HIV are forced to navigate a wider maternal culture that espouses "breast is best" (Hausman; Thulier; Wall). This gives almost everyone from healthcare provider to perfect stranger permission to police the infant feeding practices of all women. Women who "choose" not to breastfeed (regardless of reason) are held suspect. This also puts mothers living with HIV in Canada in a no-win situation because breastfeeding can, in fact, be a formal route to criminalization. Thus, in the case of breastfeeding recommendations and policies in Canada, women with HIV are potentially criminal if they do and viewed as deviant if they don't.

The policing of mothers with HIV continues. For mothers with a history of child protection system involvement, the surveillance process starts in pregnancy and continues until long after the birth of their baby. Historically, child protection in the context of HIV focussed primarily on guardianship, custody arrangements, and separation of mother and child prior to HIV disease progression (Blanche et al.; Forehand et al.; Rotheram-Borus et al.). Today, the epidemiology of HIV has changed significantly with the advent of cART and the increase in women with HIV choosing to become pregnant. However, the knowledge, attitudes, and policies of child protection services do not reflect these changes. Moreover, for mothers with HIV who experience the impact of housing instability, racism, colonization, immigration concerns, and partner violence, the threat of CAS involvement remains a daily concern (Greene, Chambers, et al.; Greene, O'Brien-Teengs, et al.). These fears, coupled with the very real stigma and discrimination mothers living with HIV experience (O'Brien-Teengs et al.), may prevent them from disclosing their status to child protection workers.

Alternatively, in hopes that she could create an opportunity to access supportive care, Serena chose to disclose her status to her child protection worker. Rather than the care she received from her medical team, Serena was ridiculed by her CAS worker for becoming pregnant and criticized for her desire to mother while living with HIV. This reflects earlier work by Juhasz and Sacks who suggest that placing emphasis on the "innocent" child victims of AIDS further marginalizes HIV-positive women as "selfish procreators and blameworthy" (qtd. in Gilbert 111). Although this dated view does not reflect the current paradigm of HIV as a chronic, manageable condition, this perspective may negatively impact the quality of services women receive. Child protection workers may have a strong sense of empathy for the child and little desire to engage with the mother (Gilbert; Thompson) and, in turn, shift their role from one of social support to one of social surveillance. In Serena's case, disclosing her HIV status to her child protection worker led to increased surveillance. It began a long process of ongoing interrogation about issues that would typically be addressed by a physician (i.e. when to start taking antiretroviral therapy in pregnancy and her mortality). Of equal significance here was how the child protection worker questioned Serena's choice to become pregnant and mother her child due to her assumption that Serena would either "drop dead" of AIDS and thus leave her children without a mother, or put her child at risk of acquiring HIV.

RESPONDING TO SURVEILLANCE: WHERE DO WE GO FROM HERE?

How mothers respond to social constructions of mothering with HIV and the agency they demonstrate during their encounters with surveillance and criminalization is equally significant to the processes themselves. We heard numerous stories of resilience, reframing, and revolutionizing constructions of mothering with HIV. In particular, Caroline's story best reflects the range of ways mothers living with HIV engage in this process.

Caroline's Story: "I'm an exotic creature ... paving the way for these women"

Caroline came to the town she now calls home when she was five months pregnant with her first baby. At that time she was working in the sex trade, was street-involved, and was arrested by the police. Five years later, Caroline, who was pregnant with her third child, shared with us her story of being inspired. She was connected to HIV care in her community and was giving back to the town that helped her find stable housing for her family by volunteering for a community-based outreach and education program through her local HIV/AIDS service organization. The importance and value this work held for Caroline was reflected in her stating,

> *I'm very blessed to be open with my status ... and be willing to educate.... If I reach out and only one person hears me ... that's one person who's heard me ... not a hundred who've not.*

However, getting to this place in her life did not happen overnight and has all been part of her journey toward acceptance of her HIV status, one that has involved resisting the ways that mothers with HIV come under social surveillance:

> *Probably about the third year of my diagnosis is when I just decided, you know what? I am going to be open with people. I don't care I'm an HIV-positive mom, I can't breastfeed, who cares, kind of thing, and I still have people in town who are like Ahhh!—whatever, I don't care.*

Throughout this process, Caroline came to view herself as a leader in her community and exclaims, "I feel like I'm an exotic creature 'cause it's not something, you know, people hear about.... I'm not only very open with my status I'm also very inquisitive and I'm willing to challenge people's thoughts ... so I'm kind of, in a sense, paving the way for other HIV-positive mothers." Caroline demonstrates leadership and a desire to reconstruct the ways in which mothers living with HIV are viewed because she envisions a time when they will not be considered "different" from other mothers. Caroline's hope is that surveillance of mothers with HIV will be minimized to enable them to engage in practices that society considers a "normal" part of the motherhood experience:

> *I'm hoping in 25 years people that I've mentored that have HIV can turn around and say, you know what? I'm HIV-positive and I can breastfeed because we found technology that enables us to do so ... and I'd also like to see positive women be able to have birth at home.*

Caroline's story reflects Judith Arcana's belief that "if we want girls to grow into free women, brave and strong, we must be those women ourselves" (33). By mothering against motherhood, and becoming, in Adrienne Rich's words, "outlaws from the institution of motherhood" (qtd. in O'Reilly 165), women like Caroline obtain empowerment through mothering (O'Reilly 165). But the question still remains: how do we move from a state of social surveillance, monitoring, interrogation, and criminalization of mothers living with HIV to a state of social care through which mothering with HIV is normalized, accepted, and as Pamela states "left alone"? This is a complex question that is grounded in the fact that while Caroline's commitment to openness about her HIV status is one way that people living with HIV resist HIV stigma and surveillance (Poindexter and Shippy), this is certainly not an option for many women. This is particularly the case for mothers who are confronted by the perceived dichotomy and tension between the interests and welfare of the mother (as an autonomous adult) and the well-being of the infant (mother as "protector of the fetus") (Breitbart et al.). In fact, as highlighted in the vignettes above, many Mothering with HIV Study participants experienced care as being *for the baby*, rather than for themselves, reinforcing the view of women with HIV who are pregnant and/or who mother as deviant. This raises the question of how is it possible to create spaces for women with HIV during pregnancy and the early stages of motherhood where they feel cared for and accepted, where care is offered as both separate (for them) as well as being connected to the care of the fetus/baby.

SUPPORTING MOTHERS LIVING WITH HIV

At a time when significant medical advances make it possible for women living with HIV to become pregnant and give birth without transmitting HIV to one's partner or baby, negative social and medical constructions of women with HIV during pregnancy and in their roles as mothers endure. The social surveillance against all mothers, the combination of HIV-related stigma, the HIV and criminalization debate, and a lack of understanding of what it means to live with HIV, contribute to the ongoing experience of stigma and social exclusion of pregnant women and mothers with

HIV. Ginn has argued that "rather than placing legally enforceable obligations on pregnant women that are not placed on others, we should be trying to ensure that there are sufficient social and economic supports in place such that a pregnant women will be better able to make choices that enhance her own and the fetus's well-being" (36). In this chapter we have demonstrated the need for adopting an anti-oppressive approach of supporting mothers living with HIV that must include a contextualized understanding of the biomedical, psychosocial, cultural, and economic factors that may be influencing their experience as women and mothers (Young et al.). This approach would go beyond existing recommendations and clinical practice frameworks for preventing vertical HIV transmission and would include an understanding of the structural and systemic factors that are pervasive in the lives of mothers living with HIV, including the public and private spaces where they experience health and social surveillance, as well as poverty, racism, sexism, and HIV-related stigma and discrimination. This type of support would celebrate their identities as pregnant women and mothers while acknowledging the spaces where they may bump up against social barriers and emotional concerns.

Health and social care providers can take part in challenging the surveillance of women living with HIV and reduce criminalization in two main ways. First, health and social care providers need to find new ways of supporting women throughout their perinatal care trajectory by developing creative strategies to discuss questions regarding birthing and infant feeding choices. These discussions can occur early in pregnancy and promote alternative messaging about motherhood and identity. Instead of an "interrogation," this could involve a two-way conversation that honours the unique sociocultural experiences of women in the context of HIV and pregnancy. Some mothers living with HIV may prefer to work with a trusted care provider around self-advocacy and how to actively respond to surveillance, while others may choose to engage in acts of concealment and self-surveillance. Regardless, it is important that care providers have the necessary tools and resources to fully support women and their families through these experiences.

Another important way health and social care providers can respond to the interrogation and surveillance of mothers living with HIV is to work collaboratively with researchers, HIV care specialists, and women themselves to develop education, training, and advocacy tools that normalize pregnancy for women living with HIV. It is here that it becomes particularly important to consider the "cultural safety" of mothers with HIV and to draw attention to power imbalances within systems and institutions on the basis of culture and race (Browne, Smye, and Varcoe). This suggestion aligns with the Canadian Health and Welfare Agency (Epp) and the World Health Organization ("Declaration of Alma-Ata") who advocate for equitable and comprehensive provision of healthcare to all citizens (Kirby and Wilbert; Romanow; Van Den Tillaart, Kurtz, and Cash) in addition to policies that address the complex and interrelated social, economic, and environmental determinants of health and wellness (Public Health Agency of Canada, "What Determines Health?").

We recognize, however, that health and social service practice is informed by education, cultural background(s), and social standing, combined with privilege and power bestowed on providers in their positions within institutions. Calling attention to and closing the persistent gap between service providers and those who are marginalized is essential (Van Den Tillaart, Kurtz, and Cash). In spite of public and professional education campaigns about HIV, deep-rooted stigma and discrimination amongst healthcare providers continues to impede reproductive choice and violate fundamental human rights for women and mothers with HIV (Ahmed, Hanssens, and Kelly; Lawson, Bayly, and Cey). Furthermore, the concern for increased awareness on the part of child protection workers is heightened given that few child protection workers in public systems have any formal training in social work (Gilbert 110). The culture of power and privilege within health and social service institutions perpetuates and encourages the increased surveillance and monitoring of mothers living with HIV. There is an immediate opportunity and need to reframe the pedagogical and structural systems that enable this culture of power and privilege over those who are marginalized to flourish.

NOT THE END OF THE STORY....

O'Reilly argues that motherhood is specifically and fundamentally a cultural practice that is continuously redesigned in response to changing economic and societal factors, and that as a cultural construction, its meaning varies with time and place and there is no essential or universal experience of motherhood (O'Reilly 4). The narratives of mothers shared herein demonstrate the critical need to establish dialogue and collaborative working relationships between all stakeholders aimed at supporting mothers with HIV and their families, including child protection workers, clinicians, community-based service providers, and community leaders (Boland et al.; Forehand et al.; O'Brien-Teengs et al.). This dialogue is critical to shaping ongoing collaborative training, practice, and policy initiatives within the child welfare, healthcare, social service, and non-profit sectors, as well as academic institutions that are training the next generation of physicians, nurses, social workers, and other allied health professionals. It is also critical that mothers living with HIV themselves are involved in the discussion and treated as equal partners with health and social care professionals to ensure their unique historical and current day realities are integrated within the development, implementation, and evaluation of training, practice, and policy initiatives (O'Brien-Teengs et al.). In this, mothers living with HIV must lead the way.

ENDNOTES

[1]This excerpt and all subsequent excerpts from transcripts are from interviews conducted by the Mothering with HIV Study (study funded April 1, 2010 to March 31, 2014; data collection completed in 2014).

WORKS CITED

Ahmed A. "HIV and Women: Incongruent Policies, Criminal Consequences." *Yale Journal of International Affairs* 6.1 (2011):

32-42. Print.

Ahmed, A., C. Hanssens, and B. Kelly. "Protecting HIV-Positive Women's Human Rights: Recommendations for the United States National HIV/AIDS Strategy." *Reproductive Health Matters* 17.34 (2009): 127-134. Print.

Allard, P., C. Kazatchkine, and A. Symington. "Criminal Prosecutions for HIV Non-Disclosure: Protecting Women from Infection or Threatening Prevention Efforts?" *Women and HIV Prevention in Canada*. Ed. J. Gahagan. Toronto:Women's Press, 2013. 195-218. Print.

Arcana, Judith. *Every Mother's Son*. New York: Anchor Press/ Double Day, 1983. Print.

Balfour, G. and E. Comack. "Introduction." *Criminalizing Women: Gender and (In)Justice in Neoliberal Times*. Toronto: Fernwood Publishing, 2006. Print.

Bitnun, A., J. Brophy, L. Samson, A. Alimenti, F. Kakkar, V. Lamarre, D. Moore, C. Karatzios, S. Seigel, L. Sauve, W. Vaudry, M. Yudin and D. Money (for the Canadian Paediatric and Perinatal AIDS Research Group and the Infectious Diseases Committee of the Society of Obstetricians and Gynaecologists of Canada). "Prevention of Vertical HIV Transmission and Management of the HIV-Exposed Infant in Canada in 2014." *Canadian Journal of Infectious Diseases and Medical Microbiology* 25.2 (2014): 75-77. Print.

Blanche, S., M. J. Mayaia, F. Veber, A. Landreau, C. Courpotin, E. Vilmer, N. Ciraru-Vigneron, C. Flock, J. Tricoire, G. Noseda, J. M. Retbi and C. Rouzioux. "Separation Between HIV-Positive Women and Their Children: The French Prospective Study, 1986 through 1993." *American Journal of Public Health* 83.3 (1996): 376-381. Print.

Boland, M. G., T. J. Allen, G. I. Long and M. Tasker. "Children with HIV Infection: Collaborative Responsibilities of the Child Welfare and Medical Communities." *Social Work* (1988): 504-509. Print.

Breitbart, V., W. Chavkin, C. Layton and P. Wise. "Model Programs Addressing Perinatal Drug Exposure and Human Immunodeficiency Virus Infection: Integrating Women's and Children's Needs." *Bulletin of the New York Academy of Medicine* 71.2

(1994): 236-251. Print.
Browne, A. J., V. L. Smye, and C. Varcoe. "Postcolonial Theoretical Perspectives and Aboriginal Health Research." *Canadian Journal of Nursing Research* 37.4 (2005). 16-37. Print.
Burdge, D. R., D. M. Money, J. C. Forbes, S. L. Walmsley, F. M. Smaill, M. Boucher, L. M. Samson and M. Steben (and the Canadian HIV Trials Network Working Group on Vertical HIV Transmission). "Canadian Consensus Guidelines for the Management of Pregnancy, Labour and Delivery and for Postpartum Care in HIV-Positive Pregnant Women and Their Offspring (Summary of 2002 Guidelines)." *CMAJ* 168.13 (2003): 1671-1674. Print.
Burton-Jeangros, C. "Surveillance of Risks in Everyday Life: The Agency of Pregnant Women and its Limitations." *Social Theory and Health* 9.4 (2011): 419-436. Print.
Campbell, N. D. "Regulating "Maternal Instinct: Governing Mentalities of Late Twentieth-Century U.S. Illicit Drug Policy." *Journal of Women in Culture and Society* 24.4(1999): 895-923. Print.
Canadian HIV/AIDS Legal Network. "Women and the Criminalization of HIV Non-Disclosure." Fact Sheet. 2012. Print.
Catholic Children's Aid Society of Hamilton v. J.I., I.N. and V.I.O. (2006). O.J. No. 2299 Court File No. C-1707-04.
Chen, H., K. A. Phillips, D. E. Kanouse, R. L. Collins and A. Miu. "Fertility Desires and Intentions of HIV-Positive Men and Women." *Family Planning Perspectives* 33.4 (2001): 144. Print.
Cooper, E. R., M. Charurat, L. Mofenson, I. C. Hanson, J. Pitt, C. Diaz, K. Hayani, E. Handelsman, V. Smeriglio, R. Hoff and W. Blattner (Women and Infants' Transmission Study Group). "Combination Antiretroviral Strategies for the Treatment of Pregnant HIV-1-Infected Women and Prevention of Perinatal HIV-1 Transmission." *Journal of Acquired Immune Deficiency Syndrome* 29.5 (2002): 484-494. Print.
Criminal Code, RSC 1985, c C-46 s 215(1)(a) & (2). Print.
Csete J., R. Pearshouse and A. Symington. "Vertical HIV Transmission Should Be Excluded from Criminal Prosecution." *Reproductive Health Matters* 17.34 (2009): 154-162. Print.
Davies, B. and D. Allen. "Integrating 'Mental Illness' and 'Motherhood': The Positive Use of Surveillance by Health Professionals. A Qualitative Study." *International Journal of Nursing Studies*

44 (2007): 365-376. Print.
Department of Health. *HIV and Infant Feeding: Guidance from the UK Chief Medical Officers' Expert Advisory Group on AIDS.* UK National Archives, 2004. Web.
Elston, D., and Ion, A. "Examining the Healthcare Experiences of Women Living with HIV and Perceived HIV Related Stigma." *Canadian Journal of Infectious Diseases and Medical Microbiology* 24.Suppl 1 (2013): 122A. Print.
Epp, J. *Achieving Health for All: A framework for Health Promotion, for Health and Welfare Canada.* Fact Sheet. 1986. Print.
Forbes, J. C., A. M. Alimenti, J. Singer, J. C. Brophy, A. Bitnun, L.M. Samson, D. M. Money, T. C. K. Lee, N. D. Lapointe and S. E. Read (Canadian Pediatric AIDS Research Group). "A National Review of Vertical HIV Transmission." *AIDS* 26.6 (2012): 757-763. Print.
Forehand, R., R. Steele, L. Armistead, E. Morse, P. Simon and L. Clark. "The Family Health Project: Psychosocial Adjustment of Children Whose Mothers Are HIV Infected." *Journal of Counseling and Clinical Psychology* 66 (1998): 3. Print.
Foucault, M. *Discipline and Punish: The Birth of the Prison.* New York: Random House, 1991. Print.
Gilbert, D.J. "In the Best Interest of the Child." *Journal of HIV/AIDS Prevention & Education for Adolescents & Children* 3.1-2 (1999): 99-117. Print.
Ginn, Diana. "The Supreme Court of Canada and What It Means to be 'Of Woman Born.'" *From Motherhood to Mothering.* Ed. Andrea O'Reilly. Albany: State University of New York Press, 2004. 27-43. Print.
Greaves, L., C. Varcoe, N. Poole, M. Morrow, J. Johnson, A. Pederson and L. Irwin. "A Motherhood Issue: Discourses on Mothering under Duress." Status of Women Canada. 2002. Web. 01 Aug 2013.
Greene, S. "Embodied Exclusion: Young Mothers' Experiences of Social Exclusion from Formal and Informal Sexual Health Education." *Atlantis* 32 (2008): 2. Print.
Greene, S., L. Chambers, K. Masinde and D. O'Brien-Teengs. "A House Is Not a Home: The Housing Experiences of African and Caribbean Mothers Living with HIV." *Housing Studies* 28.1

(2013): 116-134. Print.

Greene, S., D. O'Brien-Teengs and W. Whitebird, A. Ion. "How HIV-Positive Aboriginal Women (PAW) Talk about Their Experiences with Child and Family Services in Ontario." *Journal of Public Child Welfare* 8 (2014): 467-490. Print.

Hausman, B. L. *Viral Mothers: Breastfeeding in The Age of HIV/AIDS* University of Michigan Press, 2011. Print.

Hendry, P. "The Future of Narrative." *Qualitative Inquiry* 13 (2007): 487-499. Print.

Huisman, W. "Corporate Crime and Crisis: Causation Scenarios." *Sociology of Crime, Law of*
Deviance 16 (2011): 107-125. Web. 01 Aug 2013.

Ion, A. and D. Elston. "Examining the Healthcare Experiences of Women Living with HIV and Perceived HIV-Related Stigma." Submitted for publication. (2014). Print.

Ion, A., S. Greene, K. Mellor, G. Kwaramba, S. Smith, F. Barry, V. L. Kennedy, A. Carvalhal, M. Loutfy (for the Mothering with HIV Study Team). "Perinatal Care Experiences of Mothers Living with HIV in Ontario, Canada." Submitted for publication (2014). Print.

Ingram, D. and S. Hutchinson. "Defensive Mothering in HIV-Positive Mothers." *Qualitative Health Research* 9 (1999): 243-258. Print.

Ingram, D. and S. Hutchinson. "Double Binds and the Reproductive and Mothering Experiences of HIV-Positive Women." *Qualitative Health Research* 10 (2000): 117–132. Print.

Kirby, M. J., and J.K. Wilbert. "Out of the Shadows at Last. Transforming Mental Health, Mental Illness and Addiction Services in Canada." Ottawa, ON: The Standing Senate Committee on Social Affairs, Science and Technology. 2006. Web.

Kleinmann A. *The Illness Narratives.* New York: Basic Books, 1988. Print.

Krentz, H. B., S. Dean, and M.vJ. Gill. "Longitudinal Assessment (1995-2003) of Hospitalizations of HIV-Infected Patients within a Geographical Population in Canada." *HIV Medicine* 7 (2006): 457-466. Print.

Lawson, K.L., M. Bayly, and E. Cey. "Judgements Regarding the Acceptability of Childbearing and Parental Fitness Made towards Women Living with HIV." *AIDS Care* (2012): n.pag. Web. 15 Dec 2012.

Lekas, H-M., K. Siegel, and E. W. Schrimshaw. "Continuities and Discontinuities in the Experiences of Felt and Enacted Stigma among Women with HIV/AIDS." *Qualitative Health Research* 16 (2006): 1165-1190. Print.

Little, K. M., D. J. Hu, and K. L. Dominguez. "HIV-1 and Breastfeeding in the United States." *Advances in Experimental Medicine and Biology* 743 (2012): 261-270. Print.

Loutfy, M. R., T. A. Hart, S. S. Mohammed, D. Su, E. D. Ralph, S.L. Walmsley, L. C. Soje, M. Muchenje, A. R. Rachlis, F. M. Smaill, J. B. Angel, J. M. Raboud, M. S. Silverman, W. E. Tharao, K. Gough and M. H. Yudin (Ontario HIV Fertility Research Team). "Fertility Desires and Intentions of HIV-Positive Women of Reproductive Age in Ontario, Canada: A Cross-Sectional Study." *PLoS One* 412 (2009): e7925. Web.

O'Brien-Teengs, D. M. E. Vaccaro, S. Greene and A. Ion. "I Guess She Just Needs To Do Her Homework: HIV-positive Mothers' Interactions with Child Protection Services across Ontario." *Ontario HIV Treatment Network Research Conference.* November 12-13, 2012, Toronto, Ontario. Conference presentation.

O'Reilly, Andrea. "Mothering against Motherhood and the Possibility of Empowered Maternity for Mothers and their Children." *From Motherhood to Mothering.* Ed. Andrea O'Reilly. Albany, State University of New York Press, 2004. 159-174. Print.

Poindexter, C. C. and R. A. Shippy. "HIV Diagnosis Disclosure: Stigma Management and Stigma Resistance." *Journal of Gerontological Social Work* 53 (2010): 366-381. Print.

Pryce, A. "Frequent Observation: Sexualities, Self-surveillance, Confession and the Construction of the Active Patient." *Nursing Inquiry* 7 (2000): 103-111. Print.

Public Health Agency of Canada (PHAC). "HIV/AIDS Among Women in Canada." Chapter 5. PHAC, 2008. Web. 30 May 2012.

Public Health Agency of Canada (PHAC). "At a Glance—HIV and AIDS in Canada: Surveillance Report to December 31, 2011." PHAC, 2011. Web. 6 Aug 2013.

Public Health Agency of Canada (PHAC). "What Determines Health?" PHAC, 2011. Web. 6 Aug 2013.

Riessman, C. K. "Analysis of Personal Narratives." *Handbook of Interview Research: Context and Method.* Ed. J.F Gubrium and J. A. Holstein. Thousand Oaks, CA: Sage Publications, 2002. 695-710. Print.

Robinson, J. "Health Visitor or Health Police." *AIMS Journal* 16.3 (2004): n. pag. Web. 25 March 2013.

Romanow, R. "Commission on the Future of Health Care in Canada. Building on Values: The Future of Health Care in Canada." Final Report. Ottawa: Federal Government. 2002. Web.

Rotheram-Borus, M.J., B.H. Draimin, H.M. Reid, D.A. Murphy. The Impact of Illness Disclosure and Custody Plans on Adolescents Whose Parents Lived with AIDS. *AIDS* 11 (1997): 1159-1164. Print.

Ruddick, Sara. *Maternal Thinking: Toward a Politics of Peace.* New York: Ballantine Books, 1989. Print.

Sandelowski, M., J. Barroso, and C. I. Voils. "Gender, Race/ Ethnicity, and Social Class in Research Reports on Stigma in HIV-Positive Women." *Health Care for Women International* 30.4 (2009): 273-288. Print.

Sandelowski, M., C. Lambe, and J. Barroso. "Stigma in HIV-Positive Women." *Journal of Nursing Scholarship* 36.2 (2004): 122-128. Print.

Smart, C. "Disruptive Bodies and Unruly Sex: The Regulation of Reproduction and Sexuality in the Nineteenth Century." *Regulating Womanhood: Historical Essays on Marriage, Motherhood and Sexuality.* Ed. C. Smart. London: Routledge, 1992. 7-32. Print.

Thompson, M. "Drug-exposed Infants and Their Families: A Coordinated Services Approach." *Families Living with Drugs and HIV: Intervention and Treatment Strategies.* Ed. R.P. Barth, J. Pietrazk, and M. Ramler. New York: Guilford Press, 1992. 238-252. Print.

Thulier, D. "Breastfeeding in America: A History of Influencing Factors." *Journal of Human Lactation 25* (2009): 85-94. Print.

Van Den Tillaart, S., D. Kurtz, and P. Cash. "Powerlessness, Marginalized Identity, and Silencing of Health Concerns: Voiced Realities of Women Living with a Mental Health Diagnosis." *International Journal of Mental Health Nursing* 18 (2009): 153-163. Print.

Vasas, E. R. "Examining the Margins: A Concept Analysis of Marginalization." *Advances in Nursing Science* 28.3 (2005): 194-202. Print.

Walkerdine, V., H. Lucey, and J. Melody. *Growing Up Girl: Psychosocial Explorations of Gender and Class*. Houndmills: Palgrave, 2001. Print.

Wall, G. "Moral Constructions of Motherhood in Breastfeeding Discourse." *Gender and Society* 15 (2001): 592-610. Print.

Weait, M. "The Criminalisation of HIV Exposure and Transmission: A Global Review." *Global Commission on HIV and the Law*, Working Paper prepared for the Third Meeting of the Technical Advisory Group, 7-9 July 2011. Web.

Webel, A.R., and P.A. Higgins. "The Relationship between Social Roles and Self-Management Behavior in Women Living with HIV/AIDS." *Women's Health Issues* 22.1 (2012): 27-33. Print.

Wingood, G. M., R. J. Diclemente, I. Mikhail, D. H. McCree, S. L. Davies, J. W. Hardin, S. Harris Peterson, E. W. Hook, and M. Saag. "HIV Discrimination and the Health of Women Living with HIV." *Women Health* 46.2-3 (2007): 99-112. Print.

World Health Organization (WHO). "Declaration of Alma-Ata." Geneva: World Health Organization. International Conference on Primary Health Care, Alma-Ata, USSR, 1978. 1-2. Web.

World Health Organization (WHO). "Guidelines on HIV and Infant Feeding." WHO, 2010. Web. 01 Aug 2013.

World Health Organization (WHO). "HIV Transmission through Breastfeeding." WHO, n.d. Web. 01 Aug 2013.

Worth, H., C. Patton, and D. Goldstein. "Introduction to Reckless Vectors: The Infecting Other in HIV/AIDS Law." *Sexuality Research and Social Policy* 2 (2005): 3-14. Print.

Young, S. L., M. N. N. Mbuya, C. J. Chantry, E .P. Geubbels, K. Israel-Ballard, D. Cohan, S. A. Vosti and M. C. Latham. "Current Knowledge and Future Research on Infant Feeding in the Context of HIV: Basic, Clinical, Behavioral, and Programmatic Perspectives." *Advanced Nutrition* 2 (2011): 225-243. Print.

11.
"Do You Have My Son?"

Criminalization and the Production of (Un)Relatedness in Brazil

HOLLIS MOORE

IN THIS CHAPTER I describe and analyse the "disappearance" of a toddler, the son of a female remand prisoner (Ivete). I situate this occurrence within the broader context of Ivete's life. One woman's experiences of care reveals a great deal about criminalized women's struggles and the demanding conditions in which marginalized women mother. This analysis is based on sixteen months of ethnographic fieldwork conducted in and around a penal compound in Salvador da Bahia, Brazil. The predominantly Afro-Brazilian city of Salvador is the capital of Bahia, the largest state in Northeast Brazil. With a population of 2,675,656, Salvador is Brazil's third most populous city.

I employ the analytic of (un)relatedness, building on Carsten's notion of relatedness, to grasp criminalized mothers' *attempts* at social reproduction under conditions of crisis. I attend to messy and often incomplete processes of disconnection in order to understand how unrelatedness is produced through and despite actors' struggles. Rather than take the existence or absence of meaningful ties for granted this processual approach highlights the ongoing situated labour involved in making, maintaining, severing, and forestalling relationships. It also draws attention to broader assemblages—of institutions, discourses, structures, etc.—that shape and are shaped by practices of (un)relatedness.

My analysis is divided into three sections. First, I trace the co-development of the Lemos Brito Penal Complex and the neighbourhood of Mata Escura in order to situate the case study and illustrate key characteristics of this prison-neighbourhood nexus. Second, I consider a raciological discourse that helps us to understand Ivete's crisis of care and, more generally, the production of criminalized (m)Others. Finally, I turn to the ethnographic case study.

THE EMERGENCE OF A PRISON-NEIGHBOURHOOD NEXUS

In 1549, Portuguese settler colonists founded Salvador and the northeastern coastal city became the commercial and administrative hub of an Atlantic-orientated economy based on the enslavement of Africans and the export of sugar and other plantation products. Following the abolition of slavery (1888) many ex-slaves migrated from the countryside to the state capital. Some found housing in the city center while others settled in the urban periphery (Vasconcelos 26). Between 1930 and 1940, the city of Salvador modernized and local industry expanded. Working-class housing and subdivisions (often "clandestine") emerged on land surrounding industrial areas on the outskirts of the city (Caldas et al. 21). Mata Escura typifies this process yet the neighbourhood is also distinctive in at least one crucial respect: it emerged in direct relation to the establishment of Bahia's primary prison complex.

Women in Salvador were not historically confined in a distinct women's prison. In 1986, 43 *presas* (women prisoners) were confined in a wing of the Casa de Detenção, a prison for men. In 1990, on International Women's Day, Bahia's first women's prison—Penitenciária Feminina de Salvador—was opened in response to the growing population of imprisoned women and the perception that this population has special needs. Between 2000 and 2005, the number of women in Brazilian prisons increased from 10,112 to 20,264 (from 4.3 to 5.6 percent of the prison population) (Walmsley 3). In 2005, the women's prison was renamed Conjunto Penal Feminino (CPF) to reflect the fact that women assigned to all security levels are confined within this single institution (de Oliveira Almeida 38). Currently, CPF is in the midst of a protracted and periodically stalled renovation; *presas* are therefore "provisionally" confined in the penal complex's Centro de Observação Penal (COP). COP was originally envisaged as an entry point into the prison system for sentenced male prisoners, a place where they would be temporarily held for evaluation.

During the second half of the twentieth century as the penal complex expanded so did the neighbourhood of Mata Escura. And, like other Brazilian *favelas* (slums), a significant portion of Mata Escura's growth was informal and unplanned, occurring through a series of "invasions" of forested, unused land, and gradual auto-construction. Brazilian cities developed in an unjust, disorderly and illegal way. As elites modernized city centers, "they expelled the working poor and forced them to reside in undeveloped hinterlands ... in precarious and typically illegal conditions" (Holston 8). Yet, rapidly expanding *favelas* also frightened urban elites (Skidmore 138); their association with the illicit extends beyond the issue of usurped land. Historically, the *favela* has been represented "as a perversion of the city's social, moral, and economic order, characterized by crowded, unsanitary conditions that bred disease; harbouring illegal activities ... and populated by vagrants, drunks, criminals, prostitutes, and other social undesirables" (Hayes 81). In the case of Mata Escura, the taint of the illicit exceeds even these terms: the neighbourhood was formed, in part, as ex-prisoners and prisoners' families settled in the area. Today, it is characterized by lack of adequate infrastructure, high population density, and poverty.

Contrary to the "myth of racial democracy" (the myth that, in Brazil, miscegenation resulted in nonracist social relations), national studies emerging in the late 1970s began to reveal clear patterns of racialised inequality in Brazil (Skidmore 199-200). For example, Salvador's urban landscape is dived into *áreas nobres* (noble or wealthy areas) and *bairros populares* (low-income neighbourhoods). Although only 23 percent of Soteropolitanos (residents of Salvador) identify as white, whites represent over half the population of Salvador's wealthiest neighbourhoods. By contrast, roughly 80 percent of Mata Escura residents identify as Afro-descendent (Moreira de Carvalho and Sá Barreto 259, 265).

RACIOLOGICAL THINKING AND THE CRIMINAL OTHER

In this section I discuss a discourse that, arguably, contributes to the interpellation of criminalized (m)Others and "dissapearable" children in contemporary Brazil. I suggest this gendered "neo-racist" discourse of social difference differs from previously hegemonic modes of naturalizing, thereby (re)producing social inequality.

Brazilian society recognizes a wide range of identities for people who are perceived as neither white nor black. In Brazil, ethno-racial categorization is not organized around dichotomous racial exclusivity but, rather, around a spectrum of intermediary categories, such as *moreno/a* (Penglase 312). For example, research participants consistently classified President Obama as *moreno* (light skinned with straight hair). In Brazil, ethno-racial categorization takes criteria such as skin tone, facial features, and hair texture into account. Though perceptions can vary according to the perceived social position of the person being categorized, "African-associated physical traits, such as kinky hair, very dark skin, and broad facial features, generally are considered unattractive" (Hayes 48).

Ethno-racial identification (of the self and others) is not a straightforward process. Class, race, gender, and status intersect in important ways. For example, a defining feature of middle-classness is the ability to pay someone else to perform your manual labour (Goldstein). While upper-class people are often placed into "whiter" categories (Penglase 312), domestic workers (overwhelmingly women) are symbolically associated with the "dirty" jobs they perform in a household. This interrelated set of deep-seated associations significantly influences "how even the lightest-skinned domestic worker is perceived" (Goldstein 73) and perceives herself. Relations of servitude cultivate and sustain a sense of inferiority among domestic workers, many of whom are poor Afro-Brazilian women (Goldstein 69).

In Brazil, a plethora of colour terms and a celebration of racial mixture do not entail "racial harmony" or an absence of racisms. Throughout most of the twentieth century, Brazil's national self-image has celebrated ethno-racial *mixture*. The discourse of "racial democracy," extolling the virtues of miscegenation, has obfuscated but not obviated the existence and effects of racisms. I build on Penglase's claim that there has been a shift away from this hegemonic ethno-racial narrative (of mixture) towards a discourse of crime and security in which social and urban boundaries are envisioned as increasingly impermeable and their transgression as threatening (308). In order to grasp this emergent mode of raciological thinking we must suspend commonsense assumptions that (1) "race" does not *divide* people according to ancestry, skin colour etc. and (2) raciological thinking provides justification for hierarchical relationships, naturalizing difference and explaining social inequality in terms of essences.

In Brazil, the mid-1990s were characterized by national concern with public safety and deepening anxieties about democratization (an authoritarian military dictatorship ruled Brazil from 1964 to 1985). From this context, a new media-driven discourse of social difference emerged (Penglase) which approximates "racism without race" (Balibar) and which may be understood as a form of raciological thinking. This discourse centres on images of criminality and transgression that perform the work of racism and raciological thinking without seeming racist. Moodie describes a similar process occurring in El Salvador whereby social threats came to be recognized through "different kinds of deviant physicality" (199). By the turn of the century, the media were "parading ominous images of baggy-pantsed, tattoo-faced youths, cameras lingering in a kind of Lombrosian leer over their defiant, degenerate physicality" (182).

Certainly, in El Salvador as well as Brazil, conventional markers of race continue to structure images of criminality. However, as Penglase has argued, the criminalization of non-white youth from the urban periphery has contributed to neo-racist ideologies of social difference and exclusion that do not rely on the racialization of "criminal" behaviour or the racialized Other. Social difference is indexed, explained, and justified by a set of signs which seem to reveal an inner *essence* of criminality though they do not draw directly from biological markers of racial difference (Balibar). A set of bodily signs, signalling difference and marginality (i.e. tattoos, clothing, modes of speech and conduct, etc.) has come to mark the sites where danger to "society" is situated (viz. the *favela* and its inhabitants). And, as different types of places and people are increasingly recognized as inherently "good" or "bad"—decent or dangerous—patterns of action geared towards neutralizing this threat are normalized. Military/police occupations of *favelas* and mass imprisonment are two such interventions which, crucially, have the instrumental effect of (re)producing signs that identify the criminal Other.

Penglase argues that "the central matrix for organizing this new sense of social difference is spatial" in the sense that "stigmatized social subjects, and objects of fear, are those that are 'out of place,' violating the 'proper' organization of ... space" (307). This spatial emphasis helps us to think about the ways in which neo-racial discourses of criminality and insecurity are highly gendered. Brazilian anthropologist Roberto DaMatta distinguishes between two spheres of Brazilian cultural life—the *casa* (home) and the *rua* (street). These symbolic-material domains inform the practical understandings of working-class Brazilians.

The home is strongly associated with women and children (Hayes 53). It connotes a hierarchical moral world that represents the domestic virtues of family (i.e. ties of affection, loyalty, and mutual dependence). By contrast, the street, a site of danger and excitement, is a markedly masculine space of commerce. Inhabited by "thieves, hustlers, prostitutes, and other outlaw figures" (Hayes 53), the street is where individuals compete for dominance and hierarchies are flouted: "the poor rob the rich, women flirt with men, the young deviate from parents' rules, and people of colour disobey white people" (Goldstein 149). The street "is also a place where unprotected women become vulnerable" (Goldstein 149) and a place that is, decidedly, "not for children" (Hecht 102). These qualities make "the street' a particularly significant site of criminalized motherhood. As Hayes observes, "the faithful housewife and mother epitomizes the moral pole of femininity, while the *mulher da rua*, or woman of the street, embodies its immoral pole" (113).

Without access to the moral, female, and relatively secure domain of the house, such women end up "out of place." They are doubly judged for their own positioning (as unruly women of the street) and for exposing their children to the dangers of the street. Given the contemporary mode of raciological thinking, which (re)produces social inequality by identifying embodied signs that index a threatening essence, a woman *in* the street, or a mother who is *not* in proximity to her children, does more than reveal herself to be morally suspect or a poor mother. Her out-of-placeness may be read as evidence of criminality, evidence of her status as an intra-national criminal (m)Other posing a distinct threat to the social body. Her already-compounded transgression of gendered spatial-ethical boundaries is further magnified if she is additionally seen to embody signs of (masculine) marginality/criminality (e.g., involvement with illegal drugs or imprisonment).

Raciological thinking about the criminal Other is profoundly gendered. Working-class mothers are vulnerable in particular ways to a play of signs and circumstances that reveal/constitute them as criminal, inherently immoral. The mother-child dyad is central to concerns about deficient psychologies and spiritual inheritances (Balibar 24). The disruptive presence of out-of-place criminalized m(Others) not only threatens the present social order, but also has the capacity to "infect" her children (by denying her children *a home* in the broad material-symbolic sense of the term) and thereby contaminate the future. Thus, interventions geared towards neutralizing the threat posed by the out-of-place criminal (m)Other are shaped, in more and less direct ways, by the figure of the child, which is understood as both "at risk" and as a potential future enemy. The relationship between mother and child is often problematized by officials, experts, and trustees and, thus, is constituted, more and less formally, as an object of intervention.

The ethnographic story I recount in the final section of this paper reveals how, within Salvador's prison-neighbourhood nexus, a young woman comes to be discursively positioned as a criminalized (m)Other. The narrative begins with one of my regular visits to CPF which, at the time of my research, imprisoned approximately 120 *presas*. On Thursday afternoons I accompanied a small team of religious volunteers from the Catholic prison pastoral to visit *presas*.

AN ETHNOGRAPHIC ACCOUNT OF CRIMINALIZATION AND UNRELATEDNESS

The Prison as Context of Research and Care

The team meets at the prison entrance around 2:00 pm. Once our names have been logged in the ledger, a guard manually searched through the items we hoped to bring with us. She flipped through the volunteers' bibles and my notebook. She partially unfolded a set of donated bed sheets before returning them to a plastic shopping bag. She didn't bother with a stack of photocopied newsletters. Once the guard was satisfied that we were not bringing any contraband into the prison we headed through an open doorway into the restricted area of the prison.

A freshly painted nursery stands at one end of the administrative passage. Infants up to six months of age stay in ordinary cells with their mothers. In 1999, the Childhood and Youth Court of Bahia prohibited children over six months of age from staying with their imprisoned mothers. It also ruled that infants remaining in the prison must be sheltered in a separate area. Though the institution does not comply with the latter regulation, the statute limiting children's presence in the prison is enforced. Although the recent opening of the nursery was a highly publicized affair, ostensibly due to staff shortages, the room remains unused.

Studies comparing mothers and fathers imprisoned in the U.S. indicate that women are more likely to have custody of children prior to imprisonment. Furthermore, children of imprisoned men are much more likely to be cared for by men's partners whereas children of imprisoned mothers tend to be cared for by other female relatives (Schafer and Dellinger; Mumola). These trends also occur in Brazil. However, it should be noted that a significant number of *presas* were neither primary nor exclusive caregivers of some or all of their children prior to arrest. Ivete's life history provides an excellent vantage point onto this somewhat neglected dimension of motherhood. It reveals how intersections of criminalization and motherhood are experienced within a milieu in which dispersed reproduction and care arrangements (practices of "child circulation") are relatively common (see also Fonseca 2006).

Beside a metal gate, mounted on bars in plain view and within earshot of the guards, is a pay phone—the *only* phone that *presas* have regular access to. This phone is almost always in use and, typically, there is a long line of *presas* awaiting their daily three-minute turn. I understand phones, especially in the prison context, as "vectors of relatedness" in that they allow prisoners to build and maintain relationships and do their best to parent at a distance. Within the context of CPF, the existence of contraband cell phones seems to have been successfully criminalized and controlled. By contrast, at the neighbouring men's prison where I also conducted fieldwork, many if not most prisoners had regular access to illicit cell phones. While it is not within the scope of the present chapter to theorize the complex causes and implications of uneven gendered access to this crucial vector of relatedness, it is worth noting that, at CPF, imprisoned mothers' opportunities to communicate with and about their children are highly circumscribed and unequally distributed depending on each *presas'* differential level of access to money and other resources.

Today the patio is busier than usual owing to the recent arrival of approximately 30 women recently transferred from a police lockup in the wake of a suspicious death. In low, anxious voices visitors and prisoners say "the girl" died of meningitis. They are concerned that the problem has not been adequately addressed or contained and that others will die. As I circulate through the courtyard, a young Afro-descendent woman whom I have not met before, approaches me. She is short, has smooth, clear dark skin (she would almost certainly be identified as "*negra*" rather than "*morena*"), and sports an eyebrow ring. Her eyes are bright and alert. Her gaze is intense. The young woman—Ivete—places her hand on my forearm and asks: "You work there at that shelter right? *Do you have my son?*"

Ivete's Carceral Trajectory: Death, Disappearance, and (Disappointed) Expectations of Care

Ivete's son, Robison, is a baby, just over a year old. Before arriving at CPF she had been imprisoned at the police lockup where she had shared an overcrowded cell with the "girl who died." They slept next to one another on the floor with only a thin sheet separating them from the concrete. One night the girl got sick. Her cellmates repeatedly called for assistance. The girl died on the floor, next to Ivete.[1] In this instance, criminalization brings death to the fore of Ivete's experience. As a *presa,* Ivete feels particularly vulnerable. The state, it seems to her, does not adequately care for its wards.

While imprisoned at the police lockup, the *only* visit Ivete received was from a man she recognized as a state representative. He came to inform her that Robison had been left at the entrance of a day care but was now in state custody. The man interviewed

Ivete, reassured her that Robison was safe, and promised to be in touch. Ivete recognized the man as a state representative by his uniform, a black vest. Ivete can't remember the man's name but she tells me: "He was from FUNDAC" (the state agency responsible for delivery of "socio-educative measures"—including detention—to youth in conflict with the law).

From 1927 until 1990, under Brazil's "Minors' Code," it was legally possible to institutionalize Brazilian children and adolescents indefinitely regardless of whether or not they had broken the law (Drybread 335). Distinctions were rarely made between courts' treatment of orphans (or "abandoned" children) and children involved in criminal activity (Drybread 336). In 1990, in full knowledge of principles enshrined in the United Nations Convention on the Rights of the Child (1989), Brazil adopted the Statute of the Child and Adolescent, incorporating a rights-based understanding of childhood into the nation's new democratic constitution (Rizzini and Rizzini 3). The statute defines the rights of children and the obligations that the state and families have towards all people under the age of eighteen (Drybread 332). This legal shift reflects and (re)produces a new vision for assisting youth as rights-bearing subjects rather than objects of intervention. Central to this new vision is a rejection of policies and practices that deprive youth of their liberty or separate them from their families and communities (Rizzini and Rizzini 7). Institutionalization (for the purposes of "resocialization" rather than "punishment") is forbidden except for adolescents who have committed crimes. Otherwise, the provision of shelter must constitute an exceptional and temporary measure.

While laws and intentions regarding the use of institutions have certainly changed, it is unclear how much—or in what specific ways—the practice has been transformed (Rizzini and Rizzini 2). A significant number of marginalized youth still end up in institutions *neither* because they have committed criminal acts *nor* because they have been orphaned or abandoned (Rizzini and Rizzini 14-15). Fonseca observes that poor, urban, Brazilian mothers consider institutions for the welfare of minors as sites where children may be (temporarily) placed and that this should not result in a loss of legal parental rights (Fonseca "Orphanages" 16; "*Circulação*" 26). According to Rizzini and Rizzini, loving parents "seek out the courts and institutions to get their children placed either because of poverty or because they have difficulty disciplining them" (14). Indeed, I have found that mothers or other caregivers of children may institutionalize a child when faced with "exceptional" circumstances (e.g., inadequate housing or loss of lodgings; resource scarcity; hospitalization; imprisonment; an acute risk of violence etc.). This practice is often construed as a temporary measure to last only until the caregiver's situation stabilizes or an alternative caregiver is found.

For a child to be legally available for adoption, they must be either *declared* "abandoned" or parents must give consent. In practice, however, such procedures are highly discretionary and involve prejudicial value judgments (Fonseca, "*Circulação*" 26). Concepts such as "consent" and "abandonment" must be interrogated from the position of the Brazilian poor. However, the discourse that constructs the poor as criminal (m)Others delegitimizes their actions, claims, and understandings. For example, the legal definition of "abandonment," already vague in the European context, is even more problematic within Brazil's prison-neighbourhood nexus (see art. 23 of the Children's Code – Estatuto da Criança e do Adolescente 1990). Furthermore, social workers have tended to equate extreme poverty with abandonment and neglect (Fonseca, "Politics of Adoption" 212, 211). Discourses that operate to criminalize poor parents, especially poor mothers, conceal the role of poverty as they construct parents as *criminally responsible* and *morally depraved*. Thus, the figure of the criminal (m)Other legitimizes social workers' assessments of the "best interests of the child."

When I met Ivete at CPF, roughly three months had passed since her first (and only meeting) with the man in the black vest. Ivete had received no further news of her son. When Ivete arrived at CPF, and other *presas* heard about her situation, they informed her of a nearby shelter where an Italian nun takes care of children of prisoners. She logically assumed that this place *must* "have her son." Well aware of my affiliation with this shelter (I lived there for a year while conducting fieldwork), *presas* directed Ivete to speak with me.

The shelter or Centro Nova Semente ("New Seed Centre" heretofore "the centre") is located 200 meters from the prison complex.

An Italian nun founded the centre in 1999 to shelter children of prisoners. The centre began as a somewhat improvised response to a "crisis." In 1999, the judge overseeing the execution of penal sentences prohibited children of prisoners from living with their imprisoned mothers beyond the age of 6 months. At the time of the judge's decision there were several children living within the ordinary cells of CPF. The centre emerged to shelter these children and maintain relatedness between prisoners and their children. The implication is that, if these children had been expelled into the general system of shelter-orphanages, the continuation (and cultivation) of their relatedness to their imprisoned mothers would have been an *unlikely outcome*. Although rupturing ties between criminalized mothers and their children may not have been an official state policy or objective, it seems to have been understood as an unsurprising—if not inevitable—outcome.

Unfortunately, as soon as Ivete shared Robison's age with me, I was certain he was not at the centre. I did, however, think that he might be on his way. There is generally a consistent but low-intensity trickle of children arriving at (and leaving from) the centre. I assured Ivete that I would look into it. That night, as soon as I returned to the centre, I sought out the nun and learned that she was not expecting any new arrivals.

It seems inconceivable to an outside observer that Ivete had been imprisoned for four months and had only received a single update about her son. Clearly the state agent in the black vest knew both her and Robison's status, why had he not returned? Where was Robison? Before proceeding with an account of our search for Robison within Salvador's tangle of state and state-like institutions, I will share Ivete's life history. Her experiences reveal how criminalized women care for their children (and are cared for as children) as well as highlight the complex assemblage of processes that influence mothering. Through a focus on Ivete's crisis of care I highlight conditions that give rise to "disappearable" children.

Ivete's Story: The Social Production of "Bad" Mothers and "Disappearable" Children

Born and raised in Salvador, Ivete is 21 years old and the mother of five children by four different men. Ivete's oldest child, Felipe (6), lives with his *madrinha* (godmother), while Vitor (5) and Mateus (2), are being raised by their paternal grandmother. Ivete's only daughter (an infant) is in the care of a godmother. Ivete tells me that she doesn't plan to have more children. She always wanted a little girl and now her daughter has arrived.

This distribution of children and diffuse division of child rearing labour; the relatively early age at which Ivete first gave birth (15/16 years old); and her serial marriages (represented by the children's various fathers) are *very* typical features of research participants' lives. Studies of urban poverty in Brazil suggest that these practices of relatedness and patterns of care are relatively common among marginalized groups more generally (Heilborn and Cabral; Fonseca 1986, 2006; Goldstein; Hayes; Gregg; Rebhun). Yet, authorities consistently interpret these dimensions of Ivete's experience of motherhood as signs of her irresponsibility and personal failure to be a good, caring mother. As such, she is understood by many (e.g., prison social workers) as undeserving of sustained assistance to locate her son and, thus, undeserving of motherhood. Ivete interprets the situation quite differently:

> *Vitor and Mateus always lived with their [paternal] grandmother because I separated from their dad.... But I always went to see them, always worked as a domestic employee ... always brought money. I never let my sons go hungry, I always brought things for them and their grandmother. I never let them go without. Filipe always lived with [his] godmother. He lived with me and then.... As I was in the really horrible situation of not having anything to give him ...* eu peguei e dei *[I took and gave[2]] him to her* instead of abandoning him.... *She's still with him and she is a person that can't have kids. She became very attached to Filipe. She always suffered a great deal and I took and gave him to her.... I already knew her; I'd already lived with her and I saw that she is a person that doesn't mistreat children.... I took and gave [him to her and her husband] this one time I was living there in her house with Filipe. I always went to see him there. ... He played with me—nunca mudou [our relationship or his attitude towards me never changed].*

> *My children [note shift to plural]* nunca mudou comigo. *It's not because I lived with them that they didn't* me-estranham *[estrange from or desert me].... I always treat my children well....*

Here Ivete insists that she *chose* to circulate her children—that she did *not* abandon them. She emphasises her role as a provider of support and care not only to her children but to their (other) caregivers as well. Her account foregrounds an inclusive expansion, rather than an exclusive retraction, of relatedness. In Brazil, especially among precariat and working-class groups, it is not uncommon for children to speak of two, three, or more women as "my mother" (Fonseca, "Patterns of Shared Parenthood"). Practices of child circulation (including temporary and more long-term placements as well as informal and formal adoptions) and co-parenting are crucial strategies of social reproduction. Fonseca helps us to think about this set of practices in relation to processes of criminalization:

> *In Brazil, a mother's (or father's) separating from her child is not a criminal act. The penal code condemns anyone who "exposes" a child, that is, leaves it unassisted in circumstances that might be harmful or life-threatening (article 134). Also, at least since the 1990 Children's Code, Brazilian law expressly prohibits the "sale" of children. ... As long as the parents avoid these classifications of illegality ("exposure" or "sale"), they are technically free to give their child into the care of any responsible adult—whether a court-appointed caretaker or an adoptive parent they themselves have chosen. The question in this latter form of transaction (direct adoption) is where to draw the line between the legal giving and the criminal selling of a child. ("De-Kinning" 319)*

Before Ivete's arrest she left Robison in the temporary care of her infant daughter's godmother. Some uncertainty remains about the age of the godmother in question. Ivete insists that she is "*de maior.*" This designation could be translated/interpreted to mean "age of majority" which, in Brazil, is 18 years of age. However, throughout our interview, Ivete seems to use the term differently and it is likely that the godmother in question is younger than 18. Nevertheless, Ivete was convinced that because she had children of her own and lived independently she was a "true" adult. The "fact" that Ivete left her children with a legal minor ("not more than a child herself") was brought up by various middle-class experts, including prison social workers. Some experts characterized Ivete's statements about the godmother's age as lies and thereby (re) produced an image of her as dishonest and immoral. Her apparent attempts at deception rendered her unworthy of their assistance and, by extension, custody of Robison.

Ivete was raised by her step-mother in the Pelorinho, the colonial jewel of Salvador's historic centre. The Pelourinho (literally "whipping post") is an area where slaves were once bought and sold. It is a UNESCO world heritage site that has recently been redeveloped as a tourist attraction. Redevelopment has meant the displacement (more and less coercive) of many poor Afro-Brazilian residents from the area which, pre-redevelopment, was a centre of prostitution—known as the Maciel—largely populated by low-income families (Collins). Some families received government pay-outs and re-located to urban peripheral neighbourhoods. Many others were arrested (rumour has it, so the government could avoid pay-outs). Fatima, an ex-prisoner who currently visits her imprisoned daughter, recalls being a *presa* at CPF and pronouncing: "Look! The whole Maciel is here!" Of course, some actors (like Fatima) have managed to stay or return to the Pelourinho. Others, not originally from the area, have been attracted to the historic centre of the city by its relatively intense circulation of capital, including a concentration of tourists who willingly (and unwillingly) part with money and other items of value.

Ivete was living with her brother, father, and step-mother in the Pelourinho when she and her brother began to sleep on the streets. Although she can't recall her exact age, she remembers that she did not yet have children of her own. She insists that she stayed on the streets because she *wanted* to: "Nobody abused me, they always treated me well. It was really because I wanted to leave!" Talking about her time on the streets with her brother she becomes nostalgic, describing this period fondly, smiling mischievously as she recounts their adventures. She points out that—like many of Brazil's so-called "street kids"—she and her brother did not live on the street full-time. At times Ivete's father would send her step-mother chasing after them and would return home for a few days. She explains: "One day we slept at home, one day in the street, a day at home, a day on the street.... "

Ivete's experience as a *menina de rua* (street girl) highlights important dimension of how marginalized women relate to their children in the urban Brazilian context. During Brazil's transition from military dictatorship to formal democracy, street children assumed a prominent place in the public imagination and emerged as ideal mascots of a nascent liberal order promising universal citizenship and social protections (Drybread 331). Scheper-Hughes and Hoffman (360-361) suggest that the unarticulated, unmarked category that contrasts with the "street child" is the "home child." The latter reflects the hegemonic ideal (or "normative" model) of Brazilian childhood. The "home child," usually "white," is properly of the middle- or upper-class, from a "good" home and holds strong ties to the institutions of family and school. Even in the streets and other public places, certain children's appearances and comportment identify them as "home children." Children who are unable or unwilling to perform the role of "home children" are identified as "street children" whose dangerous or endangered status seems to demand intervention and, often, condemnation. Children ostensibly outside the normative socializing milieu of the family appear as threats to the social order and causes of urban crime and decay. However, for precariat and working-class "*favela* kids," especially males, home may not be "so much a place to eat and sleep as an emotional space, the place where one comes from and to which one returns, at least periodically ... not a permanent and dependable form of security" (Scheper-Hughes and Hoffman 359).

Seeking to explain, from the perspective of the poor, relationships between impoverished mothers and their children, Hecht identifies two varieties of "home children"—the "nurtured child" and the "nurturing child." He describes the former as coddled offspring of middle-class families who are highly differentiated from and dependent on adults. They are valued by virtue of *being* children. Conversely, "nurturing children" are poor and, from an early age, assume serious responsibilities within the home, supporting their mothers and providing or labouring for their families. To some extent, their status or value is dependent on what they *do*. Insofar as "street children" do not fulfil the obligations of either variant of home-based childhood, their status as children and citizens is threatened (Scheper-Hughes and Hoffman; Drybread) Hecht argues that street children understand themselves in opposition to nurturing children and that the essence of this difference centres on their relationship to motherhood and the moral logic of the matrifocal household.

It is helpful to situate Ivete's experiences of care within this cultural landscape of meaning and view her eventual embodiment of motherhood in relation to her own experience of childhood(s). Although Ivete does not regret her "street child" past, when asked, she is adamant that she would *not* let her own children sleep on the street *because of her current situation*. By "current situation" she is referring to her imprisonment, her missing son, and the fact that nobody is visiting her in prison. Importantly, Ivete refuses to make a reductive causal link between staying on the street, processes of criminalization, imprisonment, and strained or severed mother-child relations. However, at the same time, she seems to recognize that this cluster of experiences is complexly entangled:

> *I'm not [in prison] because I slept in the street. It's because of another thing. But, as I did that thing—a favour—it's possible that he [one of her children, if permitted to sleep on the street] could do the same thing—isn't it? He could do something worse.... If I gave him enough rope I think he'll do something worse. I don't want this for my children, for my children to go through what I'm going through here, no.... It's very difficult....*

When asked about schooling, Ivete laughs sardonically as she claims that she only went to school to mess around. She went to school one day but not every day, "one day yes, one day no...."

In this intermittent manner, Ivete "attended" school until around fifth grade. However, she describes herself as knowing "almost nothing" because she "went to mess around" and lessons "didn't connect." Today Ivete is "functionally illiterate." Ivete reports that her children *are* studying but is unable or unwilling to elaborate.

At least some of Ivete's children are not (yet) registered with the state. As I will elaborate below, the fact that Robison was not registered seems to have facilitated his disappearance in numerous senses. Not only does this make him less traceable, it is interpreted by state officials as a sign of Ivete's status as a "bad" mother and thus enables authorities to imagine Robison as categorically outside the moral universe of the matrifocal household, as a neglected "quasi-street child" that his mother let go or, effectively, *chose* to lose. This example of Ivete's "personal failure" to provide "adequate" care becomes mobilized to evince the more or less explicit claim that she does not care (enough) for her children. Though Ivete did not technically abandon her son, many middle-class actors seem to feel that she might have *eventually* done so or that she *might as well have* done so.

In Brazil, a child must be registered in order to enroll in school. Additionally, monthly *bolsa família* (federal income transfer) payments are calculated on the basis of the number of *registered* children for whom the recipient is caring. Ivete becomes quite melancholy as she explains why (some of) her children are not registered. It seems that she had lost own documents and didn't "care" to go through the process of getting new ones. The experience of imprisonment—namely, the sudden and intense foreclosure of possibility entailed by coercive confinement—may throw retrospectively visible agentive possibilities into relief. Moreover, experiential intersections between criminalization and motherhood may give rise to self blame and feelings of failure. Marginalized women—qua targets of improvement schemes—are exposed to, and encouraged to buy into, hegemonic discourses of femininity, motherhood, and *individual responsibility* (Haney). Attention to the circumstances surrounding Robison's birth disrupts such discourses, bringing structures and processes beyond Ivete's control into focus. These factors, elided by hegemonic discourses that (re) produce "unknowing" (Moodie), severely circumscribe marginalized women's parenting choices.

Ivete once worked as a maid. This is not surprising given that domestic work represents the single largest occupation among Brazilian women. In 2008, Brazil had approximately 6,600,000 domestic workers. Recently, Brazilian law has begun to recognize domestic workers' rights. The process remains incomplete. In 2008, only 25.8 percent were working formally with legally guaranteed entitlements and protections. The last time Ivete held such a position, she was pregnant with Robison. However, when Ivete's employer learned of the pregnancy she terminated her employment with the promise to re-hire her when she was ready to resume. When Ivete attempted to reclaim her job, she was frustrated to learn that her employer had hired someone else.

Working occasionally, whenever she was able to arrange a job, Ivete lived with her infant son Robison in a neighbourhood in Salvador's urban periphery (São Rafael). Soon, Ivete became pregnant again. After her daughter's birth Ivete and her children lived *de favor* (for free) in a small room. It was at this point that Ivete encountered difficulties and had to flee the neighbourhood. She explains:

> *[It] got very dangerous. ... I had a problem there and [so] I took and got out of there. ... I got myself mixed up with friendship there, with the cousin of my daughter. And this cousin put me in the* rabo de foguete *[put me at risk].... I almost died.... I saw that it was time to go and leave my children.... I left [them] with my daughter's godmother because ... I had to* correr atrás *[go after] the money I had to pay.... Then* this *happened—I* fui presa *[was arrested].*

In urgent need of money and shelter, Ivete relocated to the bustling city centre where she grew up and knows many people. Ivete repeatedly insists that she intended to send for her children as soon as possible. But, before reuniting with her son and daughter, she first needed to "find a place" because the room she was renting "didn't have a stove, it didn't have any of that." In Ivete's account, at times, she seems to suggest that she would have picked up her children on the very day she was arrested. At other moments, her reunion with her children is framed more as a taken-for-granted inevitability that was pre-empted by her arrest. It would be incorrect to assume that Ivete did not intend to resume primary custody of her two youngest children simply because her three oldest children are being (co-)raised by others. Marginalized women's levels of involvement with their various children range significantly according to an infinitely complex calculus and, additionally, change over time (also see Fonseca, "*Circulação*").

At the time of her arrest, Ivete was renting a room in a rather infamous "abandoned" building. The building had been "invaded" and occupied by the MST—the *Movimento Sem Teto* (the urban counterpart to Brazil's famous landless movement). In many cases, invasion is viewed as an effective means of gaining access to public housing: if/when state agents arrive to evict residents, evictees hope/expect they will be compensated with a space in a new, if undesirably located, social housing development.

On Christmas morning, only weeks before Ivete's move to the city centre, the MST-occupied four-story building caught fire. Although all occupants (over 36 families) managed to escape unharmed, many of their possessions were lost. The following day, families made a controversial return to the building, dividing up the bottom two "habitable" floors. City engineers directed them to leave the property citing the threat of collapse. The families refused to leave and mounted a protest in front of the building. During our interview, as we wrap up a conversation about housing, Ivete updates me on the status of the MST-building: "I just learned that they closed the [building].... That's just great! Now when I leave here I don't even know where I'll go. I don't know but I'll find a place for [the kids]." As she tries to imagine a future with her children Ivete's anxiety is palpable; she lowers her voice, shakes her head, looks down at the table, and begins grumbling to herself.

Although it is my policy to never to ask participants to disclose the charge(s) that have resulted in their imprisonment, Ivete spoke openly of her charge ("drugs") and the circumstances of her (first) arrest. The following narrative is based exclusively on Ivete's personal account of her arrest. Ivete was arrested while doing a favour for an acquaintance she had just met. Ivete was asked to deliver a snack and, unbeknownst to her, it contained drugs. The police were violent during her arrest. She considered registering their abuse with a doctor but a police officer slapped her across the face, warned her to keep quiet, and threatened her life.

At the time of our interview, Ivete had been imprisoned for roughly four months during which no family member had visited. Ivete had spoken to a prison social worker about contacting her family but didn't know their current telephone number. I asked Ivete if her family *knew* that she has been arrested. She says that they *must* know because her arrest was televised on a popular midday local news/variety program. She explains that being put on television is a horrible thing because it humiliates a person. She tried to hide her face from the cameras. She told the reporter that she didn't know the snack contained drugs—that she was "*laranjada*"[3]—but they didn't want to listen. Journalists opined, on air, that Ivete deserved punishment.

Outside of the interview context, during one of my regular visits to CPF, Ivete and I spoke again about her lack of visits. On this particular occasion Ivete was looking tired and dejected. Her hair was no longer neatly pulled back, her eyes were dull, and her posture was poor. She barely had the energy to ask after her missing son. I updated her on the status of the search and asked her how she was doing. Not surprisingly, she lamented her lack of visitors. Then she added something in a voice so low that I had to request that she repeat herself: "One time my mom told me that if I were arrested because of a fight she could visit but if it was because of drugs she'd never visit me ... and now, I'm here, needing her and not seeing her here...." Ivete's criminalization has not only undermined her status as a mother, it has also affected her status as a daughter. The conditions of Ivete's imprisonment contribute to disconnection, to practices of effective unrelatedness by Ivete's mother. Ivete is clearly hurt and upset by her mother's absence and refusal to provide care. More abstractly, Ivete's imprisonment has entailed spatial as well as social dislocation that reflects and contributes to her interpellation (and identification) as a criminal (m)Other. In prison, as a *remand* prisoner, Ivete's alienation from the moral female space of the home is perversely compounded. Like other prisoners she has lost access to the home *qua* place. She has also been denied the possibility of *proximity* to her mother and her children, thus losing access to symbols of home outlined by Hecht.

CONCLUSION: "THE SMELL OF PIZZA"[4] AND THE SOCIAL PRODUCTION OF INDIFFERENCE

To conclude this chapter I recount my role in Ivete's crisis of care. Based on the fragmentary details I was able to detect as I struggled to negotiate the "black hole" of Brazilian child protection agencies (Fonseca 2002: 214) I attempt to explain *what happened* to Robison. I contend that Ivete's interpellation as a criminal (m) Other is key to understanding Robison's "disappearance" as well as my failure (as her privileged white North American advocate with relatively strong backing from prominent local institutions) to "find" him.

In mid-April, a couple of months after Ivete's arrest, Robison was left in front of a day care. Originally Ivete had left him with her infant daughter's godmother. However, at some point, without Ivete's knowledge, it seems that Robison was transferred to the care of Ivete's mother. Such shifting care arrangements are common in situations of profound poverty and uncertainty. Households already struggling to make ends meet cannot always bear the additional strains on time, space, and resources that an additional dependent represents.

Ultimately, it is not clear who left Robison at the *creche*, what motivated them, or what exactly they intended to happen. I submit that Robison's "abandonment" was actually the enactment of a historically-constituted strategy of (temporary) institutional placement. Specifically, I understand it as a temporary stop-gap measure taken in response to the intersection of extreme scarcity with mass-mediated knowledge of Ivete's own indefinite institutionalization and ostensible involvement with drugs. In other words, the prospect of caring for Robison was practically understood in relation to Ivete's emerging status as a criminal m(Other).

Habitus (qua embodiment of a deep history of social inequality and structural violence) and situated knowledge contributed to Robison being left at a day-care centre. There, he encountered an educator who brought him to the closest branch of the Conselho

Tutelar (similar to a Children's Aid Society). At this point, when counsellor João took charge of the case, Robison's identity was unknown. On the 18th of April, João brought the boy (known only as "Junior") to a children's shelter (Eunice Weaver). He then began to conduct an investigation to identify the child. Somehow, counsellor João accomplished this. He was the man in the black vest who visited Ivete while she was imprisoned at the police lockup.

I had begun the search for Robison by trying to locate the man in the vest. Based on Ivete's recollection, I visited FUNDAC (which is a distinct organ from the Conselho Tutelar). I only managed to track down counsellor João after a few days and several wrong turns. I was ecstatic when I finally found the elusive man in the vest.

João informed me that, since visiting Ivete, he had been in contact with Robison's father and paternal relations. He was pleased to report that Robison's father is a "*trabalhador*" who intends to register and care for his son. In this context, *trabalhador* literally means "worker" but connotes an *honest* worker or a person who is not a criminal. João explained that he was just in the process of getting the necessary documents in order that Robison could finally be registered. Once registered in the name of both parents, Robison's father could have custody. João had attempted to visit Ivete at the police lockup for a second time, to update her and get her signature, but she had already been transferred. With all the confusion surrounding the death of Ivete's cellmate, police were unable to provide João with her current location. Eager to *see* Robison so that I could put Ivete's mind at ease, I left Wilson and headed to Eunice Weaver shelter.

Eunice Weaver shelter occupies a picturesque, re-purposed, colonial-era plantation house. It is relatively isolated, located in a distant low-income suburb of Salvador, surrounded by lush green forest and fields. Just beyond this verdant perimeter are tracts of newly-constructed and under-construction public housing units. As I sat waiting to meet the director I scanned old photographs and framed documents that decorate the walls of her office. In the early to mid-twentieht century, this building sheltered children of lepers. Under the Vargas administration, the leper was removed from his/her family and was forced to surrender any children to the state (Poorman). Institutions for the healthy children of lepers, like Eunice Weaver, became central to the state's approach to leprosy control. At some point it was established that severing family ties between adults with Hansen's disease and their children was not medically necessary and, in fact, might have deleterious effects on the wellbeing of the children and adults involved (Poorman). I was struck by this explicit and calculated attempt to improve society through the production of unrelatedness between marginalized parents and their children. It had an eerie resemblance to contemporary processes operating within and beyond the prison that undermine criminalized mothers' social relationships, especially their ties to children understood as "still-saveable."

My musings were interrupted by the arrival of the shelter director. She informed me that the juvenile court judge had removed Ivete's son and that she had no knowledge of his status or whereabouts. The juvenile court hearing occurred in May and the boy was removed from Eunice Weaver the same day. According to the shelter director, at the time of the hearing, none of the officers of the court knew—or admitted to knowing—the boy's identity or the identity/location of his parents. I immediately called João to share the bad news. He seemed legitimately surprised by the turn of events, insisting that he communicated the results of his investigation to the juvenile court judge. He then assured me he would look into the situation.

The following day I headed to the downtown offices of the juvenile court judge where I spent most of the day being shuffled from office to office. Just as the end of the workday was approaching, I finally made some progress. I found myself standing across from a woman employed within the records department. She was holding a manila folder containing Robison's case. The woman told me that she couldn't show me the contents of the folder until I established my authority to gain access to the file. She then lowered her voice and gravely warned me that I had better hurry. When I called João to relay the woman's cryptic warning he informed me that he had visited the juvenile court earlier in the day and had actually managed to see Robison's file. João confirmed my suspicion: Ivete's son was in the process of adoption and his file contained *no* trace of his or his parents' identities.

That night I created a document requesting authorization to act as Ivete's proxy. The catholic prison pastoral, the prison social workers, and the centre social workers each endorsed and sent separate versions of the letter to the juvenile court judge. In the letter we also summarized Ivete's situation and the findings of our investigation regarding Robison's whereabouts. Finally, we requested that adoption proceedings be immediately suspended.

I impatiently awaited a response. The following week I returned to the offices of the juvenile court judge to check on the status of my request. There was no record of my request (sent by three separate, relatively powerful, intuitions) and nobody would admit to knowing anything about Robison's case. The woman from the records department was nowhere to be found and everyone with whom I spoke said it would be impossible to locate a child's file without a case number. I called Counsellor João to obtain the case number. The secretary at the Conselho Tutelar informed me that he had been temporarily relieved of his duties and would not be back until September.

Ultimately, to my knowledge, the ("illegal") adoption proceeded and Ivete and Robison were not reunited. In late June, I was hospitalized with pneumonia. By the time I was able to return to CPF, Ivete had been released. Her trial still had not occurred. I have had no further contact with Ivete. Her crisis of care, as I have documented it, is not entirely exceptional. Within the context of Salvador's prison-neighbourhood nexus, the discourse of the criminal (m)Other naturalizes inequality, reproduces social hierarchies, and undermines meaningful relationships. *Disappearable* children are but one manifestation of the violence perpetuated by this discourse.

ENDNOTES

[1]Note that CPF is relatively more comfortable and less overcrowded than police lockups. At CPF each cell confines approximately three *presas*. Cells have a bunk bed and, typically, a mattress for the person who sleeps on the floor.

[2]Utterances i.e. "*eu peguei e saí*" (lit.: "I took and left.") place an emphasis on the second verb.

[3]The term "*laranja*" literally means orange but, in this context, it refers to a person taking the fall for someone else.
[4]This popular expression alludes to greedy actors divvying up the "pie" and refers to the sense that corruption is afoot.

WORKS CITED

Balibar, E. "Is There a Neo-racism?" *Race, Nation, Class*. Ed. E. Balibar and I. Wallerstein. London: Verso, 1991. 17-28. Print.

Caldas, Alcides et al. "Tecnologia Social: Cooperação Universidade/Comunidade Para o Desenvolvimento Urbano Regional e Local Sustentável." *Revista de DesenvolvimentoEconômico* 16 (2007): 16-25. Web. 22 September 2013.

Carsten, Janet. *Cultures of Relatedness: New Approaches to the Study of Kinship*. Cambridge: Cambridge University Press, 2000. Print.

Collins, John. "'But What if I Should Need to Defecate in Your Neighborhood, Madame?': Empire, Redemption and the 'Tradition of the Oppressed' in a Brazilian Historical Center." *Cultural Anthropology* 23.2 (2008): 279-328. Print.

DaMatta, Roberto. *A Casa & a Rua: Espaço, Cidadania, Mulher E Morte No Brasil*. São Paulo-SP: Brasiliense, 1985. Print.

De Oliveira Almeida and Maria Lúcia. "Vozes de Dentro... De Mulheres... e De Muralhas: Um estudo sobre jovens presidiárias em Salvador, Bahia." Diss. Universidade Federal da Bahia, 2006. Web. 29 Nov. 2012.

Drybread, Kristen. "Rights-Bearing Street Kids: Icons of Hope and Despair in Brazil's Burgeoning Neoliberal State." *Law & Policy* 31.3 (2009): 330-50. Print.

Estatuto da Criança e do Adolescente, Lei N° 8.069, De 13 de Julho de 1990. Web. 2 Feb. 2015.

Fonseca, Claudia. "Da circulação de crianças à adoção internacional: questões de pertencimento e posse." *Cadernos Pagu* 26 (2006): 11-43. Print.

Fonseca, Claudia. "The De-Kinning of Birthmothers: Reflections on Maternity and Being Human." *Vibrant: Virtual Brazilian Anthropology* 8.2 (2011): 306-339. Print.

Fonseca, Claudia. "Orphanages, Foundlings, and Foster Mothers:

The System of Child Circulation in a Brazilian Squatter Settlement." *Anthropologica* 59.1 (1986): 15-27. Print.

Fonseca, Claudia. "The Politics of Adoption: Child Rights in the Brazilian Setting." *Law & Policy* 24 (2002): 199-227. Print.

Goldstein, Donna M. *Laughter Out of Place: Race, Class, Violence, and Sexuality in a Rio Shantytown.* Berkeley: University of California Press, 2003. Print.

Gregg, Jessica L. *Virtually Virgins: Sexual Strategies and Cervical Cancer in Recife, Brazil.* Palo Alto: Stanford University Press, 2003. Print.

Haney, Lynne A. *Offending Women: Power, Punishment, and the Regulation of Desire.* Berkeley: University of California Press, 2010. Print.

Hayes, Kelly E. *Holy Harlots: Femininity, Sexuality, and Black Magic in Brazil.* Berkeley: University of California Press, 2011. Print.

Hecht, Tobias. *At Home in the Street: Street Children of Northeast Brazil.* Cambridge: Cambridge University Press, 1998. Print.

Heilborn, Maria Luiza and Cristiane S. Cabral. "A New Look at Teenage Pregnancy in Brazil." *Obstetrics and Gynecology* 2011: 1-7. Web. 5 Feb. 2013.

Holston, James. *Insurgent Citizenship: Disjunctions of Democracy and Modernity in Brazil.* Princeton: Princeton University Press, 2008. Print.

Moodie, Ellen. *El Salvador in the Aftermath of Peace: Crime, Uncertainty, and the Transition to Democracy.* Philadelphia: University of Pennsylvania Press, 2010. Print.

Moreira de Carvalho, Inaiá Maria and Vanda Sá Barreto. "Segregação Residencial, Condição Social e Raça em Salvador." *Cadernos Metrópole* 18.2 (2007): 251-273. Print.

Mumola, Christopher J. "Incarcerated Parents and their Children." *Bureau of Justice and Statistics Special Report* (2000). *National Criminal Justice Reference Service.* Web. 5 Mar. 2013.

Penglase, Ben. "Barbarians on the Beach: Media Narratives of Violence in Rio de Janeiro, Brazil." *Crime, Media, Culture* 3.3 (2007): 305-325. Print.

Poorman, Elisabeth. "The Legacy of Brazil's Leper Colonies." *Cad. Saúde Colet.* 16.2 (2008): 307-26. Print.

Rebhun, L.A. *The Heart is Unknown Country: Love in the Chang-*

ing Economy of Northeast Brazil. Palo Alto: Stanford University Press, 1999. Print.

Rizzini, Irene and Irma Rizzini. "Children and Youth in Institutional Care in Brazil." *Residential Care of Children: Comparative Perspectives.* Ed. Mark E. Courtney and Dorota Iwaniec. Oxford University Press, 2009: 1-26. *Oxford Scholarship Online.* Web. 15 Feb. 2012.

Schafer, N. E. and A. B. Dellinger. "Jailed Parents: An Assessment." *Women and Criminal Justice* 10.4 (1999): 73-118. Print.

Scheper-Hughes, Nancy and Daniel Hoffman. "Brazilian Apartheid: Street Kids and the Struggle for Urban Space." *Small Wars: The Cultural Politics of Childhood.* Ed. N. Scheper-Hughes and C. Sargent. Berkeley: Univ. of California Press, 1999. Print.

Skidmore, Thomas E. *Brazil: Five Centuries of Change.* New York: Oxford University Press, 2010. Print.

Vasconcelos, Pedro de Almeida. "Pobreza urbana e a formação de bairros populares em Salvador na longa duração." *GEOUSP – Espaço e Tempo* 20 (2006): 19-30. Web. 22 September 2013.

Walmsley, Roy. "World Female Imprisonment List (Second Edition)." International Centre for Prison Studies, 2012. Web. 29 Nov. 2012.

12.
Mothering at the Margins

The Case of Incarcerated Women in Trinidad and Tobago

TALIA ESNARD AND KIMBERLY OKPALA

Incarcerated mothers face major changes in their family relationships given their gender, mother-child separation, and their social status both inside and outside of prison (Enos; Shlafer and Poehlmann, "Representations of Attachment"; Easterling). For many of these mothers, the gendered nature of their incarceration, class status, and the perceived strain on or lack of a relationship with their children have a direct effect on how they function in the criminal justice system (Ferraro and Moe; Garcia-Coll et al.). Here, the complexities of this type of quandary, social victimization, and the normalization of its inherent consequences remain a common threat to maternal-child relationships, their survival during incarceration (Gabel; Poehlmann, "Representations of Attachment"; Jackson), and the way they see themselves as mothers (Scobie and Gazso). Yet, the discursive, material, and structural bases of these vulnerabilities are often underexplored and labelled as individual pathologies of what Suzanne Allen et al. called "throw away moms." This invisibility inadvertently both silences their struggles and proliferates the taken for granted paradoxes that they experience in caring for their children while navigating prison life (Enos; Morash and Schram; Young and Reviere; Raeder). Moreover, it forces them to redefine and reclaim already fractured maternal identities and practices (Easterling; Walsh and Crough). Despite this reality, few scholars have investigated existing and emerging maternal peculiarities associated with these situated contexts. Our work therefore interrogates how these related gender and class based struggles condition the identities and experiences of incarcerated mothers and their children.

In emerging economies like Trinidad and Tobago where there continues to be an alarming increase in the rate of criminal activities and a growing concern for the incarceration of vulnerable groups particularly that of women and young children (Harriott et al; Ryan et al.) such lines of questioning remain clearly deficient. We use a case study research design to give voice to the experiences of twelve incarcerated mothers in one of Trinidad and Tobago's prisons. This chapter relies on in-depth interviews to explore the ways incarcerated mothers experience multiple layers of marginality before and during incarceration and the continuing effects of such vulnerabilities on their maternal identities and practices. We contend that where incarceration of mothers is, in part, a consequence of structural marginalization related to gender and class positioning, the process of (re)negotiating and (re)defining their maternal bonds, identities, and practices become continuously coloured, complex and paradoxical.

The chapter is organized as follows. First, we discuss the potential utility of feminist post structuralist theory in the critical examination of discursive contexts, material, and or social structures within which incarcerated mothers engage and to which they respond. Next, we contextualize women's criminality in Trinidad and Tobago. Following this, we use the international literature on mothering (in the absence of related research in the Caribbean) to examine dominant ideologies related therein, its impact on discourses surrounding mothering while incarcerated and to frame the methodological orientations and procedures underlying the study. The main focus shifts to our research findings, particularly related to issues of attachment, identities, and maternal practices. Finally, we conclude with implications for policy and future research.

THEORETICAL FRAMEWORKS

Post structuralist feminist interrogation of discursive and structural contexts offer an insightful epistemological framework for understanding underlying maternal identities and practices of incarcerated mothers. In her seminal work *Gender Trouble,* Judith Butler locates gendered understandings and lived experiences within discursive and performative contexts. *Performativity* is a vocabulary for marking out those "discursive practice[s] that brings into being or enacts that which it names and so marks the constitutive or productive power of discourse" (Butler 134). This, for Butler, emerged out of "personal/cultural history of received meanings subject to a set of imitative practices ... which, jointly construct the illusion of primary and interior gendered self or parody the mechanism of that construction" (138).

We develop our theoretical analysis of gender performances, imitations of culturally defined modes of thinking, and their impact on maternal practices of incarcerated women. To make sense of maternal separation and how it affects mothers' thinking and practices during incarceration, we embrace the explanatory powers of the gendered identities construct as *performative or doing* with ongoing understanding of gendered selves (Butler; Mascia-Lees).

We also integrate theoretical assumptions and propositions of attachment theory. The objective here is to locate such theorizing within broader discursive contexts that shape social expectations and practices of mothering. Attachment theorists hold that children and parents develop unconscious and conscious bonds to each other. Using an internal working model, Bowlby (1982), for instance, argued that relationships are formed on the basis of trust gained during periods of early childhood stress. At one end, attachment theorists extend Bowlby's "working model" or "mental representations" as a way of thinking about children's attachment with the caregiver (Cox citing Bretherton), namely that of the mother. This element of monotropism in the theory or the focus on the development of attachment to the mother as the primary caregiver remains the central crux upon which mothers becomes entangled in normative discourses of motherhood. This centrality of mothers to childcare becomes further reinforced in the related attachment theorizing that directs attention to the socio-psychological consequences of its absence. Thus, researchers report that any disruption in this relationship due to separation, changing living arrangements, or non-responsiveness from attachment figures is hypothesized to produce (i) separation anxieties among others as negative but normal outcomes (Poehlmann, "An Attachment Perspective"); (ii) varied psychological problems on either side (Stalker and Hazelton) and; (iii) patterns of maternal thinking and/or practice (Cox; Arditti, Burton and Neeves-Botelho).

At the other end, what emerges is that of attachment parenting as a practice where one observes a cluster of parenting behaviours that emphasizes emotional sensitivity and responsivity to infants and young children (Cox citing the work of Ainsworth and her colleagues). These attachment ideas and parenting practices as *performed or enacted,* borrowing from Judith Butler, mirror idealized, normative, and theorized notions of mothering (Bengtsson and Psouni) that when internalized introduce many social and emotional strains on those who respond to them (Sandifer; Thompson and Harm).

Incarcerated mothers are uniquely disadvantaged within this discussion. Specifically, incarcerated mothers as well as their children carry the burden of social stigmatization as unfit and bad mothers (Ferraro and Moe; Allen, Flaherty and Ely) thereby labelling them as criminal or socially unacceptable (Hagen and Myers). This displacement of their maternal identity with that of a criminalized one (Enos) on the bases of the loss of that attachment due to incarceration can lead to intense feelings of loss, guilt, and anxiety (Sandifer; Thompson and Harm) and strained relationships with family members (Rodriguez, Smith and Zatz). When these idealized meanings are viewed through a rose-tinted glass, they also define and orient social interventions that deal with problems associated with foster families (Johnston), reunification (Brown and Bloom), and child welfare (Solomon). Moving beyond the theoretical romanticization of motherhood embedded in attachment theory (Cox citing Hays) and the absence of Caribbean research on the same, we argue for greater considerations of discursive contexts and the effects on maternal-child relationships in our understandings of mothering as a way of thinking and as a practice. It is our hope that such theorizing will give voice to those who mother outside of the dominant discourses of mothering.

CONTEXTUALIZING WOMEN'S INCARCERATION IN TRINIDAD AND TOBAGO

Located at the southernmost part of the Caribbean, Trinidad and Tobago has a population of approximately 1.3 million people with a racial and sex distribution as follows: three largest groups are East Indians (35.4 percent), Africans (34.2 percent), and Mixed (22.8 percent), with women representing 49.8 percent and males 50.2 percent of the population (GOTT "Data on Women"). At a macroeconomic level, Trinidad and Tobago's lucrative oil and gas sectors, growing economic efficiency, high level of market innovation, high income status (Harriott et al.) and wider levels of regional economic activity (which passes through the country) has drawn attention to its potential role as the economic hub of the Caribbean and the considerable degree of structural changes that it would ensue.

However, despite these notable positive economic trends, Trinidad and Tobago remains troubled by growing patterns and levels of criminality and vulnerability of critical groups, particularly children and women (Harriott et al.). In the case of the latter, most recent data shows that of the 1709 women charged or arrested for serious crime between 2007 and 2012, the major offenses were as follows: possession of narcotics (605 or 35.4 percent), other serious crimes (203 or 11.8 percent), larceny (200 or 11.7 percent), burglaries and breakings (168 or 9.8 percent), fraud (164 or 9.5 percent), and robberies (123 or 7.1 percent) (GOTT "Data on Women").

Incarcerated women are often already disadvantaged in myriad ways. In profiling incarcerated women, wider research points to those who come from low income backgrounds, are underemployed and unemployed (Ferraro and Moe; Johnston; Harriott et al.), sexually molested, and have a history of drug and alcohol abuse (Brown and Bloom; Surratt). In the case of Trinidad and Tobago, the 2004 report on "Women Incarcerated in the Trinidad and Tobago Prison" revealed that the majority of these inmates were nationals (69.1 percent), of African descent (31 percent), in their thirties (32 percent), single parents (41.7 percent), unemployed (27.6 percent), with high school education (44.3 percent), and owned a home or apartment prior to incarceration (48.5 percent)

(GOTT). At the demographic level, the data also pointed to several important differences. Women of African descent tended to be incarcerated mostly for drugs (52 percent) followed by violent offenses (26 percent). The reverse is true for women of East Indian origin: violent crimes (50 percent) followed by drug offenses (27 percent). Unemployed women were more likely to be involved in serious crimes than pre-incarcerated employed women, particularly that of property offenses, substance abuse, and other drug related charges, and a significant percentage of the inmates were physically (38 percent) and sexual (28 percent) abused (GOTT "Women in Prison").

This profile provides more compelling international support for the established economic marginalization thesis of women's criminality (Pollock; Belknap; Owen; Heimer). Yet, the contextual and discursive footings of and effects on their incarceration and maternal challenges therein remain relatively ignored (Gabel and Johnston; Chesney-Lind). Specifically, legacies of colonial past, neglect, and deprivation (Best and Levitt), persistent patriarchal ideals (Black-Chen) and its implications for criminal activity (Ryan et al.), and increasing vulnerability to criminal activity in urban centers due to the rise of the drug trade (Harriott et al.) remain sources of growing concern in the Caribbean that warrant further study. These are further complicated by the deeply rooted historical, cultural milieu (Mohammed and Perkins), and criminalization of women based on complex legislation (Pemberton) that continues to shape women's disadvantageous socio-economic and racial position, susceptibility to poverty, and primary roles as caretakers of their children (GOTT "Data on Women"; Mohammed and Perkins). Today these vulnerabilities have been further exacerbated by the feminization of poverty in the Caribbean, criminalization of women (including those in the sex and escort industry) who find ways to work against these odds, the persistence of genderless and gender insensitive policy reforms, and less tolerant judicial response to women who come in conflict with the law (GOTT *The Cabinet Appointed Task Force*). These historical, structural, and social contexts raise renewed questions on potential dilemmas related to the susceptibility of women in the Caribbean (Bailey and Ricketts), the extent to which existing legislation responds to these dynamics, and the denigrating effects of such marginality. Collectively, this sustains an unrelenting invisibility of complexities that shape the ways in and extent to which Caribbean women engage in "discursive practices."

However, while there is a burning need for further scholarship on these historical and social contexts within which gender relations operate in the Caribbean, the focus of the chapter is on making visible the ways in which these frameworks or contexts translate into the expressions and actions associated with mothering while incarcerated. In the case of incarcerated mothers, we argue that it complicates their identities and practices of mothering before and during incarceration. By centering their lived maternal experiences and giving voice to these within the discussion of the findings of this research, this chapter attempts to fill this gap.

MOTHERING WHILE INCARCERATED: A REVIEW

Notions of intensive mothering as a mainstream North American construct that has penetrated Caribbean societies continue to dominate the literature on, and understandings of what constitutes, exemplar practices of mothering. In such contexts, mothering is perceived as a child-centered, emotionally absorbing, labour intensive, financially expensive endeavour, in which the mother is responsible for the nurturing and development of the child, and the child's needs take precedent over the individual needs of the mother (Hays; Garey; Wall). Such an idealized, universalized, and institutionalized social construction in dominant discourse crafts a good mother as economically dependent, heterosexual, child-centered, and at home with the primary responsibility for child care (Hays; Kennedy). However, such normative gendered expectations of motherhood (Enos) are usually framed within understandings of patriarchal, middle class, and white nuclear families, thus affecting the quality of their interaction and relationship (Cunningham). These distort varied experiences across various classes and other ethnic groups (Collins; Glenn, Chang and Forcey) and reinforce gender and power relations (Arendell). Other styles of mothering outside that of dominant, Eurocentric, class-based constructions are silenced (Glen, Chang and Forcey). This makes invisible other socio-historical mothering practices, which rely on family and friend networks among other ethnic groups in the Caribbean (Massiah; Reddock; Mohammed and Perkins). Reynolds argued that the historicity and divergence of families and family forms in the Caribbean necessitate different theorizations of patterns and practices that are outside of normalized understandings. Attempting to disrupt these dominant discourses of mothering, motherhood, and mothers, other scholars pointed to the ways in which these institutionalized gendered expectations and stereotypes (Glenn, Chang and Forcey; Rich; Ruddick; Barriteau) continue to oppress women.

What emerges in the case of the Caribbean is a double paradox where the penetration of women in economic and social circles co-exists with persistent marginality (Barrow; Silvera; Clarke; Massiah) and where, like in other North American societies, incarcerated mothers are perceived as "normal" insofar as they bore children but are denunciated from their social title due to incarceration (Enos). Specifically, researchers contended that such dominant discourses not only place social pressures for expected ideological responses but also emotional burdens on incarcerated mothers for being a "bad mother" (Schram; McKim; Gabel and Johnston; Easterling) and a felon whose actions led to maternal separation (Morash and Schram). However, many researchers (see Gabel and Johnston; Easterling) remain troubled by the observation that despite empirical support for the incompatibility or inconvenience of their dual roles as inmate and mother and the centrality of reunification, the weight of such dominant discourse and practices around mothering intensifies. Walsh and Crough asserted that incarcerated mothers "stand at the margins of socially constructed rubrics of motherhood" (160). On the other hand, Enos reminded us that incarcerated women form their own identities as a way of responding to and renegotiating their mothering practices during incarceration.

Another source of contention in the literature of incarcerated women centres on the question of whether or not ties should be maintained between mother and children during incarceration (Hairston). At one end of this debate, some scholars emphasize the negative effects of mother-child contact during maternal incarceration (Mumola), cumulative risks and stressors (Reed and Reed), inappropriate subsequent behaviour (Henriques; Johnston), and higher rates of subsequent incarceration (Acoca; Johnston). At the other end, researchers call for greater scrutiny of the social dimensions of criminality, including discordant home characteristics and abusive parent management practices (such as child abuse) that existed prior to incarceration (Gabel). Although, we acknowledge the complexity of maternal incarceration (Seymour; Miller), we also note that very little is known about the effects on the lives of their children (Gabel). This chapter therefore responds to the need for deeper analyses of how such contexts affect incarcerated mothers' ways of negotiating and framing their identities.

METHODOLOGY: CASE STUDY APPROACH

Case study research seeks to understand the ways in which contexts or settings shape a given phenomenon (Stake; Yin). Interpretative or critical approaches allow us to "gain tremendous insight into a case by way of providing rich data on the 'why' and 'how' of a given phenomenon while taking into consideration the ways in which this phenomenon is influenced by the context within which it is situated" (Baxter and Jack 556). We utilized the intrinsic case study design in which the focus is on learning more about incarcerated mothers "as a particular ... group" (Hancock and Algozzine 34). This enabled us to capture discursive frameworks as well as cultural and structural contexts that shape identity constructions and lived experiences of incarcerated mothers.

The purpose of the study was to analyze the effects of discursive and contextual processes on the cognitive negotiations of conflicts and identities of incarcerated mothers. To this end we used purposive sampling and conducted in-depth interviews with twelve incarcerated mothers in Valley View Prison.[1] Examining the demographic profiles of these incarcerated mothers provides growing evidence for the relevance of economic marginalization in understandings of women's incarceration. These twelve incarcerated mothers were from socio-economically deprived backgrounds where most of the interviewees only completed secondary or high school entrance exams (9/12), were generally of mixed descent

(8/12), were mostly between 25-34 years old (8/12), represented an equal number of married and single women (6/6), had a mean of five children (ranging from 2-10), and were in various domestic, menial, or low paying jobs. Table 1.1 below provides further details of the distribution.

With approval from the Commissioner of Prisons and Superintendent of Prisons, interviews with incarcerated mothers were arranged through the prison system and interviewees were selected prior to the commencement of field work by the prison staff. The semi-structured interviews took place under the supervision of prison personnel but with some physical space so as to ensure full confidentiality and privacy. Interviews sought to delve into questions related to background, relationships and experiences with their children prior to and during incarceration, perceptions and experiences of negotiating identities, and practices of mothering while incarcerated. This involved asking "what, when, why, and how" questions about the meanings, practices, activities, histories, and routines of their daily lives (Halford and Leonard, citing Crossley) and situating the mothers' experiences within wider relational, temporal, economic, and socially constructed contexts.

DATA ANALYSIS AND FINDINGS

Interviews were transcribed, manually coded, and inductively, thematically and theoretically analyzed (Reissman; Creswell; Marshall and Rossman; Yin) by both researchers around the contextual and cognitive approach of the study. However, due to the sensitive nature of the alleged acts of criminality (in certain cases pending trials) and the guarded nature of institutional structures and mechanisms, our analyses were limited to the issues of maternal identity and practices. Thus, details of the institutional context that define their incarceration, reason for and length of their sentence, and explorations of the possible link of the aforementioned to their gender, race, and socio-economic status were therefore restricted. Theoretical explorations of the lived experiences of incarcerated mothers within situated contexts pointed to the salience of three important themes: 1) class, gender,

Table 1.1 Demographic distribution of sample

Name	Ages	Ethnicity	Prior Occupation	Marital status	Highest examination	Number of children	Length of Incarcerated
Sarah*	25-34 (NS)*	African	Public servant	Single	Common Entrance*	1	1year-2 months
Anna-Bella	25-34 (34)	African	Housewife	Common law	CXC*	6	7 years
Regina	25-34 (34)	Mixed	Agricultural worker	Single	Common Entrance	2	6 years- 7 months
Catherine	35-44 (42)	Mixed	Housewife	Married	Common Entrance	10	5 years
Betsy	25-34 (28)	Mixed	Self-employed	Married	Common Entrance	3	1 year-4 months
Takeyah	35-44 (37)	Mixed	Store attendant	Single	CXC	2	19 years-10 months
Zendya	35-44 (38)	Mixed	Self-employed	Single	Common Entrance	6	4 years- 6 months
Vivienne	25-34 (26)	Mixed	Sales clerk	Married	CXC	4	2 years- 3 months
Mia	45-54 (52)	East Indian	Domestic worker	Single	Common Entrance	4	5 years
Amy	25-34 (32)	African	Agricultural worker	Married	Common Entrance	7	1 year 7 months
Miranda	25-34 (32)	East Indian	Factory worker	Single	Common Entrance	2	5 years 2 months
Grace-Lyn	25-34 (26)	Mixed	Hair dresser	Single	Common Entrance	3	3 years

*NS-not stated

*Names are fictitious to protect the identities of respondents

*Common Entrance examinations are written as a pre-requisite for secondary or high school placement. In more recent times, this examination has been renamed the Secondary Examination Assessment.

*CXC means Caribbean Examinations Council. This examination issues assessments within various subject areas at the end of high school or secondary school.

and criminality; 2) social dimensions of criminality, emotional responsivity, and maternal identities, and; 3) maternal practices as situated and socially constrained.

GENDER, CLASS AND CRIMINALITY

Gender-based victimization, and inter-related sexuality, economic marginality, segregation, invisibility in the formal labour market, and social trauma, all played a role in the criminality of the women interviewed. In that regard, the data revealed that in many situations where these women served as dependent housewives prior to incarceration they expressed great dissatisfaction with their personal lives, social and familiar roles, and socio-economic situation. These defiant expressions became the subject of great discord and in many cases resulted in domestic disputes and even the cause of their incarceration. In at least five cases, the abuses the women faced emerged from their open resistance. Their way of thinking and inherent behaviour remained at variance with normative understandings of their roles as women.

On the other hand, it appeared that the cumulative effect of their economic dependence on loved ones and family members, primary responsibility for their children, low educational achievements, low paying employment opportunities, and unstable family homes led to desires for autonomy, self-reliance, financial security, need for social mobility, and alternative means of survival. Their choices were intricately linked to their assessments of these experiences as germane to their expected gender roles within the family and lack of satisfaction with their economic and social circumstances. Thus, despite some variation in the specificity of their individual litigations, the narratives implied that in cases where they attempted to respond to these marginalizing socio-economic experiences, they became increasing susceptible to acts of crime including violence and/or financial illegalities.

Existing research traces these experiences of victimization (rape, domestic violence, sexual exploitation) to patriarchal attitudes related to gender roles and identity. Few studies suggest that these women commit crimes in order to prevent being further victimized (Chesney-Lind) and to cope with broader economic and crime-gender related coercion (Raeder; Arditti and Few). In theorizing the above, Ferraro and Moe proposed that not only is violence against women under-examined but also reflects deeper structural and systematic gender dynamics, which are informed by racial and class positions in patriarchal cultures that foster female subservience, service, and subordination. While the importance of race to the experiences of abuse and subservience did not emerge as a critical factor in the criminality of interviewees due to the closed nature of their indictments, the data provide initial evidence that warrants further interrogations on the importance of gender identities, relations, and class positions.

SOCIAL DIMENSIONS OF CRIMINALITY, EMOTIONAL RESPONSIVITY, AND MATERNAL IDENTITIES

Social dimensions of criminality and emotional responsivity are also important to maternal identity. The maternal identities of the women in this study were tied to other social dimensions of their lives, like class background, femininity, social support (or lack thereof prior to and during incarceration), and how they reacted emotionally to such circumstances. In drawing on her class background, for instance, Miranda indicated that her depressed socio-economic background as well as her related need to work a few extra hours, led to fewer opportunities for framing a maternal bond with her children. Likewise, Mia stated that:

> *I had no money and no support; so couldn't give them enough love. I love them but didn't have that kind of closeness. I worked and made sure they got what they wanted. I tried my best to send them to school but I couldn't teach them because I can't read but I made sure they did their homework.*

In this case, her lack of access to more secured economic opportunities, low educational attainment, primary responsibility for her four children, and lack of social support in raising them (even from her marital partner and other proximal family members) had a direct effect on her detached relationship with her children. She also elaborated that her expressed affection towards her children prior to incarceration was further complicated by the physical abuse she faced in the home and to which her children were also exposed. In this case, her growing indifference, need for economic independence and sustainability as a means for coping with the socio-economic challenges, and gendered victimization she faced served to further deteriorate her relationship with her children. Thus, despite her professed love for her children, Mia questioned her role as a mother and by extension her maternal identity.

Theoretically, gender serves as one of the most visible stratified representations of culture. Both Mia and Miranda pointed to the broader significance of structural and cultural issues around gender and socio-economic status. They both linked lack of social support and their insubordinate status *as women* to their patterns of attachment and maternal identities prior to incarceration. In such circumstances, researchers contended that economic marginality and social trauma serve to obscure maternal relationships (Arditti and Few; La Pierre). However, while the findings confirm the importance of economic and social marginality, they also underscore the need for greater explorations that also address the role of emotional sensitivity and responsivity to such processes. Thus, Judith Lorber reminded us that as a definitive part of social structure, gender stereotypes frame economic activity, lines of authority and expectations for sexual and emotional life.

On the other hand, Betsy's narrative of her changing class status points to the situational relevance and fluid nature of class, gender, and maternal identities. In that regard, she disclosed that her prior middle class upbringing, and progressive detachment from that class background, parents, and the privileges associated with her background, led to her dominant understanding of motherhood as material rather than affective. As a case in point, Betsy spoke of the threat to her middle class status (i.e. her lack of official secured employment), the resultant need (prior to incarceration) for the maintenance of her material wellbeing, and a buying power that allowed for some endowment to her children. Thus, unlike ten other interviewees whose working class backgrounds remained a persistent structural reality, her early middle class upbringing sought not only to frame her preoccupation with strong financial security but also a way of thinking of motherhood as a proxy for her ability to provide for her children. Goodwin and Huppatz link this materiality of motherhood to contemporary class-based notions of motherhood that weigh heavily on issues of tastes, styles, access, and self-presentation.

Incarceration as an experience is also critical to the maternal identities (Ferraro and Moe; Easterling). The women in this study remained troubled by the weight of the separation from their children and its resultant strain on the relationship. Zendya, for instance, stated that "it is hard for women who love their children to be in this place." As a result, Zendya drew on the moral need to "encourage her children to do the right thing" as the basis of the way she thinks about her maternal self. Similarly, Miranda uttered: "Sure they have a roof and food but mothers need to know the details of how they are taken care of." This need for detail and freedom to nurture as normative characteristic of mothers becomes central to Miranda's maternal way of thinking.

Many other mothers also expressed great anxiety over their loss of physical engagement with their children and the social burdens associated with its absence as socially definitive of their maternal identities. Thus, Anna-Bella (like all other interviewees) pointed to the emotional trauma and psychological issues of anxieties related to the shame and blame associated with the loss of attachment to children. However, while Anna-Bella acknowledged the weight of these social burdens, she vehemently rejected the perceived loss of her maternal identity. She insisted therefore that "I will always be a mother ... separation is very hard for any real mother ... but no mother deserves to be away from children. Only mothers will know how I am dying inside. Living without them is like existing, not living." In this narrative, Anna-Bella not only stressed the emotional sensitivity to her children and the trauma of maternal separation but she also questioned the use of her incarceration as the basis for the separation. In this situation, Anna Bella saw such separation and the invisibility of her emotional sensitivity to her children as a further fracture of her maternal identity. She agonized over the strain on her bond with her children, particularly her younger son and his vulnerability to social, emotional and psychological dangers. Anna-Bella, like almost three-quarters of interviewees, attempts to move beyond the trivialization of her emotive disposition during incarceration and perceived loss of her maternal identity by reasserting her fondness or attachment towards her children. In this case, the language of attachment embedded in normative understandings of motherhood becomes her language of reassurance. For another three interviewees, the weight of maternal incarceration as well as its associated negative stereotypes resulted in either a sense of emotional withdrawal, depression, and/or refusal to practice motherhood while incarcerated.

Incarceration also engenders a sense of emotional crisis, given the multiple threats associated with the inherent strain on the attachment with their children, the replacement of that attachment with more proximal figures, and anguish over children's welfare. The twelve incarcerated mothers remained perturbed by the shifting nature of their children's attachment. For instance, Amy conveyed that she will always be their mother but the "relationship is a distant one ... we don't talk much." Likewise, Vivienne worried over the growing impartiality or coldness of her young daughter, the strained relationship with her son, and the replacement of that attachment with their caregivers. She stated that "my daughter doesn't know me. She is daddy's girl," adding that her first son is not always friendly because he has never forgiven her for breaking their relationship. She stated that they "may be angry but they still love mummy." Vivienne was emotional with us. She attempted to move beyond the pain and shame associated with this loss by reassuring herself that despite the physical and emotional distance between herself and her children, that the love bond remains. Vivienne's working model of attachment is still one based on expression of emotional responsivity as indicative of her attachment to her children.

In a similar way, Miranda remains burdened by the loss of her bond with her daughter, the chilling moments of encounter, clear signs of withdrawal, and the development of another bond with the grandmother of the child. She stated: "I am not much of a mother ... we are more like friends rather than mother and daughter ... my daughter calls her grandmother mummy but I will get my title back ... the bond is still there." Miranda likens the notion of attachment to the physical and emotional closeness between the caregiver and the child. When closeness is used as the basis for conceptualizing attachment and motherhood, she sees herself as *less than a mother*. Despite these trials, she too remains convinced that she can reclaim her respect as a mother.

Other mothers who internalized the need for physical closeness as the basis for attachment and stigmatization because of the lack thereof, sought to reconfigure their maternal identity. For instance, Regina was adamant that her children (particularly her eldest daughter) "still depended on [her] to make decisions." This need for involvement and the dependency on the mother for dealing with critical personal and social crises stands at the core of the perceived and internalized notions of attachment. Similarly, Grace-Lyn stated that the relationship is "very distant. In a way I am not a mother because I'm not there ... but when ... they are here, whole prison would fall apart and I'll only pay attention to them." Here, Grace-Lyn too assessed her own maternal identity on the lack of physical closeness and engagement in the lives of her children. This absence created a heavy sense of guilt, which she strives to ease through institutional visits. While Grace-Lyn's incarceration, like that of all the mothers, led to her questioning of her maternal identity, her children remain central to her existence. In cases like these, Cunningham advocated that children serve to reaffirm the maternal identities of their parents. Given such, Ferraro and Moe argued that while the dominant ideology of motherhood is evident in women's account of their inadequacies and failures, their possibilities of reunification served as a source of hope and survival during incarceration.

These narratives demonstrate that the strain on the maternal bond of the interviewees as well as the guilt and shame associated with their incarceration have influenced their assessments of their own maternal identity. However, in the above mentioned cases, incarcerated mothers not only attempted to hold on to their emotional ties with their children but also sought to actively reassert their maternal identity and regain the privileges associated with it. Their maternal identities emerge from the complex effects of the incarceration, including separation as well as social stereotypes and labelling associated with mothering at the margins. In such cases, incarcerated mothers bore the guilt associated with an internalized sense of what Snowden and Kotze called "mothering failure."

Alternatively, narratives in this study also suggested that the experience of being incarcerated and exposure to personal development programs can also alter and reconstruct maternal thinking and practice. Thus, Mia also drew on the role of the prison system in teaching her "how to be a better person" and how available counselling programs within the prison affect how she sees herself as a mother. In about ten of the cases in our study, these institutional rehabilitative programs presented positive mechanisms through which these women come to redefine and reclaim their maternal identities. Another two interviewees maintained that outside of personal development workshops, the thoughts of release and reunification with their children remain central to the need for self-improvement and survival. In that regard, Betsy proposed that "pain brings clarity." Whatever the driving factor, the guilt associated with their incarceration also served to reinforce the need for renewed attachment with their children such that they maintained their primary caregiving function. Where living apart from their children, "ruptures the taken-for-granted position of the mother with children, these women live outside or at the margins of mothering identity" and suffer from the pain loss of their maternal identity (Snowden and Kotze 145). These findings raise further questions about the dichotomous and crippling nature of the structural and cultural particularities of situated contexts and the ways in which these shape the moral, emotional responses and sensitivities that affect their relational experiences (Williams; Jaggar).

MATERNAL PRACTICES AS SITUATED AND SOCIALLY CONSTRAINED

Maternal incarceration is also associated with social scrutiny and stigmatization (Schram; Gabel and Johnston; Allen et al). In these contexts, incarcerated women often have to prove their worth as "good" mothers in order to negotiate access to and interactions with their children (Mc Kim; Enos). Consequently, women face many dilemmas or paradoxes in their maternal practices. While many of these mothers made sacrifices for and attempted to sustain the relationship with their children during incarceration, they remained constrained and uneasy by the institutional and cultural walls of incarceration.

Incarcerated mothers in this study were also at the mercies of institutional regulations regarding children visits. In such cases, incarceration mothers relied on the two restricted child visitation schedules for the year to maintain maternal bonds. In all cases, mothers divulged that the structured nature of the special visits (Mother's Day and Christmas), safety protocols, and the restrictive policy on physical interactions within the prison, served as a major deterrents to their hopes of reattachment. Catherine for example stated that she uses these visits to "maintain the bond ... to give them more love ... cause human beings ... need that human touch."

Cultural narratives of gender and mothering also served to define and reconstruct the women's relationships with their children during incarceration. Specifically, their *criminalized* as opposed to maternal identities often led to restrictions and in some cases denial of any input in the decision-making processes that affect where, with whom, for how long their children are cared for by other caregivers. In many of the cases examined, these incarcerated mothers remained emotional charged by this neglect and dismissal of their own concerns and rights *as mothers*. In all instances, loss of input into decisions that affect their children were related to broader concerns for the stigmatization associated with their incarceration, in particular, the perceived implications for their children and assumption that their incarceration warrants an immediate loss of their parental rights. These also shape the willingness and frequency with which their children and or family members visit or report on the status of their children.

Despite these troubling limitations, many interviewees continuously seek alternative practices that can provide a sustainable sense of maternal self. Thus, they used the visits to listen, provide support, get updates, allay fears and anonymities, and reconnect both emotionally and physically. As a case in point, Betsy indicated that "I cannot take them to beach and parks so I take complaints." However, despite the joys of being with their children, all of these mothers remain further traumatized by the fear of rejection, growing withdrawal from their children, stories of abuse and inappropriate behaviours from their children, and the growth of other attachments with their alternative families. This finding is consistent with that of Hagen and Myers, Mumola, and Poehlmann, who emphasized the relevance of the negative reactions of children on the way in which incarcerated mothers engage in maternal practices. Thus, Catherine explained that the children "start crying after visits ... the smaller ones hug while older ones feel they are now too big for that." Mia stated that "they keep asking me when it will end." Amy shared that they "don't talk much." Likewise, Regina disclosed that her son is getting "progressively quiet." However, these negative effects are dependent on the primacy of the mother and her attachment to the child/ren prior to incarceration. In cases where incarcerated mothers reflected on the perceived closeness of their children to themselves, they worry over their children's emotional state (as expressed through grief, anxiety, withdrawal), reported behavioural problems at home and in school (including fighting, stealing, lying), and the lack of any professional intervention to help their children deal with the negative effects of their incarceration. Here, separation or severing of that attachment remains deleterious for both mothers and their children (Johnston; Bloom; Arditti and Few).

Undesirable reactions or maladaptive patterns among children at times lead prison officials and mothers to stop the visitations (Bloom and Steinhart). Our findings corroborate this claim. Vivienne, on reflecting on her situation with her four children, stated that "it really breaks my heart when they become upset during the visits ... as they get older it is harder to explain ... that's why I want to stop visits." Many interviewees also implied that the younger children have a harder time communicating and dealing with the emotional strains of maternal incarceration. In "Representations of Attachment Relationships in Children of Incarcerated Mothers," Poehlmann reported that younger children are more vulnerable to effects of parental incarceration. However, these findings reaffirm our position that the disruptive effects on the children lives emerges not only from the age and class differences but also from the assignment of primary responsibility of women for child-caring in the Caribbean and the dependent relationship that develops before and during incarceration.

The women in our study remain desperate to believe that they were still performing their roles as mothers. Using the lens of attachment, one observes in such cases, that both the child and mother attempt to cope with the tragedies associated with incarceration. However, we argue that more critical feminist lens points to the noted ways in which the gendered expectations circulating around the notion of attachment and the disruption of that dependency during incarceration introduce weighted experiences of loss and longing, fears and wishes that obscure the openness and interaction between mother and children during incarcerated. Such findings not only call for greater research that can possibly unpack these social complexities of incarceration and maternal bonds but also the need for social evidence-based intervention that provides assistance to incarcerated families.

Incarcerated mothers also attempted to maintain communication as a way of sustaining these bonds and relationships during incarceration and upon release (Clark; Enos). Thus, many interviewees also relied on some form of communication (through letters, cards, messages) as limited as it may be to reinforce or sustain the mother-child bond during incarceration. Thus, most interviewees revealed that they constantly got regular information and updates on the child (through visits of another siblings, caregivers, or spouse). However, all incarcerated mothers revealed that cultural stereotypes also limited their attempt to reach their children beyond prison walls. For instance, Takeyah proclaimed that despite many efforts to reach her two children through letters and cards, these letters were withheld from them by their father who thought she may have a negative influence on the children. Her lengthy incarceration also added to an already strained relationship with her children. Three other mothers shared similar stories of shame and blame, and of fear and reprisal. In all these cases, mothers expressed great worry over the effects of associated negative feelings (related to the shame and blame of incarceration) on the growing disconnection with their children and chances of reunification. Where mother-child contact during incarceration serves as the best predictor for reunification (Johnston and Gabel), this requires parenting programs that not only connect to women's and children's emotional issues (Arditti and Few) but are also contextualized to better understand the dynamics of their relationships with their children and the possibilities for rebuilding or reframing these relationships post-incarceration.

However, limited communication and interaction during incarceration also emerged as an act of choice. In many cases, these were also associated with feelings of guilt, shame, and secrecy. For instance, Sarah consented to a peripheral role in her daughter's life. Sarah expressed that her mother has made the choice to let the daughter think that she [Sarah] is at a mental institution as opposed to prison as a way of keeping a positive image of the mother in the mind of the child. Similarly, Zendya's withdrawal and statement that she "doesn't want them to make the same mistakes," are also reflective of her own internalizations of shame, guilt, and intergenerational incarceration. By so doing, she inadvertently experiences an emotional form of imprisonment.

Other respondents attempted to remove the threat of intergenerational incarceration. Thus, three respondents also suggested that they do not think that prison is a place for children. Anna-Bella preferred the idea of children visits being held outside the prison facility to avoid the stigma associated with the prison and possible intergenerational effects. Miranda likewise thought that "children carry their parents' burdens". In such cases, the loss of attachment shapes the decisions and practices of incarcerated mothers. Specifically, these women remain increasingly concerned about the effects of these emotional traumas on their children and the relevance of the visitation since in many cases it often leads to reactive behaviours from and disruptive connections with their children. These, however, remain amenable through legislation, evidence-based social policies, and intervention (through the aegis of social workers, non-governmental organizations, and state institutions) that seek to confront the negative images of incarcerated mothers and provide feasible and sustainable ways of rebuilding healthy relationships with their children.

CONCLUSION

Beyond the present study there is much more to explore with regard to the influence of gender, social class, victimization status, and social stereotyping on maternal incarceration, identities, and practices (Easterling; Allen et al). By examining the effects of situated gender contexts, discourses, and class-based nature of incarceration, our research study adds to and empirically widens discussions on how the experience and challenges of maternal incarceration is framed within complex structural and/or cultural realities and associated social subjectivities. For Allen et al., "this multiple marginality, combined with the stigma and shame of incarceration, renders this powerless population essentially disposable in the eyes of society" (162).

In giving voice to the complex yet marginalizing experiences of incarcerated mothers, the narratives pointed to four key issues. First, the cyclical, structural, and stratified challenges, including those related to their socio-economic status, social victimization, and vulnerability to criminal activities, are significant. Two, despite their "deviant status," normative assumptions underlying expectations and ideals of motherhood are relevant to incarcerated mothers. Next, even in the context of separation dependence on mothers for children's welfare continues. Finally, the stigmatization and subsequent denial of the privileges of motherhood due to incarceration continue to impact and redefine maternal identities. These challenges illuminate the complexities of coping with and responding to experiences related to the triple jeopardy of being separated from their children, incarcerated, and voiceless.

Yet, these incarcerated mothers are conscious of, and attempt to navigate these situated contexts through the (re)negotiation and (re)configuration of their maternal identities and practices. In such cases, institutional programs appear to be both enabling and disabling and maternal responses/practices both passive and active. It is in such contexts, that these multiple paradoxes serve to perpetually marginalize their hope for, practices related to, and identities associated with their status as incarcerated mothers. The silence on these issues and experiences of incarcerated mothers is deafening.

All this points to the need not only for future interrogations of the structured and gendered relevance of incarcerated mothers' relationship to their children before and during incarceration but also for further assessments of the social and judicial systems that respond to the same. In moving forward, we also call for more relevant and gendered social policies and intervention programs that incorporate the concerns of these mothers in the rebuilding and maintaining of healthy relationships with their children under situations of vulnerability before and during incarceration. Giving voice to incarcerated mothers who remain outside the margins of the dominant discourse of mothering, one mother reminded us that "people need to hear from the mothers and know how they feel behind these bars" because as Mia positioned it, "we are humans too."

ENDNOTES

[1]This name is fictitious. The actual name and location of the prison were held for ethical reasons.

WORK CITED

Acoca, Leslie. "Defusing the Time Bomb: Understanding and Meeting the Growing Health Care Needs of Incarcerated Women in America." *Crime and Delinquency* 44.1 (1998): 44-69. Web. 26 Sep. 2012.

Allen, Suzanne, Chris Flaherty, and Gretchen Ely. "Throwaway Moms: Maternal Incarceration and the Criminalization of Female Poverty." *Journal of Women and Social Work* 25.2 (2010): 160-72. Print.

Arditti, Joyce, Linda Burton, and Lara Neeves-Botelho. "Maternal Distress and Parenting in the Context of Cumulative Disadvantage." *Family Processes* 49.2 (2010): 142-64. Print.

Arditti, Joyce and April Few. "Maternal Distress and Women's Reentry into Family and Community Life." *Family Process* 47.3 (2008): 303-21. Print.

Arendell, Terry. "Hegemonic Motherhood: Deviancy Discourses and Employed Mothers Accounts of Out of School Time Issues." Working Papers no. 1, Center for Working Families: Berkeley: University of California, 2009. Print.

Bailey, Babara and Heather Ricketts. "Gender Vulnerabilities in

Caribbean Labour Markets and Decent Work Provsions." *Social and Economic Studies* 52.4 (2003): 49-81. Print.

Barriteau, Eudine. *Confronting Power, Theorizing Gender: Interdisciplinary Perspectives in the Caribbean.* Kingston, Jamaica: University of the West Indies Press, 2003. Print.

Barrow, Christine. *Family in the Caribbean: Themes and Perspectives.* Kingston: Ian Randle Publishers, 1996. Print.

Baxter, Pamela, and Susan Jack. "Qualitative Case Study Methodology: Study Design and Implementation for Novice Researcher." *The Qualitative Report* 13.4 (2008): 544-59. Web. 17 Mar. 2013.

Belknap, Joanne. *Invisible Woman: Gender Crime andJjustice.* Belmont, Calif.: Wadsworth, 1996. Print.

Bengtsson, Hans and Elia Psouni. "Mothers' Representations of Caregiving and their Adult Children Representations of Attachment: Intergenerational Concordance and Relations to Beliefs About Mothering." *Scandinavian Journal of Psychology* 49.3 (2008): 247-257. Print.

Best, Lloyd and Kari Levitt. "Outlines of a Model of Pure Plantation Economy." *Social and Economic Studies* XVII (1968): 283-324. Print.

Black-Chen, Marsha. "The Cultural Context of Caribbean Women" Paper presented at the Annual Meeting of the 36th Annual National Council for Black Studies, Sheraton Atlanta Hotel, Atlanta, GA. All Academic Inc. Web. 17 Aug. 2013.

Bloom, Barbara. "Incarcerated Mothers and their Children: Maintaining Family Ties." *Female offenders: Meeting Needs of a Neglected Population.* American Correctional Association. Baltimore: United Book Press, Inc., 1992. 61-68. Print.

Bloom, Barbara and David Steinhart. *Why Punish the Children? A Reappraisal of the Children of Incarcerated Mothers in America.* San Francisco, Calif.: National Council on Crime and Delinquency, 1993. Print.

Bowlby, James. *Attachment and Loss. Vol. 1: Attachment.* 2nd ed. New York: Basic Books, 1982. Print.

Brown, Marilyn and Barbara Bloom. "Reentry and Renegotiating Motherhood: Maternal Identity and Success on Parole." *Crime & Delinquency* 55.2 (2009): 313-36. Print.

Butler, Judith. *Gender Trouble: Feminism and the Subversion of*

Identity. New York: Routledge, 1990. Print.

Chang, Grace and Linda Forcey. *Mothering: Ideology, Experience, and Agency (Perspectives on Gender)*. New York: Routledge, 1994. Print.

Chesney-Lind, Meda. "Reinventing Women's Corrections: Challenges for Contemporary Feminist Criminologists and Practitioners." *The Incarcerated Woman: Rehabilitative programming in Women's Prisons*. Ed. Susan Sharp and Roslyn Muraskin. Upper Saddle River, NJ: Prentice Hall, 2003. 93-106. Print.

Clarke, Edith. *My Mother Who Fathered Me*. London: George Allen Press, 1970. Print.

Collins, Patricia. "The Meaning of Motherhood in Black Culture." *The Black Families, Essays and Studies*. Ed. Robert Staples. Belmont: Wadsworth Publishing, 1999. 157-66. Print.

Cox, Suzanne. "Bridging Attachment theory and Attachment Parenting with Feminist Method of Inquiry." *Journal of the Association for Research on Mothering* 8.1-2 (2006): 83-95. Print.

Creswell, John. *Qualitative Inquiry and Research Design: Choosing among Five Traditions*. Thousand Oaks, CA: Sage, 2013. Print.

Cunningham, Lynette Ebonie. *Mothering While Incarcerated: A Multi-Level Approach to Identity Strategies, Mothering Strategies, and Child-Mother Relationships among Incarcerated Women*. Diss. Purdue University, Indiana, 2006. Web. 10 Jan. 2013.

Easterling, Beth. *Parenting Behind Bars: A Qualitative Study of Incarcerated Mothers*. Diss. University of Tennessee, Knoxville, 2012. Web. 10 Jan. 2013.

Enos, Sandra. *Mothering from the Inside: Parenting in a Women's Prison*. Albany, NY: State University of New York Press, 2001. Print.

Ferraro, Kathleen and Angela Moe. "Mothering, Crime, and Incarceration." *Journal of Contemporary Ethnography* 32.1 (2003): 9-40. Print.

Gabel, Katherine, and Denise Johnston, eds. *Children of Incarcerated Parents*. New York: Lexington Books, 1995. Print.

Gabel, Stewart. "Children of Incarcerated and Criminal Parents: Adjustment, Behavior, and Prognosis." *Bulletin of American Academic Psychiatry Law* 20.1 (1992): 33-45. Web. 18 Dec. 2012.

Garcia-Coll, Cynthia, Janet Surrey, Phyllis Buccio-Notaro, and

Barbara Molla. "Incarcerated Mothers: Crimes and Punishments." *Mothering against the Odds: Diverse Voices of Contemporary Mothers*. Ed. Cynthia Garcia-Coll, Janet Surrey, and Kathy Weingarten. New York: Guilford, 1998. 255-76. Print.

Garey, Anita. *Weaving Work and Motherhood*. Philadelphia: Temple University Press, 1999. Print.

Glenn, Evelyn, Grace Chang, and Linda Forcey. *Mothering: Ideology, Experience and Agency*. New York: Routledge, 1994.Print.

Goodwin, Susan, and Kate Huppatz, eds. *The Good Mother: Contemporary Motherhood in Australia*. Sydney: Sydney University Press, 2010. Print.

Government of Trinidad and Tobago (GOTT). *The Cabinet Appointed Task Force on Prison Reform and Transformation. Final Report*. Trinidad and Tobago Prison Service. 2002. Web. 12 Sep. 2007.

Government of Trinidad and Tobago (GOTT). "Data on Women Arrested/Charged for Serious Crimes for the Years 2007-2012." Maximum Security Prison, Arouca: GOTT, 2012. Print.

Government of Trinidad and Tobago (GOTT). National Drug Council in Collaboration with the Prison Service of Trinidad and Tobago. "Women in Prison in Trinidad and Tobago: Relationship between Drug and Criminal Offending." Drug Abuse Monitoring Project among Inmates. 2004.Web. 30 Mar. 2013.

Hagen, Kristine and Barbara Myers. "The Effect of Secrecy and Social Support on Behavioral Problems in Children of Incarcerated Women." *Journal of Child and Family Studies* 12.2 (2003): 229-42. Print.

Hairston, Creasie. *Focus on Children with Incarcerated Parents: An Overview of the Research Literature*. Baltimore, Maryland: The Annie E. Casey Foundation, 2007. Print.

Halford, Susan and Pauline Leonard, eds. *Negotiating Gendered Identities at Work: Place, Space and Time, Great Britain*. New York: Palgrave MacMillan, 2006. Print.

Hancock, Dawson and Bobb Algozzine, eds. *Doing Case Study Research: A Practical Guide for Beginning Researchers*. New York: Columbia University, Teachers College Press, 2006. Print.

Harriott, Anthony, Heraldo Munoz, Freddy Justiniano, Niky Fabiancic, and Leida Merado. *Caribbean Human Development*

Report 2012: Human Development and the Shift to Better Human Security. New York: United Nations Development Program (UNDP), 2012. Print.

Hays, Sharon. *The Cultural Contradictions of Motherhood*. New Haven, CT: Yale: University Press, 1996. Print.

Heimer, Karen. "Changes in the Gender Gap in Crime and Women's Economic Marginalization." *Criminal Justice 2000: Volume I: The Nature of Crime: Continuity and Change*. Washington, D.C., 2000.427-83. Print.

Henriques, Zelma. *Imprisoned Mothers and their Children: A Descriptive and Analytical Study.* New York: University Press of America, Inc., 1982. Print.

Jackson, Barbara. "The Lived Experience of Mothering during Incarceration." Diss. School of Nursing, University of Louisville, 2005. *Proquest Dissertation and Theses*. Web. 13 Feb. 2013.

Jaggar, Allison. "Love and Knowledge: Emotions in Feminist Epistemology." *Emotions: A Cultural Reader*. Ed. Jennifer Harding and Deidre Pribam, New York: Routledge, 2009. 50-68. Print.

Johnston, Denise. "Effects of Parental Incarceration." *Children of Incarcerated Parents*. Ed. Katherine Gabel and Denise Johnston. Lexington, MA: Lexington Books, 1995. 59-88. Print.

Kennedy, Deseriee. "'The Good Mother': Mothering, Feminism and Incarceration." *William and Mary Journal of Women and the Law* 18.2 (2012): 161- 200. Print

La Pierre, Simon. "Striving to be 'Good' Mothers: Abused Women's Experiences of Mothering." *Child Abuse Review* 16 (2010): 342-57. Print.

Lorber, Judith. *Paradoxes of Gender*. New Haven, Yale University Press. 1994. Print.

Marshall, Catherine, and Gretchen Rossman, eds. *Designing Qualitative Research*. 3rd ed. Thousand Oaks, CA: Sage, 1999. Print.

Mascia-Lees, Frances. *Gender and Difference: Globalizing World, 21st Century Anthropology.* Illinois: Waveland Press Inc., 2010. Print.

Massiah, Joycelin. *Women as Heads of Households in the Caribbean: Family Structure and Feminine Status*. Paris: UNESCO, 1983. Print.

McKim, Allison. "Getting Gut-Level: Punishment, Gender, and

Therapeutic Governance." *Gender and Society* 22.3 (2008): 303-23. Print.

Miller, Keva. "Risk and Resilience among African American Children of Incarcerated Parents." *Journal of Human Behavior in the Social Environment15.2 (2007):* 25-37. Print.

Mohammed, Patricia, and Anthea Perkins. *Caribbean Women at the Crossroads: The Paradox of Motherhood among Women of Barbados, St. Lucia and Dominica*. Kingston, Jamaica: Canoe Press, 1999. Print.

Morash, Richard, and Pamela Schram, eds. *The Prison Experience: Special Issues of Women in Prison*. Prospect Heights, Il: Waveland Press, 2003. Print.

Mumola, Christopher. *Incarcerated Parents and their Children*. Washington, DC: U.S. Bureau of Justice Statistics, 2000. Print.

Owen, Barbara. *In the Mix: Struggle and Survival in a Women's Prison*. Albany, NY: State University of New York Press, 1998. Print.

Pemberton, Rita. "Petticoats, Pathogens, Pollutants: Women, Law and Sanitation in Late Nineteenth-Century Trinidad." *Engendering Caribbean History: Cross-Cultural Perspectives*. Ed. Verene Shepherd . Kingston: Ian Randle Publishers, 1995: 491-498. Print.

Poehlmann, Julie. "An Attachment Perspective on Grandparents Raising their Very Young Grandchildren: Implications for Intervention and Research." *Infant Mental Health Journal* 24.3 (2003): 149–73. Print.

Poehlmann, Julie. "Representations of Attachment Relationships in Children of Incarcerated Mothers." *Child Development* 76.3 (2005): 679-96. Web 10 Nov. 2012.

Pollock, Joycelyn. *Women, Prison & Crime*. Belmont Ca: Wadsworth, 2002. Print.

Raeder, Myrna. "Special Issue: Making a Better World for Children of Incarcerated Parents." *Family Court Review* 50.1(2012): 23-35. Web. 10 Jan. 2013.

Reddock, Rhoda. *Women and Family in the Caribbean: Historical and Contemporary Considerations: with Special Reference to Jamaica and Trinidad and Tobago*. Guyana: CARICOM, 1999. Print.

Reed, Diane and Edward Reed. "Children of Incarcerated Parents." *Social Justice* 24.3 (1997): 152-69. Web. 10 Nov. 2012.

Reissman, Catherine. *Narrative Analysis*. Newsbury Park, CA: Sage, 1993. Print.

Reynolds, Tracey. "Caribbean Mothers: Identity and Experience in the UK." *Feminist Review* 89 (2008): 144-47. Web. 20 Apr 2013.

Rich, Andrienne. *Of Woman Born: Motherhood as Experience and Institution*. New York: W.W. Norton, 1986. Print.

Rodriguez, Nancy, Hilary Smith, and Marjorie Zatz. "Youth Enmeshed in a Highly Dysfunctional Family System: Exploring the Relationship among Dysfunctional Families, Parental Incarceration, and Juvenile Court Decision Making." *Criminology* 47.1 (2009): 177-208. Print.

Ruddick, Sara. "Maternal Thinking." *Feminist Studies* 6.2 (1980): 342-67. Print.

Ryan, Selwyn, Indira Rampersad, Lennox Bernard, Patricia Mohammed, and Majorie Thorpe. *No Time to Quit: Engaging Youth at Risk. An Executive Report of the Committee on Young Males and Crime in Trinidad and Tobago*. Multimedia Production Center, Faculty of Humanities and Education, St. Augustine: The University of the West Indies, 2013. Print.

Sandifer, Jacqueline. "Evaluating the Efficacy of a Parenting Program for Incarcerated Mothers." *The Prison Journal* 88.3 (2008): 423-45. Print.

Schram, Pamela. "An Exploratory Study of Stereotypes about Mothers in Prison." *Journal of Criminal Justice* 27(1999): 411-26. Print.

Scobie, Olivia and Amber Gazso. "It was Easier to Say I didn't have Kids: Mothering, Incarceration and Relationships with Social and Criminal Justice Policies." *Incarcerated Mothers: Oppression and Resistance*. Ed. Gordana Eljdupovic and Rebecca Jaremko Bromwich, Ontario: Demeter Press, 2013. 148-159. Print.

Seymour, Cynthia. "Children with Parents in Prison: Child Welfare Policy, Program, and Practice Issues." *Child Welfare* 77.5 (1998): 469-93. *Web*. 26 Sep. 2012.

Shlafer, Rebecca and Julie Poehlmann. "Attachment and Caregiving Relationships in Families affected by Parental Incarceration." *Attachment and Human Development* 12.4 (2010): 395-415. Print.

Silvera, Makeda. *Silenced: Caribbean Domestic Workers Talk With Makeda Silvera.* Toronto: Sister Vision, 1989. Print.

Snowden, Jenny and Elmarie Kotze. "I'm Not a Bad Mother-Stories of Mothering-on-the-Edge." *The Australian and New Zealand Journal of Family Therapy* 33.2 (2012): 142-156. Print.

Solomon, Brenda. "A Social Constructivist Approach to Theorizing Child Welfare: Considering Attachment Theory and Ways to Reconstruct Practice." *Journal of Teaching in Social Work* 22.1 (2002): 131-149. Print.

Stake, Robert. *The Art of Case Study Research.* Thousand Oaks, CA: Sage, 1995. Print.

Stalker, Carol and Rosemary Hazelton. "Attachment Theory." *Theoretical Perspectives for Direct Social Work Practice: A Generalist-Eclectic Approach.* 2nd ed. Ed. Nick Coady and Peter Lehmann. New York: Springer Publishing Company, 2008. 149-78. Print.

Surratt, Hilary. "Parenting Attitudes of Drug-involved Women Inmates." *The Prison Journal* 83.2 (2003): 206-20. Print.

Thompson, Patricia and Nancy Harm. "Parenting from Prison: Helping Children and Mothers." *Issues in Comprehensive Pediatric Nursing* 23 (2000): 61-81. Print.

Wall, Glenda. "Moral Constructions of Motherhood in Breastfeeding Discourse." *Gender & Society 15 (2010):* 592-610. Print.

Walsh, Christine and Meredith Crough. "Mothering through Adversity: Voices of Incarcerated Mothers." *Incarcerated Mothers: Oppression and Resistance.* Ed. Gordana Elijdupovic and Rebecca Jaremko Bronwich. Bradford, ON: Demeter Press, 2013. 160-174. Print.

Williams, Raymond. "On Structure of Feeling." *Emotions: A Cultural Reader.* Ed. Jennifer Harding and Deidre Pribam. New York: Routledge, 2009. 35-49. Print.

Yin, Robert. *Case Study Research: Design and Methods.* 4th ed. Thousand Oaks, Ca: Sage, 2009. Print.

Young, Vernetta and Rebecca Reviere. *Women Behind Bars: Gender and Race in U.S. Prisons.* Boulder, CO: Lynne Rienner Publishers, Inc, 2006. Print.

13.

Mothering in the Context of Domestic Abuse and Encounters with Child Protection Services

From Victimized to "Criminalized" Mothers

CAROLINE MCDONALD-HARKER

When you're abused you're under the microscope. They can see you and they have different views, different opinions, and different ideas of you. Like every society expects every mother to protect their kids, but anybody that's a mom takes care of their kids and protects them. Whereas if you've been abused then it's in question. Like other moms, it's like, okay, she's a mom, she's good. But if you've been abused it's like, okay, is she taking care of the kid? Why is she abused? Is it because she's weak? Is it because she's not smart enough? Is it because she's not educated? Is it because she doesn't have the money? ...So then if she's maybe all of that and she's not strong enough or responsible enough to take care of the kids then she can't protect the kids.... Abused moms are out there, everybody knows their story, everybody knows something. Whereas moms who are not abused, then nobody knows about that. So moms that are abused are viewed differently. Like child protection services, they haven't seen my son, but at the same time it's like, oh, you know she's in an abusive situation we're just going to have a record just in case you go back, and it's like, are you kidding me? So it's not good. But, at the end of the day, people will judge regardless of whether you're bad or you're good. It doesn't matter they always have something to say. (Quotation from Zahra, a mother of a four-month-old son who experienced verbal, physical, and financial abuse from her male partner for over six years)

MARGINALIZED POPULATIONS have always been more likely to be targeted, to come under supervision, and to experience the controls of state and non-state agencies. Today, women who find themselves mothering in the context of domestic abuse relationships face surveillance and governance through their encounters with child protection agencies and the criminal justice state. A conversation about gendered victimization and marginalized social circumstances that feminists fought to spark seems to be reduced to a woman's so-called "lack" of self-sufficiency and criticisms of her inadequate capacity to parent, given the precarious situation in which *she* has placed her child(ren). Locating the problem primarily with the women and their mothering shifts attention away from larger societal and cultural forces, and removes responsibility from the men who inflict violence. Yet, in contemporary neo-liberal times the "abused woman" is responsibilized, pathologized, and her plight decontextualized from systemic factors like gendered violence and economic marginalization that constrain her choices. Consequently, as we will see in this paper, a symbolic and at times concrete slippage occurs from "victimized" to "criminalized" mother. The ways non-criminal justice agencies perceive and treat mothers who grapple with domestic abuse situations are in keeping with a wider culture that demonizes mothers.

My aim is to underline and discuss the case of mothering in the context of domestic abuse as an example of a complicated process that both criminalizes mothering and criminalizes mothers. Mothers' narratives about their encounters with child protection services provide a window into the ways in which a woman's "choice" to mother in the context of abuse begins a process of increased surveillance and possible criminal charges. Based on my research with 29 women victims of domestic abuse, I will demonstrate how the regulatory practices within child protection services exert an influence that mirrors the law's power to criminalize insofar as mothers are re-victimized by systems purporting to help them and their children. While most of the women are not formally charged as offenders, many of them express feeling they were treated like criminals for being suspected of wrong-doing, and were consequently monitored for "potential" criminality.

WOMEN VICTIMS OF DOMESTIC ABUSE: MOTHERS AND CHILD PROTECTION COLLIDING

In recent years, the social problem of domestic abuse has been reconstructed, and this has had significant implications for the way that abused women, particularly those who are mothers, are perceived, depicted, and treated by the numerous state agencies that they encounter, access, and navigate when grappling with their situations of domestic abuse (Bullimer 4).[1] Women in abusive relationships have been stigmatized and vilified for living in circumstances of abuse when such contexts are perceived through the lens of dominant mothering ideologies. In this sense, the "abused mother" is not a "good mother" because she has failed to protect herself from the experience of violence and/or she has not prevented her child(ren) from witnessing and/or experiencing abuse (Radford and Hester). Consequently, many mothers who have experienced domestic abuse have come to the attention of extra-legal state agencies, particularly child protection services, indirectly through their involvement with the legal system as "victims."

Recent research has linked woman abuse and child maltreatment, and there is some evidence demonstrating negative consequences for children exposed to domestic abuse. This discourse has shaped child maltreatment legislation, and the policies and practices of child protection services (Osofsky). Consequently, mothers living with domestic abuse are more likely to come to the attention of child protection services because their ability to shelter, care for, protect, and provide a safe and secure home environment for themselves and their child(ren) is called into question.

Other research suggests that being the victim of domestic abuse aggravates rather than mitigates how women are perceived by officials they encounter in their attempts to ensuring the care, safety, and protection of their child(ren). When women victims of domestic abuse are deemed to be "failing" as mothers, they are held accountable through extensive scrutiny, monitoring, governance, and control—and even the possible removal of their children into state care (Nixon; Wilson).

Despite some of the research that links woman abuse and child maltreatment, Holden et al. conclude after three interconnected quantitative studies that on the vast majority of measures assessing child-rearing behaviours, women in a domestic violence refuge do not differ significantly from women in the comparison group. Holden et al. find that while many of mothers in violent marriages do indeed engage in aggressive behaviour toward their children, mothers in the community also engage in child-directed aggression, indicating that there is relatively little difference between the battered and comparison mothers when it comes to the treatment of their children (304).

Based on erroneous assumptions, child protection services may respond punitively to mothers in abusive situations in several ways, ranging from decisions about which parenting programs mothers must attend and how often, to placement decisions such as moving children into family or foster care, to criminal charges directed at mothers who fail to protect their children, if and when they fail to meet expectations of "good mothering" (O'Reilly, *Rocking the Cradle*, *Maternal Theory*, *Feminist Mothering*; Nixon).[2] Feeling the threat of, or actually being impacted by, policies, practices, and child protection service intervention is akin to that which criminal offenders experience. The parallel is that one's choices, decisions, actions, and everyday life are highly governed and regulated when women are identified as being mothers in an abusive context. In this sense, being a mother in the context of domestic abuse is constructed and "criminalized" as a particular kind of deviant mothering that offends sensibilities about how a "good mother" ought to be, and makes women vulnerable to re-victimization through the legalities, processes, and practices of child protection services.

Despite child protection services' increasing intervention and involvement in the lives of women victims of domestic abuse, there is little to no research that examines the power of child protection services as an agent in the "criminalization" of mothers outside of law –whether that "criminalization" is in the form of legally ascribing a criminal label to mothers for failure to protect, or implicitly labelling mothers as having the potential to be "criminal" for failure to protect, and therefore in need of and subject to constant monitoring, surveillance, and governance.

Some research has begun to examine the regulatory practices of child protection services and the power this extra-legal state agency has to criminalize individuals that come within its reach. Wrennall discusses how child protection services provide a "rhetoric," under the guise of protecting children, to "extend and disguise surveillance" by constructing children from "child in need," to "child at risk," and even to "potentially delinquent" to "delinquent" (304). This research suggests that the process of "criminalization, whether children are constructed as victim or transgressor, pretexts for expanding power" (305). While this research begins to point to the criminalizing power of child protections services, it continues to be child-centred and therefore does not specifically focus on mothers and processes through which they too may be criminalized.

Brown and Bloom (2009) specifically focussed their research on mothers, examining patterns of criminalization and child protection services' control among Hawaiian families in corrections. This research finds that "Native Hawaiian families, as a legacy of colonialism, are especially at risk as targets of this control due to strategies of regulation and control coincident with the rise of neo-liberal politics," whereby "penal and welfare practices attempt to shift the responsibility for structural disadvantage onto individuals in marginalized populations" (151). This research begins to examine the criminalizing power of child protection services to monitor, regulate, and penalize incarcerated mothers, as one group of marginalized mothers. However, this research focusses on mothers who are offenders, and does not examine the unique experiences of mothers who are victims.

Given the limited research, little is known about how mothering is "criminalized," in either sense of the term (legally or implicitly) in the context of abused women's victimization. This limitation raises a number of important questions which this paper will attempt to address. (1) What are the processes through which mothers who are victims become "criminalized" by child protection services, either legally through referral to the criminal justice system for failure to protect, or unofficially through heightened surveillance and control for suspected or potential failure to protect? (2) Are some mothers more likely to come to the attention of, and experience the intervention and involvement of child protection services in their lives than others? (3) How do mothers experience the intervening practices of child protection services in both their and their children's lives? This study provides a conceptual space where the experiences, challenges, struggles, and difficulties of being a mother and mothering in the marginalized circumstances of domestic abuse can be discussed freely by putting mothers' experiential knowledge at the forefront and making their subjectivity visible.

METHODS

This research is based on 29 face-to-face in-depth interviews that I conducted with women who are victims of domestic abuse. These women were recruited from nine different abused women's shelters located in various parts of the city of Calgary, Alberta and outlying areas. The interviews ranged in length from one and a half hours to three and a half hours. All interviews were recorded, with the women's permission, using a digital voice recorder, and were then transcribed verbatim. Using Nvivo 8, I coded and analyzed the data based on patterns that emerged, and built arguments through creating an ongoing exchange between the data and existing critical feminist theory on motherhood and mothering in an effort to reconstruct this existing theory (Burawoy et al. 10)

PARTICIPANTS

The 29 mothers that I interviewed have various abuse experiences, relationship status, ages, educational backgrounds, race/ethnicities, and incomes. Each woman experienced abuse from her current intimate male partner, which ranged from emotional, psychological, financial, verbal, physical, and sexual abuse. The most common forms of abuse were physical, verbal, and psychological abuse, and all of the women but one mentioned experiencing multiple forms of abuse at the same time. The majority of the women (22 out of 29 women) lived with their abusive male partner in either a common-law or a marriage relationship. The women's ages ranged between 24 and 66 years, with the average age being 37 years. Most of the women had a high school education and above, with three women having Bachelor degrees from university, two women having college diplomas, three women having technical certificates, and ten women having high school diplomas. The women's racial/ethnic background varied: 15 were Aboriginal, 9 were Caucasian, and the rest were landed immigrants from various countries. Almost all of the women (27 out of 29) at the time of the interview were unemployed and receiving social assistance. Finally, all of the women had children, and the number of children ranged from one to seven children, with the average being 2.79 children. The women's children ranged between the ages of three months and 40 years.

FINDINGS AND DISCUSSION

Child Protection Services: The Greatest Power to "Criminalize" Mothers Living with Domestic Violence

The findings of this study indicate that in both the legal and extra-legal state agencies that mothers encounter, access, and navigate when grappling with domestic abuse (including the criminal justice system, domestic abuse resources, and social services), there occurs a symbolic and at times concrete slippage from "victimized" to "criminalized" mother. That is, despite being victims, mothers experience "criminalization," either in the form of being legally ascribed a criminal label for failure to protect, or being implicitly labelled as having such potential, and therefore constructed as needing constant monitoring and governance.

However, the mothers in this study overwhelmingly experience the greatest extra-legal "criminalization" through the policies, practices, and actions of child protection services. The majority of the mothers (24 out of 29) in this study, when discussing their experiences with extra-legal formal institutions, stated that they felt the most amount of judgment, criticism, and blame from child protection services. This is well illustrated by one mother's quote provided at the beginning of this paper. In this quote, Zahra states "when you're abused you're under the microscope, they can see you and they have different views, different opinions, and different ideas of you. ... Anybody that's a mom, they take care of their kids and protect them. Whereas if you've been abused then it's in question.... So moms that are abused are viewed differently." Her comment reveals how mothers who are victims of domestic abuse are often automatically brought to the attention of, and scrutinized by child protection services solely for having been victims of domestic abuse. The assumption appears to be that they are not adequate mothers. Therefore, their mothering is called into question and they are subject to observation and monitoring by child protection services.

The fact that the majority of the mothers in this study felt most denigrated by child protection services is not that surprising given recent and increasing neo-liberal influences on the mandate, guidelines, and procedures of child protection services. Increasingly, child protection services have begun to reflect, reinforce, and perpetuate a neo-liberal responsibilization strategy, whereby mothers are viewed and constructed as active subjects who are responsible for both their own and their children's well-being under any and every circumstance. This is evident in recent child welfare legislation and policies in Canada that have been amended to include child exposure to domestic abuse as a form of child maltreatment, which includes children seeing, hearing, or being aware of abuse by one intimate partner against another (Nixon).[3] These reforms have detrimental consequences for mothers who are victims of domestic abuse (Profitt 3). Mothers are held responsible for their children's exposure to domestic abuse, even when this abuse is not perpetrated by them personally as mothers but by their male partners, and even when the abuse perpetrated by their male partners is not directed towards the children, but is solely directed at them. As such, mothers who are victims of domestic abuse are held responsible for protecting their children from witnessing and/or experiencing abuse. These mothers are then constructed as, and treated like "criminals." These mothers are labelled and categorized as deficient mothers who pose a risk and a threat to their children's safety and well-being, and who need to be managed, controlled, and rehabilitated. Rehabilitation involves teaching them how to adequately care for their children, while scrutinizing and monitoring the family to ensure children are safe.

We see this with the policies, practices, and actions of child protection services when dealing with mothers living with abuse which include holding them responsible for: (1) personally protecting themselves and their children from domestic abuse; (2)

removing themselves and their children from the abusive context; and (3) regulating and governing themselves so that they follow the intervention programs laid out for them in order to deal with and overcome the abuse. In this sense, these mothers are required to prove to child protection services that they can effectively care for, provide for, nurture, protect, and ensure the safety and well-being of their children. When they do not conform to these standards, they face the serious threat and consequence of having their children apprehended, or not having their children returned to them (for those who have already had their children apprehended). Below I discuss these three ways that child protection services (CPS) has the power to "criminalize," whether formally or informally, mothers who are victims of domestic abuse.

1) Holding Mothers Personally Responsible for Protecting Themselves and their Children from Domestic Abuse

One of the ways that CPS has the power to criminalize mothers who are victims of domestic abuse is by holding them individually responsible for their own and their children's exposure to abuse. Several mothers discussed how societal beliefs and expectations of the maternal role and instinct of women to care for their children are reflected and reinforced in the practices of CPS. These mothers stated that child protection workers often hold mothers solely accountable for the well-being of their children. Because they are in an abusive relationship, they felt they were accused of failing to protect their children from witnessing and/or experiencing abuse. For example, Coreen stated that when she came in contact with CPS, the main focus was on her deficiencies in caring for and protecting her children, as opposed to her male partner's abusive behaviour. This made Coreen feel like her ability to mother her children was called into question:

> *Child welfare, the way they deal with mothers that are going through this, like they're just, they don't even go on the fathers. The father gets away with everything. The mother, it's just like, you're bad, you're not good, you're doing this, you're doing that wrong. Yeah, cuz I had five kids ... they were forever telling me what I did wrong, but*

they weren't looking at what I did right, and then they weren't looking at his part.

Placing "all the responsibility for protecting children" on "mothers because they are deemed the main caregivers" of children "obscures the gender inequalities that underlie domestic abuse relationships," that is, that males are the perpetrators and females are the victims (Hester). CPS is more preoccupied with what mother victims of domestic abuse could have done and should have done as mothers to care for and protect their children. This results in much emphasis being put on these women's failures as mothers.

Other mothers discussed how CPS's preoccupation with their failure to protect their children overshadowed the fact that domestic abuse is the actual problem which needs to be addressed, and not the abused women's mothering. Carly stated that CPS was concerned with how and why she and her children were in an abusive situation, and how she failed to protect her children by remaining in an abusive relationship. To her mind, they should have been more concerned with putting an end to the domestic abuse. This made Carly feel like her victimization experiences were minimized and disregarded. She felt personally blamed for the abusive context in which she and her children found themselves, as opposed to holding her male partner, who was the actual perpetrator of abuse, responsible for creating this abusive context:

You know what, I think that child welfare looks at an [abused] mother that's let themselves or their children be abused.... I think, like I said, I feel like a lower class citizen. I feel like they're treating me like a lower class citizen. You know, they're looking down at me, where that's bullshit. They should not be looking down at me, you know ... stop the abuse, do something to stop the abuse! ... I'm still here for my babies, you know, I've never once left them alone, I've never once, you know.... My kids are not being harmed, you know, and like I was at Chuck E Cheese's a month and a half, two months ago, and some kid turned around and told my girlfriend to fuck off. This kid's like seven or eight years old, where are the parents to that? You know.... Looking down their nose at me, you know. ...Because you know ... being with ... child welfare and stuff and ... you know, like, bullshit, you know, just back off.

A gender bias permeates child protections services: even though men are the perpetrators of abuse they are not also held responsible for failing to protect their children. Rather, mothers who are the victims of abuse are the ones who are solely held accountable for failing to protect their children (Hester 134). Domestic abuse has been constructed in such a way that, as Strega describes, "a mother being beaten [is not] a problem in its own right," but is only a problem when children are exposed to it (37). As a result, mothers who are victims of domestic abuse are not only blamed for failing to protect their children, but are also blamed for being abused.

Some mothers stated that child protection workers often assume that because they have been in an abusive relationship, they are at risk of becoming abusers themselves. Assuming the potential abusive behaviour of mothers subjects them to unfounded and unwarranted labelling, scrutiny, and monitoring. April said that she felt like CPS was always watching her, just waiting for her to slip-up and make a mistake. Consequently, April felt like she was under constant examination and judgment because of this suspicion that she would "turn into the abuser":

Because we were abused, and most people think that if you are abused or have been abused, you turn into the abuser, you know, and that's what they are just waiting for, you to start abusing them [children].... Once Kylie had a bruise on her arm ... and Easter morning, knock, knock, knock, child welfare was at my door. I said, can I help you, and they're like well, you know the school called and said that your daughter had a bruise on her arm, and I was like yeah, I said look at the size of me. If I was abusing my daughter she'd have more than a bruise this big on her arm, look at the size of her. The lady said, well I have to investigate, and I said, so investigate, ask her if I hit her. I can tell you on seven years on one hand how many times I've hit my daughter ... I was just like, you know, are you going to come back for every bruise that she has, cuz you're gonna be here, five, fifteen times a week, you know (laughs). So I just feel like once child welfare's been called on you once, they're waiting. Well my file's closed. It was never actually really open, it was just, they came, they investigated, they seen no point, and they closed. But, I just feel like they know that. So, they're just waiting for the wrong mess up. I don't know.... Cuz they say if you're abused, then you turn into the abuser right?

Similarly, Zahra echoed the view that CPS suspected that she would begin to abuse her children simply because she was a victim of abuse. This made Zahra feel like she was viewed as a completely different person as a result of being abused, and was therefore unable to properly mother her son, which she claimed was definitely not the case:

So they might think if you've been abused you're gonna abuse your kid, or you know you're gonna let that abuser that abused you, abuse them and, stuff like that.... Just by, you know, being you [an abused mother] ... I still know what I'm supposed to do and I'm still the same person I was and, so it's not like I'm gonna forget all of a sudden to take care of my son, to feed him, to change him, to love him and cuddle him. I still have those qualities in me.

When CPS scrutinizes mothers who are victims of domestic abuse for their potential to harm their children, they are unjustly stigmatizing, but also wrongfully condemning mothers for something they did not do. As such, mothers are blamed for failing to protect their children, blamed for being abused, as well as blamed for potentially becoming "abusers" merely because they are victims of domestic abuse.

CPS "criminalizes" living in the context of abuse by holding mothers individually responsible for their own and their children's exposure to and protection from abuse. Criminalizing the "Abused Mother" in this way is detrimental as it fails to recognize that most mothers love, care for, and meet the needs of their children despite the fact that they victims of domestic abuse.

2) Holding Mothers Responsible for Removing Themselves and Their Children from the Abusive Social Context

CPS also has the power to criminalize mothers who are victims of domestic abuse by holding them responsible for removing both themselves and their children from the abusive social context. Several mothers discussed how CPS expects and requires them to personally leave their abusive male partner, if they have not already done so. Mothers in abusive relationships who do not leave their abusive male partners are viewed as not putting their children first, are accused of failing to protect their children, and are at risk of losing their children. Indeed, child protection workers often threaten the removal of children as a means of forcing women to leave abusive relationships, which many mothers view as unfair treatment. For example, April claimed that mothers who are victims of domestic abuse, by virtue of being abused, are often viewed as incompetent mothers who are unable to care for their children or make good decisions for themselves and their children. April stated that, as a result, there is the assumption that mother victims of domestic abuse will not leave their abusive male partner, even though April herself had left her abusive male partner without being asked or coerced to do so. April felt like she was constantly being not only underestimated, but also watched and criticized:

> *Because mothers are abused, people think they don't have the best problem solving skills. Um, and they're not putting their kids first, you know, because if you put your kids first, then you know, if you are in an abusive situation you'd get your kids and you'd leave, right ... and I did leave.... But I feel like I'm under tooth and nail.*

Even though male partners are the perpetrators of domestic abuse, it is the mother victims who are faced with the expectation and responsibility of leaving their abusive male partner in order to properly care for and protect their children. As such, this reflects a dichotomy of staying versus leaving—good mothers leave and bad mothers stay, choosing not to protect their children (Strega). Mothers face the negative stigma of being in an abusive relationship, and therefore are labelled as irresponsible mothers. In this light, CPS wrongfully allocates the responsibility to put an end to children's exposure to domestic abuse on the mother victims, as opposed to the abusive fathers.

Some women felt that being held responsible for leaving their partners was not fair. They saw it as demeaning and unjust because it failed to recognize their victimization. The requirement that the women leave their abusive male partner and all of their belongings in order to start a new life puts women at risk of additional problems such as further violence, homelessness, and lack of support. Arika stated that it was unjust for her to have to leave home with her children and "leave everything behind," while her abusive male partner remained in the home. Arika expressed her discouragement: "The bad thing about it is, I don't know why women have to get up and go and leave everything behind and they get to stay ... it's just totally not fair. It's happened to me so many times and I'm just so tired of it. I get angry, I get sad."

Similarly, Eden points to victims of abuse being treated like the perpetrators of abuse because they are the ones who are expected to leave the abusive relationship and make many sacrifices to start a new life, whereas the abusive male partners get to carry on with their lives as they were:

> *I just find so many mothers just get the short end of the stick so many times. They have to leave the house, they have to go find a new job, they have to go back for training for school, they have to come up with finances for their whole family while the husband gets the house, gets the vehicle, sits in this house with two, three bedrooms and no one's in them cuz the kids left. Then he gets to party, cheat, do whatever he wants, and all the time why does the mother have to leave with the children when the men, they just like la-di-da in their own life. It's so unfair, I see*

it all the time.... I find it's still like a man's world, the man still gets the house, the everything and, yeah.

Putting the onus on mothers to control, predict, and manage the violence of their abusive male partner places the focus on mothers and what they need to do to stop the violence in their lives, rather than on the male partner's abusive actions and what they personally need to do to stop their abusive behaviour (Edleson). CPS often focuses on the mother, omitting intervention plans for the aggressor that would attempt to ensure the safety of women and children alike without marginalizing women (Edleson).

Several of the mothers also discussed how CPS's practice of requiring them to leave the abusive relationship fails to recognize that for many mothers not leaving is a way to protect their children. That is, they wait until it is a safe time to leave, or wait until they can leave with their children, or wait for when they have found somewhere safe to go, and they can ensure that leaving will not expose them to even more abuse, among other reasons (Magen). Maggie stated that she had tried on numerous occasions to leave her abusive male partner, but he would not allow her to take the children with her. As such, the primary reason she remained with her abusive male partner was because she did not want to leave her children as she feared that her children would be harmed. Nonetheless, Maggie was viewed as failing to protect her children, which was the exact opposite of how she perceived her actions:

It seemed like I wasn't protecting my kids but I wasn't allowed to leave even when I tried. Like when I tried to walk out of the room whenever he was abusing me, he wouldn't let go of me. Or if I wanted to leave, I would have to leave on my own, like without my kids. And that was a lot of the reason why I didn't leave on my own, it's because I didn't want to leave my kids. It seemed like my son, like our oldest together, was always the one that was getting into trouble, and, when he would get mad at him, um, I would feel like I couldn't stick up for him, and when I did he would turn around and get mad at me.... It's not

> *that I didn't want to [leave], it's just that I couldn't, I was unable to, you know.*

CPS's practice of requiring mothers who are victims of domestic abuse to leave the abusive relationship, regardless of the circumstances in which they find themselves, assumes that they have control over whether or not they are abused, are easily and safely able to leave an abusive relationship, and have the ability to successful put an end to the abuse merely by leaving. Leaving is presumed to be a solution to violence that is appropriate and available to all women (Mahoney). However, leaving as a strategy to keep children safe is not always successful since children are often exposed to still more violence from abusers after separation (Magen).

CPS has the power to criminalize mothers who are victims of domestic abuse by holding them responsible for removing themselves and their children from the abusive social context. This ignores the fact that abused women are the victims and not the perpetrators of abuse, and also ignores the complexity of both living in and exiting an abusive relationship. This is detrimental as the difficult conditions under which mothers carry out their mothering in the context of domestic abuse are overlooked, and the numerous ways that mothers actively protect their children despite mothering in the context of domestic abuse are ignored.

3) Requiring Mothers to Regulate and Govern Themselves

Another way that CPS has the power to criminalize mothers who are victims of domestic abuse is by requiring them to regulate and govern themselves so that they follow the intervention programs laid out for them in order to deal with and overcome the abuse. The mothers in this study vocalized the assumption that all mothers are negatively impacted by their experiences of abuse, and a misperception that all mothers are personally responsible for addressing and dealing with these negative consequences that abuse has on both themselves and their children. Several of the women discussed how CPS assumes that because they are a victim of domestic abuse they do not have the skills or the ability to ensure their own and their children's welfare, and therefore they need professional help and assistance. For example, Maggie asserted that child protection workers constantly told her that because she had been abused she needed to go for counselling in order to deal with her experiences. However, Maggie did not feel comfortable being told to share her personal experiences with people (counsellors) that she did not know:

> *Abused women they always look at them like they need counseling and, like that they should go for counseling and, um, just stuff like that.... I think they just look at it as like, just to go for counseling, you know ... they told me that I should go for counseling.... I was told that a lot.... But I won't just talk to anybody and let my feelings out to anyone.*

Likewise, child protection workers also told Arika that because she was a victim of domestic abuse she needed to go for counselling in order to properly care for her children. Arika claimed that her child protection worker assumed that if she did not deal with her experiences of abuse, it may have a negative influence on her children's lives long term. Arika felt that CPS's involvement in her life was unwarranted and very intrusive. She felt like the abuse had not impacted her mothering:

> *They expect us to go for counseling, and if something goes wrong in the child's life ... it's because of abuse, it's always cuz of abuse. And the mothers that aren't abused don't have to go through what abused women go through. ...Everything that goes wrong in the child's life is because your mom was abused, your mom was abused. They blame everything on abused women! ... They say abused women should go for counseling, you feel that ... I just don't think I've ever changed as a mother....I think I've always been the same way ... they say oh you have to go to counseling because I might make wrong decisions with my children. I just think that's very forceful and really an invasion.*

When child protection workers constantly tell mothers that they need to go for counselling, the women get the message they are a deficient mother, incapable of properly mothering their children, and in need of formal help. All of this undermines how they view themselves as mothers. This reinforces the assumption that women are responsible for playing the primary role in sustaining the family life, and that when dysfunction occurs in a family, such as in cases of domestic abuse, it is a result of a mother's failure in some capacity, and consequently she needs help.

Another issue concerns CPS requiring women to follow a specific personal intervention program, such as finding their own housing and employment, taking parenting programs, undergoing alcohol and drug testing, among others. If they do not follow this personal intervention program they risk losing their children, or not having their children returned to them (for those who already lost custody). Oftentimes these mothers claim that the programs they are required to access are not necessary and are not useful to them, but that they only accessed them because they were told to do so by CPS. Emma stated that CPS removed her children from her home and put them into foster care because she was living with her abusive male partner. She explained that CPS assumed she needed help to improve her mothering, so they informed her that if she wanted to regain custody of her children she had to find her own housing, take a parenting program, and undergo drug testing to ensure that she was not using illicit substances. Emma claimed that she met all these requirements set out by her child protection worker, but "learned nothing," because she did not voluntarily choose to take these intervention programs, but rather was forced to.

> *I was involved with child welfare and I don't know, like they expect you just to be a better mom.... But I never learned anything when I went to child welfare, when I was dealing with them, because I was made to do these things, and you don't learn nothing when you're made to do things. Like, if they ask me to go to treatment, I went, and the only reason why I did it was just to get my kids out of the system. I ain't gonna lie ... I got my own place and I took that parenting program.... I did what they expected me to do. And they wanted some of my drug tests to come*

> *back clean. I did all of that.... All the women I'm around basically go through the same thing with child welfare.... But everybody has a different way of parenting.*

Coreen was instructed by CPS to take programs to assist her with improving her mothering abilities because she was told that she wasn't living up to "standards of what a mother should be." Coreen stated that the programs (parenting and anger management) were not useful, as she did not need help in these areas of her life. Coreen felt like she was being treated harshly by CPS:

> *I think they think they [abused mothers] are really weak. Can't stand up for themselves, you know, can't say what they need. But they can, and they do, but nobody listens. A lot of like, people don't listen. Because that's what happened to me with my kids. Like I was asking for this help, yet they were giving me help in a way I didn't need help (laughs), you know like, what meals to feed my kids. Like hello!!!!! ... I don't need you to tell me how to cook for my kids, I know how to cook for them. I know what they like and what they don't like, like, you know. And then they're giving me, like um, telling me to go to programs for like anger management, and I was like, um excuse me I think he [abusive male partner] needs to go not me. So. Yeah. ... Pretty much because I was being told I wasn't living up to standards of what a mother should be (laughs). Like child welfare ... would tell me. So child welfare ... I felt like they really were harsh on me.*

CPS expects mothers to be actively and fervently taking all measures to improve their mothering, implying that the way they currently mother is not "good enough." When dealing with CPS, abused women's mothering is subject to moral regulation. Programs that abused women are required to take, like a parenting program, reinforce intensive mothering. In this view, mothering ought to be child centred, emotionally consuming, and self-sacrificing, a standard unrealistic for any mother to achieve, let alone mothers who are trying to escape and deal with domestic abuse (Hays).

Furthermore, several mothers mentioned that they are constantly being observed, monitored, and scrutinized by CPS to ensure that they are following child protection conditions. When abused women do not meet CPS's conditions, which are often demanding and unrealistic, they are criticized, rebuked, and threatened with the removal of their children from their home. The threat of child apprehension, especially in the name of not living up to the "ideal mother," re-victimizes mothers. Aliya stated that she took her son and left her male partner the first time he was abusive, went to an abused women's shelter, and contacted CPS to help protect both herself and her son. However, once Aliya contacted CPS, all of a sudden her mothering abilities were scrutinized and called into question. She was criticized and reprimanded on several occasions by her child protection worker for not effectively protecting her son. She told a story of almost having her son apprehended after she left him with a babysitter for the day (quoted below). This impacted Aliya so much that she constantly questioned her mothering practices, always feeling "tested" by CPS, fearing she was going to lose her son:

> *I constantly second-guess myself, if I'm doing the right thing or not. Because of his dad I went to child welfare, and I said I have to get away and I need your help to do it. But now child welfare's involved, and so now I'm scared for everything I do.... The worker ... is a male, who I don't even think has children.... There's times where, you know, he said he got a phone call about something and I'm sure it's completely made up because it never even happened. I said I've never even had that conversation with somebody so how could that be, and I said can you give me a name, and he said oh I don't have a name, I don't remember. I feel like, yeah, like I'm being tested right now and it's like don't try to make me feel like a bad mom when I know I'm a good mom. I feel like I'm walking on eggshells right now and that really bothers me. He says well my biggest interest is Dimitri (her son) and keeping Dimitri with you and so forth and so forth. What do you mean keeping my son with me? That should not even be in question. Do you*

know what I mean? I take care of my son.... So I mean what bothers me. There's women out there that sell crack and constantly beat on their children or molest their children. I don't do those things. I bathe him every day, I feed him every day. I went to you to help keep us safe.... You know like I got in trouble from child welfare because I left my son with a 16-year-old friend of mine to babysit for 8 hours. There were some things I had to take care of, and it was 8 hours, but I almost got my son apprehended for that. I didn't think I was doing anything wrong. I didn't know I was doing anything wrong, because I had left him, you know I had milk and uh you know food with him.... And, he had said to me, you really need to watch who you leave your son with and, and so forth. And I thought to myself I didn't even know I was doing anything wrong. And so I feel like there's, more of a spotlight on us. ...That's what bugs me about child welfare. If you think you would be doing me a favor by taking him away when I'm all he's had ... you're gonna make him sick.

Likewise, Brandy had three children, but these children had been apprehended and put into foster care by CPS several years ago. Brandy turned to abusing alcohol and drugs in order to cope with the pain of not having her children. However she had recently decided to change her life around so that she could regain custody of her children. Brandy stated that the first thing she needed help with was overcoming her substance addiction. Her child protection worker did not agree, and wanted her to look for employment. According to Brandy, she was not yet ready to get a job, and instead thought that she needed to first and foremost work on overcoming her addiction, if she were to be successful in the other areas of her life. Brandy constantly felt looked down upon and humiliated when her child protection worker questioned her judgment.

I was telling her [child protection worker] the stuff that I was working on, and I remember, it's always the looks eh. It's always the eyes that I remember. It wasn't a sympathetic look it was more critical ... demeaning.... I was

> *telling her the stuff that I work on and she goes well you have to get a job, you have to do this, you gotta do this, and this, and this, and I'm like, I remember using the word I was overwhelmed ... and, I'm telling them I'm working on me right now. I'm working on you know, recovering from alcoholism, um and being an addict, and that's why I wanna go to treatment, and they want me to work, work, work and everything, and I'm like do you realize how hard it is for me to just get out of bed sometimes, you know? There's people in life that you know don't give a shit basically. You know, I give a shit, otherwise I wouldn't be pushing myself as hard as it is at times to do the simplest thing to get out of bed.*

CPS's constant surveillance of mothers who are victims of domestic abuse to ensure that they are following intervention programs, standards, and rules for their mothering, presupposes that they are lacking the appropriate and necessary skills to carry out their mothering. CPS's practices narrowly interpret the principle of the best interests of children in ways that work against the needs of mothers (Magen et al.). That is, the assumption that helping to improve abused women's mothering skills is the most effective way to ensure the well-being and protection of children ignores the actual needs that mothers may have, given that children's and women's needs do not always coincide (Whitney and Davis 160).

CPS has the power to criminalize mothers who are victims of domestic abuse by holding them personally responsible for accessing resources in order to overcome the consequences of living in an abusive context, regardless of whether or not they have been negatively impacted by their abuse experiences. CPS assumes that all mothers are in need of formal help and assistance, and deem that such interventions are needed or wanted. Criminalizing mothers in this way is detrimental as it suggests that domestic abuse always impacts abused women's mothering, regardless of their experiences or circumstances. This denies the fact that many abused women do not need help with their mothering, but rather merely need safety and protection from their abusive partner—a need that often goes unrecognized and unmet.

CHILD PROTECTION SERVICES' POWER TO CRIMINALIZE AND INTERSECTIONS OF GENDER, CLASS, AND RACE

The findings of this study reveal that mother victims' social location based on gender, social class, and race influences the extent and the degree of their "criminalization," both formally or informally, by CPS. Single, poor, and Aboriginal women in abusive relationships are subject to greater and more widespread processes of "criminalization" when dealing with CPS. In fact, the more visible abused women's marginalizations are, the more severely they as mothers and their mothering are criminalized. A disproportionate number of single, poor, and Aboriginal mothers come to the attention of CPS. These mothers are often brought to the attention of CPS because they do not meet the ideals of motherhood, which are based on married, middle-class, white women's experiences.

Being a single mother affected some women's interactions with CPS. Cultural stereotypes that prevail and portray single mothers as promiscuous, irresponsible, and negligent are reinforced in the practices and actions of CPS (Chant, *Diversity*, *Poorest*). Mothers who are single are viewed as constantly changing intimate male partners, as lacking stability in their lives, and as going against conventional familial configurations. Yet, many mothers choose single motherhood (by leaving their abusive male partner) for their own and their children's safety and protection. Nonetheless, neoliberal ideologies punish these mothers for their status as single mothers, understanding lone parenting as a personal problem she created for herself (Scobie and Gazso). This is echoed in the practices of CPS, as mothers who are single are subject to greater scrutiny and chastisement because they are viewed as providing an insecure and volatile family environment for their children. Maggie discussed how single mothers are viewed as constantly changing intimate partners, as emotionally unstable, and therefore are looked down on as mothers.

> *It seems like, everybody thinks that, like ... always leave their husbands and ... they're looked at as people in pain.... It just seems like that's how we're looked at, because we're single that's why, because we were abused, and it seems*

> *like the ones that aren't abused are in happy relationships and it kind of makes me feel like we're looked at like ... we're not happy.*

Carly also discussed how, despite the fact that she personally contacted CPS for help and was taking all the necessary steps to get help, CPS still treated her as though she was incompetent.

> *On the ninth of January, that was the final day that I left, I phoned child welfare and found out where I could go, what I could do ... and I didn't know what to do.... So since then they [child welfare] are telling me as a single mom that I need to seek this, this, and this, you know.... But they don't even need to tell me I've got to do this, this, and this, because I've been asking to do this, this, and this, and to get the ball rolling.*

These accounts demonstrate how being single exposes women to more inquiry and criticism. The women felt they were seen as "unfit mothers," simply because they were parenting on their own. As such, CPS constructs and treats single mothers battling abuse as in need of more monitoring and assistance, based on cultural stereotypes of single motherhood.

The ways that living in poverty influenced mothers' interactions with CPS also routinely came up in discussions with mothers. Mothering presents a challenge for women living at the economic margins because they often must rely on support from the state. These mothers "encounter the negative economic effects of neoliberal inspired social policies and programs," as they face substantial "social, financial, and logistical barriers" when they leave their abusive male partner, yet this is not taken into consideration, and they are themselves blamed for their poverty (Scobie and Gazso 148). Most mothers, by virtue of leaving their abusive partners, also suffer from poverty, yet neoliberal ideologies again place the responsibility for getting out of poverty on mothers themselves, despite their social circumstances (Scobie and Gazso). The practices of CPS reinforce this when accusing poor and abused women of failure to provide. Mothers living with domestic violence experience poverty for a number of different reasons, including leaving their abusive male partner on whom they relied financially, escaping the abusive environment and leaving behind all of their belongings, or foregoing employment in order to stay home with their children. However, they are held responsible for the impact of this poverty on their children. In these instances, mothers are at risk of having charges laid against them, or having their children apprehended by CPS. Leena discussed how mothers who receive social assistance are viewed as incapable of providing and caring for their children, and therefore are looked down on as mothers.

> *Because I'm low income and then I go to donation centers and food banks and stuff ... people are just looking down at me ... like I'm a bum and just real poor. Yes, I am on welfare, but I'm not so poor that I don't have no place or whatever. Like it pays my rent and my utilities, but not my food, so I get food bank. You know when I was with him I felt like a bad mother because it was hard being in an abusive situation and trying to take care of my kids ... but now I'm a good mother and I'm a survivor, and I'm a strong mother.*

Shyan also discussed how she was looked down upon because she experienced poverty as a result of leaving her abusive male partner. As such she was categorized as a "welfare case" for relying on governmental assistance. She was, to her mind, viewed as being an unfit mother who is at risk of having her children apprehended by CPS, which also came with stigmatization and left her feeling hopeless and discouraged:

> *I think you're pinpointed like aww poor thing and low income, that sorta thing to me.... They think oh no another welfare case. They'll be on welfare, government, taxes, blah blah.... I probably drink, and you know my kid's probably apprehended.... So I'm already categorized.... That's the way I look at it, you know what I mean? ...I'll still be judged like this ... I'm already pinned right there.*

Being poor came with much stigmatization and labelling, which impacted these mothers' interactions with CPS. These mothers already felt "categorized" as unsuitable mothers because they were living and mothering in conditions of poverty, causing them to feel hopeless and discouraged. CPS constructs and treats mothers who are poor as failing to provide for their children, neglecting to recognize the abusive context and other social conditions that led to their poverty in the first place.

Finally, many mothers talked about how their race impacted their interactions with CPS. Specifically, mothers who are Aboriginal asserted that they feel judged more harshly than other mothers, and therefore their mothering is subject to greater surveillance and scrutiny by CPS. Aboriginal mothers' experiences cannot be understood outside colonialism and the historical characterization and treatment of Aboriginal women and children (McCausland and Baldry). Indeed, the greater surveillance and scrutiny of Aboriginal mothers by CPS is a contemporary manifestation of centuries old colonial patriarchal impetus to control Aboriginal women and their children, as well as practices that enable the forcible removal of Aboriginal women's children on the basis of racist assumptions about the children's welfare (McCausland and Baldry 121-122). Even though mothers who are Aboriginal continue to face racist and discriminatory constructions and practices when it comes to their mothering identities and rights, neoliberal ideologies place the responsibility for these negative views and treatments on the Aboriginal mothers' themselves. That is, mothers who are Aboriginal are blamed for failing to assimilate and live up to white mainstream ideals of motherhood. Eden asserted that Aboriginal mothers who are abused have to prove a lot more that they are competent, given racist stereotypes that depict Aboriginals in a negative light:

> *When you're abused a lot of times they expect you work extra hard, to prove to everyone that you're not bad, that you're not doing drugs or alcohol, and that you can have a good life too. ... I know this comes from, I hate to say it, a little bit of racism. Like everyone thinks that Native mothers from the reserve are, all drunks, poor and whatever.*

Mackayla also discussed how discrimination and unfair treatment characterized her experience with CPS. Mackayla believed that her children were not apprehended by CPS because she could not care, provide, or protect them children, but rather because she was Aboriginal, and therefore was lacking the supposed ability to raise her children.

> *There was one incident where the kids were actually taken from my home, and that wasn't because of lack of food, or the house was messy, or the kids were dirty ... it was because we were Native. There's two different ways—there's Native and there's White. I've been in the White people's homes and they're just absolutely disgusting, and Natives' [homes] will be like clean. And I'm thinking, well how come they've got their kids and I have to fight for mine you know like, it's stupid.*

These two mothers' accounts demonstrate that abused women who are victims of domestic abuse and who are also poor and non-white are subject to much stigmatization and labelling, which impacts their interactions with child protections services. They indicate that they are already "categorized" as unsuitable mothers because they are living and mothering in conditions of poverty. This all left them feeling hopeless and discouraged.

CONCLUSION

This chapter examined the power of child protection services to "criminalize" mothers living in the context of abuse. This power is revealed not only by legally ascribing a criminal label to mothers for failure to protect, but also by implicitly labelling them as having the potential to be "criminal" for such failure. Consequently, mothers living in the context of domestic abuse are subjected to constant monitoring and control. The findings of this study (based on in-depth interviews with 29 mothers residing in shelters) reveal that CPS has the power to criminalize mothers living in or fleeing from domestic abuse by holding them responsible for circumstances over which they have little control. This involves: (1) personally protecting themselves and their children from domestic abuse; (2) removing themselves and their children from the abusive context; and (3) regulating and governing themselves so that they follow the intervention programs laid out for them in order to deal with and overcome the abuse. The marginalization of women living with abuse is based on gender, social class, and race relations, which influence the extent and the degree of their criminalization by CPS. Mothers who are abused and single, live in poverty, and/or are Aboriginal found themselves with more intrusive practices of stigmatization and "criminalization" when dealing with CPS.

Interestingly, although CPS's mandate is based on a welfare approach that is centered on protecting children from abuse, their policies, practices, and actions are increasingly reflecting a neo-liberal approach, whereby abused women who are victims are blamed for having mothered in an abusive social context. As such, like other neo-liberal state-sponsored systems of control, child protection services contains, regulates, controls, monitors, and even attempts to "rehabilitate" abused women, particularly those who are the most marginalized. When formal social institutions, such as child protection services, "criminalize" abused women for having mothered in the social context of abuse, they are re-victimizing the victim. Indeed "criminalizing" the "abused mother," whether through formal or informal practices, has detrimental impacts not only on mothers' lives and experiences, but also on the actions and strategies of dealing with the larger social problem of domestic abuse. If we blame the very victims of domestic abuse, how can we ever hope to understand, support, help, and empower them? Our conceptions, understandings, and discussions of mothers living in the context of abuse need to be reframed to account for the challenging conditions under with these women perform their mothering, and must attempt to empathize as opposed to accuse each and every abused mother who is, as one of the mothers I interviewed stated, a "good mother in a bad situation."

ENDNOTES

[1]Prior to the 1970's, domestic abuse was viewed as a private and

individual problem. Women who were emotionally, verbally, physically and sexually abused by their intimate male partners had no means of obtaining help, support, resources, or legal protection or recourse. In the early 1970s, the topic of domestic abuse emerged as an important and central topic of public attention and inquiry. Public awareness of the social problem of domestic abuse as a public matter requiring intervention grew as a result of feminist activists and scholars' efforts in the amorphous "battered women's movement," a movement, in turn, often credited to the general women's movement. The goal of the battered women's movement was to "bring into the public realm an everyday event that had been hidden by the ideology of privacy surrounding the patriarchal family" (Bullimer 3). Feminist activists and scholars' argued that domestic abuse needed to be redefined from a private problem to a public problem, because abusive behaviours perpetrated by male partners towards their female partners provided a powerful illustration of the systematic oppression of women in the context of male domination, was morally intolerable, and required public awareness and action (Dobash and Dobash). By the late 1970s and early 1980s, the tenets of neoliberalism began to influence and shift state policy. This shift significantly affected the already established battered women's movement in its "attempts to reform the criminal justice programs and build up victim services" for abused women (Bullimer 4). The "call for state responsibility for preventing and treating" women who were victims of domestic abuse "was in direct contrast to the new ethics of personal responsibility that was the cornerstone of the neoliberal agenda" (Bullimer 4). As such, in recent years, the state's commitment to social welfare has been quickly eroding, and services for domestic abuse victims have been slowly decreasing. Domestic abuse is increasingly being viewed once again as a private/individual problem.

[2]"Intensive mothering," which emerged in the 1980s, is the current and dominant discourse of mothering. According to O'Reilly, intensive mothering defines and promotes mothering in the following ways: (1) children can only be properly cared for by their biological mothers; (2) mothering must be provided 24/7; (3) mothers must always put their children's needs before their own; (4) mothers must turn to experts for instruction; (5) mothers are

fully satisfied, fulfilled, completed, and composed in motherhood; (6) mothers must lavish excessive amounts of time, energy, and money in the rearing of their children. Intensive mothering requires more than mere physical proximity between mothers and their children. Mothers are "expected to spend 'quality time' with their children" where "they are told to play with their children, read to them, and take classes with them" (O'Reilly *Rocking the Cradle* 40). Women who conform to the intensive mothering discourse are considered "good mothers", while women who do not conform to the intensive mothering discourse are considered "bad mothers."
[3]Six provinces and one territory have amended the statutory definition of child maltreatment to include child exposure to domestic abuse (Nixon et al.).

WORKS CITED

Bullimer, K. *In an Abusive State: How Neoliberalism Appropriated the Feminist Movement Against SexualViolence.* Durham: Duke University Press Books, 2008. Print.

Brown, M. and B. E. Bloom. "Colonialism and Carceral Motherhood: Native Hawaiian Families under Corrections and Child Welfare Control." *Feminist Criminology* 4.2 (2009): 151-169. Print.

Burawoy, M., A. Burton and A. Ferguson et al. *Ethnography Unbound: Power and Resistance in the Modern Metropolis.* Berkeley: University of California Press, 1991. Print.

Chant, S. *Women-Headed Households: Diversity and Dynamics in the Developing World.* Basingstoke: Macmillan Press, 1997. Print.

Chant, S. "Women-Headed Households: Poorest of the Poor?Perspectives from Mexico, Costa Rica and the Philippines." *IDS Bulletin* 28.3 (1997): 26-48. Print.

Dobash, R. E. and R.P. Dobash. *Women, Violence and Social Change.* London: Routledge, 1992. Print.

Edleson, J. L. "Responsible Mothers and Invisible Men: Child Protection in the Case of Adult Domestic Violence." *Journal of Interpersonal Violence* 3.2 (1998): 294-298. Print

Hays, S. *The Cultural Contradictions of Motherhood.* New Haven, CT: Yale University Press, 1996. Print.

Hester, M. *Who Does What to Whom? Gender and Domestic Violence Perpetrators*. Bristol: University of Bristol in association with the Northern Rock Foundation, 2009. Print.

Holden, G. W., J. D. Stein, K. L Ritchie, S. D. Harris, and E. N. Jouriles. "Parenting Behaviors and Beliefs of Battered Women." *Children Exposed to Marital Violence: Theory, Research, and Applied Issues*. Ed. G. W. Holden, R. Geffner, & E. N. Jouriles. Washington, DC: American Psychological Association, 1998. 185-222. Print.

Magen, R.H. "In the Best Interest of Battered Women: Reconceptualizing Allegations of Failure to Protect." *Child Maltreatment* 42.2 (1999): 127-135. Print.

Magen, R. H., K. Conroy, A. Paniera and B. L. Simon. "Identifying Domestic Violence in Child Abuse and Neglect Investigations." *Journal of Interpersonal Violence* 16.6 (2001): 580-601. Print.

Mahoney, M. "Legal Images of Battered Women: Redefining the Issue of Separation." *Michigan Law Review* 90.1 (1991): 1-94. Print.

McCausland, R. and E. Baldry. "Incarcerated Indigenous Australian Mothers: Maintaining Patriarchal Colonization" *Incarcerated Mothers: Oppression and Resistance*. Ed. G. Eljdupovic and R. J. Bromwich. Toronto: Demeter Press, 2013. 121-136. Print.

Nixon, K. L. "Intimate Partner Woman abuse in Alberta's Child Protection Policy and the Impact on Abused Mothers and their Children." *Current* 8.1 (2008): 172-193. Print.

O'Reilly, A. *Rocking the Cradle: Thoughts on Motherhood, Feminism, and the Possibility of Empowered Mothering*. Toronto: Demeter Press, 2006. Print.

O'Reilly, A. *Maternal theory: Essential Readings*. Toronto: Demeter Press, 2007. Print.

O'Reilly, A. *Feminist mothering*. Toronto: Demeter Press, 2008. Print.

Osofsky, J. D. "Prevalence of Children's Exposure to Domestic Violence and Child Maltreatment: Implications for Prevention and Intervention." *Clinical Child and Family Psychology* 6.3 (2003): 161-170. Print.

Profitt, N. J. *In the Best Interests of Women and Children: Exploring the Issue of "Failure to Protect" in the Acadian Peninsula.*

Fredericton, NB: Muriel McQueen Fergusson Centre for Family Violence Research, 2008. Print.

Radford, L. and M. Hester. "Overcoming Mother Blaming? Future Directions for Research on Mothering and Domestic Violence." *Domestic violence in the Lives of Children: The future of Research, Intervention, and Social Policy.* Ed. S.A. Graham-Bermann and J. L. Edleson. Washington: American Psychological Association, 2001. 135-156. Print.

Scobie, O. and A. Gazso. "'It was easier to say I didn't have kids': Mothering, Incarceration, and Relationships with Social and Criminal Justice Policies." *Incarcerated Mothers: Oppression and Resistance.* Ed. G. Eljdupovice and R. J. Browich. Toronto: Demeter Press, 2013. 148-159. Print.

Strega, S. "The Case of the Missing Perpetrator: Improving Child Welfare Interventions When Mothers are Being Beaten." *Envision: The Manitoba Journal of Child Welfare* 4.1 (2005): 23-42. Print.

Whitney, P. and L. Davis. "Child Abuse and Domestic Violence in Massachusetts: Can Practice Be Integrated in a Public Child Welfare Setting?" *Child Maltreatment* 4.2 (1999): 158-166. Print.

Wilson, C. "Domestic Violence in the Child Protection System: Seeing Double." *Journal of Interpersonal Violence* 13.2 (1998): 289-293.

Wrennall, Lynne. Surveillance and Child Protection: De-mystifying the Trojan Horse. *Surveillance and Society,* 7.3/4 (2010): 304-324. Web. 3 November 2014.

14. Marginalization and Hope

Personal Narratives of Previously Incarcerated Mothers

RENITA L. SEABROOK AND HEATHER WYATT-NICHOL

> *Nowhere is the marginalization of women more tragic than in prisons and jails in the United States.* (Pimlott and Sarri 55)

INCARCERATION AMONG WOMEN in America's correctional system has dramatically increased over the past several decades, an increase of approximately ten percent each year (Laux et al.). Not surprisingly, the majority of imprisoned women, approximately 70 percent, are mothers with dependent children (Poehlmann). Women have an average of two to three children living with them prior to incarceration (Laux et al.; Pollock). Within state institutions, 64 percent of incarcerated women had at least one child under the age of eighteen prior to incarceration—the number increases to 84 percent in federal prisons (Laux et al.; Figueira-McDonough and Sarri; Morash and Schram; Moses; Snyder; Tuerk and Loper).

Both incarcerated and previously incarcerated mothers re-entering society experience numerous challenges that contribute to "multiple marginality" (Chesney-Lind). For example, they are disproportionately low income, women of colour, undereducated, unemployed (Bloom, Owen, and Covington), convicted of drug-related crimes (Davis), young mothers with the primary responsibility of the children, and on welfare (Henriques and Manatu-Rupert). Based upon the obstacles these women confront they are more likely to become involved in the criminal activity. The intersection of race, class, and sex marginalize women in the criminal justice system as they are subjected to unique challenges at every phrase, from conviction to incarceration and re-entry into society. Once in the penal system, women are labelled as bad mothers because they do not fit the dominant ideology of motherhood. This coincides with Figueira-McDonough and Sarri's assertion that "female criminals are worse than male criminals and, therefore, worthless magnifies distortions regarding their capacity for motherhood" (19). During the incarceration phase, women often experience institutional barriers to maintaining contact with their children and struggle with the "bad mother discourse," while during the reentry phase, mothers are often punished again through obstacles to successful transition into the community—barred from assistance programs, finding meaningful employment, and in reestablishing the mother-child relationship.

This chapter serves as a voice for sixteen previously incarcerated women enrolled in a re-entry program that we refer to as Positive Pathways[1] in Baltimore City, Maryland. We use critical race theory and feminist standpoint theory to examine the plight of previously incarcerated mothers and the marginalization they have experienced throughout their lives as they re-enter society. The women in our case study maintained hope for a positive future and reunification with their children.

EXPLANATIONS FOR THE MARGINALIZATION OF INCARCERATED AFRICAN AMERICAN MOTHERS

African American women are disproportionately represented in the criminal justice system and generally receive longer sentences than their Caucasian counterparts (Stringer). Although African American women represent 13 percent of the U.S. population, they represent 50 percent of the incarcerated population (Bloom, Owen and Covington). According the U.S. Bureau of Justice Statistics report *Prison Inmates at Midyear 2009*, only one in 1,099 White females are incarcerated, compared to one in 704 Hispanic females and one in 300 Black females (West).

Critical race theory (CRT) provides an important framework to interpret the intersection of race and class in relation to the incarceration of African American women (Alfred and Chlup). One of the principles of CRT is that racism is embedded in American society (Delgado and Stefancic) in ways that are often opaque yet reflect the dissymmetry of power. For example, legislation is often accepted at face value as legitimate because we have governing structures and processes in place. However, an examination of the impact of a particular law might reveal that the legislation passed by a privileged few negatively impacts African Americans—this was the case with race disparities in sentencing for crack cocaine until President Obama advocated and signed the *Fair Sentencing Act* in 2010.

While the policy process may appear "objective" on the surface, it is often a reflection of dominant discourse among those in power in the legislative, executive, and judicial branches of federal and state branches of government (Schur). In other words, deviant behaviour and crime are social constructs. Schur asserts that "...who will be defined as deviant, and for what, is 'a question of political and economic power'" (17). The hidden assumptions and stereotypes bound up in the policy narratives of the privileged perpetuate disparities along the lines of class, race, and sex—intentional or not. The stigma resulting from incarceration marginalizes the opportunities of individuals re-entering society. According to Schur, "numerous studies have demonstrated that when individuals are 'seen' in terms of a deviant status and identity (past or present)—be it 'criminal,' 'homosexual,' 'madman,' 'prostitute,' 'drug addict,' 'cripple,' or 'retardate'—other people's responses to them are heavily influenced by that identification. The tendency is for that to be all the other persons see" (24). For example, the criminalization of drugs places individual users as behaviourally defective and lacking moral standards; as a result the view of our society is that such individuals are undeserving of any reform efforts funded by taxpayers (Alfred and Chlup; Tonry).

The racial disparities in incarceration rates lend evidence to a common narrative in CRT that "racism constantly changes in form but not in effect" (Harris 11). We contend that racism in the US can change form through government policy. Alfred and Chlup assert that the increase in female incarceration is attributed to the following policy shifts: "the war on drugs, mandatory minimum sentences, and get-tough-on crime attitude" (242).

THE WAR ON DRUGS AND MANDATORY MINIMUM SENTENCING

The history of alcohol and drug laws in the U.S. provides a perfect example of crime as a social construct. For example, marijuana use was not illegal until the 1937 *Marihuana Tax Act*, and mandatory minimum sentences for the distribution of marijuana were established through the 1951 *Boggs Act*. Similarly, prior to 1914, heroin and other opiates could be purchased at drugstores throughout the U.S. (Reiman 40). The prohibition of various drugs that were once legal results in higher crime rates as drug users are now labelled and treated as criminals and prohibition shifts distribution to criminal organizations.

Racial disparities are evident in the war on drugs and mandatory minimum sentencing guidelines in the United States although there is no evidence that Blacks are more likely to use or sell drugs than Whites. Reiman conducted a study on mandatory sentencing in federal courts and found that between 1984-1990 whites consistently received sentences less than the minimum. In 1988, African Americans were 30 percent more likely to receive mandatory minimum sentences (Reiman 131). Disparities persist decades later. According to the U.S. Sentencing Commission (2009), among the offenders sentenced for crack cocaine in federal court, 79.8 percent were black and only 10.4 percent were white (Tonry).

Criminal justice practitioners and researchers also acknowledge that drug-related offenses are linked to the increase in women offenders (Bloom). Sudbury indicates that females are arrested and convicted for various types of "*non-violent survival crimes*," such as prostitution and drug possession. The war on drugs prompted legislators to formulate and pass laws and policies which resulted in a large proportion of women being charged and sentenced on drug offenses (Bloom, Owen and Covington; Morash and Schram; Stringer). The rapid rise in women and mothers' imprisonment has resulted from changes in sentencing rather than from changes in crime (Steffensmeier et al.). Furthermore, the changes in sentencing laws for drug-related crimes have resulted in the increased incarceration among African American women (Alfred and Chlup; Stringer). In fact, African American women are cited to have the highest incarceration rate for drug-related activities than any other racial-gender group (Alfred and Chlup; Henriques and Manatu-Rupert; Stringer).

GET TOUGH ON CRIME DISCOURSE

The mainstream discourse on crime in the United States emphasizes personal responsibility and retribution. By personal responsibility, we mean that the "offender" is typically faulted as having a character flaw or moral defect. According to Curtis, "Barry Goldwater equated the crime problem with a failure of our national morality. Republican candidates ever since have promised to get tough on crime, and as the 1988 election revealed, being perceived as soft on crime is extremely damaging to a campaign" (146). It is easier for our society to address crime when we place all responsibility on the individual and fail to address the power asymmetries and structural inequities that often result in criminal activity in the first place. The emphasis on retribution fails to consider the larger social, political, and economic factors that are attributed to criminal activity (Snyder). For example, the majority of incarcerated women were raised by a single parent (Conway and Hutson 205), lack a high school diploma (Feston et al. 7), and earned less than $600 per month at the time of arrest (Alfred and Chlup 243). Many incarcerated women (43-57 percent) report prior physical or sexual abuse (Greenfield and Snell). As a result, incarceration as retribution rather than rehabilitation only perpetuates a cycle of broken families, poverty, and crime. According to David Cole (2013), much of the injury that high incarceration rates inflict on African American communities results from the system's impact on Black mothers who need treatment for substance abuse, shelter from domestic violence, and support for children. This emphasis on retribution has severely limited a holistic approach to reentry initiatives for incarcerated mothers.

THE MOTHER CHILD RELATIONSHIP

Incarcerated and previously incarcerated women have been labelled deviant and in violation the social construction of the ideal mother, which portrays mothers as the primary caregiver, with ample resources, who place the needs of their children above themselves (Walsh and Crough). Incarcerated mothers are antithetical to the cultural concept of an ideal mother, particularly the ideology and practice of "intensive mothering," characterized by Andrea O'Reilly as:

> •children can only be properly cared for by the biological mother;
> •care must be provided 24/7;
> •the mother must always put children's needs before her own;
> •mothers must turn to the experts for instruction;
> the mother is fully satisfied, fulfilled, completed, and composed in motherhood;
> •mothers must lavish excessive amounts of time, energy, and money in the rearing of their children.
>
> The discourse of intensive mothering becomes oppressive not because children have needs, but because we, as a culture, dictated that only the biological mother is capable of fulfilling them. (O'Reilly 43)

Our societal emphasis on retribution reinforces "bad mother" discourse and women are punished twice—for the crime convicted and for not living up to the ideal standards of motherhood. Kennedy asserts: "Criminal justice and child welfare policies that fail to prioritize family preservation and social workers and child-caretakers who fail to aggressively foster the mother child bond may be unconsciously reflecting a stereotyped view of incarcerated mothers that deems them unworthy of the extensive support they need to parent from prison" (88). During the incarceration phase women often experience institutional barriers to maintaining contact with their children and struggle with their identity. Role strain also results as incarcerated women are unable to perform their role as mothers in a traditional sense (Berry and Eigenberg 103) and is magnified as contact is discouraged by policies and personnel within the criminal justice system that label women as bad mothers. "Many social workers may feel it is traumatic for the child to see their mother in prison and resist accommodating such visits" (Pollock 136). These barriers are further illustrated at the federal level via the 1994 *Family Unity Demonstration Project Act* which would have allowed individuals convicted of non-violent offenses to serve time in residential facilities with their children as opposed to traditional prisons. Although Congress authorized annual funding, the funds were never appropriated (Allard).

Children of incarcerated mothers are also more likely to be placed in foster care than children of incarcerated fathers, given that in the majority of cases when men go to prison mothers continue to be primary caregivers. This is significant as the mandatory drug sentencing guidelines (typically over 15 months) conflict with the permanency hearing timeline of 12 months after a child enters foster care. The *Adoption and Safe Families Act* of 1997 (AFSA) terminates parental rights if a child has been in foster care for 15 months. Furthermore, a perverse incentive under AFSA that works against reunification is the monetary bonus distributed to states for each child adopted above a baseline (Allard; Kennedy).

Despite the institutional barriers to maintaining the mother-child relationship, only three states (New York, Minnesota, and California) allow children to live with their mothers in prison until eighteen months of age (Henriques). Mothers who participated in prison nursery programs, as well as women who maintained regular contact with their families had lower recidivism rates than mothers who were denied contact with their infants or children (Snyder).

Re-entry phase

Incarcerated women typically have multiple and complex problems that must be addressed to enable reentry and sustained success in the community after release. Economic difficulties are often an important part of this challenge. During the re-entry phase mothers are often punished twice through barriers to successfully reintegrate into the community. They may be barred from assistance programs and experience difficulties in finding meaningful employment. Under the auspices of reentry programs, policymakers have identified substantial obstacles surrounding offender reentry, such as employment, substance abuse, housing, low levels of educational and vocational skills, mental health, and other health-related problems such as hepatitis B and C, tuberculosis, and HIV/AIDS (Baer et al; Golembeski and Fullilove; Lattimore and Visher; Shivy et al.).

There is often a disconnect between corrections and human service agencies to smooth the transition for individuals reentering society because there is no overarching public agency responsible for coordinating necessary services for successful reentry (Feston et al.). Moreover, because of their lack of preparedness for community reintegration, previously incarcerated individuals are not well connected or familiar with community social services (LaVigne et al; Uggen et al).

PERSONAL NARRATIVES

Feminist standpoint theory, specifically, black feminist standpoint theory, is used as an epistemological framework to present the personal narratives of the women in this study. Feminist standpoint theory recognizes the active role of the researcher and participant in knowledge production from the perspectives of the persons being studied, particularly marginalized populations. Flavin (2001) contends that feminist standpoint theory provides an opportunity to construct knowledge that is less distorted when perspectives of marginalized or oppressed groups are presented. Similarly, Patricia Hill Collins (2007) asserts that "we must distinguish between what has been said about subordinated groups in the dominant discourse, and what groups might say about themselves if given the opportunity" (314). The importance of black women in developing knowledge and understanding of black women's experiences is encapsulated within black feminist standpoint theory.

This project is a case study of an intensive re-entry program in Baltimore City, Maryland. In order to protect the confidentiality of the organization and the ongoing research with individuals in the organization it will be referred to as *Positive Pathways*. According to the Maryland Public Safety and Correctional Services, 1,313 women were released from incarceration in Maryland in 2010 and 65 percent of the women returned to the six poorest neighbourhoods in Baltimore City. *Positive Pathways* is a non-profit organization that has provided re-entry services for over 25 years and is geographically located to meet the needs of the clients it serves. This organization provides civil legal pro-bono services to those in prison and comprehensive case management to those returning to their communities. In response to the need for community-based transition programs for women, *Positive Pathways* entered into a cooperative relationship with the State Department of Corrections to provide comprehensive transitional services in the correctional facility and after care services in the community. Over the past 14 years, *Positive Pathways* has worked directly with the Maryland Parole Commission to provide intensive case management to previously incarcerated women. One of the strengths of this program is that the Assistant Director and one of the Counsellors were formerly incarcerated. Having been in the position of the women they serve provides in-depth understanding and greater empathy. In addition, *Positive Pathways* educates the public and policy makers about the barriers former prisoners experience when reentering society.

Positive Pathways is also unique because it focusses on the whole woman, not just job-placement. The program categorizes reentry into three distinct phases. During the first phase of initial release and treatment the organization works to identify factors that contributed to the client's criminal behaviour in an effort to minimize the risks of recurrence. Upon release from prison, clients are placed in either a 28-day inpatient drug treatment program or a community-based substance abuse program. The second phase of reentry is considered the transition phase. During this time women are placed in transitional housing for a typical period of six months. The location is tailored to the specific needs of each client. The third phase consists of developing a permanence plan which emphasizes independent living, family reunification, and employment.

We conducted in-depth focussed interviews with sixteen previously incarcerated women who are current clients of *Positive Pathways*. Each of these personal and social challenges presents a systemic issue that is not only relevant to the successful reentry for the individual, but to the community at large. The following questions were used to guide the interview process:

- Who assumed responsibility for your child or children while you were incarcerated?
- Did you maintain contact with your child or children while you were incarcerated?
- Were there any services available to you while you were incarcerated?
- What were the top three obstacles in your life when you were released from incarceration?
- What types of support services were available to you upon reentry?
- What has been your relationship with your child or children upon reentry?
- Has participation in the current program eased your transition back into your family and community?
- What additional types of programs would you like to see to assist mothers upon reentry?

DISCUSSION

The combined stories of the women we interviewed represent desperation, hope, and resilience. Some had strong mothers or grandmothers in their lives, while others had no relationship with their mothers. Most have battled with abuse, as well as alcohol and drug addiction. All of the women experienced adversity fairly early in life and continue to face challenges as they transition back into society.

Demographically, the women ranged in age and by race, fifteen of the sixteen women were African American and one was Caucasian. We have provided pseudonyms for each client to protect confidentiality. The women served time for various crimes. We did not question why the women were incarcerated, however, they often volunteered that information. Donna stated that physical, mental, and sexual abuse led her to the corner and that she has used drugs (heroin and cocaine) for 30 years daily. She has been in and out of prison since 1994 and tested positive for HIV in 2004. Donna also reports being raped three times—inside and outside of prison. Mary had also cycled in and out of prison as offenses have snowballed from battery to theft to taking the life of another (we did not seek clarification on whether the charge was for manslaughter or murder). Erica had taken the fall for a crime committed by her friends at the time.

When asked about services available during incarceration, most women cited GED classes and vocational training. Cindy noted that she attended plumbing, wiring, and painting classes, and built benches. Donna stated, "While there were GED classes, there were distractions because not everyone is in class to learn." Mary and Erica shared their broader experiences of incarceration itself. Shortly after citing the availability of job readiness training, Mary stated, "[Prison] really did something to my spirit. Never really saw the mental capacity as some of the people there. Sometimes we go through something and allow it to take us too far. I had two nervous breakdowns."

In addition to sharing her emotional mindset at the initial phase of incarceration, Erica revealed the shortcomings of the job readiness programs:

> *I was so angry—I learned how to turn off at Jessup in order to do time and get out. I worked and went to college classes. I was gullible until prison ... bitter toward the system, corrections officers. There is no real rehabilitation in prison/slave labor. Emphasis for women is also on sewing and kitchen—you can't market those skills. I worked in data entry—top paying at time in prison—about $200 to $300 per month. I sent it home to my brother for my child.*

Relationship with Children

Three women did not have any children. The other women had one to four children at the time of incarceration with ages ranging from one to fourteen years. Most of the women had placed their children in the care of a family member during incarceration. In contrast, Cindy's children (ages one, give, six and eight) were placed in foster care and separated. Donna's children were eight, nine, and fourteen at the time of incarceration. She gave her mother guardianship and was blindsided when her own mother placed her children in foster care: "I felt hurt and betrayed. Now trying to correct the mistake that she made—they are scarred for life. My mom had no reasonable explanation for the action." Her children are grown now, with the oldest 33 years of age.

Twelve of the thirteen women with children reported that they maintained contact during incarceration. The main source of contact was through phone calls and letters, although visitation did occur. For example, Cindy's children were placed in foster care and the various foster parents brought the children to visit. "I constantly had contact with baby son and the five year old. My daughter was brought in to visit every two to four weeks. All kids visited at least once a month." Lena stated that her children were grown at the time of incarceration and that three of her four children were also incarcerated. Erica's daughter was 4 when Erica was incarcerated: "My child would cry when she did visit because she didn't want to leave." In contrast, Donna reported that she had no contact with her children. She would send letters but they did not write back. Similarly, Betty replied that her oldest son's father has both children, but when she tried to send letters to her children the letters were mailed back. The father sent the letters back because he was tired of her being in and out of prison.

Most of the women continue to work on building relationships with their children since reentry. Erica reported that she has a good relationship with both and that her daughter is about to get married. Betty hasn't seen her kids since 2011 however her twelve-year-old is friends with her on Facebook. Donna asserted, "You have to give kids time." Her first daughter was angry at her absence. Donna now has eleven grandchildren (her oldest daughter has five children). Cindy reported that her children "accepted her and pulled her in." Similarly, Lena indicated that the relationship with her daughter is strained because her daughter is still angry over her mother's incarceration—but they do talk. Andrea noted that her drug use limited her vision for love and her thinking. She found her children through an online search on the computer because she never had a relationship with them. Andrea stated that now her children know that she loves them and "to have them in one room is great!"

When asked what additional programs the women would like

to see to assist mothers upon reentry half of the women cited parenting classes. Betty and Mary highlighted the importance of communication and visitation. Mary asserts:

> *More child care and reuniting children with mothers, family gatherings, helping kids understand why mommy was incarcerated. A lot of children don't get chance to spend time with mother while incarcerated. Tell child the truth rather than mommy's off on vacation. Open communications with children is the best thing to have. Break the mold and tell them before they go out in street and hear it.*

Reentry Obstacles and Adjustments

Getting a job was cited as one of the top obstacles the women are experiencing. They indicated that it is tough to find work with a felony record even when federal bonding is available. However, as noted by Jan, the greatest adjustment is often mental rather than physical. She stated:

> *Although physically free, not mentally free. Inside you say you are not institutionalized and refuse to be institutionalized but when you come out you realize that you are. For example, when in prison I had to have a badge on at all times. On the way out the door at the X house I ran halfway upstairs to get my badge when I realized I didn't need one.*

In contrast, two participants are continuing their education. Julie is currently enrolled in Business Administration at Coppin State University and Lena is enrolled in Nursing at Morgan State University. Other participants acquired skills training in trades such as plumbing, welding, and software certification.

Resilience can be defined as "the ability to become strong, healthy, or successful again after something bad happens" (Merriam-Webster, n.p.). Collectively, the stories of the women in this study represent positions of desperation during the phases of conviction and incarceration, as well as hope and resilience upon re-entry into society. All sixteen women reported the importance of *Positive Pathways* in garnering necessary services such as transitional housing, substance abuse treatment, and therapeutic programs to assist in rebuilding themselves and their relationships. The coordination of essential services and the support provided by *Positive Pathways* eased the transition back into the community for all participants. Andrea stated, "R. has really been supportive—she is my counsellor. She is a wonderful person. She comforts me and makes me feel better when I'm going through something." Lena maintained that by *Positive Pathways* not giving up on her she could not give up on herself. She has finally forgiven herself because the program supported her heavily and encouraged her to move on, especially since her relapse—*Positive Pathways* "loves and supports [her]."

CONCLUSION

The extraordinary growth in the number of women behind bars has made the United States the nation with the highest proportion of female prisoners (Pimlott and Sarri) and warrants further attention in criminal justice scholarship. This manuscript presents research that is part of a continuous project to understand the plight of previously incarcerated mothers and the marginalization they face from mainstream discourse on crime and motherhood. Although this case study represents the experiences of sixteen previously incarcerated mothers, standpoint theory empowers the women to share their lives, struggles, and support systems (or lack of) during incarceration and reentry. Incorporating the standpoint feminist epistemological framework, the authors were able to draw from the women in the case study very rich, detailed, descriptive, and diverse narratives that would otherwise not have been available through alternative means of data collection.

It is our hope that the existing data coupled with the lived experiences of the women enrolled in *Positive Pathways* enhances policy changes necessary for successful reentry programs of previously incarcerated mothers. Furthermore, we aim to enhance social activism by expanding the dialogue on laws within our society that marginalize African American mothers in the first place.

ENDNOTES

[1]The name of the organization and participants have been changed to protect confidentiality.

WORK CITED

Alfred, Mary V. and Dominique T. Chlup. "Neoliberalism, Illiteracy, and Poverty: Framing the Rise in Black Women's Incarceration." *The Western Journal of Black Studies* 33.4 (2009): 240-249. Print.

Allard, Patricia E. "Research to Action: Informing Policy Makers About the Needs of Mothers and Children at Risk of Separation." *Women & Criminal Justice* 17.2 (2006): 27-42. Print.

Baer, Demelza, Avinash Bhati, Lisa Brooks, Jennifer Castro, Nancy La Vigne, Kamala Mallik- Kane, Rebecca Naser, Jenny Osborne, Caterina Roman, John Roman, Shelli Rossman; Amy Solomon, Christy Visher, and Laura Winterfield. *Understanding the Challenges of Prisoners Reentry: Research Findings from the Urban Institute's Prisoner Reentry Portfolio.* Washington, DC: The Urban Institute, Justice Policy Center, 2006. Print.

Berry, Phyllis E. and Helen M. Eigenberg. "Role Strain and Incarcerated Mothers: Understanding the Process of Mothering." *Women & Criminal Justice* 15.1 (2003): 101-119. Print.

Bloom, Barbara. "Gender-responsive Programming for Women Offenders: Guiding Principles and Practices." *Forum on Corrections Research* 11.3 (2000): 22-27. Print.

Bloom, Barbara, Barbara Owen and Stephanie Covington. *Gender-Responsive Strategies: Research, Practice and Guiding Principles for Women Offenders.* Washington, DC: U.S. Department of Justice, National Institute of Corrections, May 2005. Print.

Chesney-Lind, Meda. "Patriarchy, Crime, and Justice: Feminist Criminology in an Era of Backlash." *Feminist Criminology* 1 (2006): 6-26. Print.

Cole, David. "Getting Past Tough on Crime." NYR Blog. n.d. Web. 5 October 2013

Conway, Tiffany and Rutledge Hutson. "Parental Incarceration: How to Avoid a Death Sentence for Families." *Journal of Poverty Law and Policy* 41 (2007): 212-221. Print.

Curtis, Craig. "An Exploration of Critical Criminology and the Policy Making Process." *Race, Gender & Class* 10 (2003): 144-162. Print.

Davis, Angela. "Masked Racism: Reflections on the Prison Industrial Complex." *ColorLines: News for Action* Sept. 1998. Web. 10 January 2013.

Delgado, Richard and Jean Stefanic. "Critical Race Theory and Criminal Justice." *Humanity & Society* 31 (2007): 133-145. Print.

Festen, Marcia, Michelle Waul, Amy Solomon, and Jeremy Travis. *From Prison to Home: The Effect of Incarceration on Children, Families, and Communities: Conference Report*. The Urban Institute, Justice Policy Center. 2002. Web. 10 January, 2013.

Figueira-McDonough, Josefina and Rosemary C. Sarri. "Increasing Inequality: The Ascendency of Neoconservatism and Institutional Exclusion of Poor Women." *Women at the Margins: Neglect, Punishment, and Resistance*. Ed. Josefina Figueira-McDonough and Rosemary C. Sarri, New York: The Haworth Press, 2002. 5-30. Print.

Flavin, Jeanne. "Feminism for the Mainstream Criminologist: An Invitation." *Journal of Criminal Justice* 29 (2001): 271-285. Print.

Golembeski, Cynthia and Robert Fullilove. "Criminal (in) Justice in the City and Its Associated Health Consequences." *American Journal of Public Health* 98.1 (2008): 185-190. Print.

Greenfeld, Lawrence and Tracy L. Snell. *Women Offenders*. Washington, DC: Bureau of Justice Statistics, 1999. Print.

Harris, Angela, P. "Critical Race Theory. The Selected Works of Angela P. Harris." Selected Works. n.d. Web. 10 January 2013.

Henriques, Zelma W. "Imprisoned Mothers and Their Children: Separation-Reunion Syndrome Dual Impact." *Women & Criminal Justice* 8.1 (1996): 77-95. Print.

Henriques, Zelma W. and Rupert N. Manatu. "Living on the Outside: African American Women Before, During, and After Imprisonment." *The Prison Journal* 81.1 (2001): 6-19. Print.

Hill Collins, Patricia. "Shifting the Center: Race, Class, and Feminist Theorizing About Motherhood." *Maternal Theory: Essential Readings*. Ed. Andrea O'Reilly, Toronto: Demeter Press, 2007. 311-330. Print.

Kennedy, Deseriee A. "Love Behind Bars: The Darker Side of

Incarcerating Mothers." *Incarcerated Mothers: Oppression and Resistance.* Ed. Gordana Eljdupovic and Rebecca Jaremko Bromwich.Toronto: Demeter Press, 2013. 82-92. Print.

La Vigne, Nancy G., Cynthia A. Mamalian, Jeremy Travis, and Christy Visher. *A Portrait of Prisoner Reentry in Illinois.* Washington, DC: Urban Institute, 2003. Print.

Lattimore, Pamela K. and Christy A. Visher. "The Multi-site Evaluation of SVORI: Summary and Synthesis." SVORI Evaluation, 2009. Web. 15 January 2013.

Laux, John, M., Stephanie Calmes, Jeffry L. Moe, Paula J. Dupuy, Jane A. Cox, Lois A. Ventura, Celia Williamson, Barbaranne J. Benjamin, and Eric Lambert. "The Career Counseling Needs of Mothers in the Criminal Justice System." *Journal of Offender Rehabilitation* 50.3 (2011): 159-173. Print.

Merriam-Webster Dictionary. n.d. Web. 10 November 2014.

Morash, Merry and Pamela J. Schram. *The Prison Experience: Special Issues of Women in Prison.* Prospect Heights, IL: Waveland Press, Inc., 2002. Print.

Moses, Marilyn C. "Children of the Incarcerated Must Be Studied, and Responded to, Comprehensively." *Corrections Today* June (2010): 58-60. Print.

O'Reilly, Andrea. *Rocking the Cradle: Thoughts on Motherhood, Feminism and the Possibility of Empowered Mothering*, Toronto: Demeter Press, 2006. Print.

Pimlott, Sheryl and Rosemary C. Sarri. "The Forgotten Group: Women in Prisons." *Women at the Margins: Neglect, Punishment, and Resistance.* Ed. Josefina Figueira-McDonough and Rosemary C. Sarri, New York: The Haworth Press, 2002. 55-85. Print.

Poehlmann, Julie. "New Study Shows Children of Incarcerated Mothers Experience Multiple Challenges." *Family Matters: A Family Impact Seminar Newsletter for Wisconsin Policymakers* 3.2 (2003). Web. 15 September 2013.

Pollock, Joyce M. "Parenting Programs in Women's Prisons." *Women & Criminal Justice* 14.1 (2002):131-154. Print.

Reiman, J. *The Rich Get Richer and the Poor Get Prison.* 6th ed. Boston: Allyn and Bacon, 2001. Print.

Schur, Edwin M. *Labeling Women Deviant: Gender, Stigma, and Social Control.* New York: McGraw-Hill, 1984. Print.

Shivy, Victoria A., J. Juana Wu, Anya E. Moon, Shay C. Mann, Jo G. Holland and Christine Eacho. "Ex-offenders Reentering the Workforce." *Journal of Counseling Psychology* 54.4 (2007): 466-473. Print.

Snyder, Zoann K. "Keeping Families Together: The Importance of Maintaining Mother-child Contact for Incarcerated Women." *Women & Criminal Justice* 19 (2009): 37-59. Print.

Steffensmeier, Darrell, Hua Zhong, Jeff Ackerman, Jennifer Schwartz, and Suzanne Agha. "Gender Gap Trends for Violent Crimes, 1980 to 2003: a UCR-NCVS Comparison." *Feminist Criminology* 1.1 (2006): 72-98. Print.

Stringer, Ebonie Cunningham. "'Keeping the Faith': How Incarcerated African American Mothers Use Religion and Spirituality to Cope with Imprisonment." *Journal of African American Studies* 13 (2009): 325-347. Print.

Sudbury, Julia. *Global Lockdown: Race, Gender, and the Prison-industrial Complex*. New York: Routledge, 2005. Print.

Tonry, Michael. *Punishing Race: A Continuing American Dilemma*. Oxford: Oxford University Press, 2011. Print.

Tuerk, Elena H. and Ann B. Loper. "Contact Between Incarcerated Mothers and Their Children: Assessing Parenting Stress." *Journal of Offender Rehabilitation* 43.1 (2006): 23-43. Print.

Uggen, Christopher, Sara Wakefield, Jeremy Travis, and Christy Visher. "Weaving Young Ex- Offenders Back into the Fabric of Society." *Network on Transitions to Adulthood*. Feb. 2005. Web. 15 January 2013.

Walsh, Christine A. and Meredith Crough. "Mothering Through Adversity." *Incarcerated Mothers: Oppression and Resistance*. Ed. Gordana Eljdupovic and Rebecca Jaremko Bromwich. Toronto: Demeter Press, 2013. 160-172. Print.

West, Heather. *Prison Inmates at Midyear 2009: Statistical Tables*. Washington, DC: Bureau of Justice Statistics, 2010. Print.

15. "Something Worth Living For"

Young Criminalized Mothering

BRYAN HOGEVEEN AND JOANNE MINAKER

POPULAR TWENTY-FIRST CENTURY FILMS and television programs like *Knocked-up*, *Juno*, *Sixteen and Pregnant* and *Teen Mom* glorify teenage pregnancy. Nevertheless, dominant discourse on unplanned, unwed, single, early motherhood in North America continues to castigate young mothers (Wilson and Huntington; Duncan). The trope of the bad, uncaring mother casts a dark shadow upon mothers who deviate from limited socio-cultural scripts of good mothering and appropriate femininity. Such logics obfuscate the precarious social realities and the constrained choices these women are forced to make in the context of chronic instability and social exclusion.

When it comes to Canada's child welfare and youth justice systems, marginalized young mothers are among the most disadvantaged. We understand marginalized young mothers to be between 15 and 24 years old and who, on the basis of age, gender, class, race, ethnicity, economic status, criminal history, and child welfare involvement live on the periphery of society. These women are marginalized and stigmatized for opposing the traditional and widely accepted family structure (Ruddick; McMahon; Hanna; McDermott and Graham; Warnes and Daiches). The stereotypical image of these mothers as "difficult to manage" and "at risk" obscures the richness of their lives, their potential, and their accomplishments.

This chapter emerges out of Joanne Minaker's larger systematic investigation of young marginalized mothering in Edmonton, Alberta, Canada, where advocates claim that the number of cases involving pregnant and parenting females in youth justice and family court is becoming increasingly acute. These mothers share a background of chronic instability and a history of encounters with the child welfare and youth justice systems (Minaker). In this way, we understand their experiences as occupying the criminalized social position of young, marginalized mothers. With its intimate ties to world energy markets, Edmonton is tightly integrated into the processes of globalization. While the conclusions we reach emerge from this distinct local context, they hold relevance well beyond the geographical borders of Western Canada. Drawing on ethnographic interviews with young women who experienced early motherhood at the social margins, we highlight how young criminalized mothers navigate the demands of early motherhood while attempting to break the fetters of street life, addictions, and abuse. But, perhaps more importantly, we demonstrate how, far from burdening their young lives, pregnancy and motherhood propelled many young women to make meaningful and positive changes. Our analysis in this chapter is framed primarily around the life history of one street-involved young mother we named Jenna[1] who was 23 at the time of our interview.

We begin by describing Jenna's material conditions of life before she became pregnant. Next, we demonstrate how motherhood, far from being associated with exclusively dreadful outcomes (Reid and Meadows-Oliver), motivated Jenna to take necessary steps to leave the street lifestyle and a criminal way of life (Warnes and Daiches). We conclude with a call for additional care services that are supportive, flexible, and open to the unique needs of these women.

Jenna's young life was characterized by heavy involvement in crime, periods of homelessness, and chronic instability. Her official record shows convictions for drug offences, break and enter, assault, and mischief. Throughout her journey to become a mother "on her own terms," she grappled with addictions and dysfunctional relationships, especially with her mother, boyfriend, and almost-absent father. Like all the women in this study, Jenna spent a considerable amount of her life involved in the criminal justice and child welfare systems. The responsibility of taking care of her unborn son, in Jenna's case, was a call to transform her life (Duncan, Edwards and Alexander; Rolfe).

In addition to the inherent challenges of motherhood, Jenna and the mothers in this study faced stigma, poverty, lack of support, physical and emotional abuse, fear of criminal victimization, inadequate living situations, disquiet about child apprehension, and tenuous ties with their own family members. They share much in common with other similarly situated, marginalized young moms who, as a group, are entangled in the child welfare system, have a history of chronic instability and abuse, have low educational attainment, live in poverty, and are located at the political margins of society (Rolfe; Hobcraft and Kiernan; Smid, Bourgois and Auerswald). Unlike mothers who have familial stability and income security, young marginalized and criminalized mothers routinely confront these issues and anxieties as part of their daily round of life. We argue that caring for themselves and their child(ren) becomes possible to the extent that support networks and resources are available and appropriate.

These mothers have unique needs that remain unmet. Existing social services typically do not attend to their ways of being. Strategies tailored to their needs as marginalized pregnant and parenting teens—strategies that are open and hospitable—might better assist them in their transition to new motherhood. By demanding that these mothers act according to foreign logics, many contemporary projects close down upon these young marginalized mothers. As we will see, Jenna attempted to secure assistance from a government-sponsored program but quickly left the group after she felt rejected and excluded from meaningful involvement in their activities. In place of strategies that promote alien norms of being that close down upon the other, we promote the creation of projects that are attentive to the unique needs of young criminalized mothers and extend an unconditional welcome. Social service agencies and wider publics must embrace a new ethic of being that opens out to these women and supports their mothering practices.

JENNA'S STORY: UNDERSTANDING FROM EXPERIENCES OF MARGINALIZED, YOUNG MOMS

Jenna longed to feel worthy of love, belonging, and part of a community of care (Klodawsky, Aubry and Farrell). Humans share a common need to feel loved and to experience being the recipient and giver of care. Ideally, within our earliest social relationships we begin to learn that we are worth being cared for and capable of caring. Like many other young women who take to the streets, Jenna did not feel this worthiness (Novac, Eberle and Brown).

Jenna was conceived in a refugee camp in her mother's home nation, an Eastern European country, shortly before her mother left for Canada. Once in Canada, Jenna's mom was beset by struggle and strife. She found it difficult to gain meaningful employment, make friends, and otherwise adjust to the alien culture. When Jenna was two years old her mother sent for her father and agreed to sponsor him. Things at home took a turn for the worse shortly after his arrival. He brought increased hardship to the family and burden on her mother. Jenna's father also found life in Canada alienating. To cope, Jenna explains, "...he started getting into the drugs, of course, and into that bad lifestyle and it was scary. I just remember being a kid and he was always banging on the door and trying to get in all strung out and I just would hide in the closet. I was scared of my own dad."

From the outset, Jenna's life was uncertain and precarious. Her father's extreme drug use only added to the chaos. Jenna recalls one occasion when she was six and travelled with her mother to visit family in Europe. They returned home to nothing.

> *My cat was dead in my toilet and there was needles everywhere. I was starting grade 1 right after we came back. I was traumatized. Like, all the—my mom had a bunch of Disney movies for me—I just loved those. All my Doctor Seuss books, gone! Like everything I owned. Me, as a six-year-old, was gone.*

With the stresses of immigration, and her husband's abuse and almost constant drug use, Jenna's mother turned to alcohol to cope. It was around this time that Jenna recalls that her mother began physically abusing her. She recounts:

> *Beating the shit outta me because I looked like my dad.... On the streets, people would ask, "Why don't you go*

home?" I was just like, "Do you wanna go to my house?" I'm like, "Do you wanna get beat up with a fricking blind turner?" She would take it off [of the window blinds] and whip the shit outta me with it.

Despite the violence she endured Jenna craved her mother's acceptance and support. On the numerous occasions when Jenna appeared in court to answer a charge or for a child welfare hearing she would peer around the room in anxious anticipation that her mother would be there for support. The only time her mother made an appearance, "she was on such a long binge that she had a seizure in court. And the social worker was like, 'She's faking it' and I was like, 'No she's fucking not faking it.' I was fourteen at this time. I was like, 'She's not faking it. She's having a seizure because of the alcohol.'"

Pain enveloped Jenna. Her suffering from the abuse, from being abandoned, and from street life was overwhelming. Marginalized groups, other researchers confirm, may medicate the pain associated with past trauma with drugs and alcohol (Comack). For Jenna, drugs provided an escape and dulled the torment that was welling up inside her. She says, "Well, the drugs make me feel good. This is better than this bullshit getting abused."

Drug addiction is not entirely an individualized problem (Aboriginal Healing Foundation; Waldram, Herring and Young; Denov and Campbell). Rather, it is indicative of a number of social, economic, psychological, or emotional factors at work in all of the young women's lives. Chloe, for her part, "started getting into shit" when she was thirteen. From that point until she had her third child, she was in and out of youth detention: "It was a continuous thing. Monthly ... I had a few car chases, a few stolen vehicles, and some thefts more or less there was two assault I think...." When we met Chloe she had recently regained custody of her daughter and was fighting to have her three sons returned to her care. She has been in and out of jail her entire life and, in the interest of her children, is now making a concerted effort to, in her words, "go straight." But her efforts have been constantly confounded by her addictions. When Children's Services removed her children from her custody for apparent neglect, Chloe turned to "the bottle" to numb her pain in this "dark time." While she loved her children immensely, she recalls that in the two-week period they were gone she "...drank all thirteen days because I didn't know what to do. Yeah. It was like every time I went to drink, I was like 'I want to drink and party and have fun' to get this shit off my mind."

Like Chloe, Jamie used drugs to silence the "demons that haunted her waking and sleeping hours." She says of the taunting voices in her head that said she was nothing:

> *I would fall asleep to that voice. I would wake up to that voice. I would live out my day wanting to get drunk to make that voice be quiet for a little while. It was just like everyday kinda happening. As soon as I would start to sober up I'd hear that voice again. It just got to be so repetitive.*

Free from alcohol's intoxicating effects, the demons would return to remind her of her inadequacies and past mistakes. "That was the first month that I was sober in like years and years," she explains. "It was awful because all the memories started coming back, all these shame feelings, all that kinda stuff just started coming back."

In combination with their numbing effects, drugs serve a utilitarian purpose for the young mothers we met. Like the women Moe and Ferraro interviewed, Jenna turned to drug dealing as an alternative to starvation and homelessness. She explains: "I was living a hard lifestyle and you gotta do what you gotta do to survive." In the absence of more legitimate and societally approved means of fulfilling their shelter, clothing, and sustenance needs, these girls turned to the only means at their disposal. When Chloe was fifteen, she was pregnant and homeless. She describes this time in the following manner:

> *I woke up one morning after whatever and my mom comes upstairs and says "Pack up your room. Take everything outside and put it on the lawn." I said "Okay." So I packed up everything and put it on the lawn. She said, "Well you know I don't know where I am going. Take care of yourself. I know you can take care of yourself so I'll see you*

whenever I see you." I was like, "Okay."

With no more-appealing options, drug dealing satisfied Chloe's need for economic and physical survival.

Unlike many of the young mothers in this study, Jenna maintained a relationship (albeit stormy) with her son's father. Together, they traversed the many challenges of the street. Peter is several years older. In fact, when they first met he told her she was too young to seriously consider her being his girlfriend. Jenna was persistent and after a couple years they were together. She maintains that when living on the street it is essential that someone is there to support and protect you (Gaetz; Smith): "We were on the street, homeless, selling drugs and smoking drugs and doing what we had to do to survive. And we did it together. We didn't let anything tear us apart. 'Cause like when you're out there, you need somebody."

Under the influence of drugs and alcohol, Jenna and Peter were physically and verbally abusive toward each other. Jenna says, "We would fight all the time." When they weren't involved in this or that battle Peter was in and out of jail. Chloe's relationship with her partner was similarly vicious. She says, "I physically abused him and he would physically abuse me, verbally, emotionally, mentally, everything. We were just horrible to each other."

Despite the abuse, both women were convinced that they were vulnerable to other, more insidious, ill-treatment and victimization that typically accrues from a street-involved life. These marginalized women (consistent with patriarchal values) viewed their significant others as "protecting them" from future trauma (even if these men were at times the cause of them). In part, this helps to explain why, after she found out she was pregnant, Jenna insisted that she and Peter marry.

That she desired a more "normal" life where a father and husband played a significant role also helps us to understand her firm stance on the matter. As we will see in the next section and throughout the remainder of this chapter, learning she was pregnant was transformative. She shared this:

> *I want to give my son everything I didn't have. I want to be the parent I never had. I want him to have a proper*

> *family with a mom and dad and that's why I made my husband marry me. I was like, "You knocked me up! You have to marry me!" I was eight months pregnant when we got married. I was like, "I need my son to have a proper family."*

Jenna was familiar with struggle, with abuse, with the child welfare system, and with the pain associated with a street-involved life. She wanted to shield her son from the agony and despair that characterized her own childhood. To this end, Jenna desired solace and peace that she understood would be hard won.

MATERNAL RESPONSIBILITY

Becoming a mother often radically alters a woman's sense of self and her life trajectory (Rolfe). It frames many women's lives. Once they learned of their pregnancy, many of the young women in our study felt an overwhelming responsibility to this other growing inside of them. The recognition of their responsibility to care for another who is separate from, though intimately connected to them was often the initial impetus for changing a destructive life course.

Echoing other research on street-involved young mothers, the moms in this study marked finding out they were pregnant as a key turning point in their lives (King et al. 139). Chloe, for example, expressed it this way: "Fuck, I want to be a good parent!" Sienna, engaging in what King et al. calls "identity work," stated that "my children are my first purpose in life" (147). For Jenna, a positive pregnancy test became a spark that flamed into her awareness that *something* was different. Her responsibility for and to her unborn child burned a hole through her being in the world. Awash with the knowledge that she was now accountable to someone else, Jenna took the first steps toward leaving the street and all the negativity that came with it (i.e. crime, instability, addictions, and precariousness). As we shall see, getting out of harm's way and rebuilding a new—what she refers to as "straight"—life was fraught with difficult choices and onerous challenges.

It is not pregnancy *per se* that is transformative, but the promise of a favourable future to come that expecting a child represents for young mothers living in marginalized circumstances. Consider that this was not the first instance that Jenna took a positive pregnancy test. Minaker and Hogeveen (204) maintain that "a salient feature of life on the streets for young women is pregnancy and motherhood." Smid, Bourgois and Auerswald report that, "homeless young women are almost five times more likely to become pregnant and far more likely to experience multiple pregnancies than housed women" (140). The first time Jenna learned she was pregnant she was strung out on drugs, with no job prospects, heavily involved in the drug trade, and without any positive and supportive role models. Estranged from her own kin and scared and confused, she turned to her street family for advice. They were unanimous in their counsel to terminate the pregnancy. Telling this story Jenna reveals her impressionability and hedonism. Fresh on the street and only fifteen she made the decision to abort the pregnancy. Looking back on this point in her life she is full of regret and yearns for a chance to do it over. However, and as she maintains, her life at that point was chaotic. Daily, she was consuming and dealing vast quantities of drugs without remorse or reflection on a possible future beyond what dealing and the street offered. Reflections on the meaning another life held for her would have to wait.

It is no mean feat that she survived the intervening years, let alone emerged from this deep well. Two years later, again at a tremendously young chronological age, she found out she was expecting. This time her response was considerably different. She recalls thinking: "Well now I have a baby coming!" and "All of a sudden I was like 'Oh! I have to protect this baby and keep it healthy!' I had to quit. I was just like 'I'm not doing this anymore.'"

The call of her unborn child interpolated her as a mother and began to erode her street-toughened being (Levinas). She now had another direction brought on by the sense of responsibility she felt welling up from within. *This* call she had to answer. This time it demanded that she acknowledge the presence of another to whom she needed to respond. This other would not go away, but instead interrogated her very being.

Answering this call demanded that Jenna undergo a process of transformation. For the first time in her life, she looked closely at her current conditions and saw them as not inevitable, but open to change. he became, at first in the imaginary, aware of her future to come. She desired a different, healthier, happier one. Jenna vowed to make this vision materialize. Here we are not insisting that her responsibility was the fulfillment of a duty or a way of acting that can be externally validated through law or an ethical code. Jenna's responsibility to the call of the other goes beyond this calculation. Responsibility for the other did not come at the end of a social worker's lecture—or, for that matter from a pamphlet disseminated by this organization or that one. It was not from a police officer's admonitions. Rather, as her growing baby encroached upon her former independent and hedonistic self, she was an active agent taking on a new responsibility. The invocations of her rapidly growing child triggered an answering response. This call held enormous power to divert Jenna's attention from life on the street and toward altering her present reality.

It is disingenuous to think that once Jenna heard and responded to the call life would be uncomplicated and unchallenging. Hearing and responding favourably to the call of this unborn other was just the beginning, however. In addition to attending to the voice of her unborn child, there were other calls lingering that came up against her burgeoning identity as a mother. Interjected alongside positive and forward-looking sentiments were trappings of her past that attempted to nudge her away from a newly imagined way of being. In variance to her sentimentality toward her growing baby, residues of the past—childhood memories and an unstable present—contoured her path into motherhood.

Growing up, marginalized young mothers frequently bounce between parental homes, the street, jail, and foster placements. Jenna was no different. Toxic effects of alcohol and drugs infringed upon her mother's ability to care and provide for her. When she was seven, the child welfare system intervened and placed Jenna with a family. In placement after placement she felt as if she didn't belong. As bad as life was with her Mom, Jenna was traumatized by being taken away and forced to live in a strange home. Here began her struggle with belonging and acceptance. She felt awkward, alone, and, as she says, "scared shitless. I didn't know what to do. It was like a foster mom with a bunch of kids in a house. I was like, 'Can I do this? Am allowed to go to the fridge?' I didn't feel like I was allowed to do anything. Like I just felt like ok, this is awkward."

More placements would follow, but none would provide the kind of open, caring, and hospitable environment she craved. She felt unwelcomed. Shielding her own children from this unfortunate reality was a prime motivator for Jenna. She laments her time in foster care and never wants her children to experience the uncertainty, trepidation, and tremendous discomfort of being uprooted. She explains the chaos this way:

> *I do not want children's services in my life because I grew up in the system and I know it's hard. Because sometimes your social workers can only do so much and it's not up to them, right? They tried and you're like, "This sucks." So I don't want my son to be in that situation ever. To be taken from me, be scared and traumatized like I was when I got taken away.*

Being in foster care and living on the street throughout her formative years left Jenna without positive role models upon which to base her parenting or through which to envision her identity as a mother.

At the same time, Jenna realizes that the example her mother (and foster parents) set was less than ideal. In many ways, she employs her mother as a foil for her own mothering. She says: "I don't want to be like that. I don't want to be like my mom. I don't wanna be an alcoholic. I don't wanna live unhealthy. I want to provide for my child the best way I can." She vows that her son is going to receive the opposite kind of parenting. To vow that one will parent in opposition to their experiences Byng-Hall (1993) terms "corrective transgenerational script" (cited in Warnes and Daiches 119). Obscured in this vision, however, is that her mother may have been raising her the best way she could, given the resources available. Jenna's mother was extremely poor, a recent immigrant, a single parent, lacking extended family support, and struggling with addictions. Jenna's mother certainly made decisions about how she would parent Jenna, though she did not freely choose the mothering context in which those choices were determined (Minaker).

Nevertheless, living in extreme poverty with an alcoholic and abusive mother meant that Jenna lacked many of the advantages many middle class children take for granted. Her mother did not own a car—let alone two. There were no summer trips to the lake or Disneyland. Her daily needs (i.e., food, love, sleep, and exercise) often went unmet. Even the rather simple experience of playing at a park was rare. Instead of running around, climbing, and jumping she was frequently confined to the balcony of the pocket-sized apartment she co-habited with her mom. Jenna explains:

> *My backyard was a balcony. I never got to go to the park. My mom always kept me on the balcony. That was my playground and it sucked 'cause I never played with anybody. Or, she would ground me to my room for the whole summer. She did! And my window faced the playground. And I was in my room for six months. I want him [her son] to have the opposite.*

Jenna's resolve to be a positive and nurturing force in her son's life, her responsibility for his welfare and growth, was conditioned not only by his beckoning call, but also through the deleterious experiences of her home life. She mined the negativity for inspiration and a contrarian template. Jenna remarked, "I want to give [him] everything I didn't have. I want to be the parent I never had. I want him to have a proper family with a mom and dad."

Bringing a child into the world is one thing, caring for and supporting this being is another thing all together. Jenna was and is acutely aware of this reality. The following quotation evidences her colliding emotions.

> *I'm gonna be a mom. I'm gonna have a baby. Like what's gonna go on? What's gonna happen? How are we going to afford to feed this baby and give it clothes? And that's all that I could think about. I was like, "Oh my gosh! This is a lot of responsibility."*

Responsibility for a baby can be overwhelming. Even families with significant cultural capital and financial and familial resources struggle to navigate their parenting obligations and are at pains to build caring relations with their child(ren). Imagine the uphill battle fought by marginalized street youth whose parenting role models have oscillated between changing state actors and being non-existent.

Surely, solid and renewable resources are in place to assist marginalized young moms as they traverse the early days of motherhood? Tragically, as state policies aimed at reducing government spending roll along, far too few programs are in place to responsively attend to the unique needs of these young moms as they attempt to transition from the street into more pro-social roles. Leaving the street on its own accord is arduous. Without supportive social systems, which include respectful practices and strategies that are tailored to the unique needs of the growing population of pregnant street-involved and criminalized young moms, transitioning toward pro-social, healthier and/or empowered modes of mothering are elusive.

"I COULDN'T KEEP IT TOGETHER ANYMORE:" MOTHERING AND SOCIAL SERVICES

Since the 1990s, the provincial government in Alberta has whittled away at social services. Evisceration of social supports shows no sign of stopping. Consider that former Premier Ralph Klein's first order of business when taking the helm in 1995 was to slash social service spending nearly to the bone (Taft). Even in more robust economic years the cuts continue. Nevertheless, while social service funding continues to corrode under the weight of contemporary economic logics that privilege the proverbial bottom line over providing meaningful help, governments sweep social problems and structural inequality under the rug. Social problems such as poverty, homelessness, drug addiction, and (but not limited to) gender violence remain, yet governmental assistance is harder to access and less likely to provide the resources required to move beyond survival and basic subsistence. Insufficient education, job insecurity, extreme poverty, and a lack of childcare options are realities for young women mothering at society's margins. Western governments seem more content to allow these underlying problems to fester while investing more heavily in the most coercive end of the criminal justice and social welfare state. Tragically, the institutions most readily available and primed to intervene in the lives of young people like Jenna are those that extend punishment, control, and regulation. Policing and corrections remain one of Canada's most extensively funded resources dedicated to governing the street-involved and marginalized other (Hogeveen and Freistadt).

When Jenna found out she was pregnant, she and her boyfriend were financially propped up through drug dealing, fencing stolen property, and her boyfriend's medical disability support. Shortly after learning she was pregnant and about the same time she made the decision to leave the streets, the couple's only legitimate source of income (medical disability support) ran its course. Under these conditions, and with no promising future and a government unwilling to provide meaningful subsistence assistance, the couple might have descending into the drug-induced stupor of street life or upped the ante with more lucrative forms of criminal activity.

On the street Jenna could easily parlay her previous experience into fast cash. She reports that whatever she needed could readily be acquired through theft or selling drugs. Laptops, for example, could easily be attained. She says, "I would just sell a ten piece of crack and get a laptop." Committed to providing a functional home environment and a healthy pregnancy for her son, Jenna doggedly sought out means to this end. Nevertheless, being steadfast in her responsibility meant the road ahead would be wrought with trials and tribulation. During our interview she expressed tremendous gratitude and sense of accomplishment after she purchased her first "straight" computer. When her hard-earned bicycle was stolen, she felt a sense of remorse because she then understood what it felt like to have someone take something for which she worked hard.

Marginalized young mothers who lack education and the cultural capital to otherwise find success in the capitalist job market have immense difficulty securing meaningful employment and tracking down affordable childcare. Jenna's education in hustling on the street worked against her finding the kind of legitimate employment that would provide her means to guarantee all of her needs would be met. Nevertheless, the call of the other, the responsibility she felt for her child, trumped the beckoning of the street and the promise of (relatively) easy money. She often weighed the allure of quick cash against the example she would be setting for her son, and continued to take small, incremental steps toward self-sufficiency.

Struggles associated with transitioning from the street and attempting to escape the grip of street entrenchment cannot be overstated. It is like a ghost that haunts the being of those who once dwelled there. At times, the gnawing of their past was far too strong for some of the women in this study who ended up getting pulled back into its depths time and again. When Jenna's mother, for example, was trying to get "straight" she "ended up hanging out with people who are negative from her past, family members, all that crap and they ended up pulling her back into that lifestyle after whatever odd years, right?" Jenna explained. It is not only the absence of more legitimate and societally sanctioned means of securing resources to meet their needs that draws these women back to their former selves, but the real connections to friends and their street family that keeps them entrenched in the street lifestyle. Exiting the street means turning your back on a former way of being and, along with it, acquaintances, friends, and a street family.

Cutting ties with a former self and turning a deaf ear to the street's haunting call is arduous. Deep-seated behavioural patterns are difficult habits to break. But, for Jenna and others, a louder call brought her back and silenced the demons in her head. Chloe echoes this sentiment when she says:

> *After I had my daughter, things were totally different. I could never get sucked back in ever. I decided that was when I wanted to change. It is easy to get sucked back in* but when you're more aware of what is your life now and you have that kind of where you want to go, who you want to be type thing. (emphasis added)

The connection to her baby and the responsibility Chloe (like Jenna) felt towards him was definitive. Jenna explains that whenever she slipped up or felt the street's pull she would sense her son's need for her. On these occasions she would hear an inner voice calling to her: "I'm like 'I have a baby,' you know? I'm like, 'I have a child. I have a child.'"

Jenna was resolute and took a series of low paying jobs to help make ends meet. For example, she accepted a job at local dollar store. She reminds us that she "barely made any money" at this job. Such retail establishments are infamous for their low pay, lack of status, and dearth of benefits. Working at Dollarama was anything but an economical and emotional boon. Although it was certainly "a job," the long hours and low pay left her unfulfilled. She still required further financial assistance. However, that help was not entirely forthcoming, sufficient, or readily available. After paying rent, electricity, and other bills, there was little left over from her meager income to buy groceries. To make up for the shortfall, Jenna says, "We relied on the Food Bank a lot back then right? They give you a week's worth of food and it's supposed to last a month because everything is perishable that they give you. You have to eat it, right?"

In the absence of supportive and ameliorative services Jamie, another young mom in this study, ran back to the cold comfort that alcohol and the street provided. Jamie, for her part, was attempting to make her way in life and get back on her feet, but with only limited financial and emotional support. She reports feeling

> *...trapped. I totally felt stuck. It's like you're on survival mode and in your mind you're like, "Okay! I get $1000—600 goes to rent" and this is going on your head all the time—and like, "I get to buy like $200 worth of groceries, what do the babies need? The babies need diapers. Okay. I better go buy a $100 worth of diapers."*

Services to help her mediate the stress and make sense of her unique situation of a former street-entrenched youth were too few and far between.

Erosion of social services under the weight of global economic restructuring has meant that far too often help is unavailable for those who could benefit the most. Or, innovative programs that could meaningfully attend to the needs of the structurally disadvantaged never leave the drawing table—or when they do get up and running are far too underfunded to handle the demand placed upon them (Hogeveen and Woolford). For Jenna, many of the supports she sought to help make up for the shortfall in her resources were inadequate and ill-equipped to meet her unique needs. Other organizations instituted barriers to her involvement. To make-up for the lack of governmental funding, some programmes have instituted user fees. Even a nominal fee is a barrier to accessing services for young marginalized mothers for whom every nickel is accounted. She recounts: "I looked into some [parenting programs] and they were like, 'You have to pay to go' and it's like, 'Seriously?' It's a parenting group and you have to pay to go?"

Parenting groups are intended to foster the creation of support networks. Many women find meaningful connections through these ad hoc groups. Mothering groups can be very important for maternal identity and helpful to new mothers, that is, when participants feel welcomed and accepted. Despite assurances on their website that "each centre provides services based on the needs of families in its particular community" (Alberta Human Services), Jenna felt ostracized and alienated when she attended the Government of Alberta sponsored *Parent Link*. She says:

> *I felt awkward because I was the high risk youth, coming out of the high risk lifestyle with all these normal people.... I was like "I can't sit here and talk about my life because they are probably gonna judge me." Or, like, "We don't want you here" and that's how I felt.... I just wanted some interaction. I didn't get it. I was like, "I'm just gonna stay home then."*

Existing social services rarely, if ever, attend to the singular needs of pregnant street-entrenched girls (McDermott and Graham).

Police officers typically receive no training for dealing with the unique circumstances of pregnant street-involved youth. In the absence of meaningful and relevant services some misguided, but paternalistic officers have remanded these girls to custody when they encountered them on the street. Sienna, for example, reports how an arresting police officer sent her to jail because he didn't feel there were any other options available. She spent several months in detention awaiting trial. While she maintains that being in jail helped her to "straighten out," it is a sad statement on our society that the only place that Sienna found meaningful was in Canada's most austere and intrusive institution. At least in prison, she says, "I learned a lot about pregnancy and stuff." Well-meaning though the staff at the detention centre might have been, they neglected some important prenatal preparation. Sienna complained that, "Nobody told me about labour. Nobody told me that hurts or what to do! Nobody told me any of that. I was like, 'Why didn't they fucking tell me!?!' I was really angry about that!" What more can we expect from an institution designed and intended to deliver pain?

Marginalized and pregnant youth need positive role models and guidance if they are to make it through what is often a terrifying and uncertain time. Punishment and pain only adds to the stress these women experience. A more hospitable approach guides rather than forces or coerces young women through their transition. In the absence of widely available programs that are tailored to the complex needs of at-risk or high risk mothers, young moms attempting to leave a street-entrenched lifestyle might find themselves entangled within state agencies. If state agents are able to reach them, these young women have an opening for a supportive space. More often the case, however, a lack of trust and conditional care might push these women back to the streets. As we have seen already, Jenna and others were forced to negotiate the familiar call of the street. While Jenna was able to find meaningful connections that helped her quiet this shaming voice. Jamie, for example, fought these forces as long as her personal resources allowed. In the end, however, the influence of the street unfortunately won out. She recalls that battling the call of the street and drugs

> *...was harsh. I did it for two years by myself. But by the end of that two years I was totally burnt out and I had just given up hope. The easiest thing to do was to just start drinking and then it didn't seem so bad. And then after the drinking then everything else just follows it. Everything*

else just started slowly falling apart. I couldn't keep it together anymore.

All that Jamie wanted, desired, or says she needed was for "one person just to walk by me and just say: 'Do you want help? Do you want to do something different?' I would have jumped right then and there and just said, 'Just show me where to go! Show me how!'" Regrettably, social services and helping organizations that might have mitigated the call of the street did not materialize and she spent the next several years in and out of prison.

Social services that are attendant to the singular needs of street-involved moms and those that are open and hospitable to their unique ethos are tragically underfunded and too few in number. Today, funding cuts and precarious funding relations with governments are the reality for far too many social service providers. In this ethos programmes are forced to become increasingly creative as they attempt to navigate the contemporary funding climate (Hogeveen and Woolford). Many smaller agencies have been forced out of the industry and have left gaping holes. Larger organizations with more diversified funding structures are left to pick up the slack. As a result, significant areas of need remain unaddressed and people (read: the marginalized and oppressed) are left to suffer.

CREATIVE CARE: THE CASE OF WOVEN JOURNEY

In Edmonton, as elsewhere, strategies that provide an open and hospitable welcome to young street-involved pregnant moms have been lacking (Hanna). The needs these women present are unlike any other group and demand a hospitable approach that confronts their addictions, alienation, and (but not limited to) abuse history while at the same time providing the necessary skills to navigate their contemporary ethos.

Edmonton's Woven Journey (WJ) works with women like Jenna, Chloe, Sienna, and Jamie. WJ is a support group operating out of iHuman Youth Society in Edmonton for young mothers (14 to 24 years) who are currently or have in the past lived high risk lifestyles. It provides both practical parenting advice as well as a safe, caring space where young women can support each other and learn from one another without judgment. In addition to offering seminars on infant feeding and parenting strategies, the group addresses issues of emotional support and holistic wellness for the young mothers (e.g., yoga). A social worker named Brianna Olson facilitates the group, which emerged organically from a previously street-involved mom searching for a program that met her needs. The group meets twice a week and participants receive a $50 monthly gift card that they can spend on groceries or other household items. WJ is a site where young mothers like Jenna can find mentorship and share their experiences of mothering with others in similar situations.

An overriding responsibility for the other growing inside of her spurred Jenna to move away from her destructive street-involved lifestyle and toward a healthier and happier existence. A hospitable and helping social service that was attuned to her unique needs and situation buoyed her efforts:

> *And ever since [I started attending* WJ*], I've been like straight. Religiously coming every week. I have to. It's good for me. It's good for [my son] to get out and meet new kids and talk to the other moms who I've built lots, big relationships with. We all help each other out. Kids are from different ages so the older, the kids with mom's the older kids can tell us what the younger kids, what to do, what to prepare for, the terrible two's and like, you know? Sicknesses they get, how they grow at that age, when they're not even that age yet.... Now I just, if I didn't come here, I'd go crazy! Like that one week, one night a week is my salvation. It's good.*

All of this begs questions about how we ought to relate to marginalized young mothers who dot the contemporary urban landscape.

Programmes that shunt these women into an existing paradigm close down upon their unique needs and shape negotiations according to a logic foreign to their being (e.g., standards that exist outside of their experience). Feeling judged, shamed and blamed, many young girls, like Jenna, resent this lack of attention to their individual needs. The demand to act according to strange norms is alienating to young women who are attempting to escape their former selves. When too many agencies close down upon the otherness of these women, the women fall through the proverbial cracks and are unable to obtain the assistance that they require. Jenna was unable to find the unique help and assistance she required when she sought out *Parent Link*. While the officials were courteous and cordial, she felt alienated and out of place. Had WJ not come into her life to singularly support her, she, like Jamie, might have ended back on the streets, in jail, and again consuming drugs.

Creative care strategies like WJ that attend to the unique needs and realities of street-involved or formerly street involved mothers are needed now more than ever. Supportive and caring spaces hold much promise in assisting young mothers traverse the rocky shore of motherhood as they attempt to transform their lives. In the absence of such strategies, another generation of children will be growing up on the streets, in state care, addicted, "at-risk," and otherwise in trouble. We must insist that strategies that open out to marginalized mothers as they arrive without asking them to conduct themselves according to foreign ways of being hold more potential for transformative change. Such an effort demands pushing against contemporary wisdom that manifest tension between programme officials and those they purport to help. These are important concerns. The very existence of numbers of pregnant, young, marginalized moms that are living precarious lives should be cause for disquiet. It concerns the vital questions of life and death. Open and welcoming spaces attendant to the uncommon needs of this population are imperative for the survival, welfare, and dignity of these women and their children.

CONCLUSION

> *Something that was worth living for. You know? Cause we were just doing our thing. We had nothing really special going on.* (Jenna)

Against a life history of struggle, poverty, drugs, abuse, neglect, and the street, Jenna finally found "something that was worth living for." As we have seen, the hardship she and other similarly situated mothers face cannot be attributed to individual pathology, but emerged in a particular socio-cultural landscape and unequal structural context that limits some mothers' access to resources. Young mothers like Jenna struggle to access appropriate social support networks. At the same time, when we listen to these women's stories we hear tales of hope, resilience, and the courage to care (Kennedy).

Jenna spent a considerable period of her formative years struggling with addictions and the harsh realities of street life. However, learning that she was pregnant and now ready to assume the overwhelming responsibilities associated with bringing another human being into the world inclined her toward making significant and pro-social changes in her life. The call of her unborn child and the responsibility this invoked sparked a determination that otherwise might have been muted. A positive pregnancy test interpolated her as a mother. The call of her unborn child and her status as soon to be mother impelled her to radically alter her life-course.

Learning that she was pregnant propelled Jenna to find ways to escape the street and all that it meant in her life—addictions, abuse, crime, etc. Nevertheless, she did not emerge from this quagmire alone. Meaningful connections to the women in WJ formatively aided and guided her efforts. In the absence of caring role models things might not have turned out as positively. In contemporary times there is a pressing need to reflect on how we ought to *be* with and support young marginalized mothers in ways that do no reproduce their inequality (i.e. through further criminalization). Creative strategies (like Woven Journey) that are open, supportive, and respectful hold potential to offer young mothers meaningful alternatives to contemporary social service logics. They require sustainable funding, multiplication, and extension. There is much work to be done to identify the gaps in services for marginalized young mothers and their children. Young women like Jenna deserve care that enables them not just to survive but to flourish. We echo Smid, Bourgois and Auerswald's conclusion:

> More research is needed to understand better the window of opportunity that pregnancy presents, regardless of

> outcome, to engage youth at a time when they strongly desire support. Such research could inform the design of wrap-around services that meet their needs at this vulnerable time. (154)

Respecting the voices of young mothers and honouring their stories is an essential step in better understanding their needs and the supports they require to empower them to care for themselves and their child(ren).

With the support of the WJ group Jenna and her son are doing exceptionally well. In the fall of 2014, she began a vocational programme at a local college. She is rightfully proud of the work that has gone into getting herself to this point in her life. We end with Jenna's own words about her transformation:

> *We went from street to straight. Now we're going up. Going up the stairs, slowly, slowly. It's a lot of hard work. So much hard work.... I want a house so bad! That's my biggest goal right now! In the next five to seven years, a house! That's mine ... that I can call my own.*

Like other similarly situated mothers, Jenna, over everything else, aspires to belong, to be what she calls a normal and contributing citizen: "I just want to be normal, a contributing citizen that supports the community."

ENDNOTES

[1]To protect the anonymity of our research subjects all names have been changed.

WORKS CITED

Aboriginal Healing Foundation. *Aboriginal Domestic Violence in Canada*. Ottawa: Anishinabe Press, 2003. Print.

Alberta Human Services. *ParentLink*. Web. 6 August 2014.

Byng-Hall, J. *Rewriting Family Scripts. Improvisation and Systems of Change*. New York: Guildford, 1997. Print.

Comack, E. *Women in Trouble*. Halifax: Fernwood Publishing, 1996. Print.

Denov, Myriam and Katheryn Campbell. "Casualties of Aboriginal Displacement in Canada: Children at Risk among the Innu." *Refuge* 20.2 (2002). Print.

Duncan, Susan, R. Edwards and C. Alexander, ed. *Teenage Parenthood: What's the Problem?* London: Tufnell Press, 2010. Print.

Duncan, Susan. "What's the Problem with Teenage Parents? And, What's the Problem with Policy?" *Critical Social Policy* 27 (2007): 307-334. Print.

Ferraro, Kathleen J., and Angela M. Moe. "Mothering, Crime and Incarceration." *The Journal of Contemporary Ethnography* 32.1 (2003): 9-40. Print.

Gaetz, Stephen. "Safe Streets for Whom? Homeless Youth, Social Exclusion, and Criminal Victimization." *Canadian Journal of Criminology and Criminal Justice*, 46.4 (2004): 423-456. Web. 6 May 2014.

Hanna B. "Negotiating Motherhood: The Struggles of Teenage Mothers." *Journal of Advanced Nursing* 34.4 (2001): 456–464. Print.

Hobcraft, J. and K. Kiernan. "Childhood Poverty, Early Motherhood and Adult Social Exclusion." *British Journal of Sociology* 52.3 (2001): 495-517. Print.

Hogeveen, Bryan and Andrew Woolford. "Cold Cities: Care and Control in Inner City Edmonton and Winnipeg." *Radical Criminology* (forthcoming 2015).

Hogeveen, Bryan and Josh Freistadt. "Hospitality and the Homeless: Jacques Derrida in the Neoliberal City." *Journal of Philosophical and Theoretical Criminology* 5.1 (2013): 39-63. Print.

Levinas, Emmanuel. *Ethics and Infinity*. Trans. Phillippe Nemo. Pittsburgh, PA: Duquesne University Press, 1985. Print.

Kennedy, A.C. "Resilience Among Urban Adolescent Mothers Living with Violence: Listening to Their Stories." *Violence against Women* 11 (2005). 140-1514. Print.

King, Katharine, Lori E. Ross, Tara L. Bruno, Patricia G. Erickson. "Identity Work among Street-Involved Young Mothers." *Journal of Youth Studies* 12.2 (2009): 139-149. Print.

Klodawsky, Fran, Tim Aubry and Susan Farrell. "Care and the Lives of Homeless Youth in Neoliberal Times in Canada." *Gender, Place and Culture*. 13.4 (2006): 419-436. Print.

McDermott, E., and H. Graham. "Resilient Young Mothering: Social Inequalities, Late Modernity, and the 'Problem' of 'Teenage' Motherhood." *Journal of Youth Studies* 8 (2005): 59-79. Print.

McMahon, Martha. *Engendering Motherhood: Identity and Self-Transformation in Women's Lives*. New York: Guilford Press, 1995. Print.

Minaker, Joanne. "The Space Between: Mothering in the Context of Contradiction." *Moms Gone Mad Oppression and Resistance*. Ed. Gina Wong. Toronto: Demeter Press, 2012. 124-140. Print

Minaker, Joanne and Bryan Hogeveen. *Youth, Crime, and Society: Issues of Power and Justice*. Toronto: Pearson, 2009. Print.

Moe, Angela and Angela Ferraro. "Criminalized Mothers: The Value and Devaluation of Parenthood from Behind Bars." *Women and Therapy* 29.3/4 (2006): 135-164. Print.

Novac, S. L., M. Eberle and J. Brown. *On Her Own: Young Women and Homelessness in Canada*. Ottawa: Canadian Housing and Renewal Association, Status of Women Canada, 2002. Print.

Reid, V. and M. Oliver Meadows. "Postpartum Depression in Adolescent Mothers: An Integrative Review of the Literature." *Journal of Pediatric Heath Care* 21.2 (2007): 289-298. Print.

Rolfe, Alison. "'You've Got to Grow When You've Got a Kid': Marginalized Young Women's Accounts of Motherhood." *Journal of Community and Applied Social Psychology*. 18 (2008): 299-314. Print.

Ruddick, S. "Procreative Choice for Adolescent Women." *The Politics of Pregnancy: Adolescent Sexuality and Public Policy.* Ed. A. Lawson and D. Ann. Arbour: Yale University Press, 1993. 126-143. Print.

Smid, Marcela, Philippe Bourois and Colette Auerswald. "The Challenge of Pregnancy among Homeless Youth: Reclaiming Lost Opportunity." *Journal of Health Care for the Poor and Underserved* 21.2 (2011): 140-156. Print.

Smith, Hilary. "Searching for Kinship: The Creation of Street Families among Homeless Youth." *American Behavioral Scientist* 51.6 (2008): 756-771. Print.

Taft, Kevin. *Shredding the Public Interest: Ralph Klein and 25 Years of One Party Government*. Edmonton: University of Alberta Press, 1997. Print.

Waldram, James, Ann D. Herring, and Kue T. Young. *Aboriginal Health in Canada: Historical, Cultural, and Epidemiological Perspectives*. Toronto: University of Toronto Press, 1995. Print.

Warnes, Jan and Anna Daiches. "'Rebuilding After the Storm': Stories of Young Motherhood." *Narrative Inquiry* 21.1 (2011): 109-129. Print.

Whitbeck, L. and D. Hoyt. *Nowhere to Grow: Homeless and Runaway Adolescents and their Families*. New York: Aldine de Gruyter, 1999. Print.

Wilson, Helen and Annette Huntington. "Deviant (M)others: The Construction of Teenage Motherhood in Contemporary Discourse." *Journal of Social Policy* 35.1 (2006) 59-76. Print.

16.
My Mothering Story

A Mother, a Daughter, a Fighter

MELISSA BIGSTONE

HI, MY NAME IS MELISSA. I was asked to share some of my story with you. We cannot all understand each other fully nor can we take away the pain and hurt some of us may have endured but we can support each other and embrace our differences in a positive way. I was born into a life of dysfunction and violence. I was in and out of care and through some unfortunate events I continued that cycle with my own kids. All I ever wanted was to be better than the role models I had growing up. I also wanted to beat the cycle of addiction that plagued my family. However, when one is not taught the tools to take care of oneself, let alone survive in this world, it can feel like an unsafe place.

I wanted to be taught, and I wanted to learn how to leave that lifestyle behind. When I was sixteen, I had already spent majority of my life living with and fighting against drug and alcohol abuse. I was going nowhere in life, death was knocking on my door.

I was trying to find a way out and didn't know where to start. I lacked trust, self-control, and didn't know how to love myself or anyone else. I was numb. Then, I met two very important people. They began to work with me and helped me to see the strengths I had not been able to see in myself. They opened the doors for me to recreate my life and identity. They never let my past define who I was. They had seen me—the real me.

A MOTHER, A DAUGHTER, A FIGHTER.

They said "Who do you want to be?" and "Where do you see

yourself in life?" Then, they helped me create that for myself. I'm forever grateful for these people. For once in my life they showed me a way out and guided me through it. But not by their words. It was their actions that really, truly meant more to me than anything.

They didn't have to come to court with me, and they didn't have to come to my graduation, or help me move into a new place. They didn't have to keep advocating for me after my son went PGO (permanent guardianship order) but they did—because they acted with kindness and caring.

I am now a post-secondary student enrolled in a BA for psychology. I now have my son home with me, my son who was in care for four years and was PGO. I am over two years drug and alcohol free. I have my own car and we have not had to move in over three years, something I have never had before. Today I embrace my past, all because these people never gave up on me no matter how much I wanted to give up on myself at times.

They battled the very system they worked for to help me and taught me not to give up when times get tough, but to be tough when times get rough and always follow your dreams. I don't believe I would be where I am at today if it weren't for people like this. If it weren't for all the people that said to me they believed in me and never put barriers in my way but instead helped me find a way around the barriers being put in my path. They helped me break the cycles I was in. Today, I aim towards helping others do the same. I think we all should.

We all have good inside and even though we are all different. We all deserve a chance at life and it's our job to help break through the barriers and create a new beginning for our community and young people.

Contributor Notes

Editors

Joanne Minaker is a sociologist, qualitative researcher, and active mother of three amazing children. Joanne's body of work is rooted in her family. She and her partner Bryan share a life together with their daughter Maylah and sons, Taryk and Ayden. She received her Ph.D. from Queen's University (2003) and MA from University of Manitoba (1998). Joanne is Associate Professor at MacEwan University in Edmonton, Alberta, where she has taught courses such as Gender, Crime and Social Justice since 2002 and received the Distinguished Teaching Award in 2009. Joanne's work underscores care, human connection, and social in/justice. She co-authored the book *Youth, Crime and Society: Issues of Power and Justice* (2009) with Bryan Hogeveen. Joanne has published widely on areas such as gender violence, marginalized women, criminalized youth, and mothering. Her current research program involves studying care and marginalized, young mothering and a collaborative project on mothering in the context of disaster. Joanne spoke at TEDxGarneau Women (2013) about the transformative power of caring, *Just Care*. In 2014, Joanne founded Cared Humanity, a care-based learning resource and community that creates meaningful experiences to support practicing both self-care and care for others. She runs with her dog Riel, loves music, and makes a wicked s'more at the campfire. She blogs about her adventures in *being bold with care* at caredhumanity.com.

Bryan Hogeveen joined the Department of Sociology at the University of Alberta in 2002 and holds a Black Belt in Brazilian Jiu-Jitsu. Bryan received his Ph.D. from the Centre of Criminology at the University of Toronto (2002) and his MA(1997) from the University of Manitoba. He is co-author (along with his wife Dr. Joanne Minaker, MacEwan University) of *Youth, Crime and Society: Issues of Power and Justice* (2009). Bryan has published widely on his academic interests, which include justice, violence, epistemology, youth crime, martial arts in/and society, continental philosophy, and the sociology of sport. His Social Sciences and Humanities Research Council of Canada-funded research project examines the impact of governmental economic restructuring on the marginalized inner-city residents of Edmonton and Winnipeg. Dr. Hogeveen has a forthcoming book with McGill-Queen's press called *Cold Cities: Care and Control in the Inner City* (with Andrew Woolford, University of Manitoba). He is the father of three incredible children and enjoys coaching hockey, teaching Brazilian Jiu-Jitsu, submission grappling and self-defense—and catching fish at the lake, hanging out with his kids, and playing his guitar.

Contributors

Melissa Bigstone is a 22-year-old female emcee, mother of two beautiful children—son Traytin and daughter Lenaya—whom she raises as a single parent in Edmonton, Alberta. She's been writing and rapping her own music since 2010, something she finds a positive outlet to channel the negative energy she endured in her life. Her music speaks about the systemic issues she and other marginalized youth have faced, such as poverty, neglect, family dysfunction, peer pressure, negative relationships, abuse, alcohol abuse, violence, and young parenting. Melissa is in her third year of her psychology degree at Concordia University. She aspires to become a developmental psychologist and speaker for young mothers and children in the child welfare system. Melissa has sought back her roots as an Indigenous woman, which has helped her to heal from past trauma. She finds meaning in fancy dance, a cultural dance that symbolizes the movements of the butterfly—a fitting metaphor for her own transformation.

Rebecca Jaremko Bromwich is a mother of four, a lawyer, and a legal academic who thinks all of these aspects of her life's work do not conflict but make sense together as an activist vocation involving maternal thinking. She has a BA (Hon.) in social/cultural anthropology from the University of Calgary, an LLB and an LLM from Queen's, and a Graduate Certificate in Women's, Gender and Sexuality Studies from the University of Cincinnati. She is currently a Ph.D. Candidate at Carleton University. Called to the Bar of Ontario in 2003, Rebecca has worked as a lawyer for ten years and has previously researched and published in a variety of areas, including youth criminal justice law, law practice management and equality issues relating to women and members of other historically marginalized groups in the legal profession. She is a part-time professor at the University of Ottawa, Faculty of Law and a staff lawyer with the Canadian Bar Association. Rebecca's most recent book, published in spring 2013, is a MIRCI collaboration entitled *Incarcerated Mothers: Oppression and Resistance*.

Dawn Elston, MA, has an impressive career as a Research Coordinator, which spans over two decades working in the Social and Health Sciences. Recently, Dawn's research areas focus on social determinants of health, specifically as they relate to HIV and women's sexual health. Of Dawn's many interests and pastimes, she is most passionate about promoting senior dog adoption; in fact she runs a retirement home for three of her own!

Talia Esnard is an Assistant Professor of Sociology at the Centre for Education Programs at the University of Trinidad and Tobago. She holds a Ph.D. in Sociology from the University of the West Indies. Talia is a recipient of a BSc Sociology (First Class Honours) and a 2012 Taiwan Research Fellowship. Her main research interests include gender and entrepreneurship, poverty and entrepreneurship, mothering and entrepreneurship, entrepreneurial education, and educational leadership as it relates to Caribbean societies. Her work has been published in several journals including *Journal of Asian Academy of Management*, *Journal of Higher Education and Practice*, and *Journal of Educational Administration and History*.

Saara Greene, MSW, Ph.D., is an Associate Professor in the McMaster University School of Social Work. Her practice and research background has focussed extensively on critically analyzing how social policies and practices contribute to the continuing oppressions of mothers who are marginalized as a result of racism, ageism, sexism, and HIV-related stigma. She is particularly interested in doing community-based research and improving upon existing frameworks to support the leadership of women living with HIV at all stages of the research and dissemination process. When she's not engaging in community and research endeavours, Saara immensely enjoys hanging out with her son and daughter who remind her daily of the complexities, joys, and promises of motherhood.

Tamar Hagar teaches in the Department of Education and Gender Studies at Tel Hai College, Israel. Critical feminist methodology, art sociology, fictional and academic writing are core issues of her academic research and writing. In 2002, she published a book of short stories, *A Perfectly Ordinary Life* (in Hebrew), and in 2012 she published a second book, *Malice Aforethought* (in Hebrew), in which she attempts to reconstruct the elusive biographies of two English working class mothers who killed their babies at the end of the nineteenth century.

Michelle Hughes Miller is an Associate Professor in the Department of Women's and Gender Studies at the University of South Florida. Her academic interests are in discursive constructions of motherhood within law and policy, which merges her two areas of expertise: gender studies and criminology. Michelle also researches systemic responses to violence against women. In addition to teaching graduate courses on "The Politics of Motherhood" and "Women and Social Justice," Michelle is an active local advocate on behalf of female victims of violence and discrimination for which she served as the Chair of the President's Committee on Title IX at USF. During 2014, she is balancing her own treatment for breast cancer with the support of her partner, Rob Benford, the wedding and subsequent move to graduate school of her youngest child, and hearing all about the adventures of teaching Kindergarten from her oldest daughter.

Amy Kaler, Ph.D., is a Professor in the Department of Sociology at the University of Alberta. Her work focusses on reproduction, gender, social change, and institutions. Most of her fieldwork has taken place in central and southern Africa, in the context of the AIDS epidemic and other complex challenges to household survival, although she has also done historical work in Alberta. Her newest book, *Baby Trouble in the Last Best West: Making New People in Alberta 1900-1950,* will be published by the University of Toronto Press. Amy lives in Edmonton with her daughter.

Gladys Kwaramba has over five years of experience working as a Peer Research Associate (PRA) on a number of projects and is currently employed as a PRA with the Canadian HIV Women's Sexual and Reproductive Health Cohort Study in Toronto. Gladys' work has allowed her to work closely with HIV positive women and their healthcare providers. She is notably very proud of the work she did on The HIV Mothering Study which looked at the experiences of HIV positive women in their first year of motherhood. Her work has been mostly around women's health and well-being. Gladys is a mother of two, lives in Toronto, and loves to travel.

Laura C L. Landertinger is a Ph.D. Candidate in the Department of Social Justice Education at the Ontario Institute for Studies in Education (OISE), University of Toronto. Her work examines the intersections of race, gender, and settler colonialism in the Canadian context, focusing in particular on institutions of child welfare. She pursues this work under the supervision of Dr. Sherene Razack.

Mona Loutfy, MD, FRCPC, MPH, is a mother of two rambunctious children and loves to travel, scuba dive, bicycle, and camp outdoors. She is an infectious diseases specialist and Associate Professor at Women's College Hospital and the University of Toronto. Her clinical work and research focusses on women and HIV with specific interest in sexual and reproductive health, intersecting stigma, mental wellbeing, and quality to care. She launched the Women and HIV Research Program in 2006 and works from a community-based research model involving the people that her research will affect at all stages.

Caroline McDonald-Harker, Ph.D. in Sociology from the University of Alberta, is currently Assistant Professor in the Department of Sociology and Anthropology at Mount Royal University in Calgary, Alberta. Caroline's areas of research expertise include the sociology of motherhood/mothering, gender, and family; domestic violence; social policy; and qualitative research methods. Caroline is the mother of three young children. Working part time as a Counsellor at an Abused Women's Emergency Shelter during her MA led to Caroline's interest in studying the experiences of women victims of domestic abuse. Her doctoral dissertation examined abused women's mothering experiences and identities in relation to dominant mothering discourses. Caroline is currently conducting a three-year research study (with Joanne Minaker), funded by a Social Sciences and Humanities Research Council (SSHRC) Partnership Grant, on the impact of the 2013 High River, Alberta flood on the family, with a specific focus on mothering in the context of disasters.

Hollis Moore is a Ph.D. candidate at the Department of Anthropology at the University of Toronto. Her thesis, "Imprisonment and (Un)relatedness in Salvador, Bahia, Brazil," examines how increasing rates of imprisonment, and the concentration of carceral effects, shape social relations in low-income, heavily penalized neighbourhoods and households in Northeast Brazil.

Mrs. Kimberly Okpala received her BSc Sociology and Management Studies (Hons.) in 2004 and MSc Sociology in 2008 from the University of the West Indies. She is a recipient of the 2004 Most Outstanding Sociology student award. In 2005, she joined the academic staff at the University of the West Indies and held various research and teaching positions until 2012. Mrs. Okpala is currently a student at the University of London pursuing her Bachelor of Law degree. Her main research interests include sociology of work, social theory, and social change and development.

Keri K. O'Neal received her Master's degree in Human Development from Arizona State University and her Ph.D. in Human Development from Texas Tech University, specializing in adolescent risk-taking. She is currently an Associate Professor at California State University, East Bay in the Department of Human Development and Women's Studies. Keri teaches courses that emphasize the developing and "at risk" adolescent, cross-cultural human development, gay and lesbian development, and women's development. She lives with her husband, son, two cats, and one very large dog. Keri is active in her son's school and assists with the Spanish Immersion Program. She keeps busy wearing many hats and is confident that she will sleep again, *someday*!

Hijin Park is Associate Professor of Sociology at Brock University in St. Catharines, Ontario. Her current research on racialized female murderers examines the ways that social constructions of gender, race, class, disability, violence, and crime shape and legitimize Canadian white settler colonialism and neoliberalism. Her research areas include feminist legal studies, refugee and migration studies, differential racialization, and Asian Canadian studies. She lives in Toronto.

Josephine L. Savarese is an Associate Professor in the Department of Criminology and Criminal Justice, St. Thomas University, Fredericton, New Brunswick. Her interest in the racialized nature of the child welfare system was formed through studies in critical race, socio-legal feminist scholarship at the University of Saskatchewan. A contract with the Saskatchewan Legal Aid Commission gave Josephine "hands on" experience representing families and children, who were largely Indigenous, on protection matters. In 2009, she was commissioned to research and co-author (with the Saskatchewan Legal Aid Commission, Regina Rural Area Office) a Memorandum of Argument for an application to appeal to the Supreme Court of Canada on behalf of Laura, the mother highlighted in her chapter. Josephine is a member of the executive committee of the SSHRC-funded Urban Aboriginal Knowledge Network (UAKN) for the Atlantic Region and serves on the board of the Canadian Law and Society Association. During a 2013 sabbatical leave, Josephine completed a graduate certificate in Advanced Women's Studies at the University of Hawai'i at Mānoa. A highlight of this experience was working with the children and families of tourists and "locals" while volunteering at the Honolulu Zoo in Waikīkī.

Renita L. Seabrook is an Assistant Professor in the School of Criminal Justice at the University of Baltimore where she serves as Faculty Fellow for the Schaefer Center for Public Policy. Her interests include correctional rehabilitation, women and crime, and theory. Her research includes incarcerated mothers, ex-offender reentry services, and cognitive-behaviour treatment programs for female offenders. She received both her Ph.D. (2007) and MA (1993) in Criminal Justice from Rutgers University and her BA (1990) in Law and Society from Purdue University. She's worked in governmental agencies in New Jersey and Georgia, including a position as Program Development Consultant for the Georgia Department of Corrections. Dr. Seabrook's scholarly work reflects her passion that centers on: (1) inclusion of applied research and theoretical underpinnings; (2) synergy needed to enrich educational and experiential learning for students; (3) integrating research within the community in order to improve the lives of marginalized populations.

Stephanie Smith recently began working in the field of HIV research, having worked in the Heath Care field since she graduated in 1999 from the Personal Support Worker program at Algonquin College. Currently, Stephanie is a Research Associate on three projects: the Canadian HIV Women's Sexual & Reproductive Health Cohort Study (CHIWOS), the Positive Spaces, Healthy Places, Employment Change and Health Outcomes (ECHO), and HIV Mothering studies. Stephanie also works full time for a Home Care agency in Ottawa as a staffing coordinator. When not at work you can find Stephanie playing rugby, working out, gardening, rock climbing, or scuba diving. Stephanie also has an interest in tattoos as she has a quite a few. Her newest hobby is photography. She enjoys taking photos of nature and architecture.

Wendy K. Watson received her Master's Degree and Ph.D. in Human Development and Family Studies from Texas Tech University. She is currently an Associate Professor of Gerontology at Bowling

Green State University and Program Coordinator for both the Undergraduate and Graduate Gerontology Programs. Wendy's research interests are in midlife and older women's experiences, specifically regarding issues around individual development, relationships, sexuality, sexual decision-making, gender, and aging. Wendy and her husband have five cats and two turtles. She enjoys art journaling and knitting in her free time.

Heather Wyatt-Nichol, Ph.D., is an Associate Professor and Director of the MPA Program in the College of Public Affairs at the University of Baltimore. She earned a Ph.D in public policy and administration from Virginia Commonwealth University and an MPA from Old Dominion University. She is a Commissioner on the Commission on Peer Review Accreditation for the Network of Schools of Public Policy, Affairs, and Administration. She also serves as Chair Elect for the American Society for Public Administration's Section on Democracy and Social Justice. She has published book chapters and articles on a variety of topics in public administration and feminist journals. Her research interests include diversity management, ethics, family-friendly workplace policies, organizational justice, and social equity. She is a mother and other-mother residing in Baltimore County, Maryland, USA, with her husband, daughter, niece, great-niece, and great-nephew. Heather may be reached at hwyatt-nichol@ubalt.edu.